LOS ANGELES
CALIFORNIA

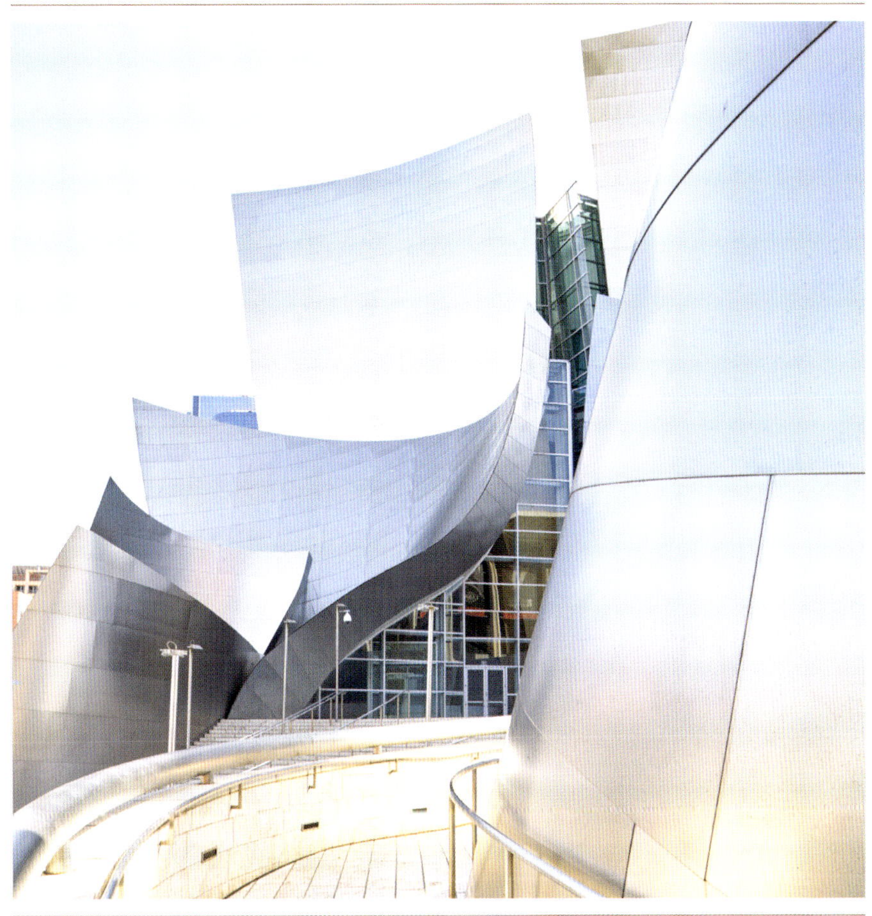

A PHOTOGRAPHIC PORTRAIT

Photography by John Chapple

Narrative by Emma Foster

TWIN LIGHTS PUBLISHERS | ROCKPORT, MASSACHUSETTS

First published in the
United States of America by:

Twin Lights Publishers, Inc.
Rockport, Massachusetts 01966
Telephone: (978) 546-7398
www.twinlightspub.com

ISBN: 978-1-934907-47-4

10 9 8 7 6 5 4 3 2 1

(opposite)
One and Two California Plaza

(frontispiece)
Walt Disney Concert Hall

(jacket front)
Getty Center

(jacket back)
Beach Front Homes and
Hollywood Tower

Book design by:
SYP Design & Production, Inc.
www.sypdesign.com

Printed in China

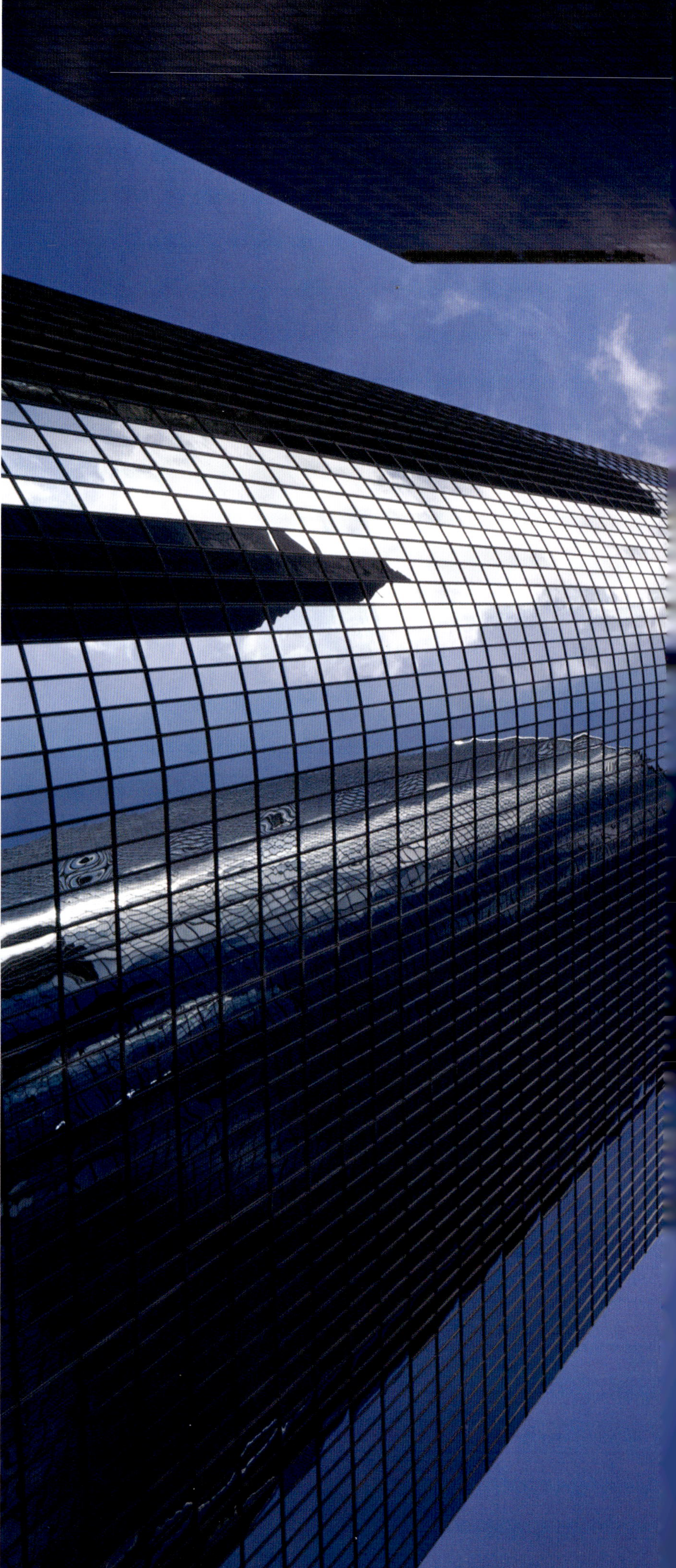

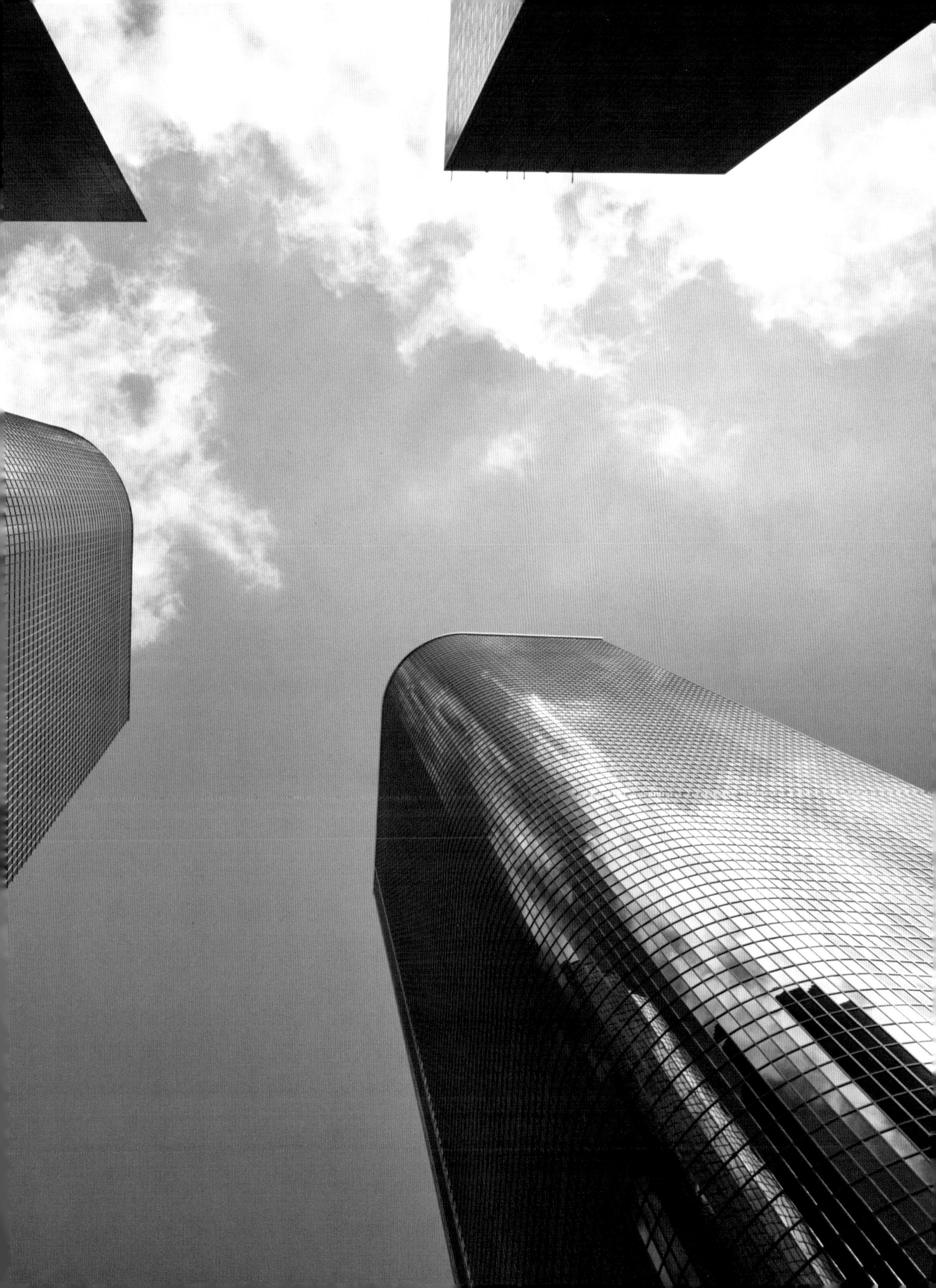

CITY OF ANGELS

From the perfect sandy beaches of Malibu to the star-struck streets of Hollywood and the urban bustle of Downtown — Los Angeles is a city of contrasts, captured perfectly by talented photographer John Chapple in this stunning series of photographs. And while this sprawling metropolis can sometimes be bewildering, it remains magical — inspiring countless songs; providing the backdrop for blockbuster movies; and enticing artists, dreamers, and free spirits from all over the world, looking for their slice of the California dream.

Walk in the footsteps of movie stars past and present on Hollywood Boulevard; ride the Pacific waves at some of the best surfing spots in the world; enjoy the street art and skater scene of Venice Beach or the rock 'n' roll legacy of Sunset Strip — there is so much to explore in this eclectic city.

Home to the Griffith Observatory with its commanding views, the Malibu beach homes of the rich and famous, and the magnificent Getty Center and Getty Villa, you'll also find other architectural marvels such as the Walt Disney Concert Hall and world-class art galleries LACMA and MOCA.

As well as being diverse in landscape and architecture, it is the different people and cultures that make Los Angeles the rich and vibrant city it is today. The fascinating stories of immigrant communities from all corners of the world who have settled and flourished in Los Angeles are told in its museums, parks, and ethnic enclaves. There's Olvera Street, a vibrant Mexican-American marketplace, which dates back to 1781, or the Biddy Mason Park, which was built in honor of the inspiring African-American slave who became a philanthropist and entrepreneur.

The city's spectacular diversity demonstrates its inclusivity - all are welcome in the City of Angels.

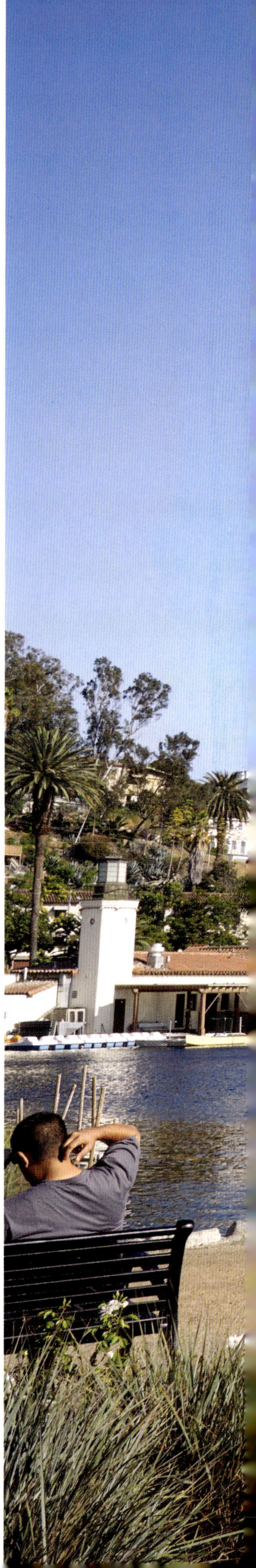

Echo Park Lake *(opposite)*

The *Queen of Angels* watches over her city. Officially named Nuestra Reina de Los Angeles, but affectionately called "Lady of the Lake" by locals, this Art-Deco-style statue is Echo Park's unofficial patron saint. She gazes over visitors to the peaceful lake, a welcome respite from the busy Downtown.

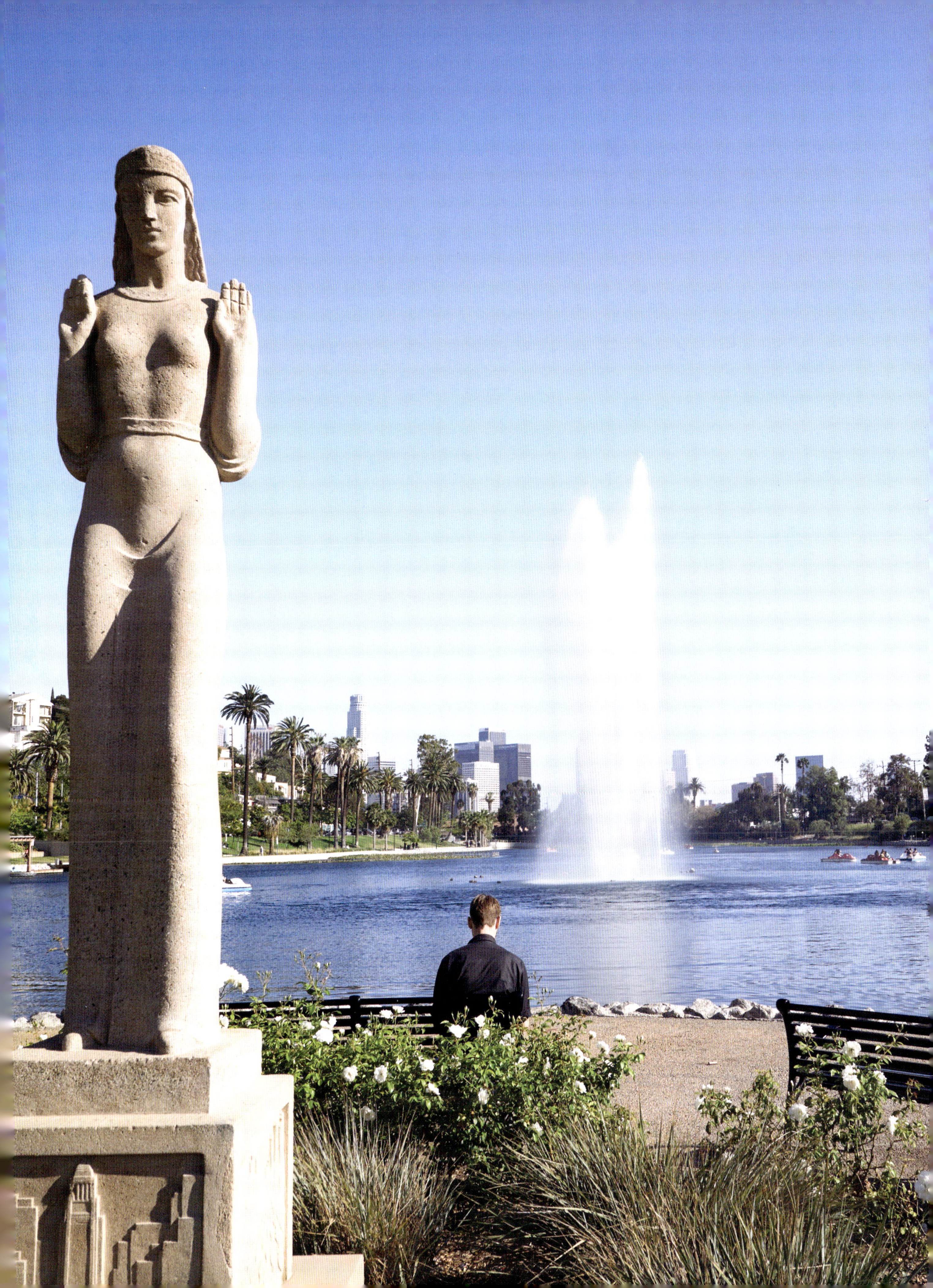

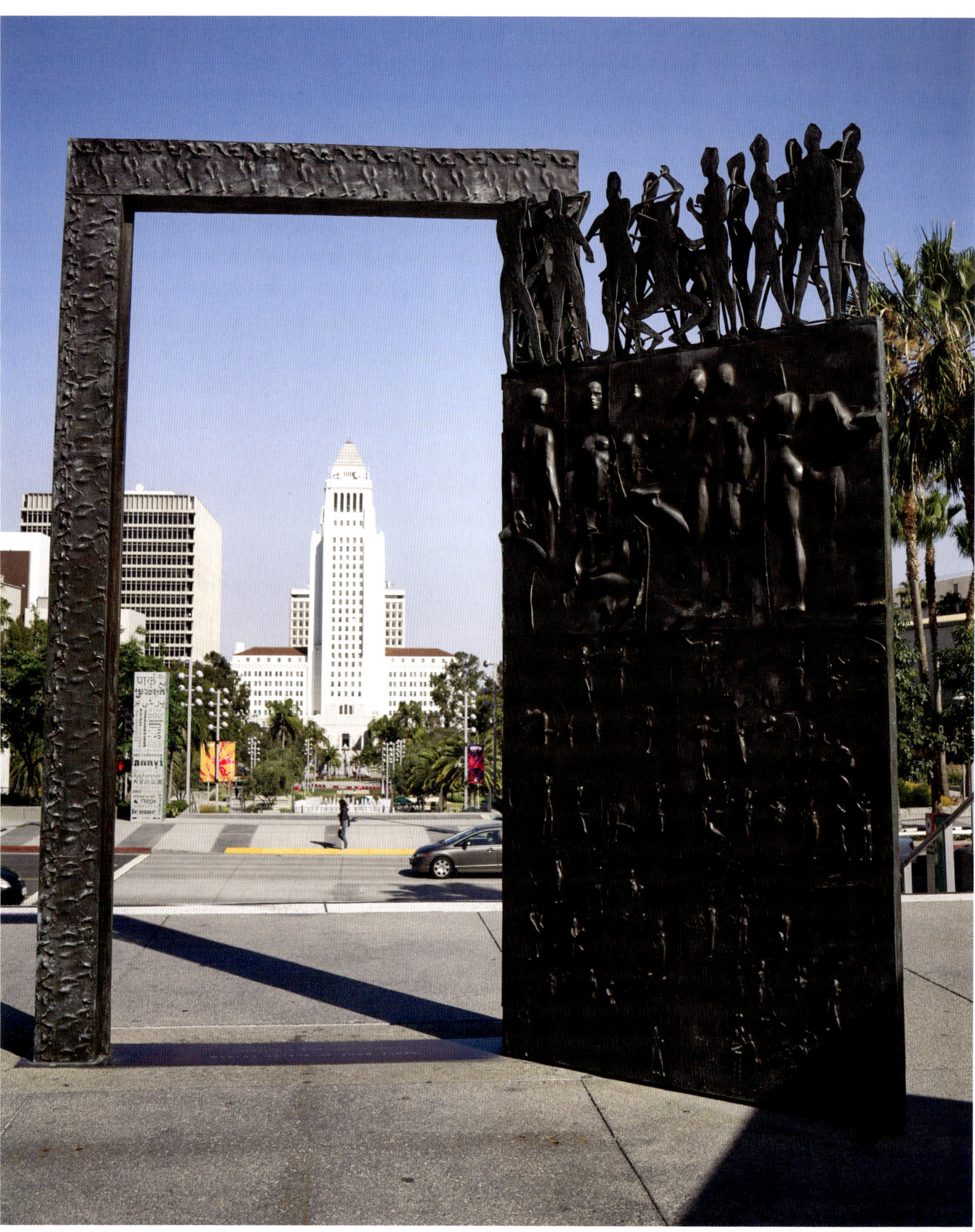

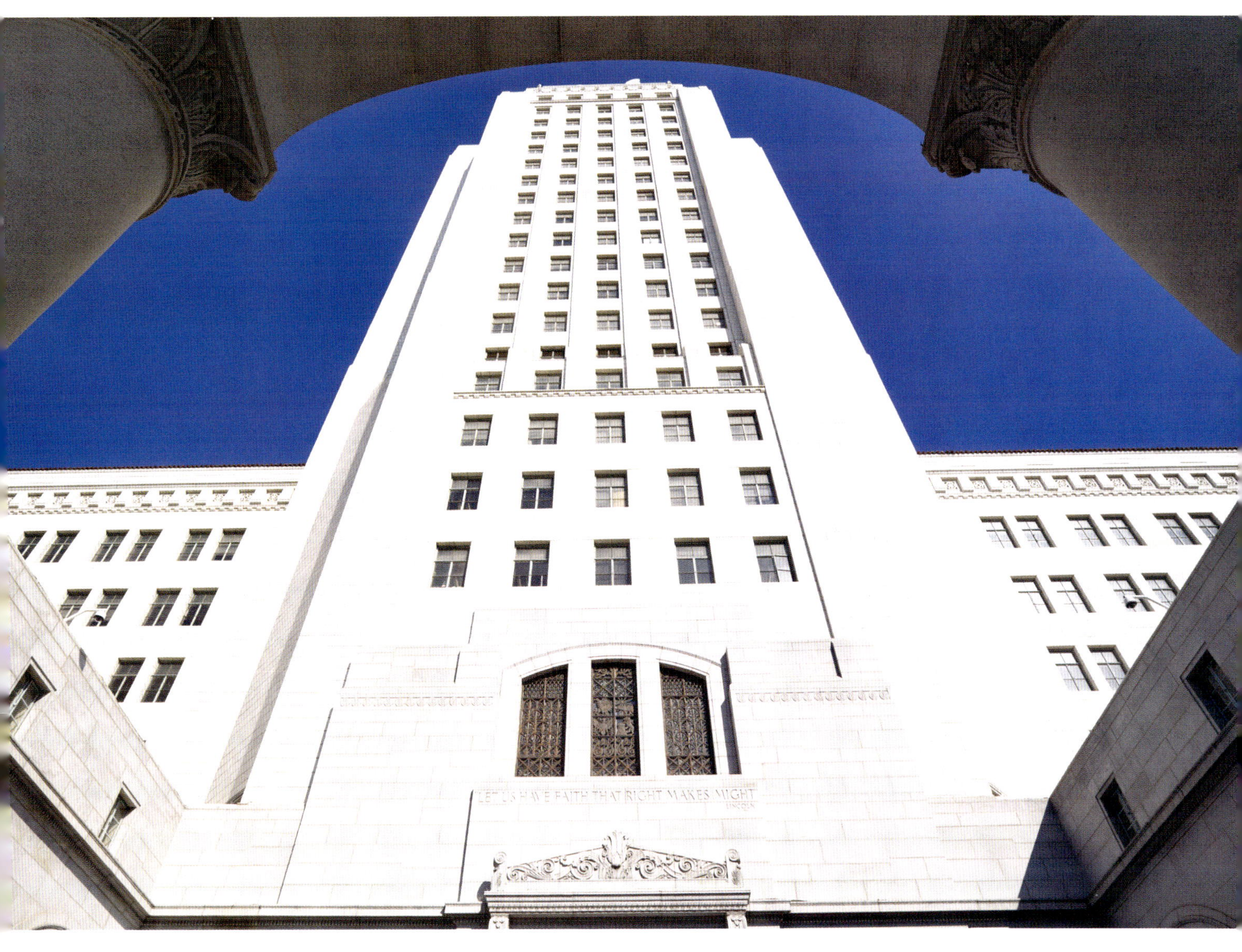

Dance Door *(opposite)*

The perpetually open *Dance Door*, a bronze sculpture by renowned artist Robert Graham, which sits outside the Los Angeles Music Center. Designed to enhance the beauty of the surrounding area, this open doorway, adorned with dancing figures, perfectly frames the majestic City Hall.

City Hall *(above)*

City Hall, with its Art Deco-style tower, is an iconic Downtown landmark. Completed in 1928, the concrete used in its construction was formed from sand taken from California's 58 counties and water from each of its 21 historic missions. Its appearances in TV and films has made it synonymous with the city.

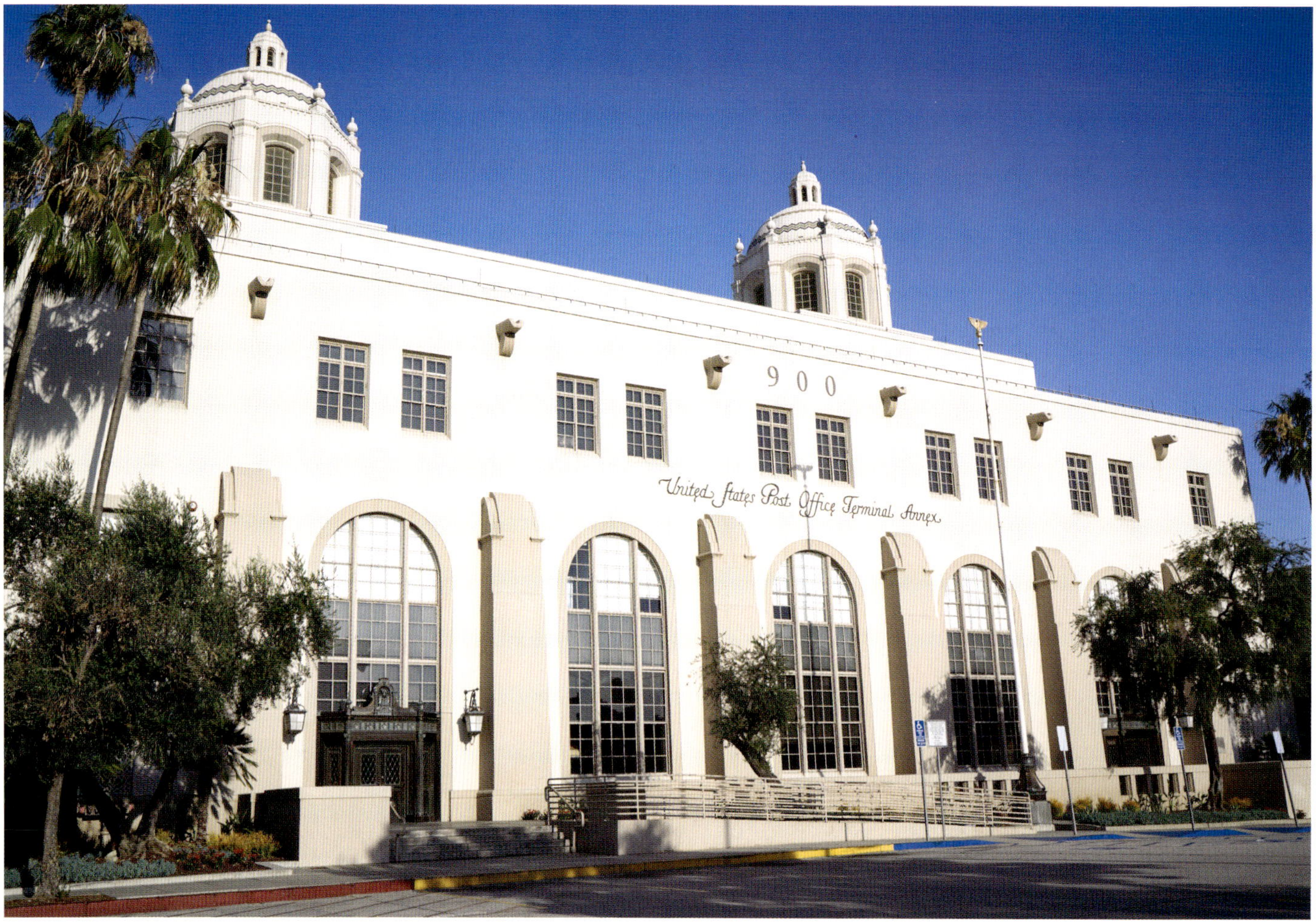

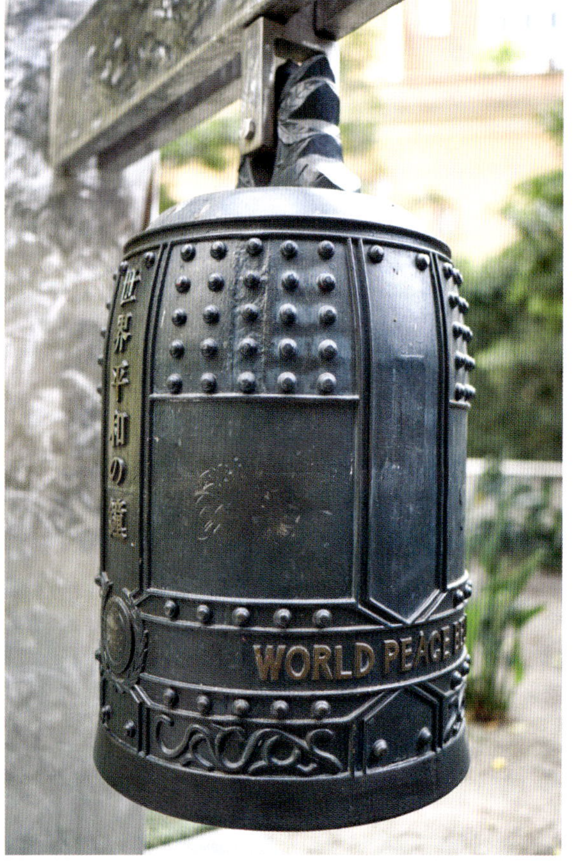

United States Post Office *(above)*

Renowned poet and author Charles Bukowski worked here for 14 years, penning his 1971 novel *Post Office* about his time here as a mail clerk. Once the central mail processing facility for Los Angeles, the Mission Revival-style Terminal Annex Post Office building is now used as a data center.

Public Library *(left and opposite)*

The historic facade of Central Library (opposite) and the World Peace Bell (left), an international symbol of peace cast from the coins of 103 countries. Built in 1926, the library's west side showcases sculptures and reflecting pools and is the third largest library in the United States.

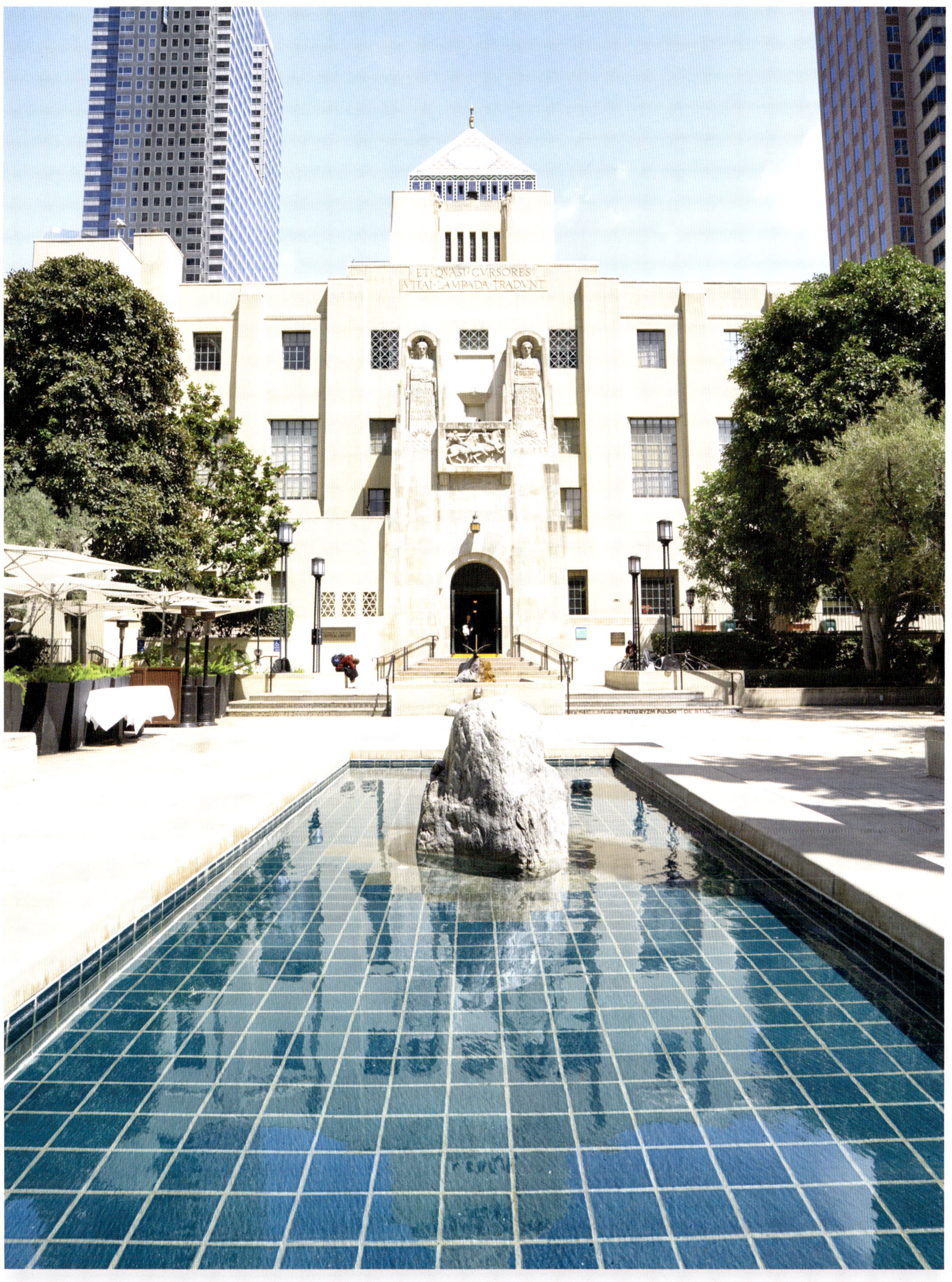
ET·QVASI·CVRSORES
VITAI·LAMPADA·TRADVNT

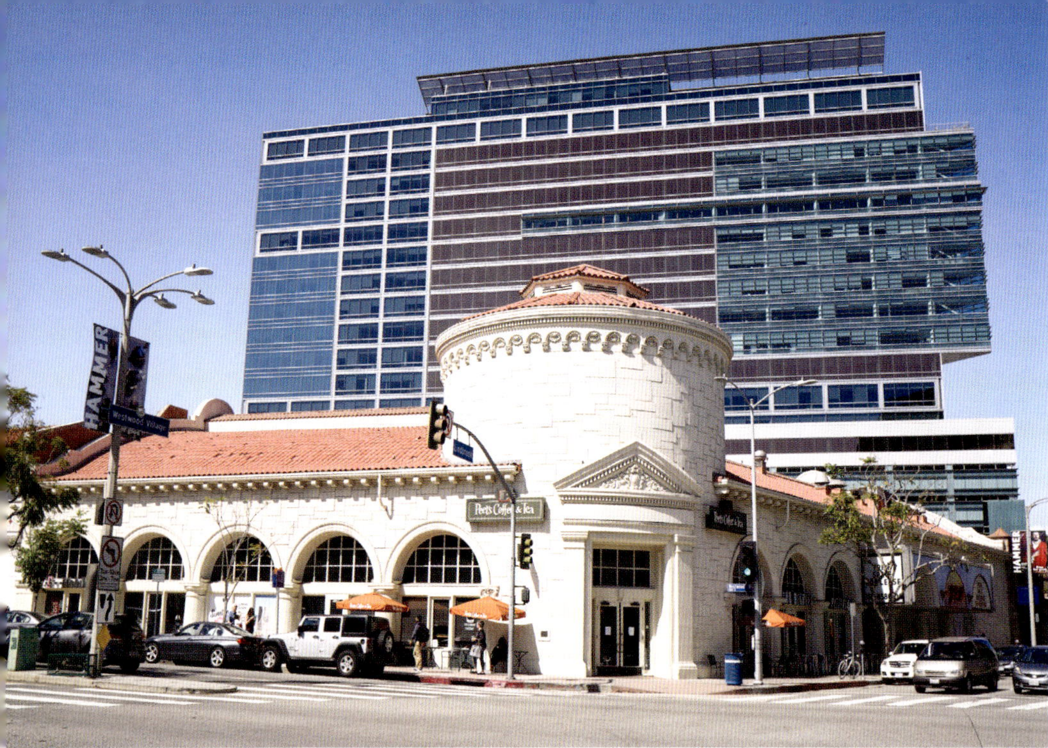

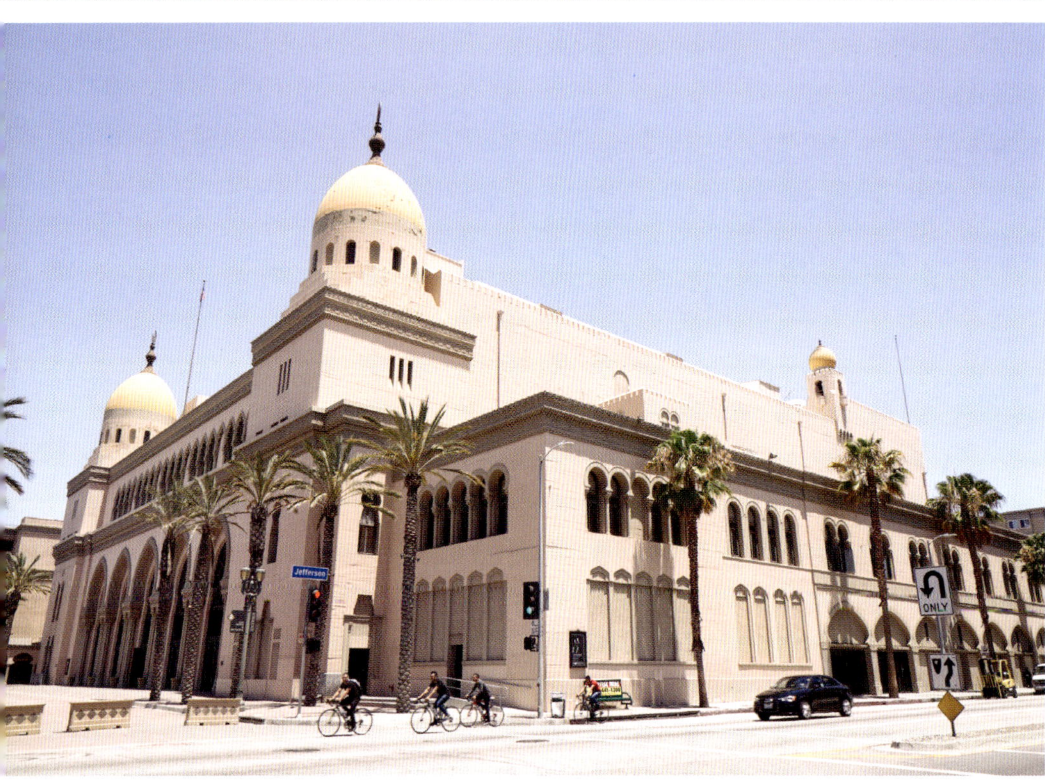

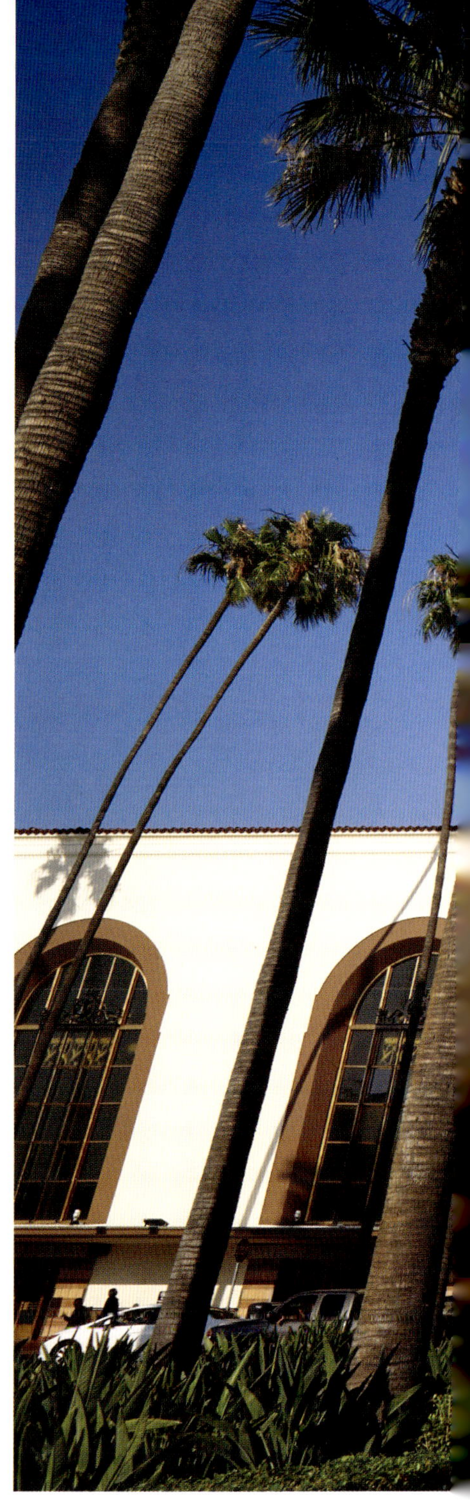

Ralphs Grocery Store *(top)*

This early 1929 branch of the SoCal supermarket chain was built in the Spanish Colonial style with a large rotunda built to house its entrance. As well as keeping Angelenos stocked with groceries, the chain store has made its mark on popular culture; featuring in movies such as *The Big Lebowski*.

Shrine Auditorium *(bottom)*

The Oscars, Emmys, and Grammys have all been hosted in this opulent Moorish Revival-style building. Opened in 1926, this unique structure was originally a civic center and club house for members of the Shriners fraternity before becoming established as a center of entertainment.

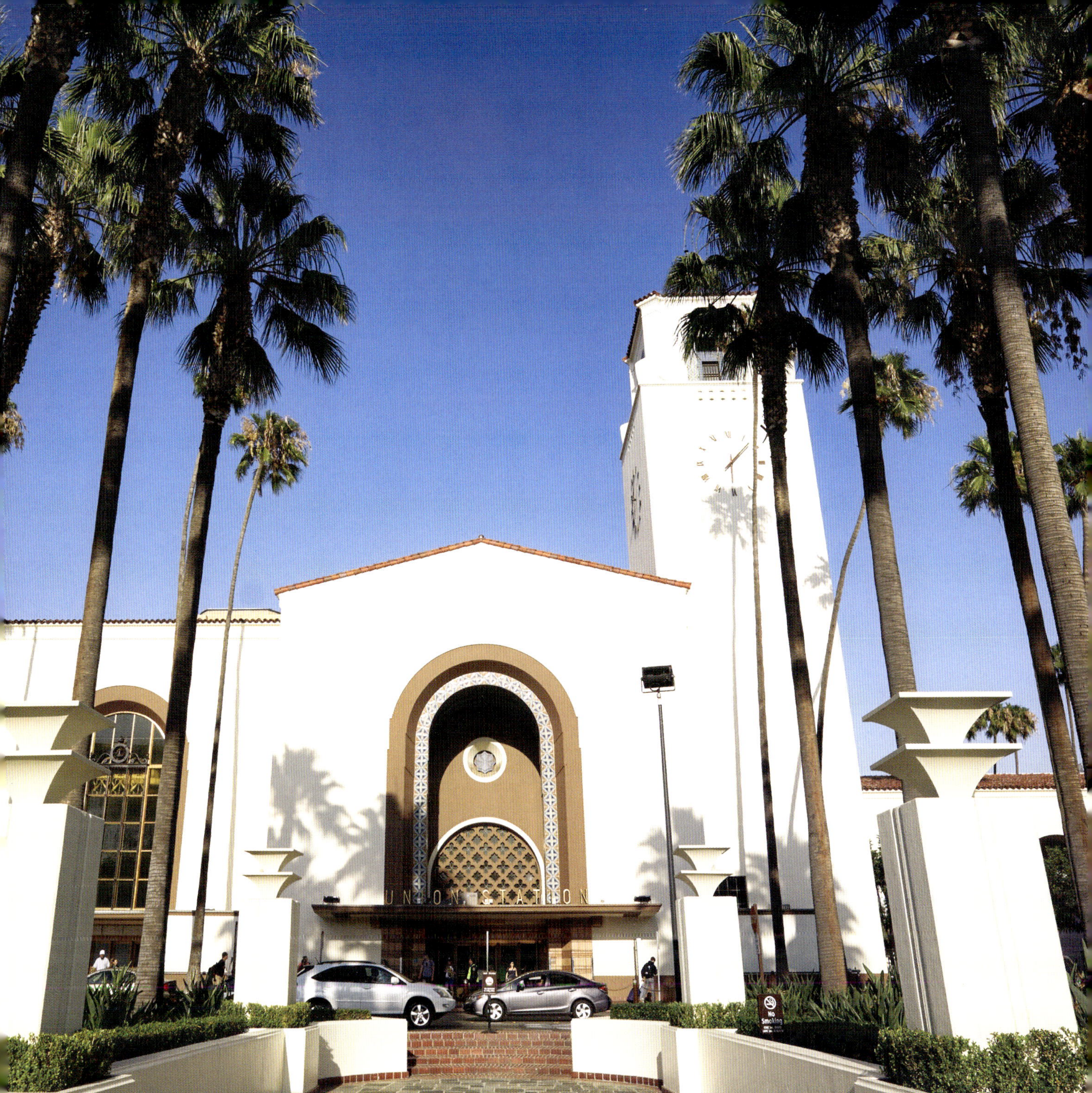

Union Station

Flanked by tall palm trees, Union Station is the largest railroad passenger terminal in the American West. Opened in 1939 as the main railway station in Los Angeles, almost 110,000 people pass through the doors of the Art Deco and Mission Revival-style building every day.

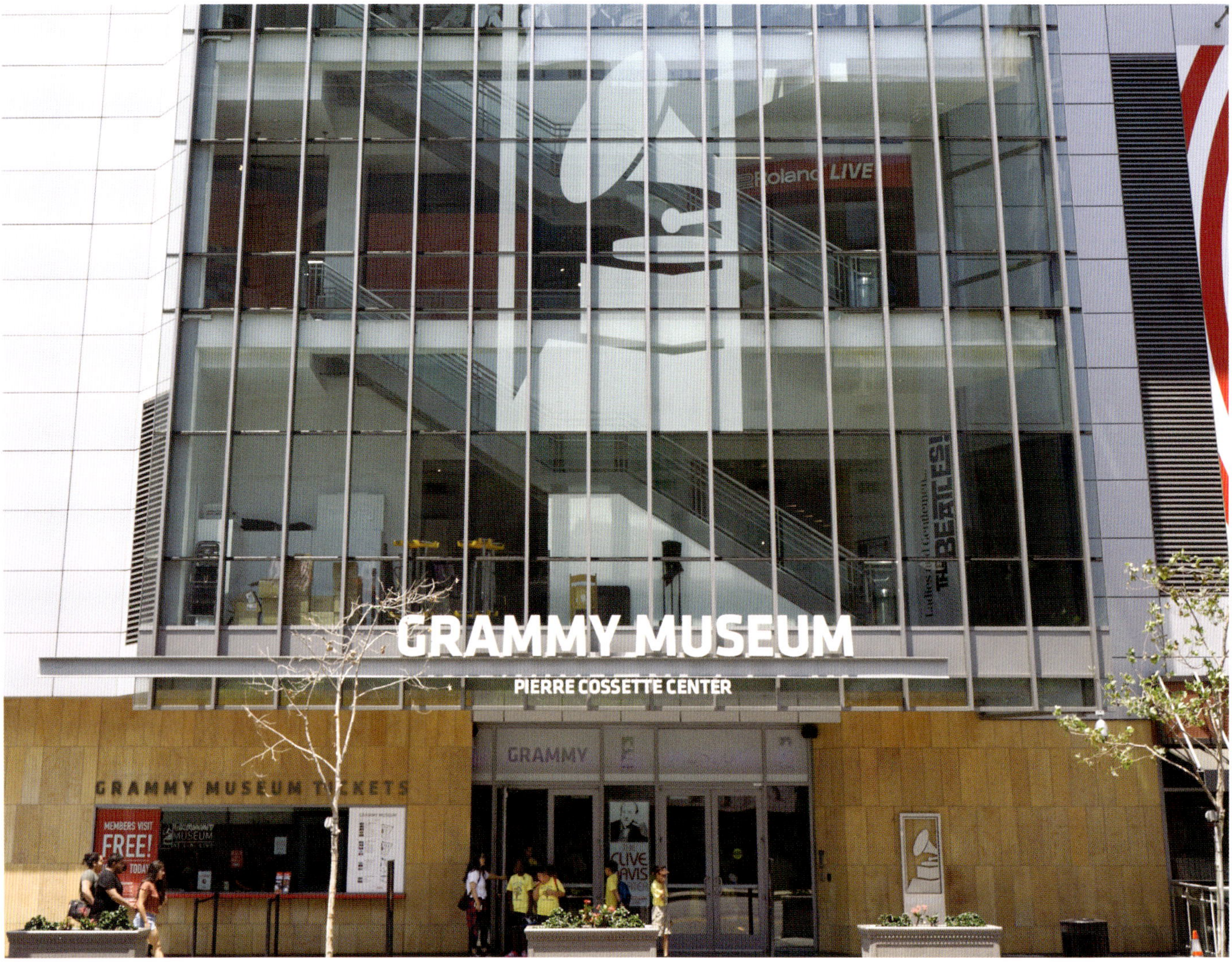

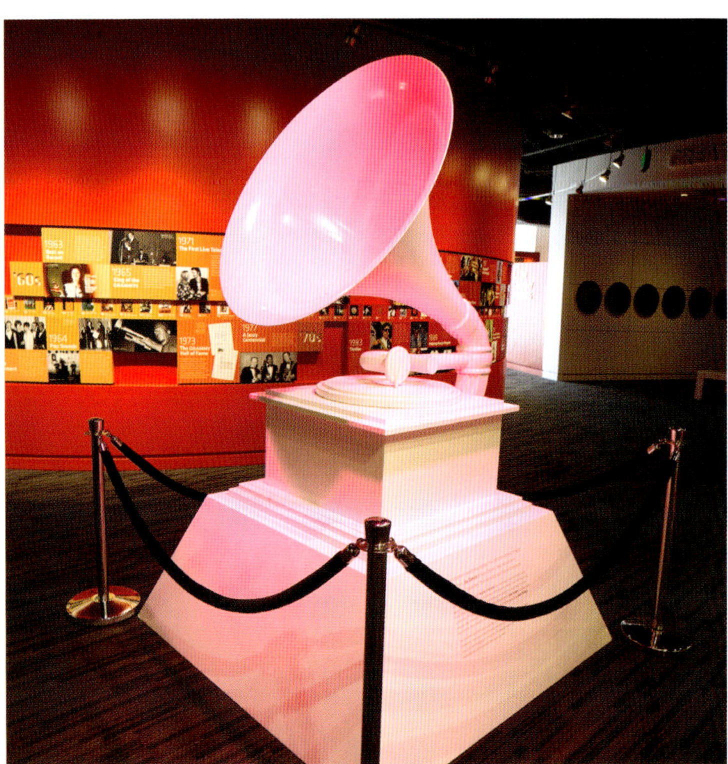

Grammy Museum *(above and left)*

Aiming to celebrate the power of all kinds of recorded music, the Grammy Museum is a four-floor treasure trove of interactive exhibits for music lovers. The trademark white gramophone — after which the Grammy awards take their name — basks in a pink glow, overlooking years of music history.

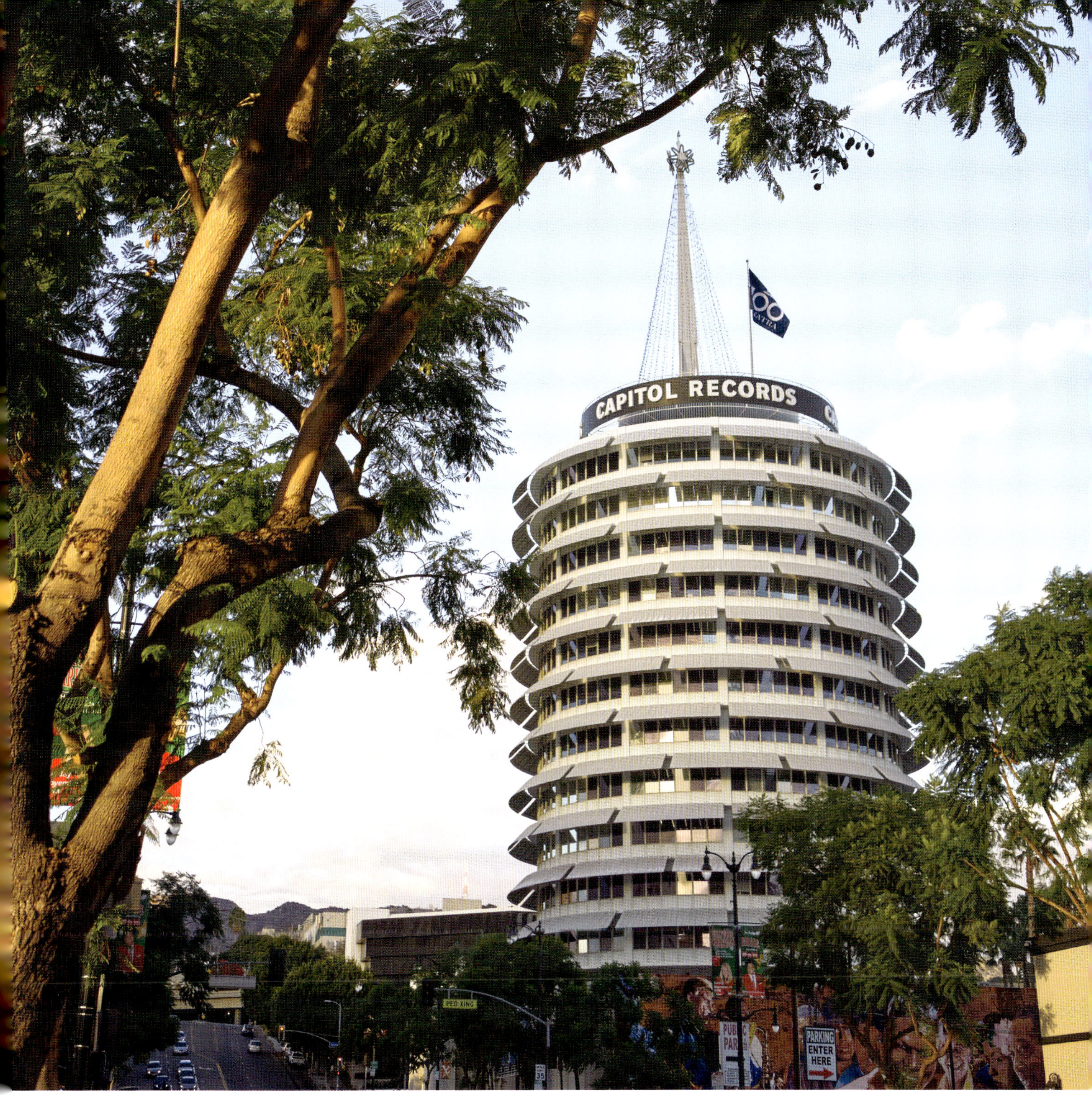

Capitol Records Building

Resembling a stack of records on a turntable, this music industry landmark houses the offices of Capitol Records and Capitol Studios, where hundreds of iconic artists from the Beach Boys to the Beastie Boys have recorded. The blinking light atop the tower's spike spells out "Hollywood" in Morse code.

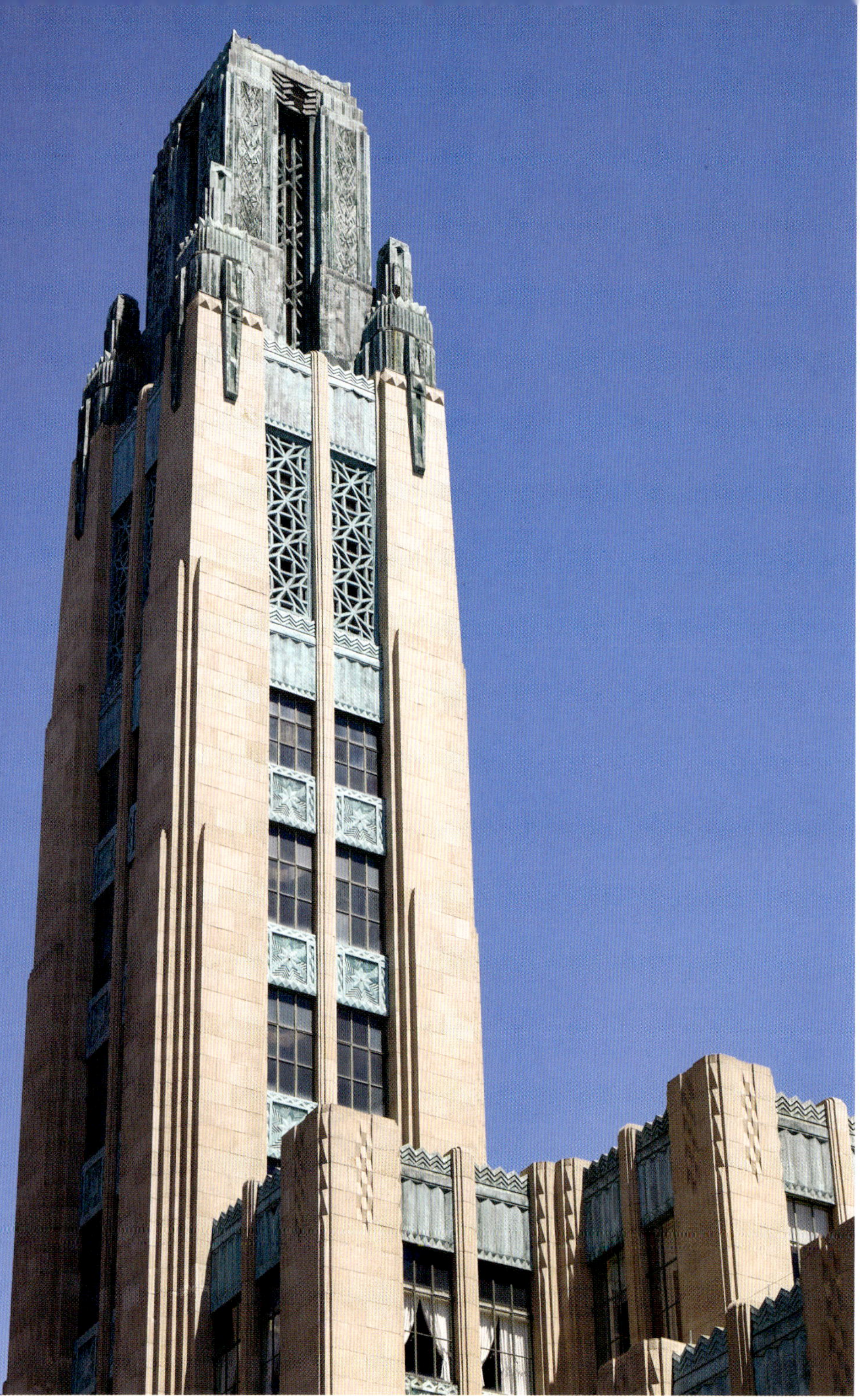

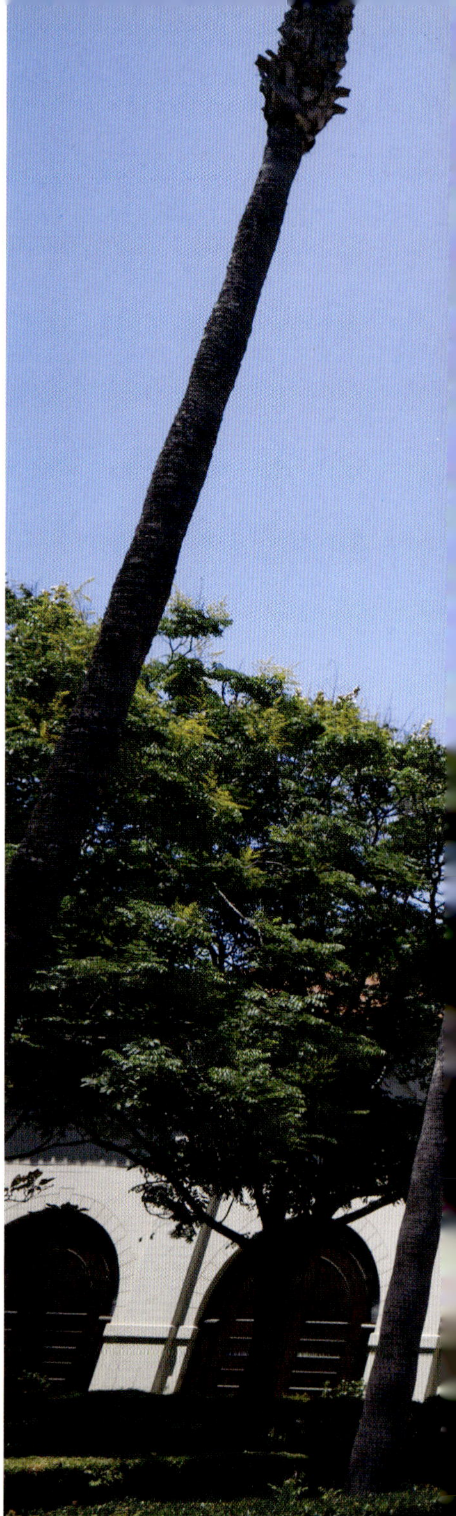

Bullocks Wilshire Building

The tarnished green copper and stone of this glamorous Art Deco tower set against a beautiful blue California sky. Originally a luxury department store frequented by the likes of Greta Garbo and Clark Gable, the Bullocks Wilshire Building now houses the Southwestern Law School.

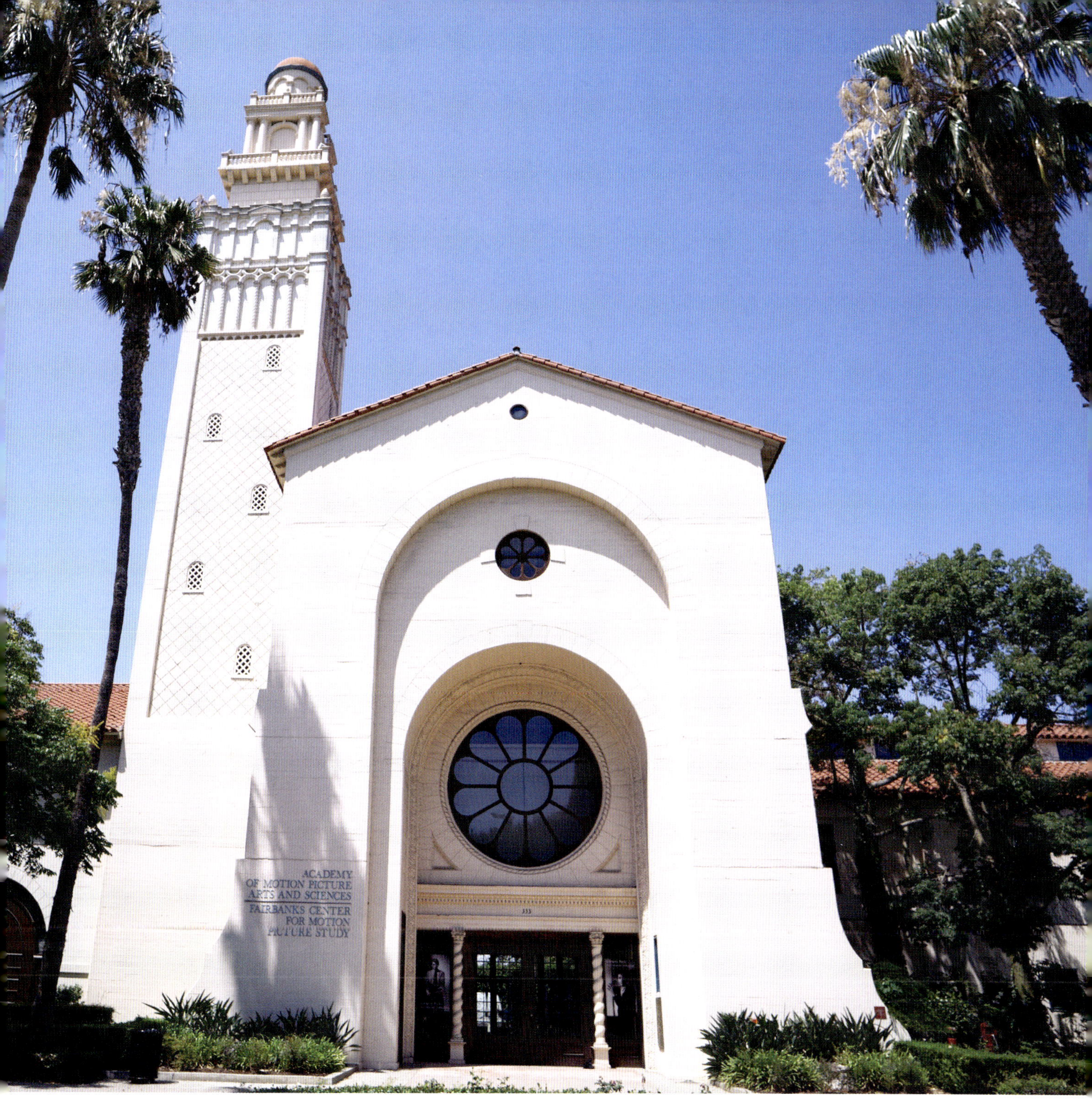

Beverly Hills Waterworks

Built in the style of a Romanesque church, this building had a less than glamorous start as the water treatment plant for Beverly Hills. Earmarked for demolition in the 1980s, the building was saved by the Academy of Motion Picture Arts and Sciences, who made it a library and film archive.

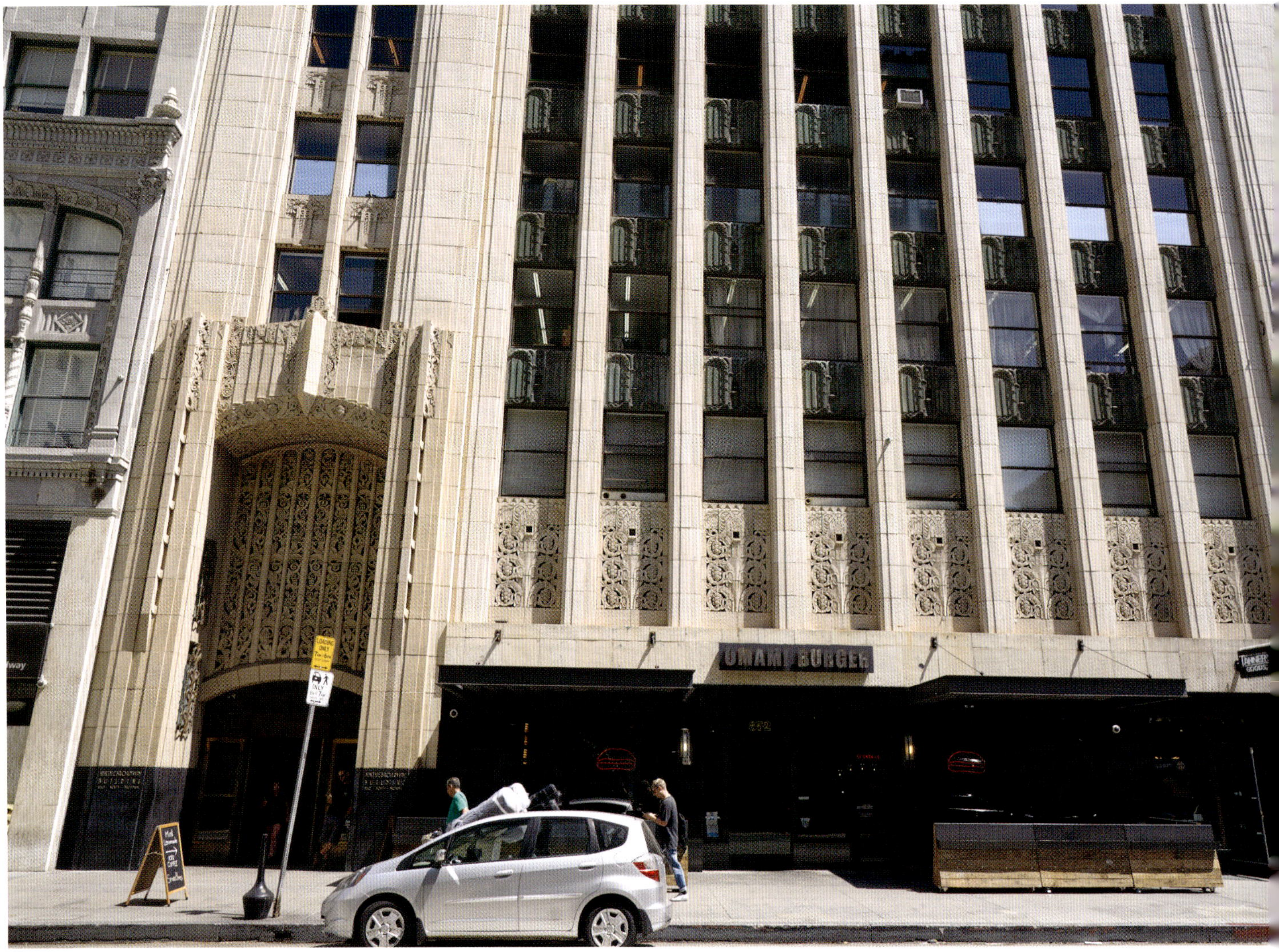

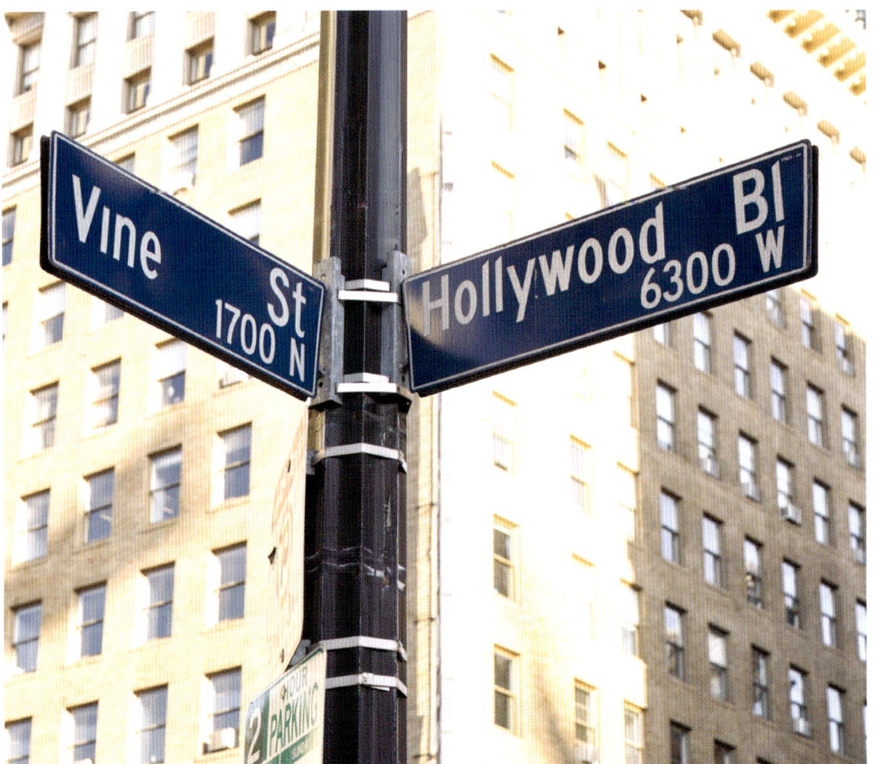

Ninth and Broadway Building *(above)*

The dramatic two-story entrance to the historic and ornate Ninth and Broadway Building is located next to Umami Burger, a gourmet burger chain. Designed by renowned architect Cloud Beelman in 1930, this 13-story office building is decorated with terra cotta panels featuring a beautiful grapevine design.

Hollywood and Vine *(left)*

It has been called "the most famous intersection in the world" and attracts hundreds of tourists each day. Home to Hollywood's Walk of Fame, this iconic district of Hollywood grew notoriety in the 1920s for its large concentration of radio and showbiz related businesses.

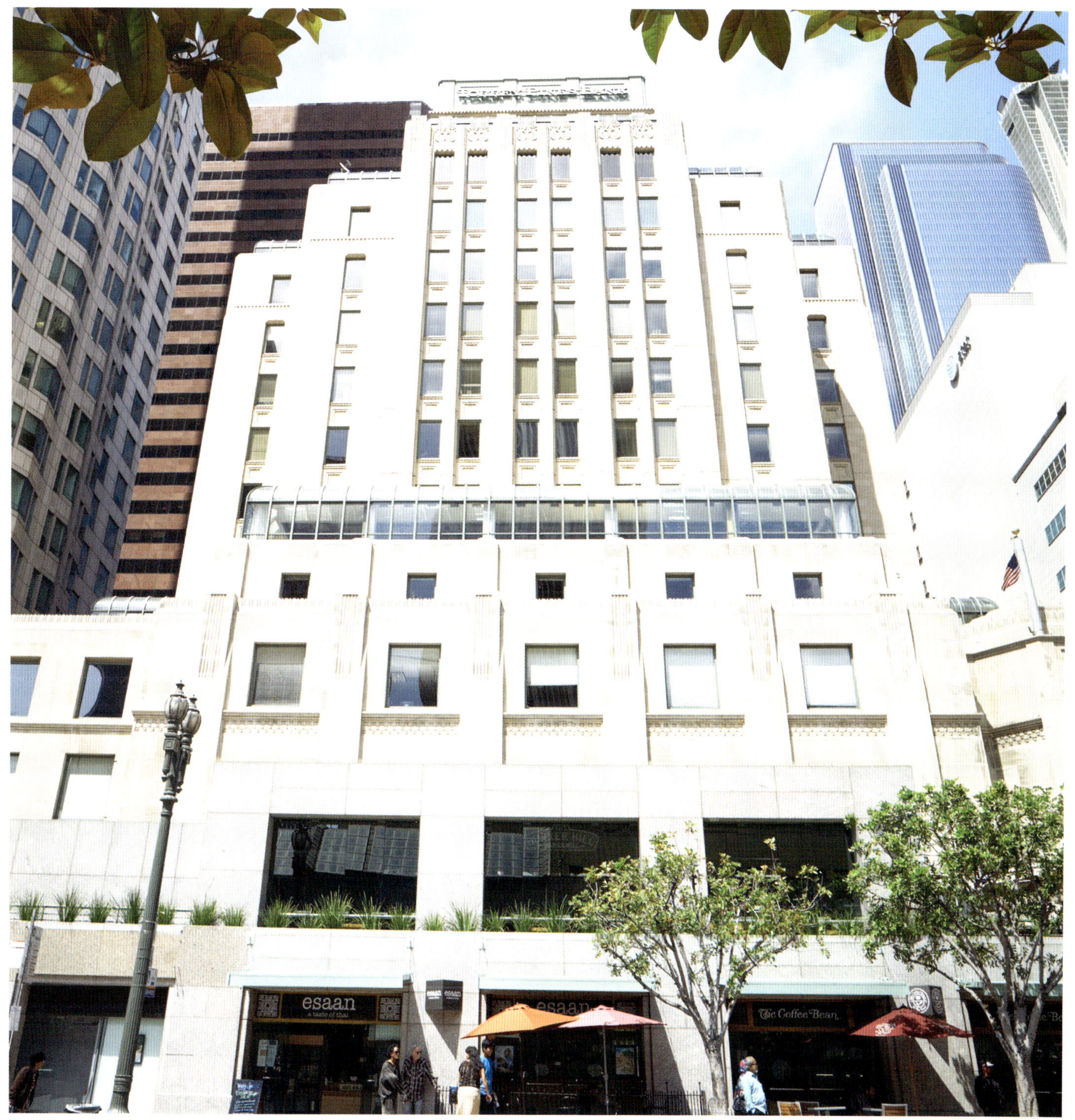

One Bunker Hill Building

This 13-story former utility company building once dwarfed its neighbors in Downtown but now sits in the shadows of the surrounding skyscrapers. One of the first fully electrically-powered buildings in the Western U.S., the beautiful zig-zag Art Deco architecture ensures it still outshines the rest.

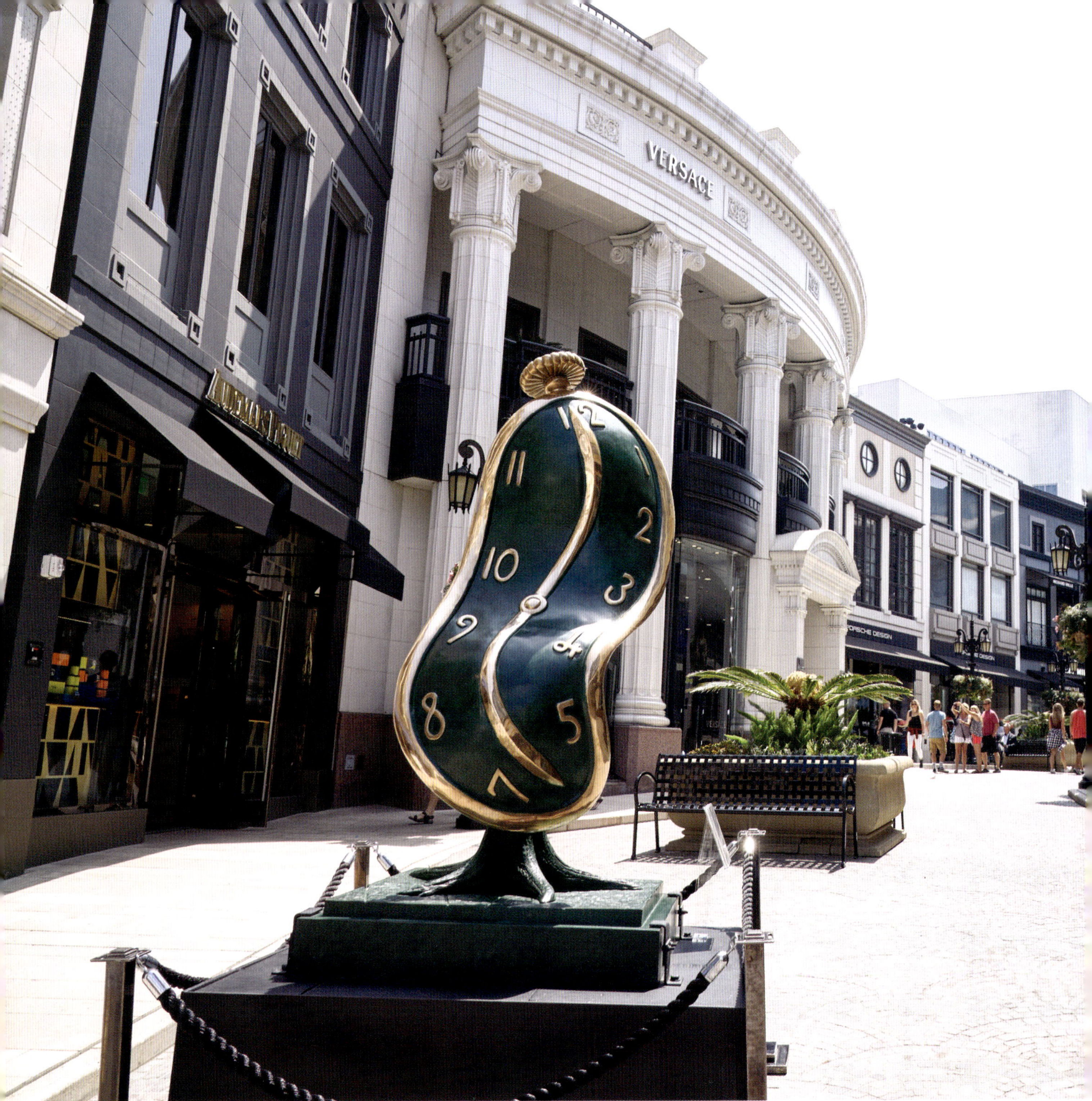

Rodeo Drive

Salvador Dali's famous melting clock sculpture *Dance of Time I* takes center stage on one of the most luxurious shopping streets in the world. Signifying how time stops for no man, many visitors would disagree as they get lost in the opulence of the designer stores lining the street.

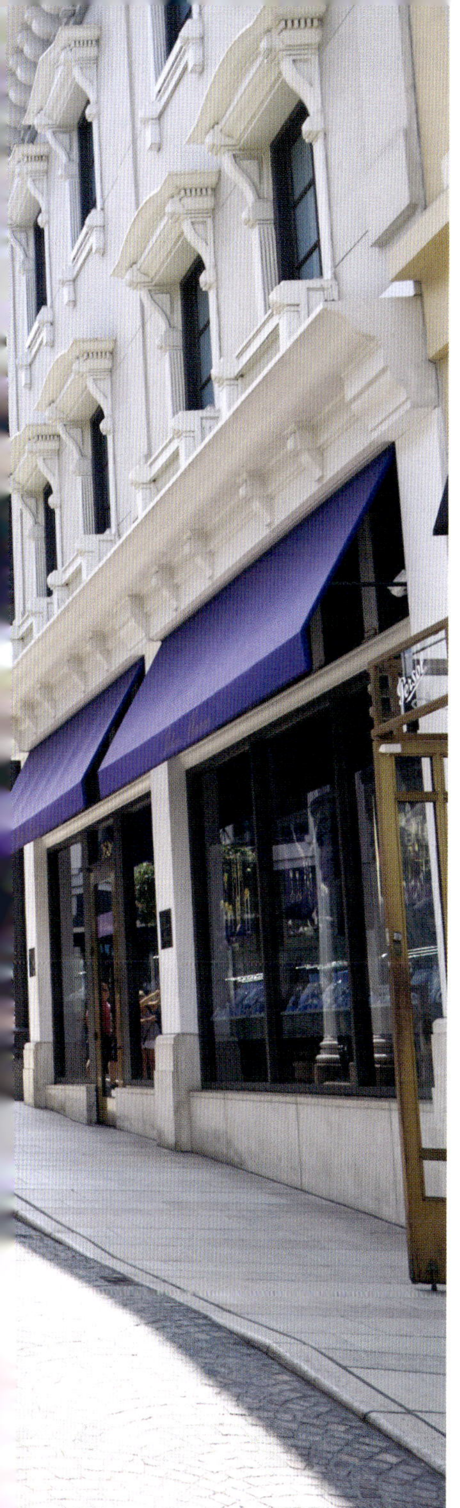

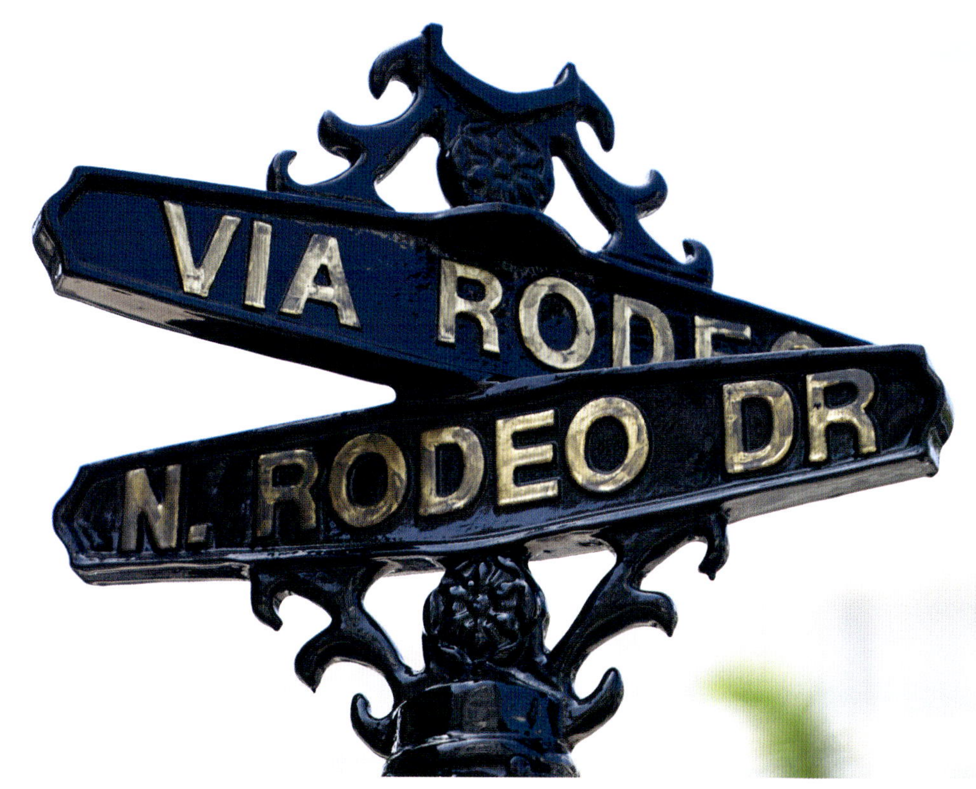

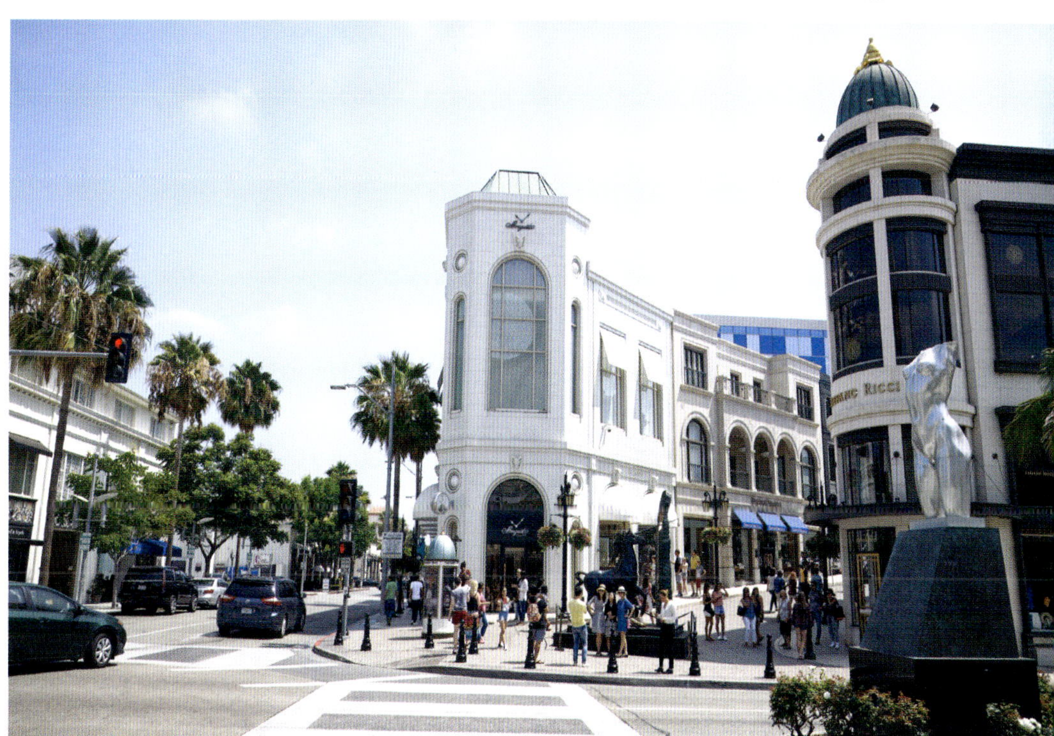

Rodeo Drive *(top and bottom)*

The area around Rodeo Drive has become so synonymous with luxury it now has its very own Walk of Style, honoring the great and good of fashion and design. The shimmering *Torso* sculpture sits on the southern end of the Walk of Fame and was created by Robert Graham in 2003.

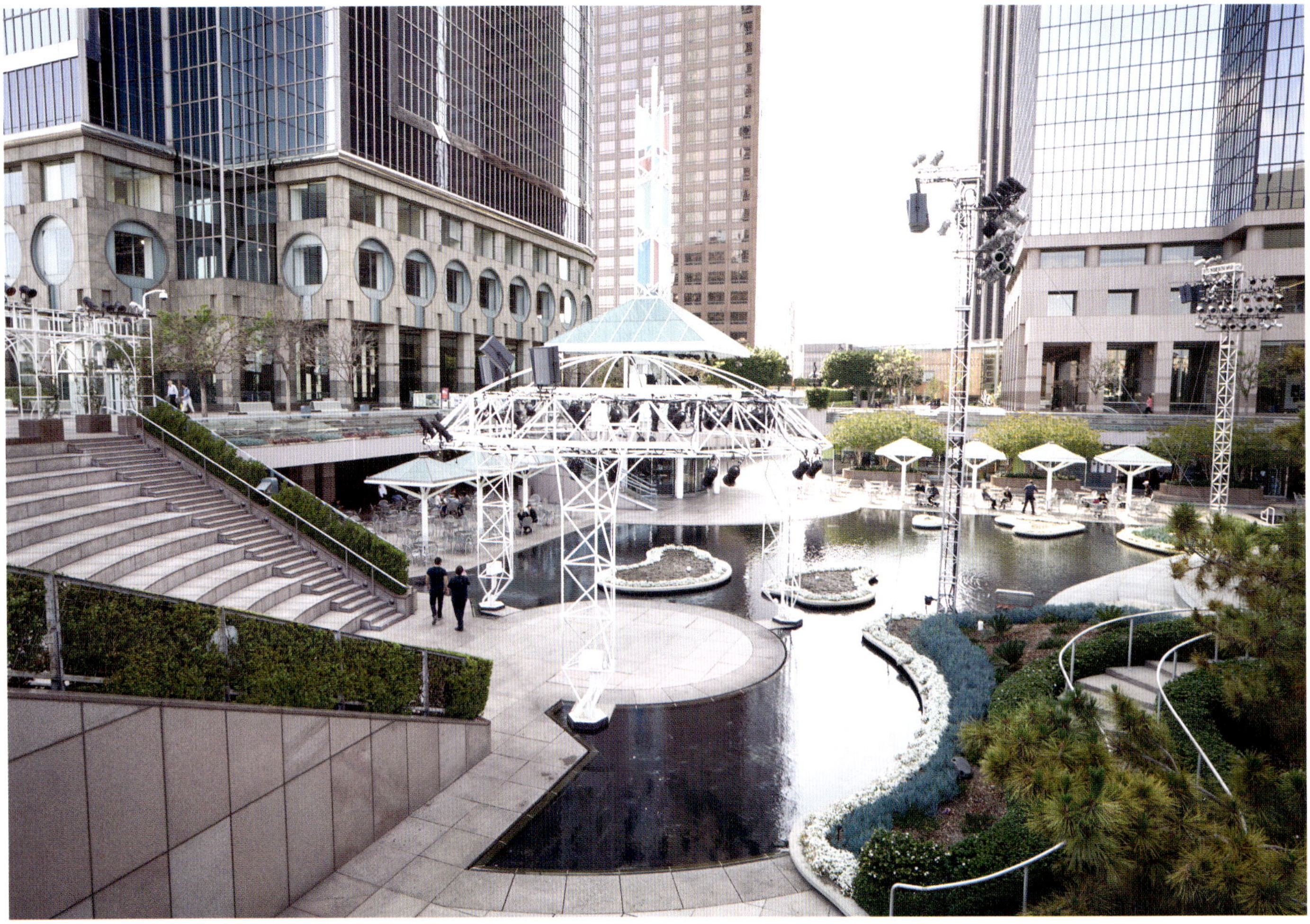

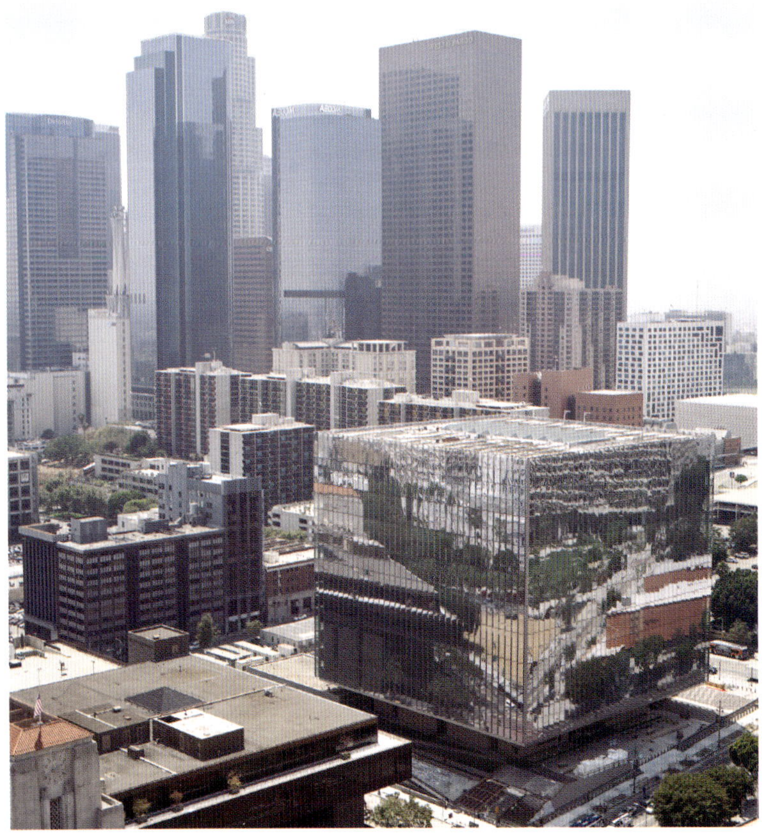

One California Plaza *(above)*

Workers and visitors are often seen enjoying lunch on the open-air seating of this lush 1.5-acre water court, which sits beneath the two California Plaza skyscrapers. At 577 feet, One California is the smaller of the two towers and is occupied by various banking and financial firms.

View from City Hall *(left)*

The famous Downtown Los Angeles skyline as seen from the observation deck on the 26th floor of City Hall. The gravity-defying floating cube in the foreground is a federal courthouse, which opened in 2016. You can almost see the reflection of City Hall in the cube's shiny tempered glass facade.

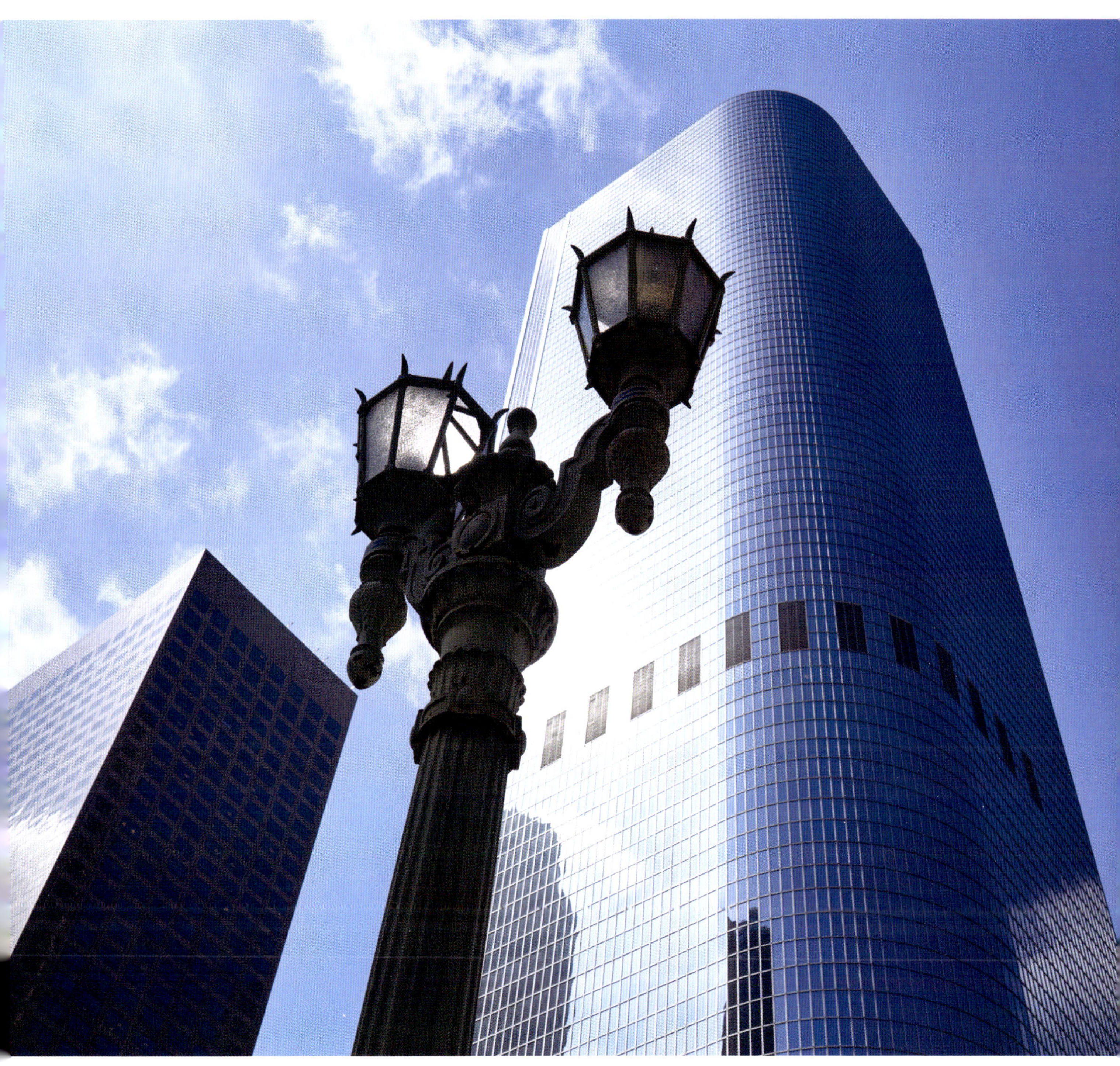

Two California Plaza

This 750-foot, futuristic skyscraper juxtaposed behind an historic 1920s street lamp post is typical of how old and new coalesce throughout Downtown Los Angeles. The gleaming office tower of Two California Plaza was designed by Arthur Erickson Architects and twice named Building of the Year by BOMA.

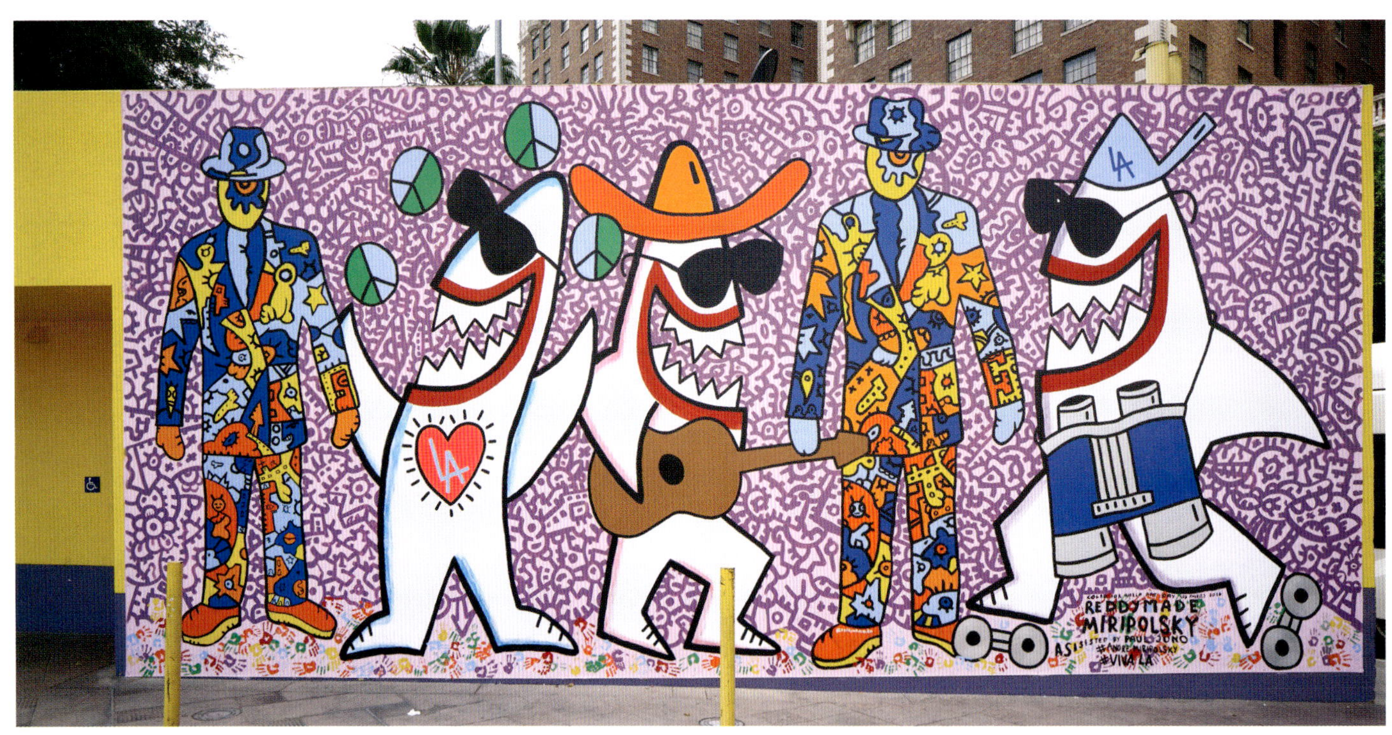

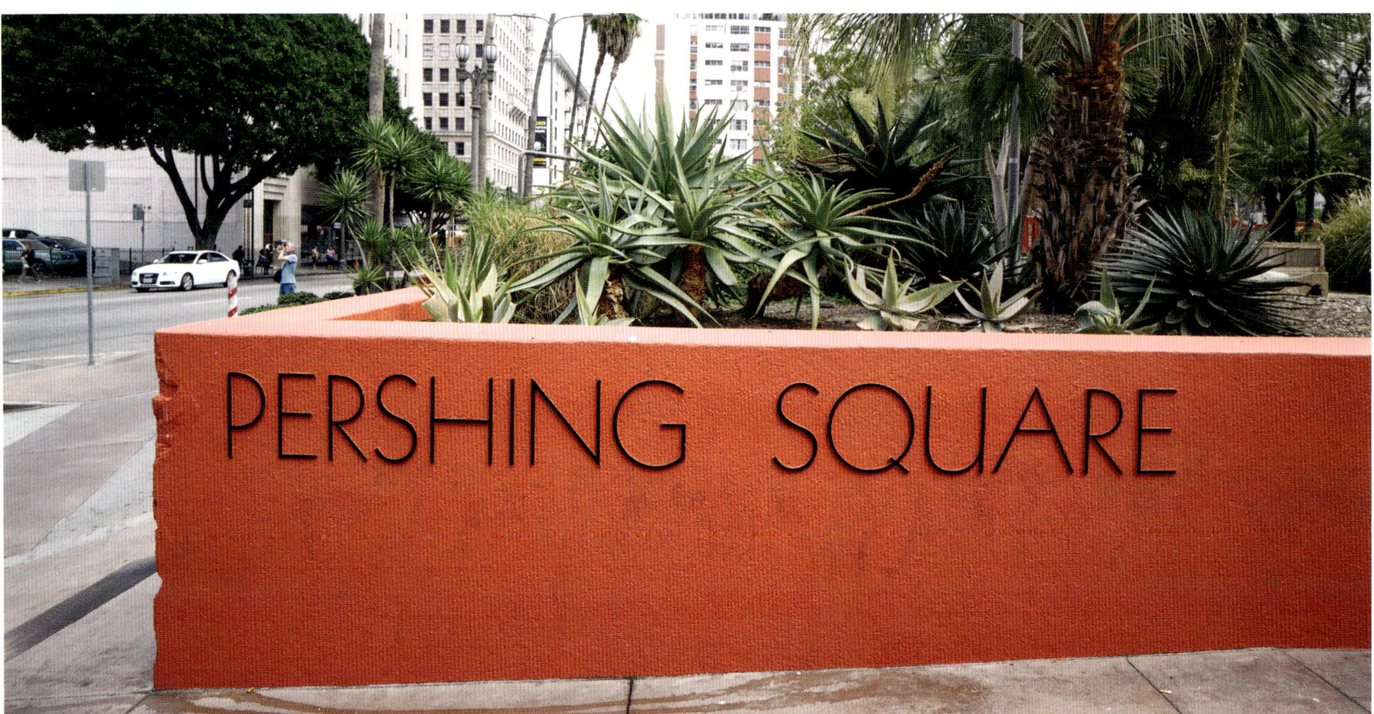

Pershing Square *(top and bottom)*

This vibrant mural by renowned Los Angeles pop artist Andre Miripolsky, which is part of his Sharks in the City collection, brightens up this section of Pershing Square, a public park that lies atop a subterranean parking garage in Downtown.

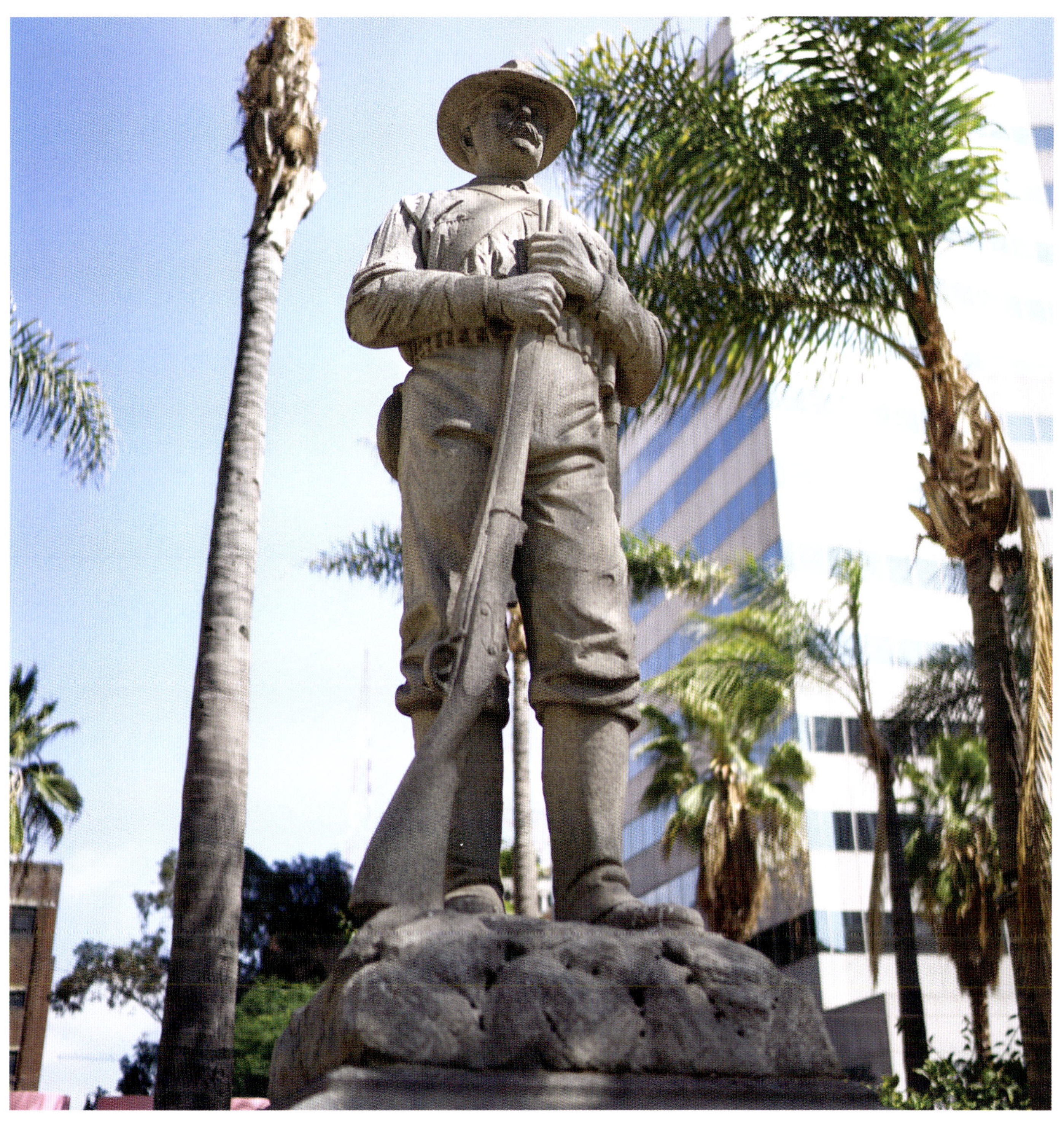

Spanish-American War Monument *(above)*

Believed to be the oldest work of public art in Los Angeles, this monument in Pershing Square to the 20 local soldiers who perished during the Spanish-American War of 1898 was erected in 1900. The statue is said to be modeled after 7th California Infantry volunteer, Charlie Hammond, of San Francisco.

Pershing Square *(pages 24–25)*

The purple structure and orange concrete spheres in this public park aim to symbolize the water flow from the Californian mountains to the citrus farmers. Now surrounded by looming skyscrapers, this heart-of-Downtown park actually dates back to the 19th century, although it has vastly changed over the years.

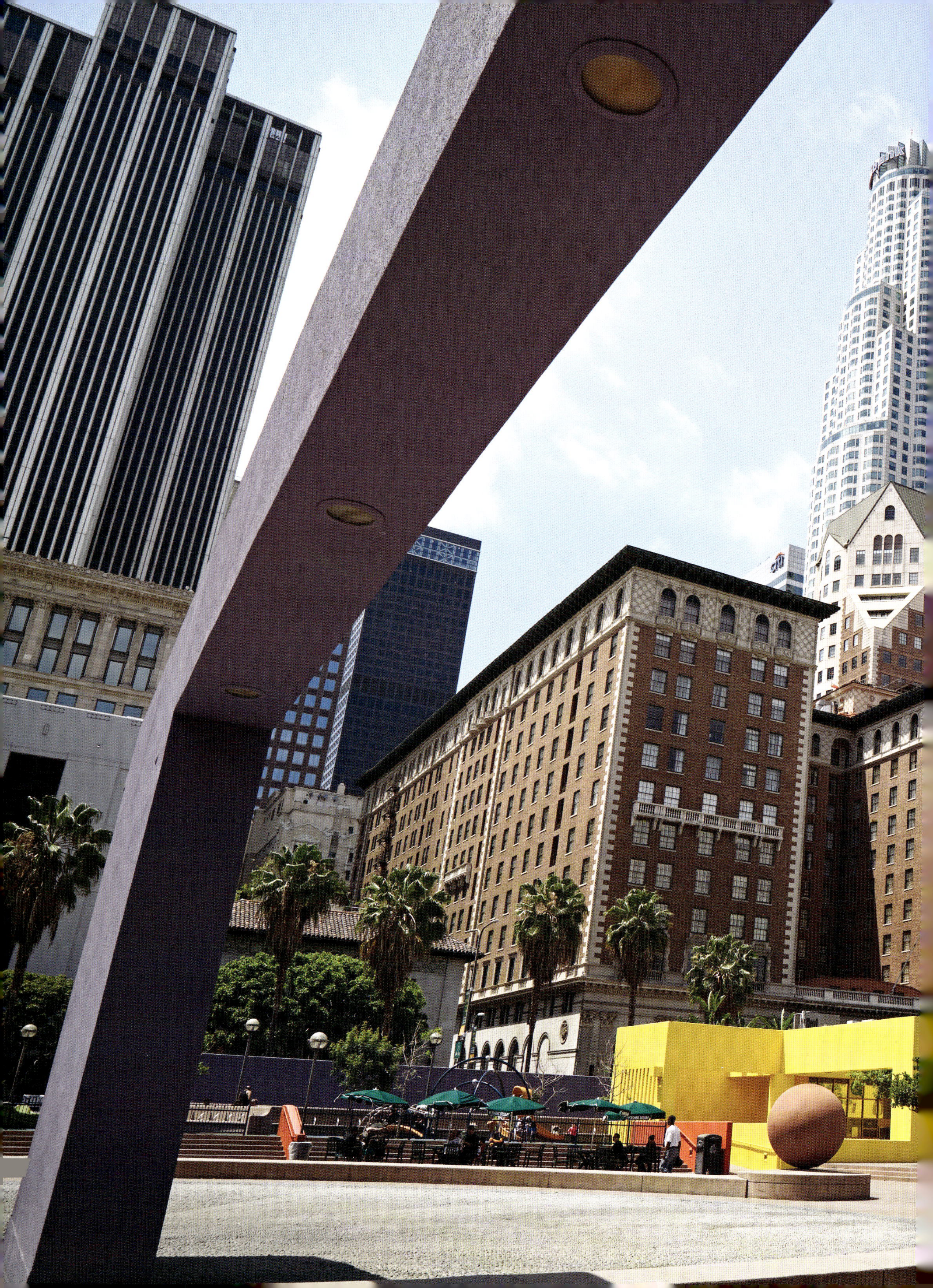

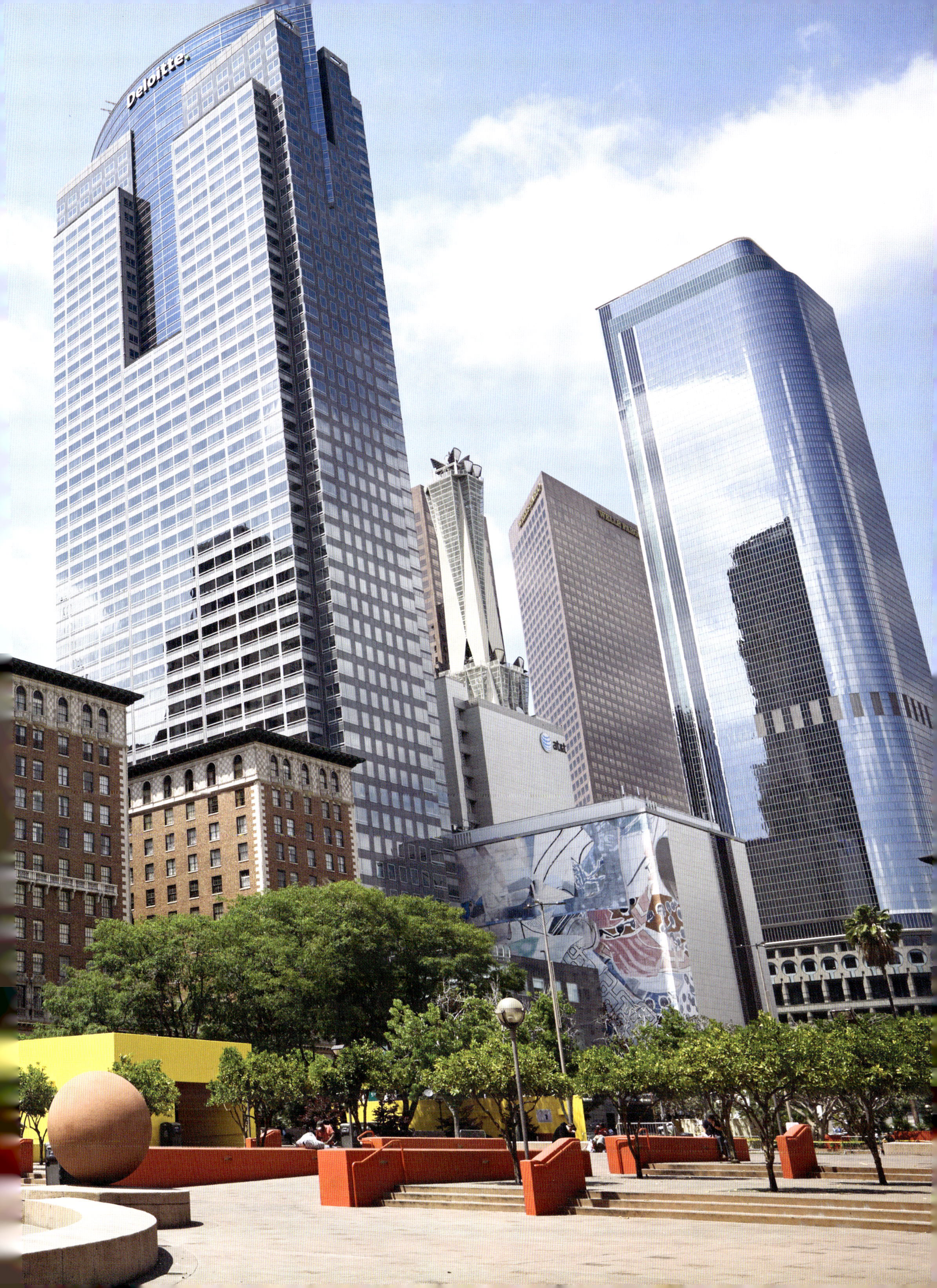
Deloitte.

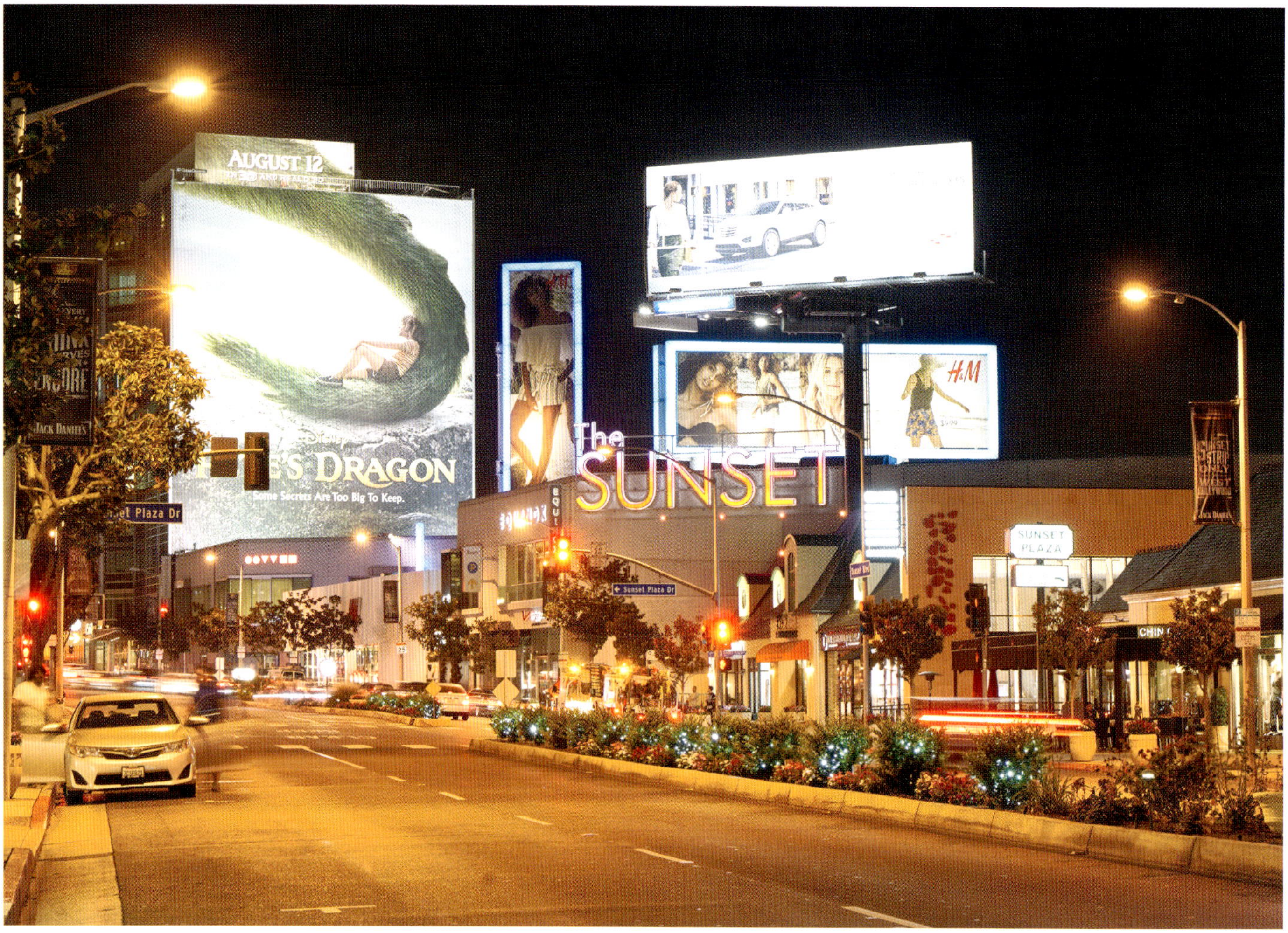

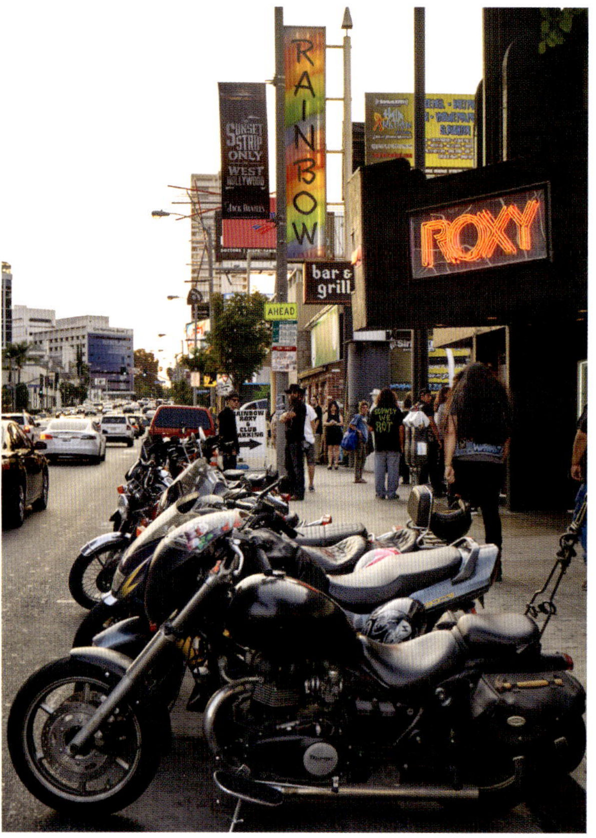

Sunset Strip *(above and left)*

With its gaudy neon lights and legendary venues such as the Roxy and Rainbow, the famous Sunset Strip is where bands such as Mötley Crüe and Guns N' Roses cut their teeth. It remains a haven for hell raisers and those in search of a good time.

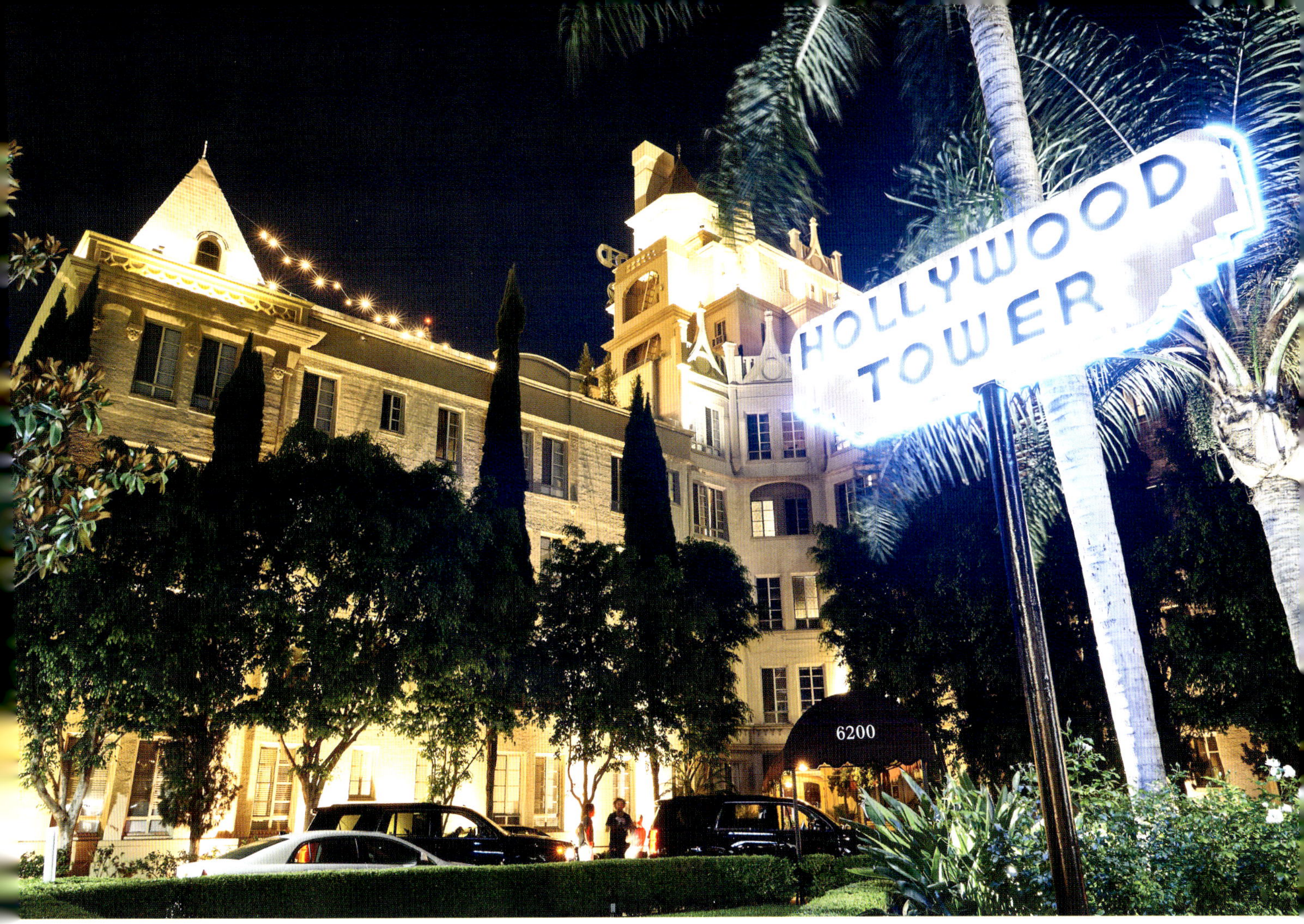

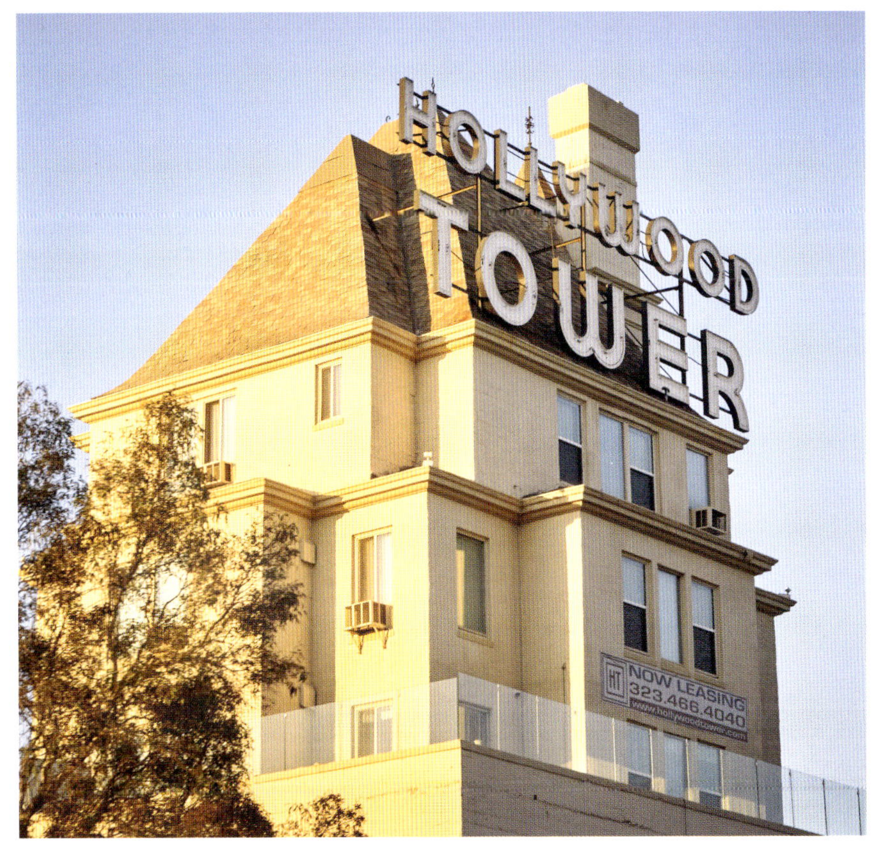

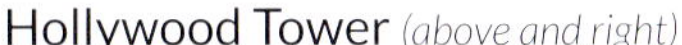

Hollywood Tower *(above and right)*

Cited as the inspiration for the Twilight Zone Tower of Terror ride at Disney's theme parks in California, Florida, and Paris, this apartment block offered "sophisticated living for film luminaries during the 'Golden Age' of Hollywood," according to a plaque on the door. It is also said to be haunted.

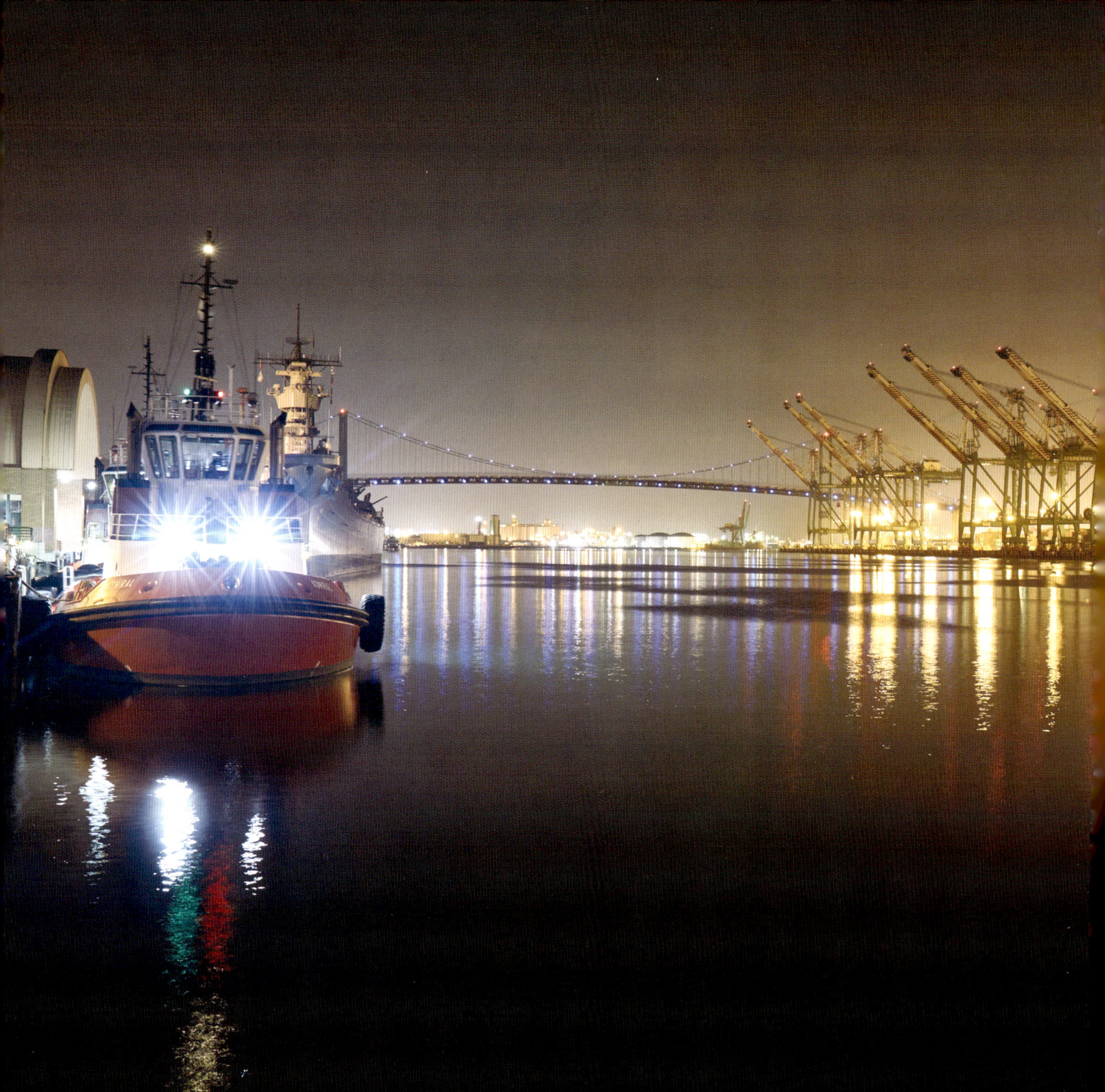

Port of Los Angeles

Evening on the Port of Los Angeles, also called "America's Port," as multi-colored lights from boats, bridges, and cranes reflect off the calm waters to striking effect. A rare moment of calm for the busy port, which sees approximtley $1.2 billion worth of cargo pass through it each day.

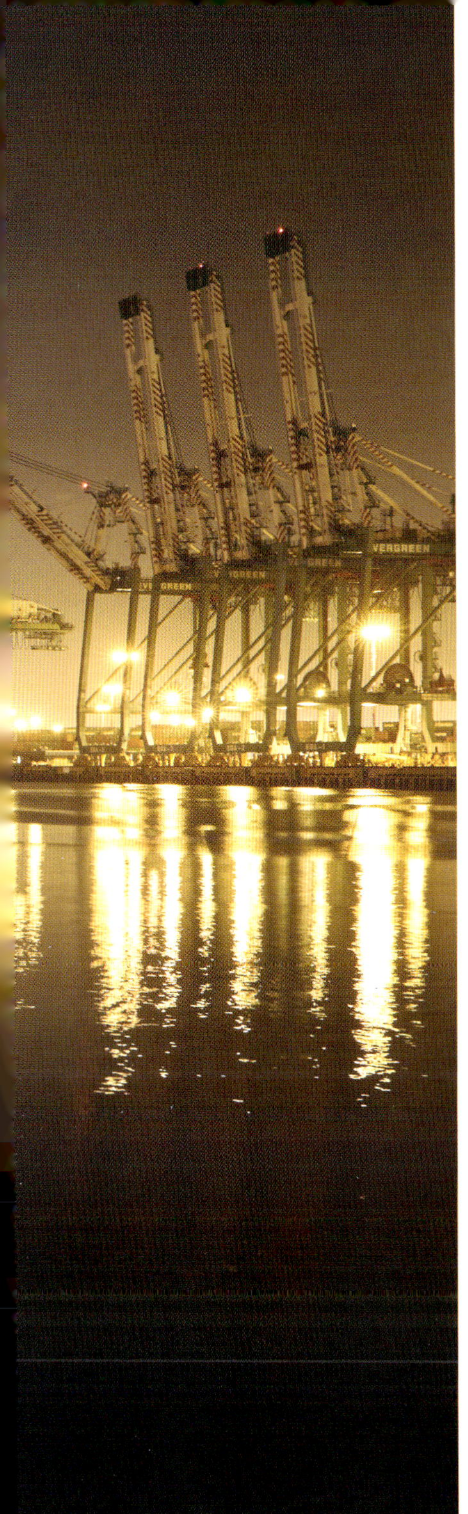

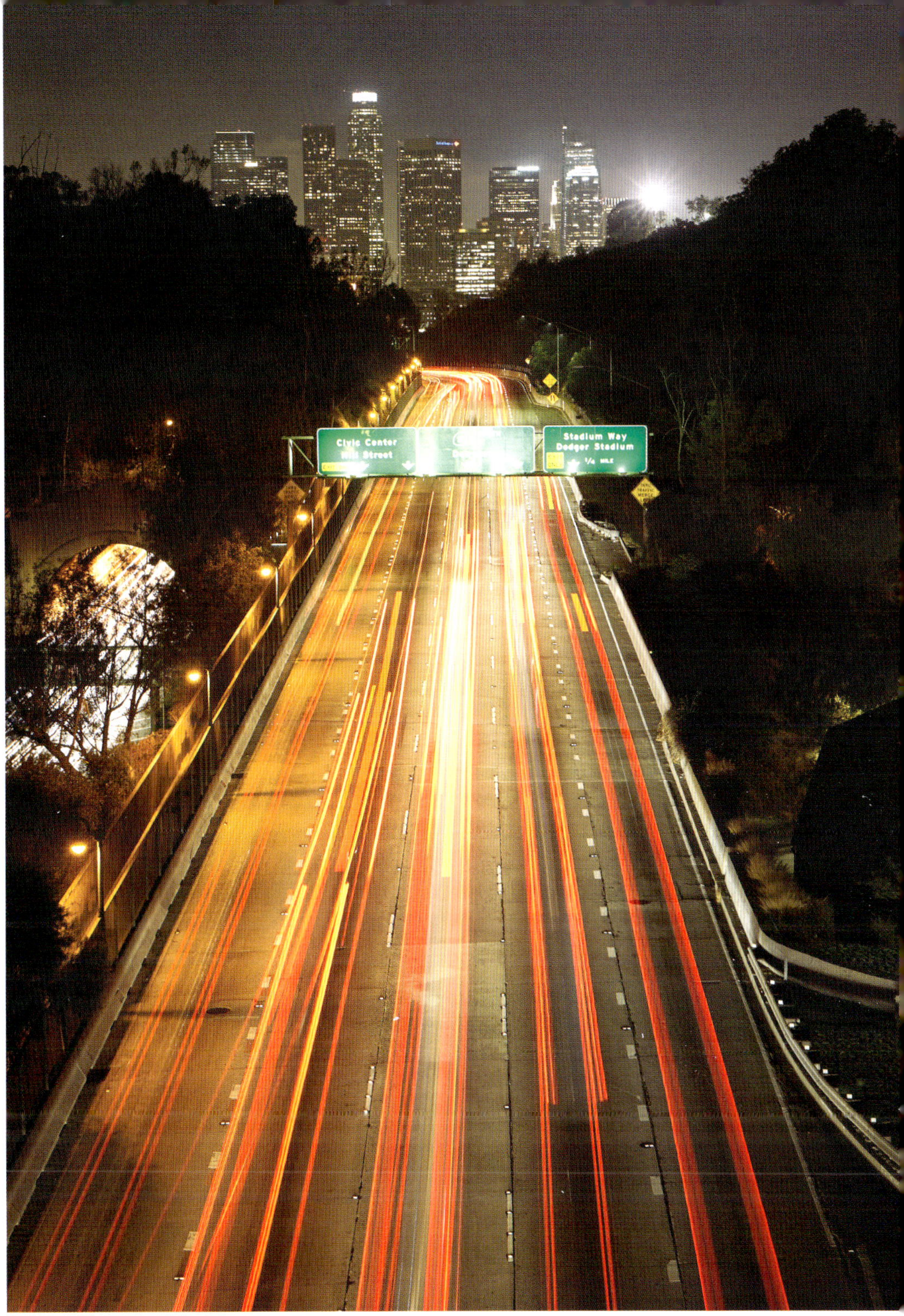

Downtown Skyline

A long exposure captures the glittering Downtown Los Angeles skyline nestled behind the frenetic 110 freeway at night. Even those who have never visited Los Angeles will most likely recognize the cityscape from movies such as *Fast and the Furious*, *Die Hard*, *L.A. Confidential*, and *Rebel Without a Cause*.

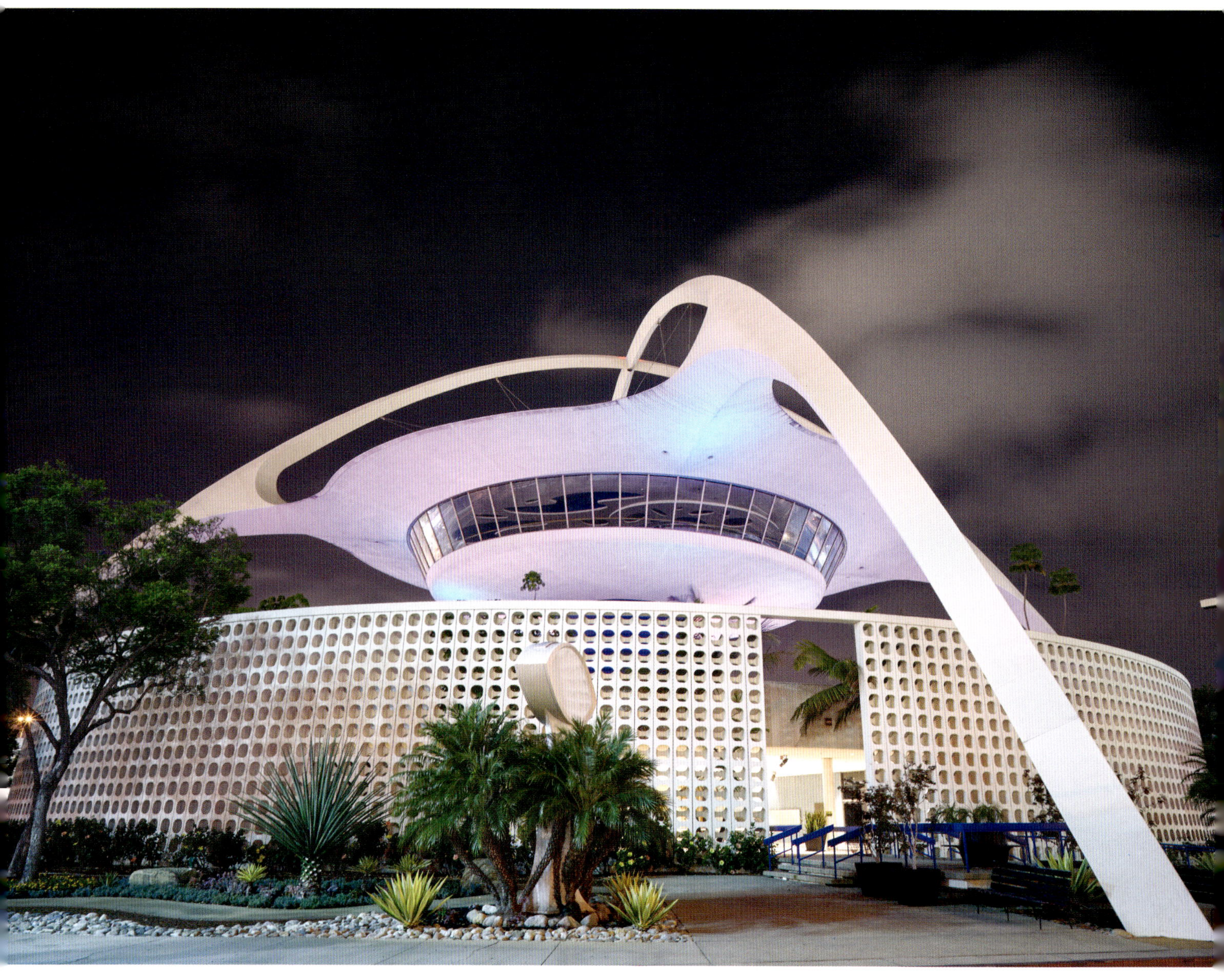

LAX Theme Building

Illuminated with purple lighting at night, the playful, space-age LA Theme Building resembles a flying saucer on four legs. The iconic structure once housed a revolving restaurant but now serves as an observation deck, open on weekends, giving visitors 360-degree views of planes landing and taking off.

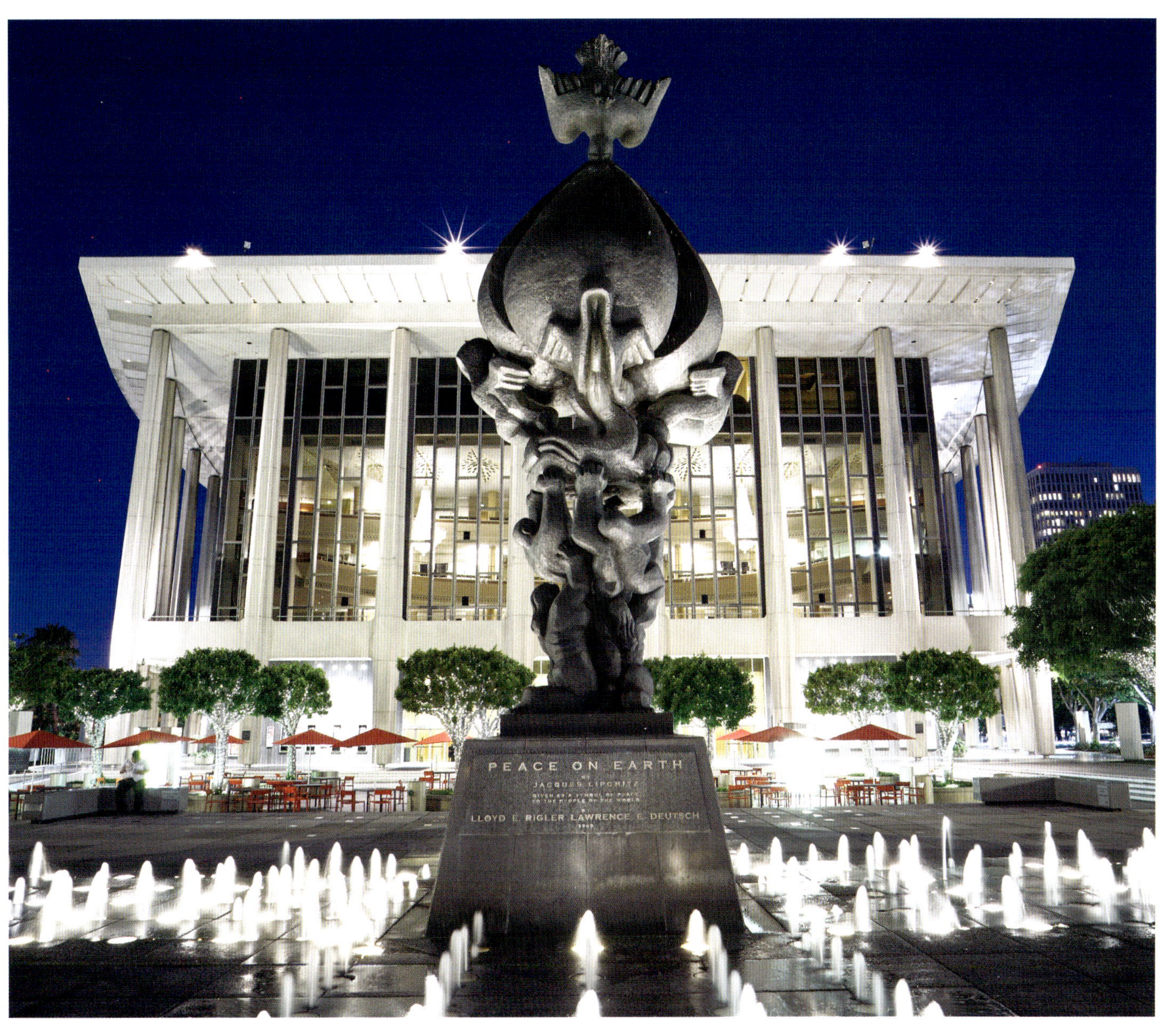

Dorothy Chandler Pavilion

Described by the artist as a "prayer for peace," the *Peace on Earth* sculpture by Jacques Lipchitz, takes center stage in front of the Dorothy Chandler Pavilion, at the Los Angeles Music Center. Surrounded by dancing fountains, the sculpture depicts a dove descending to earth with the spirit of peace.

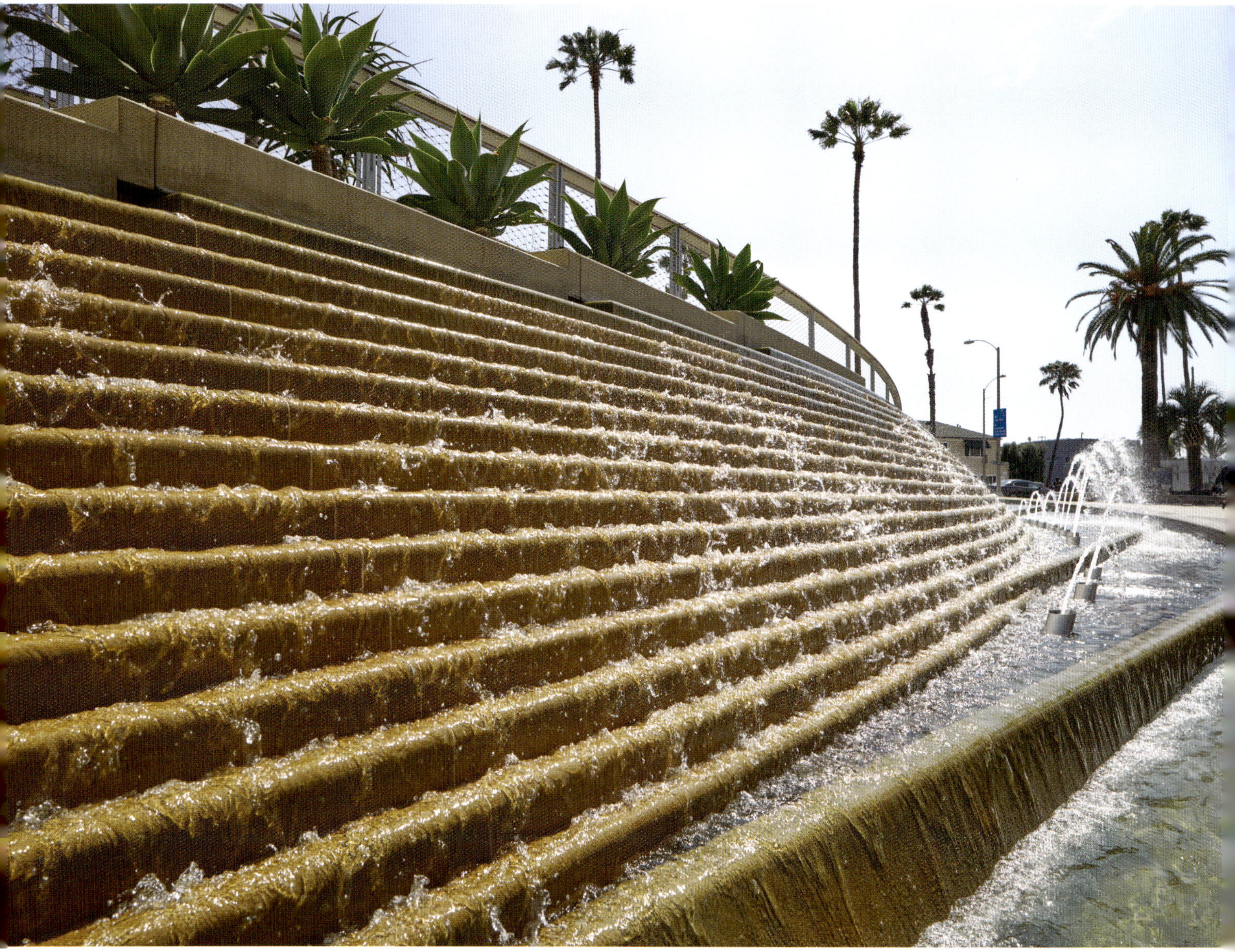

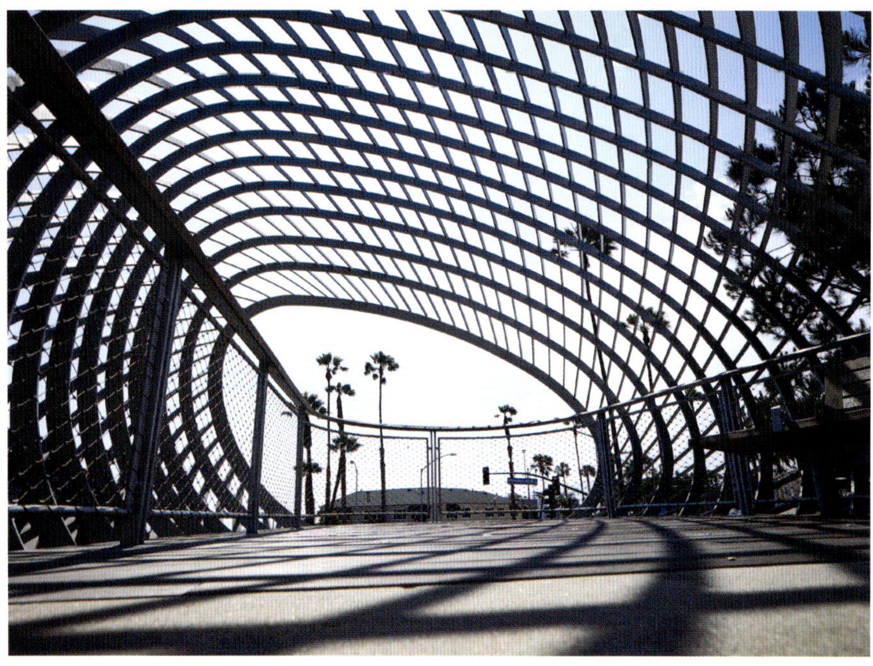

Tongva Park *(above and left)*

The cascading waters of this fountain and the curved lines of the observation deck lure visitors to the Pacific Ocean, located opposite this stunning Santa Monica park. The six-acre urban oasis is named after the indigenous Tongva people who have lived in the region for thousands of years.

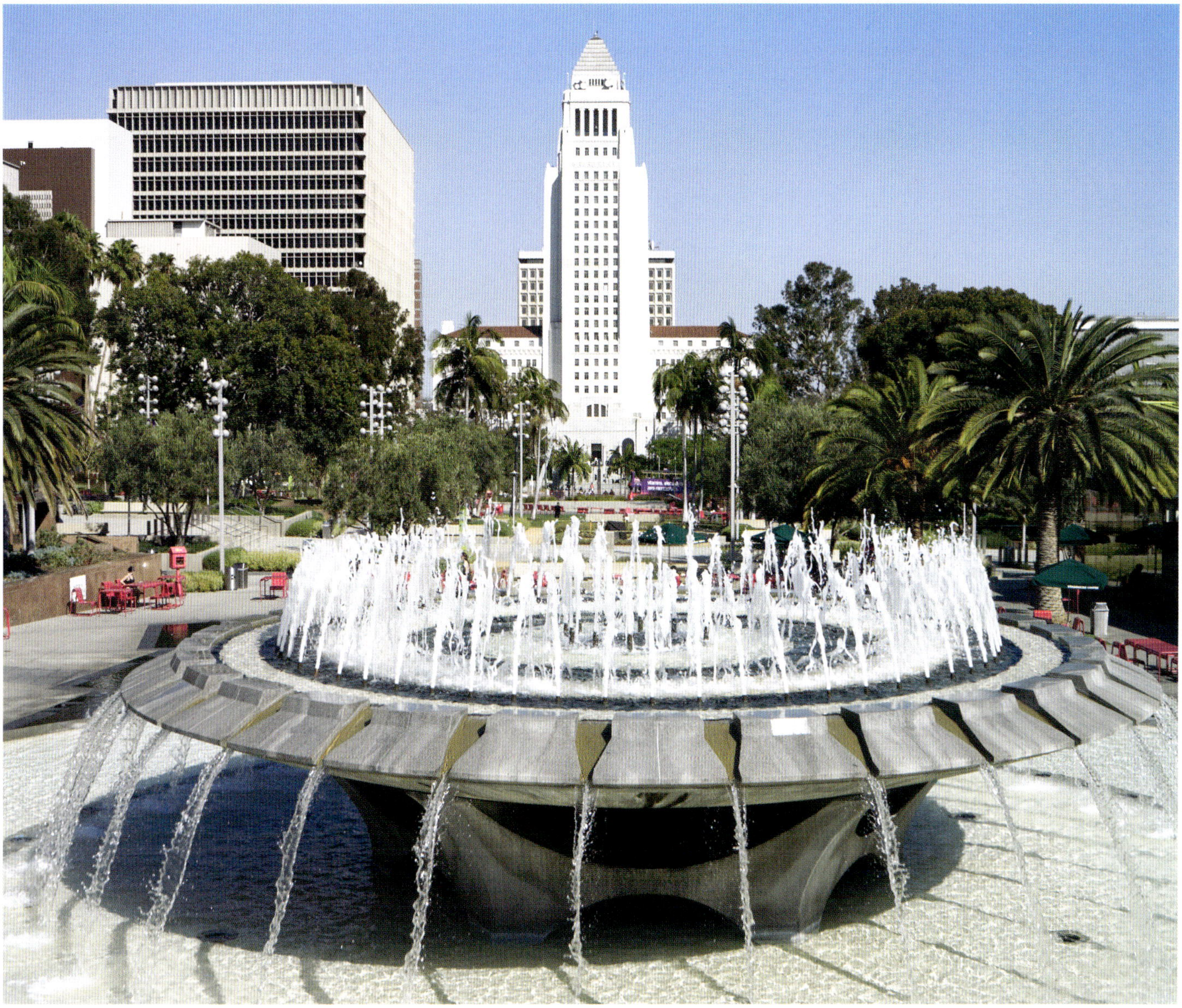

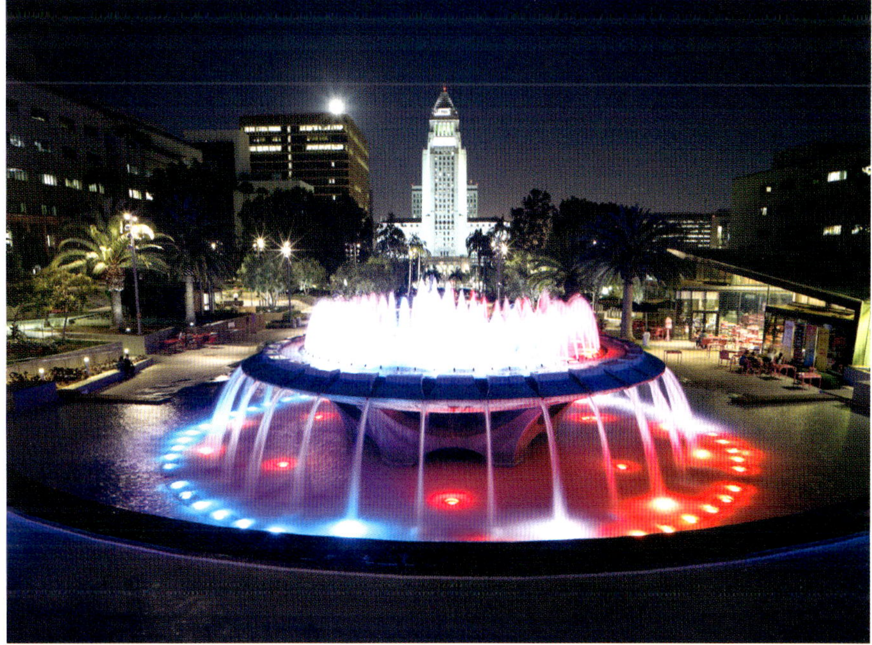

Grand Park *(above and right)*

From day to night, the stunning Arthur J. Will Memorial Fountain transforms from a tranquil fountain to an edgy neon-lit art installation. Located between City Hall and the Los Angeles Music Center, this "park for everyone" also features an interactive splash pad for children.

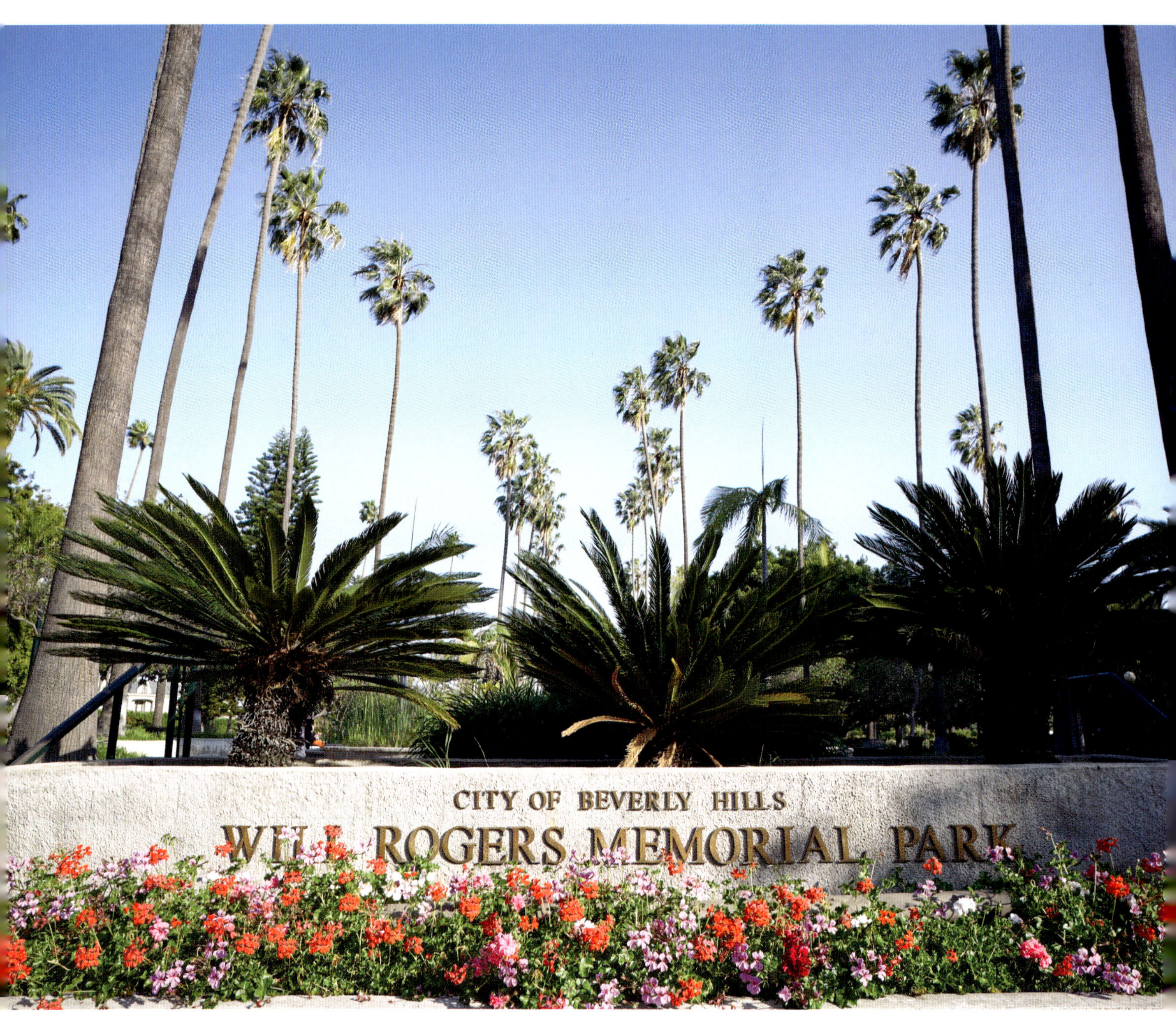

Will Rogers Memorial Park

Nothing says California like majestic rows of tall palms and these pass right through the middle of Will Rogers Memorial Park, in the heart of the affluent Beverly Hills neighborhood. The popular park has a pond with fish and turtles, a fountain, and a dragon tree.

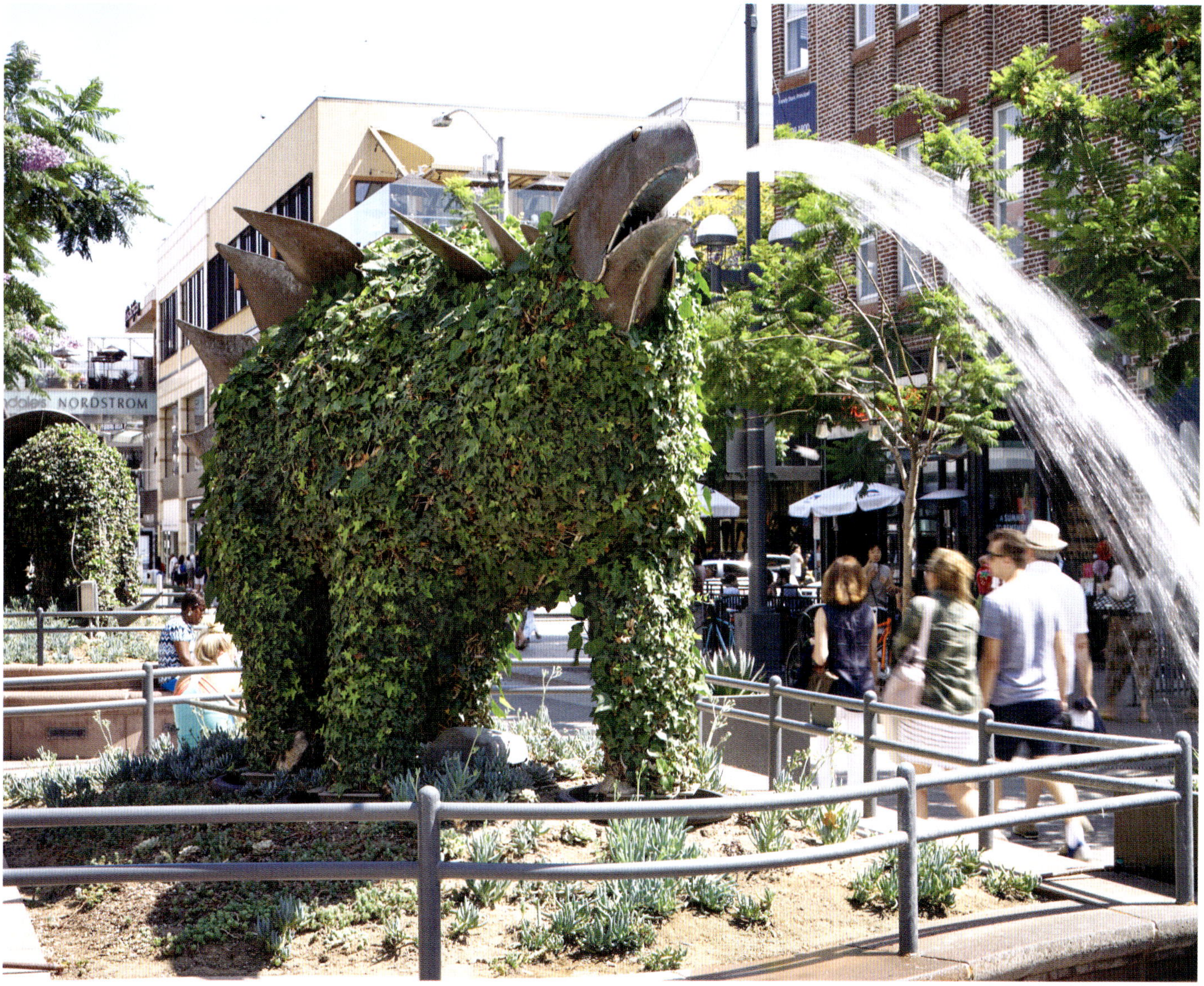

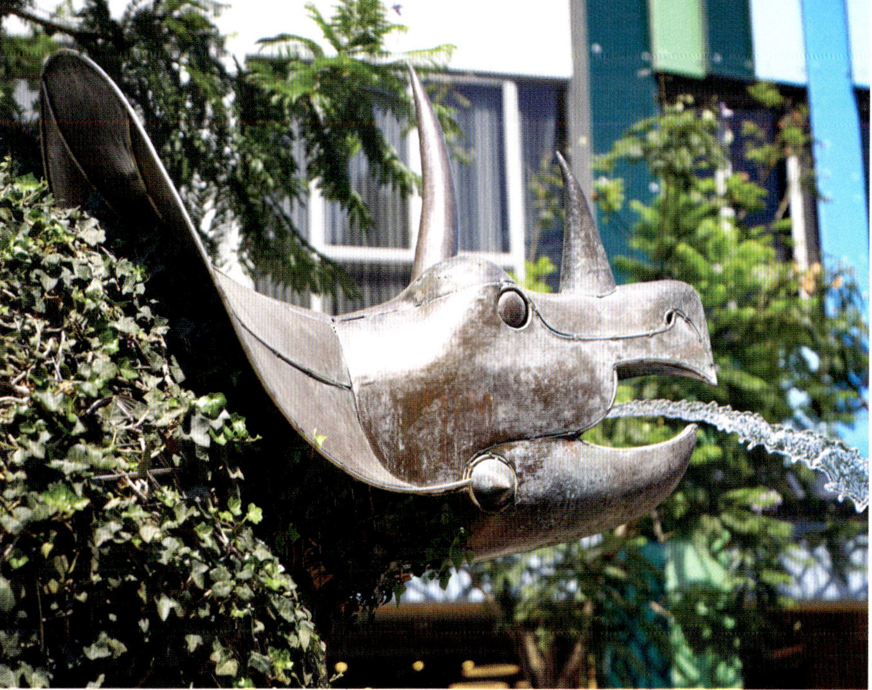

3rd Street Promenade *(above and right)*

These prehistoric beasts once spewed fire from their mouths to the delight of visitors to Santa Monica's 3rd Street Promenade shopping district. The fire was extinguished after the city's rick officials stepped in. Now the beloved copper and topiary sculptures spout the much safer alternative — water.

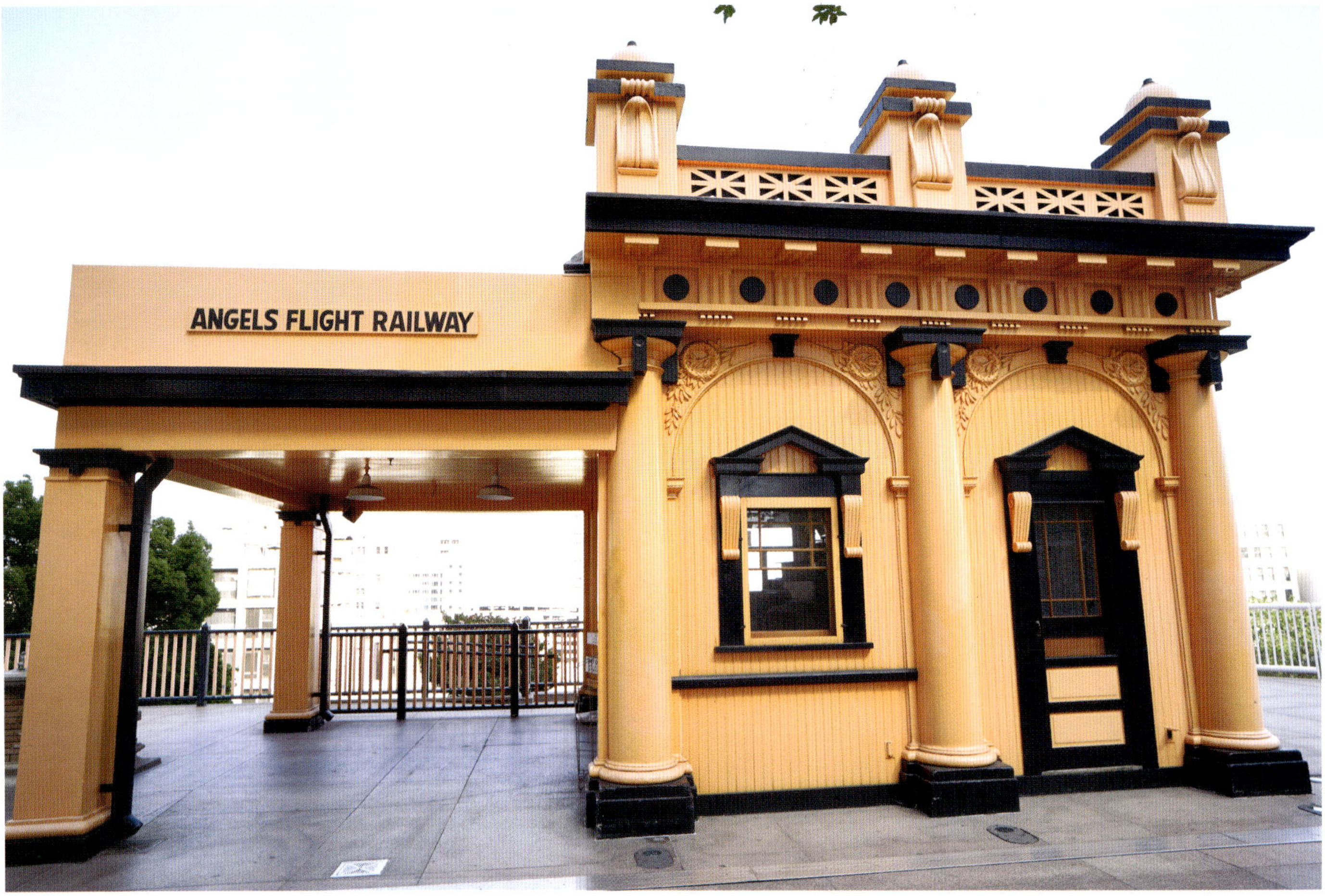

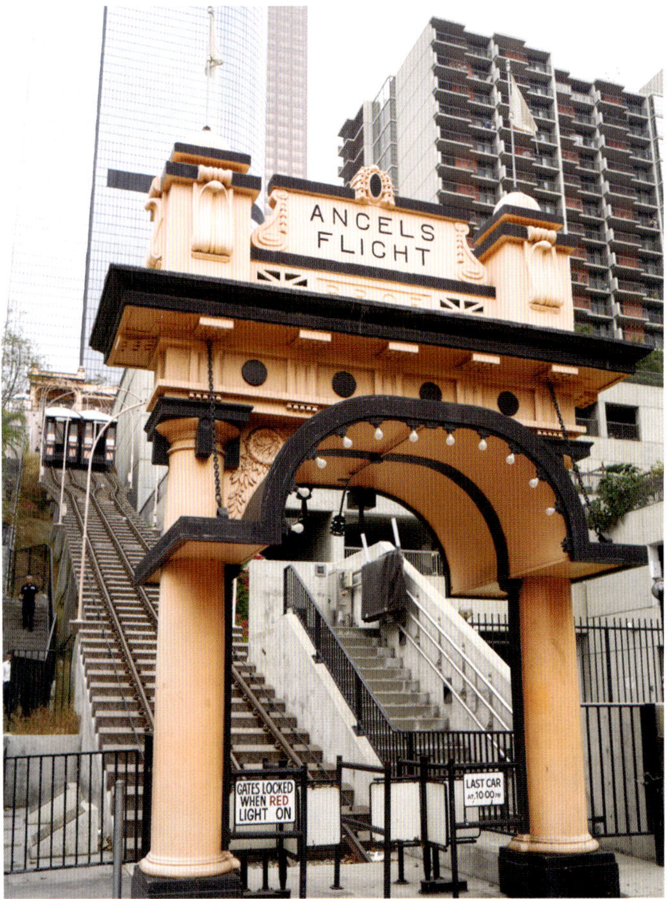

Angels Flight Railway *(above and left)*

The distinct orange and black buildings of this landmark funicular railway in the Bunker Hill district of Downtown Los Angeles now stand eerily quiet. The railway, which dates back to 1901, was originally a tourist attraction but was often used by local workers.

The Bradbury Building *(opposite)*

Illuminated with natural light and featuring ornate iron railings, marble staircases and open cage elevators, the interior of this Victorian land-mark is magical. Still stunning over a century after it first opened in 1893, it's easy to see why this remains one of Los Angeles' most photographed buildings.

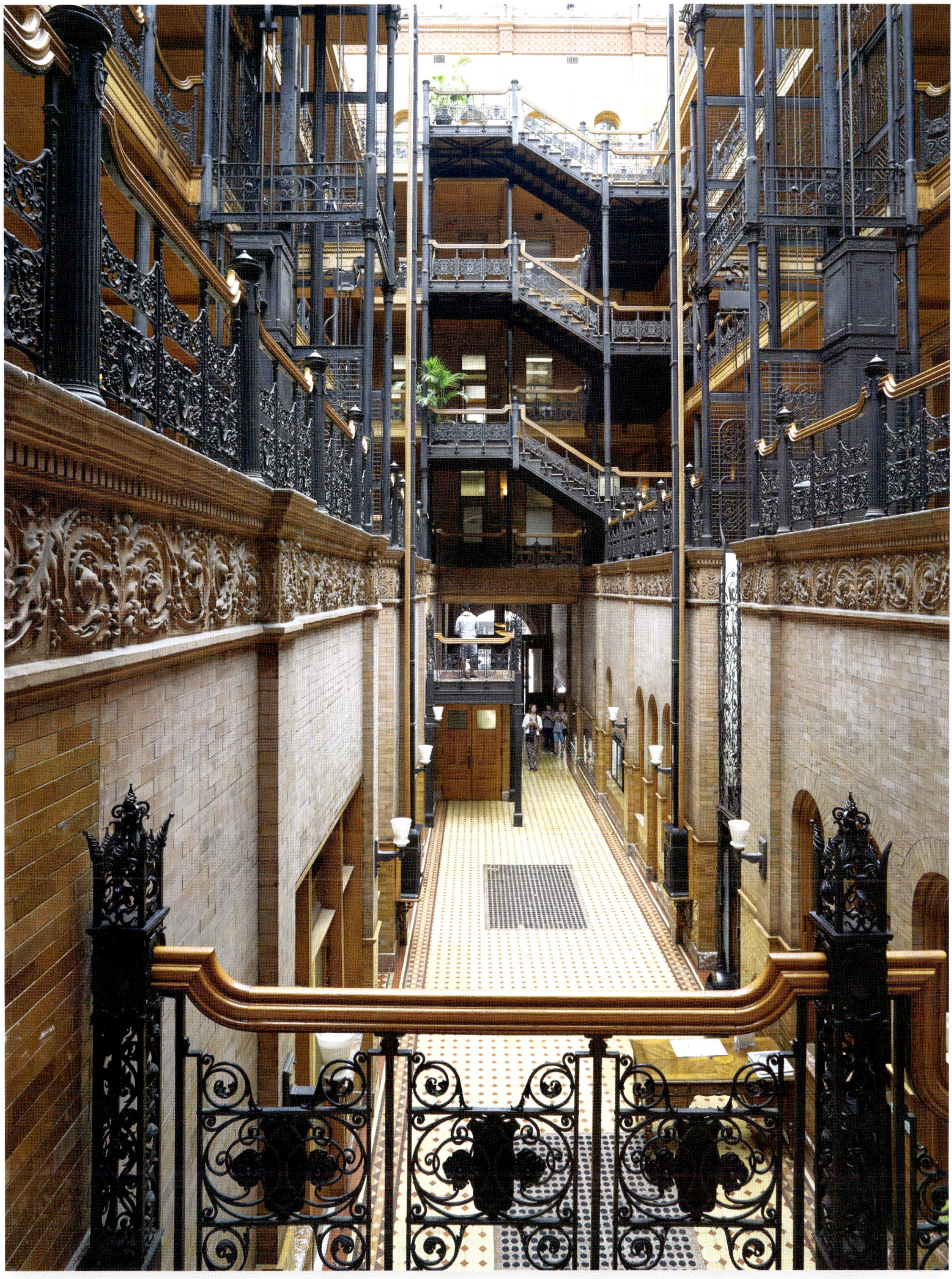

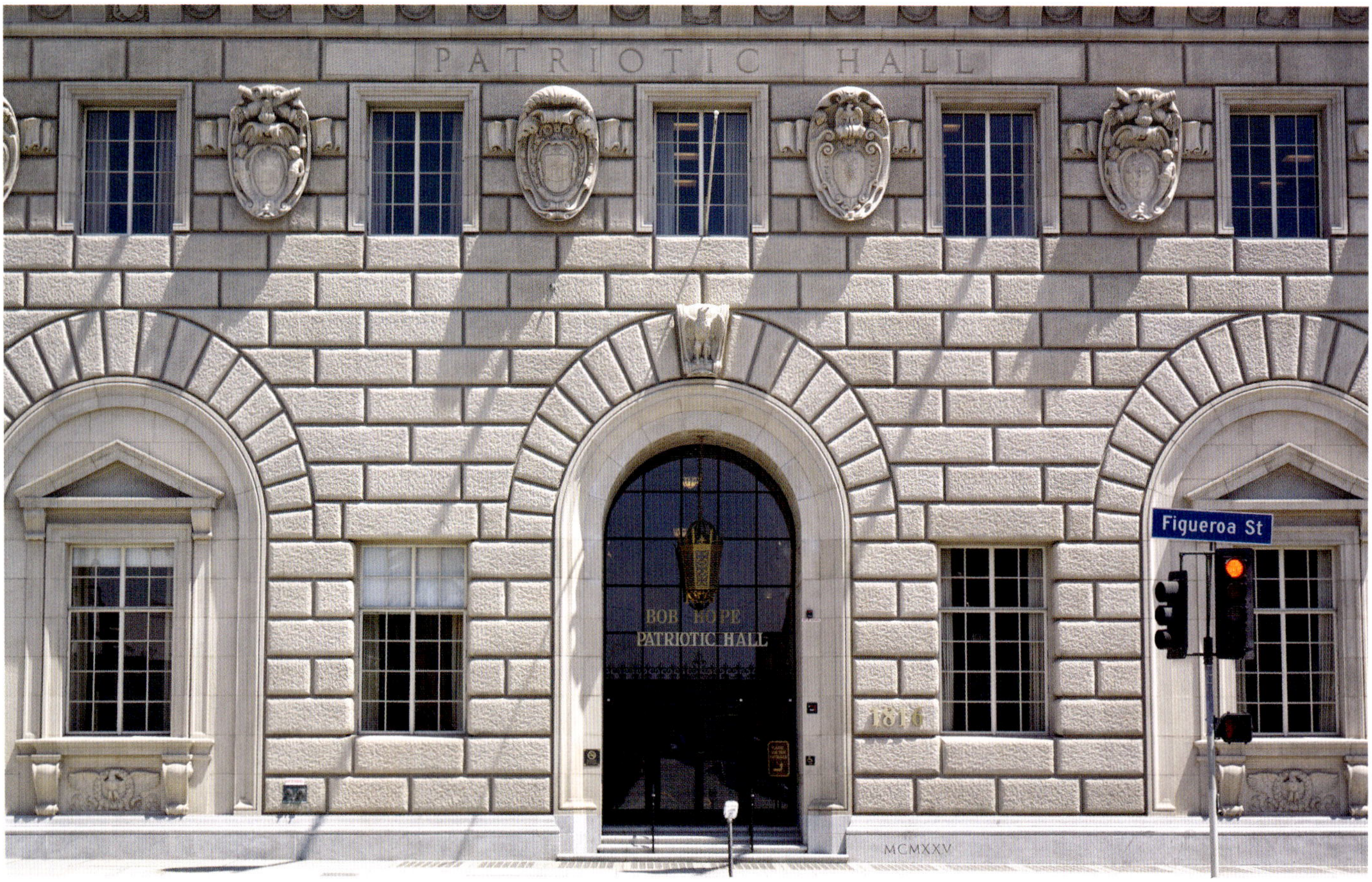

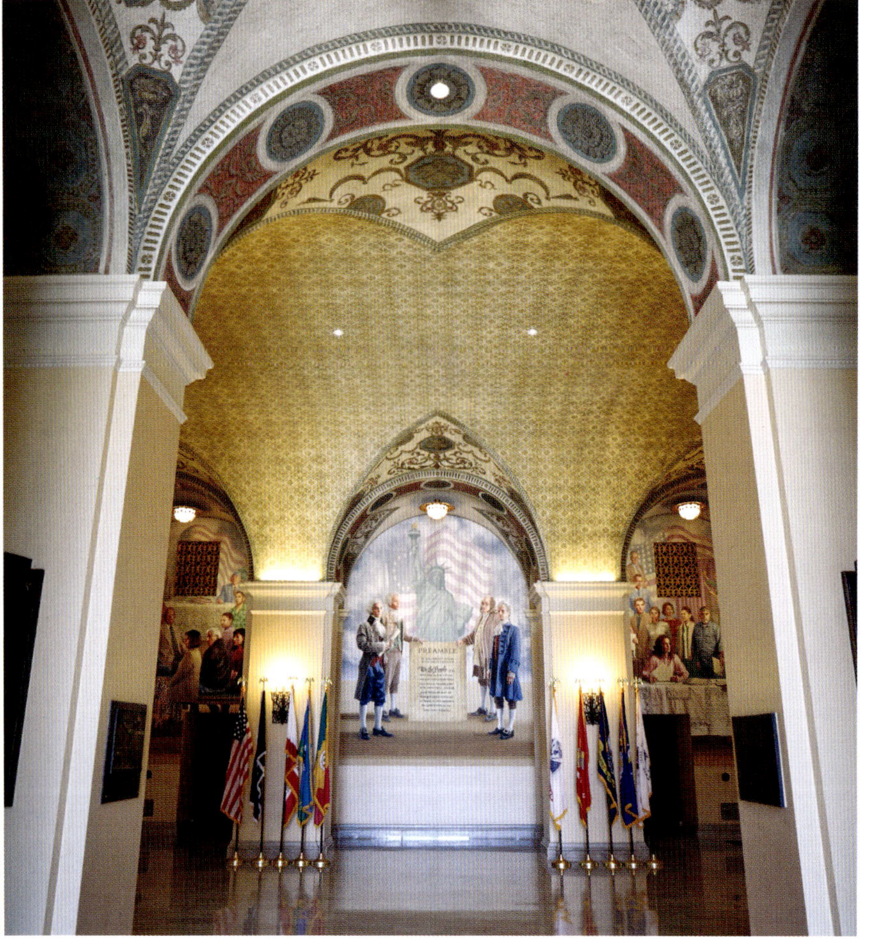

Bob Hope Patriotic Hall *(above and left)*

Once the tallest buildings in the city, this Romanesque-style hall was built as a memorial to veterans who died in the Civil War, Spanish-American War, and World War I. Three striking murals collectively titled, *We the People, Out of Many, One*, painted by artist and Vietnam veteran, Kent Twitchell, welcome visitors.

Getty Villa *(opposite)*

With its striking pillars, mosaic floors and decorative panels, the Getty Villa transports visitors back to ancient Rome. Modeled after a first-century Roman country house, this pristine museum is dedicated to the art and culture of the ancient world and home to thousands of Greek, Roman, and Etruscan antiques.

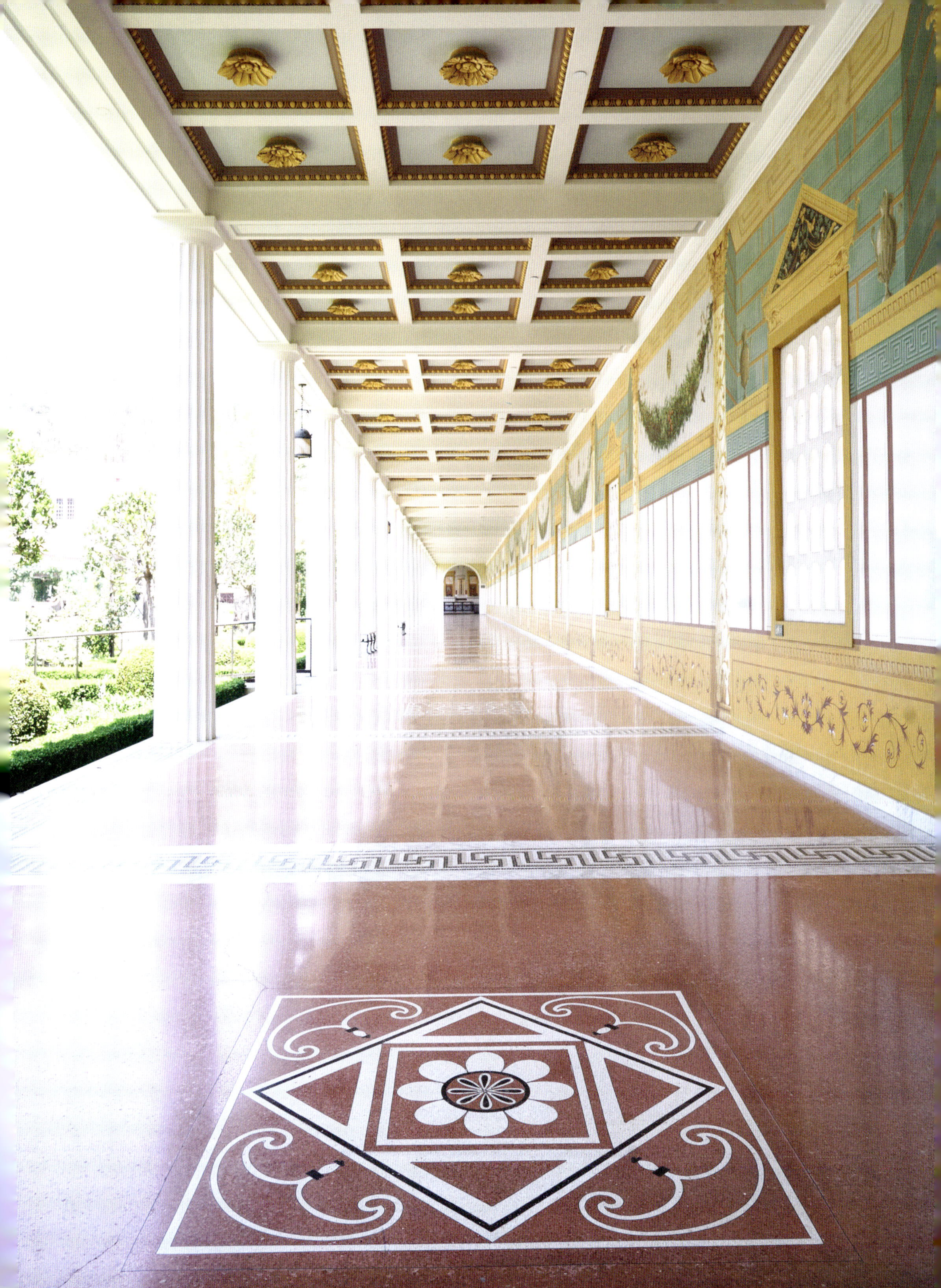

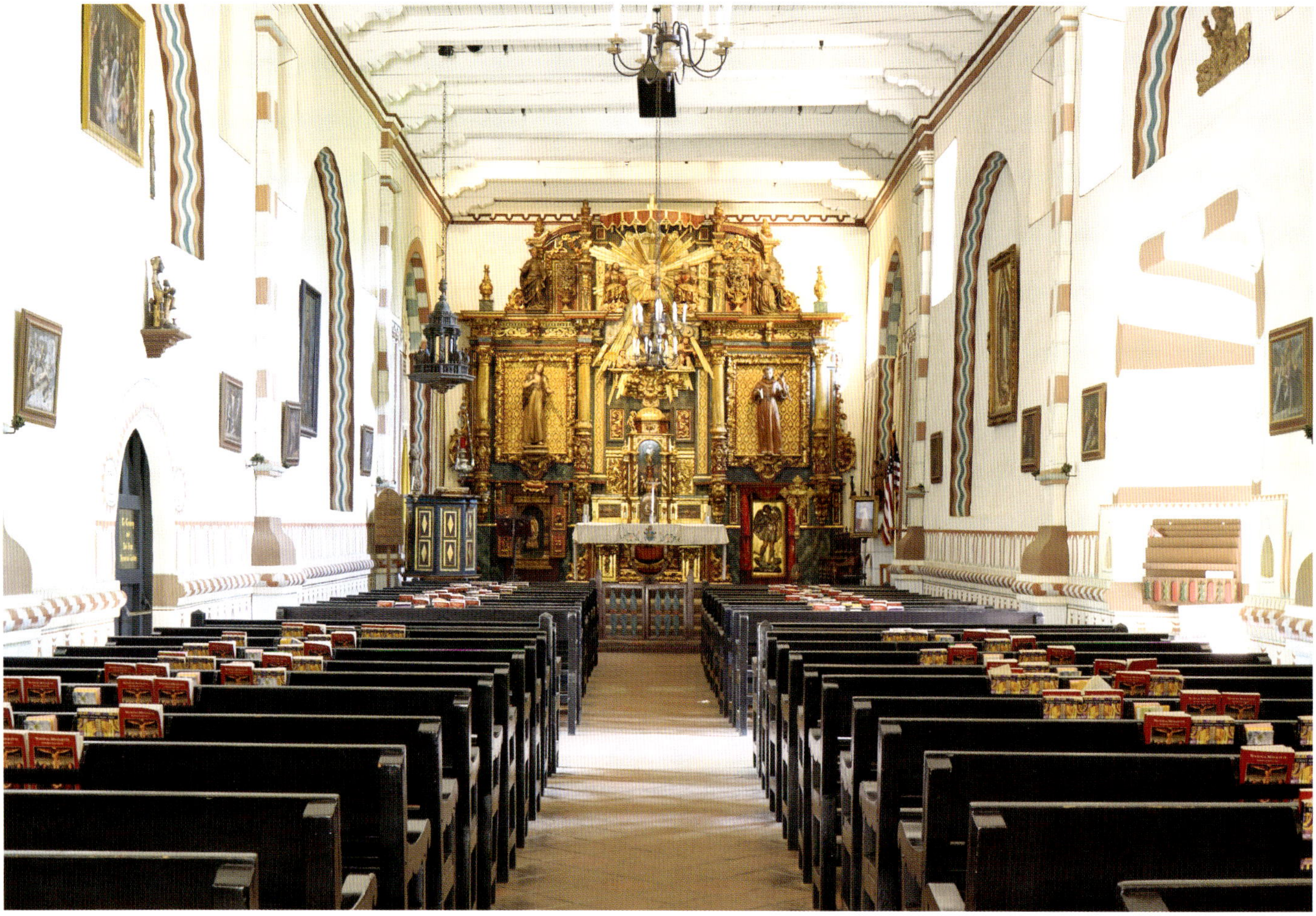

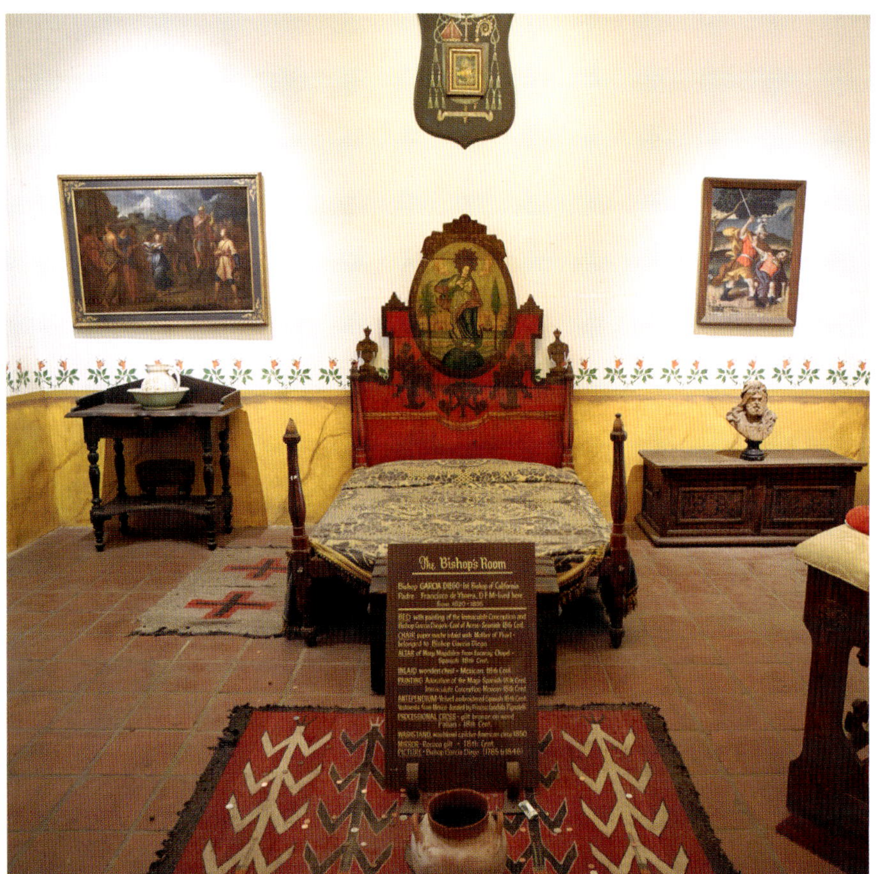

Mission San Fernando Rey de España

(above and left)

Dating back to 1797, the mission is the 17th of 21 Spanish missions founded in California. The chapel's 400-year-old Ezcaray Altar is from a church in Spain and installed in 1990. Visitors can also see the room where Bishop Francisco García Diego y Moreno, the first bishop of California, stayed.

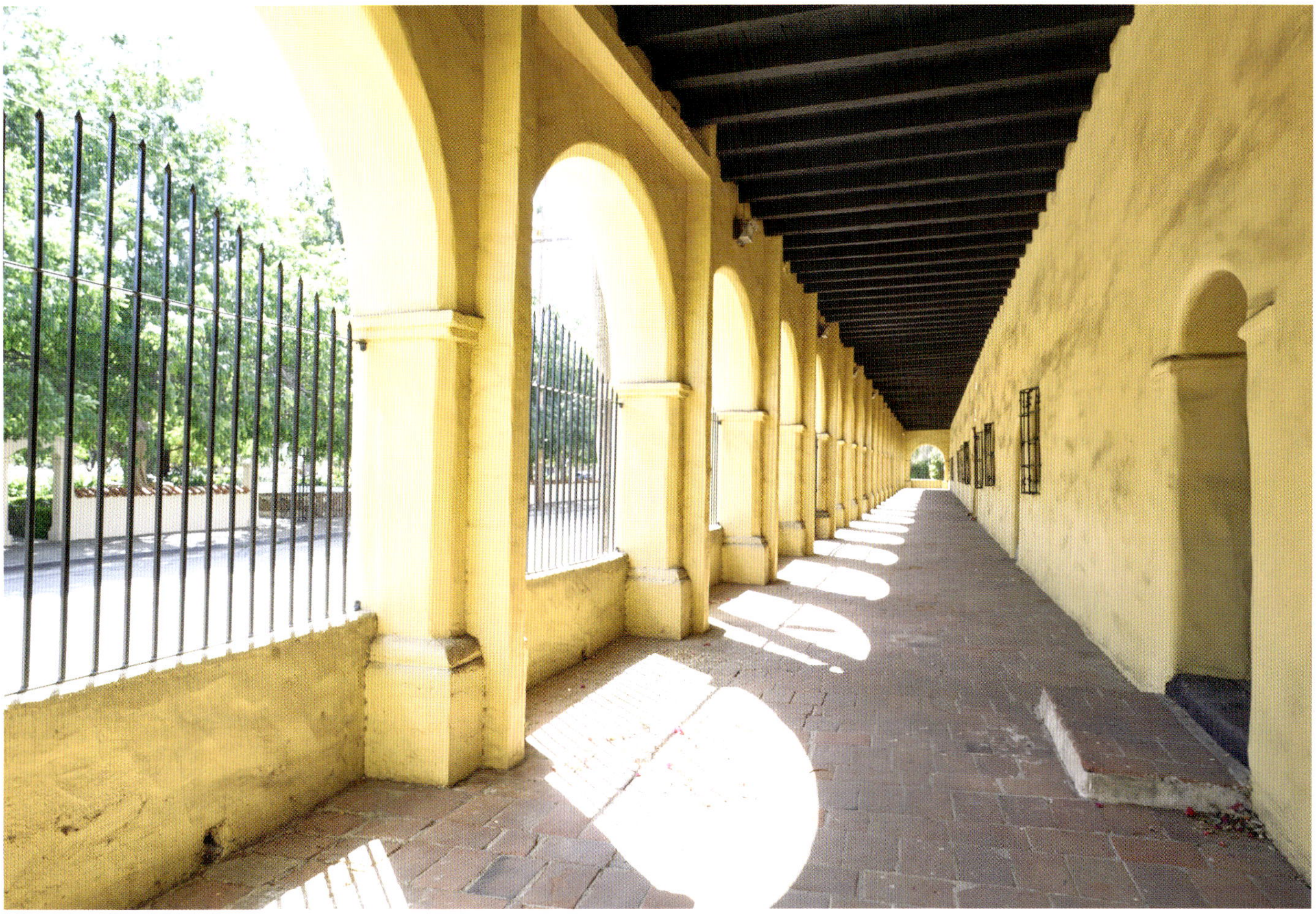

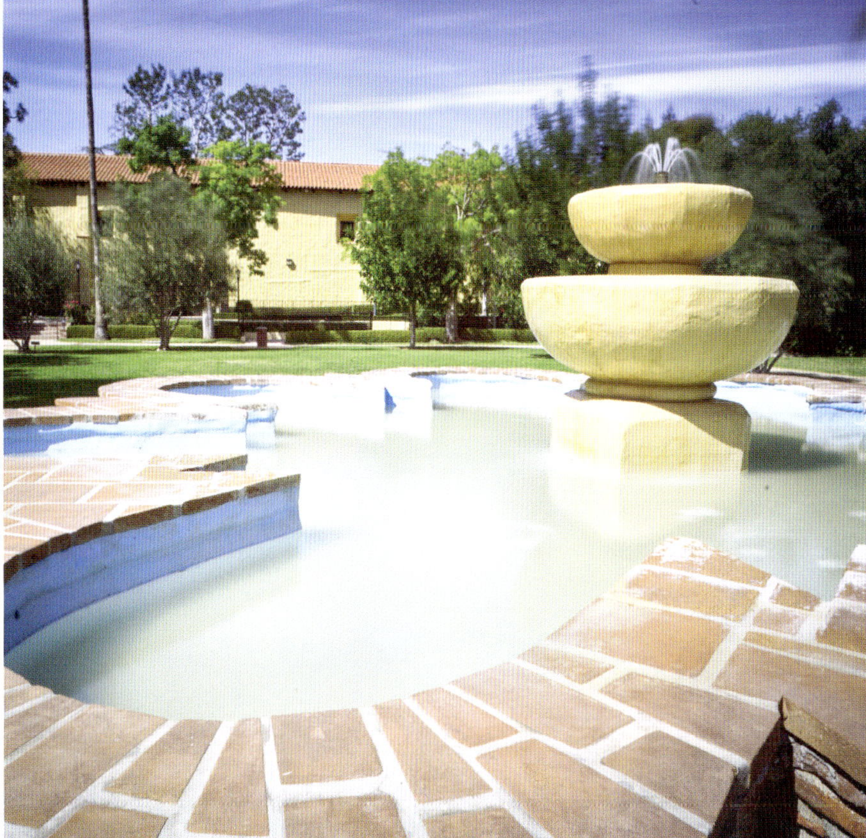

Mission San Fernando Rey de España

(above and right)

Sunlight streaks through the 19 Convento arches that border the full length of the mission's "long building," while a pleasant fountain gurgles in the peaceful gardens. The flower-shaped fountain is located in the mission's plaza.

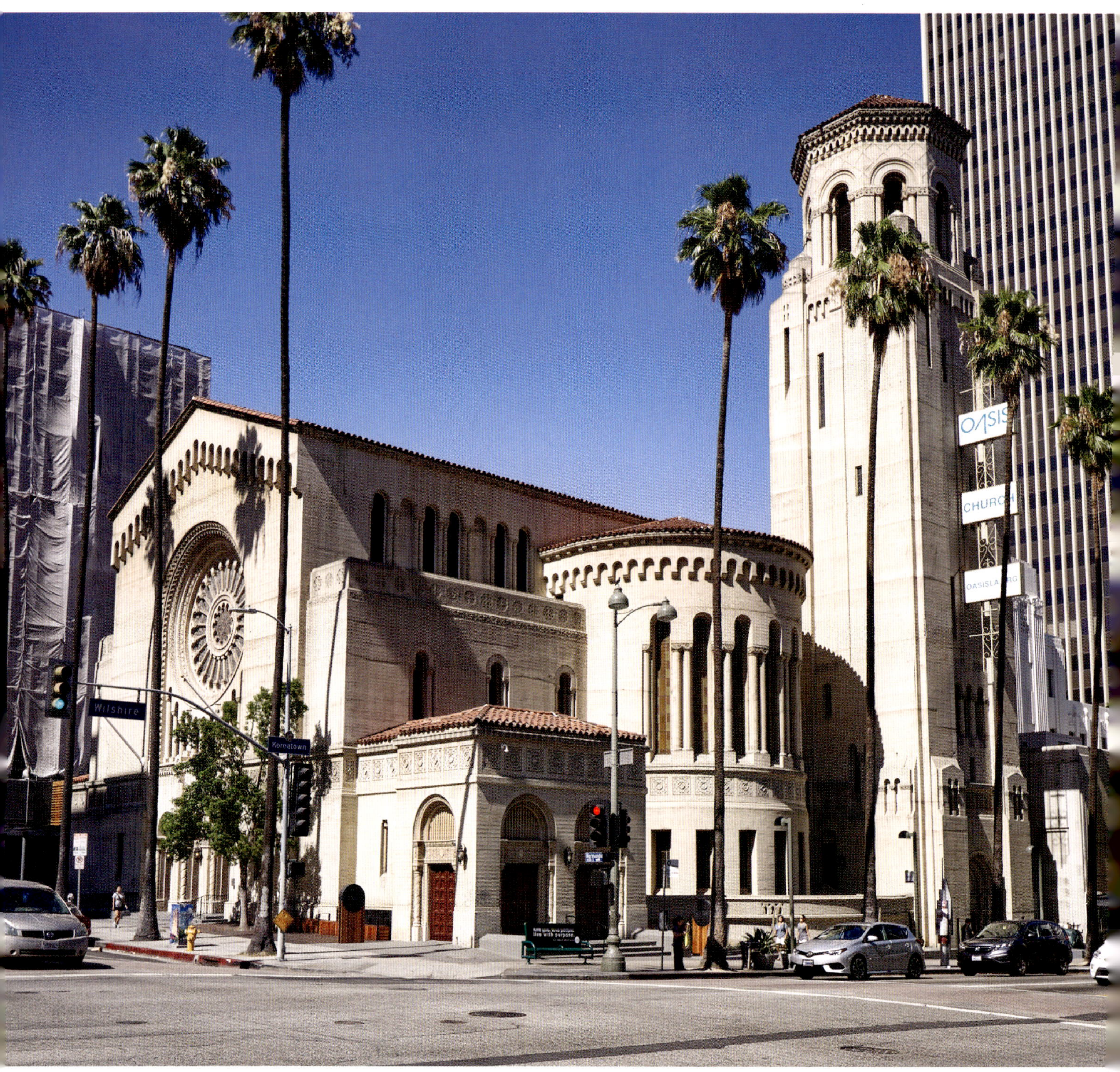

Wilshire Christian Church *(top)*

A fine example of Romanesque Revival-style architecture, the rose window is believed to be copied from the Reims Cathedral in France. The church's original congregation, which dates back to the 1870s, began to dwindle in recent times, and the building was bought by the Oasis Church in 2012.

Wilshire Boulevard Temple *(opposite)*

Beautifully framed under the branches of a large jacaranda tree, the Wilshire Boulevard Temple stands proud as the home of the oldest Jewish congregation in Los Angeles. The Moorish influenced temple, topped with an immense Byzantine Revival-style dome, was renovated inside and out in 2013.

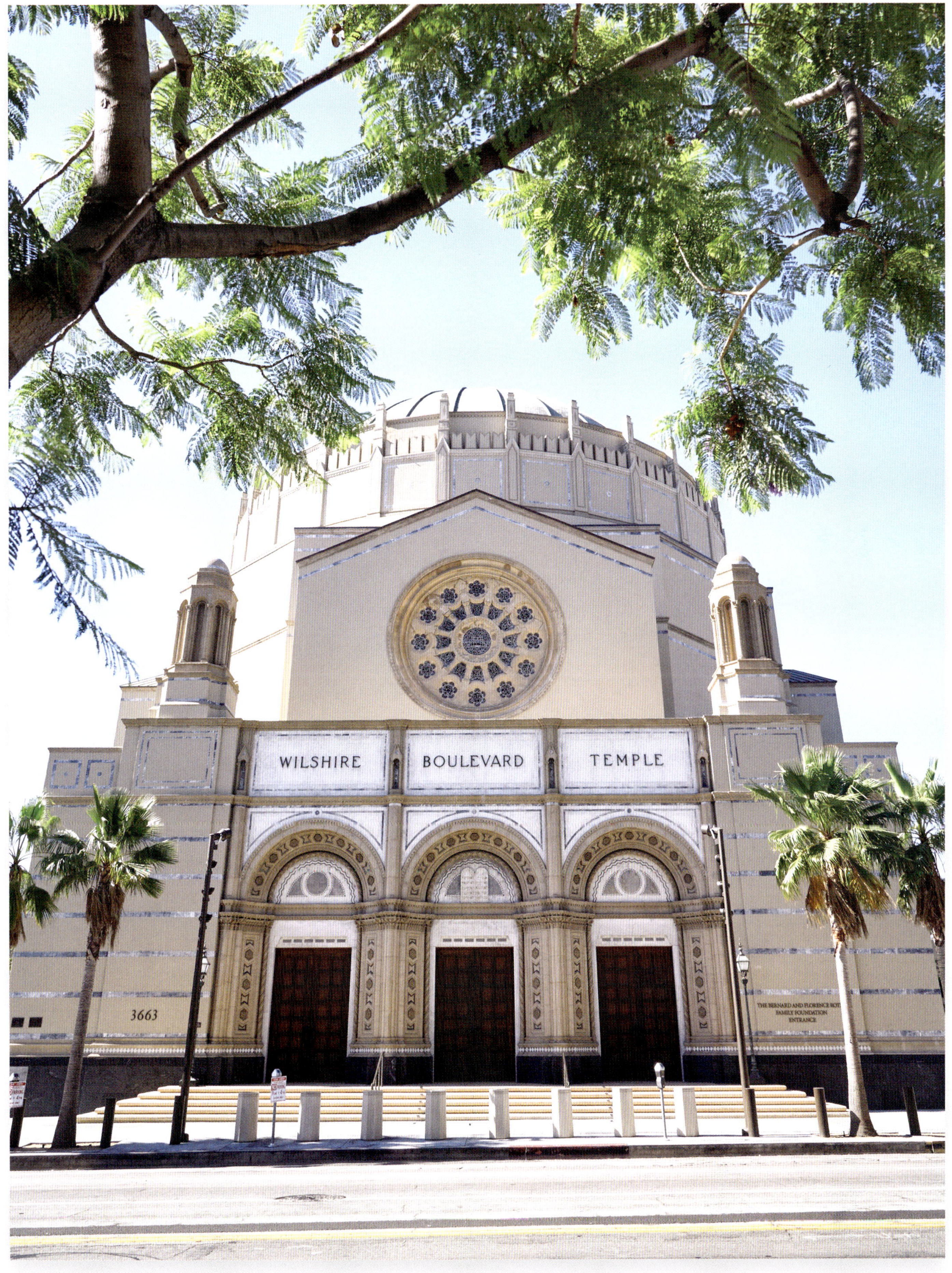
WILSHIRE
BOULEVARD
TEMPLE
3663

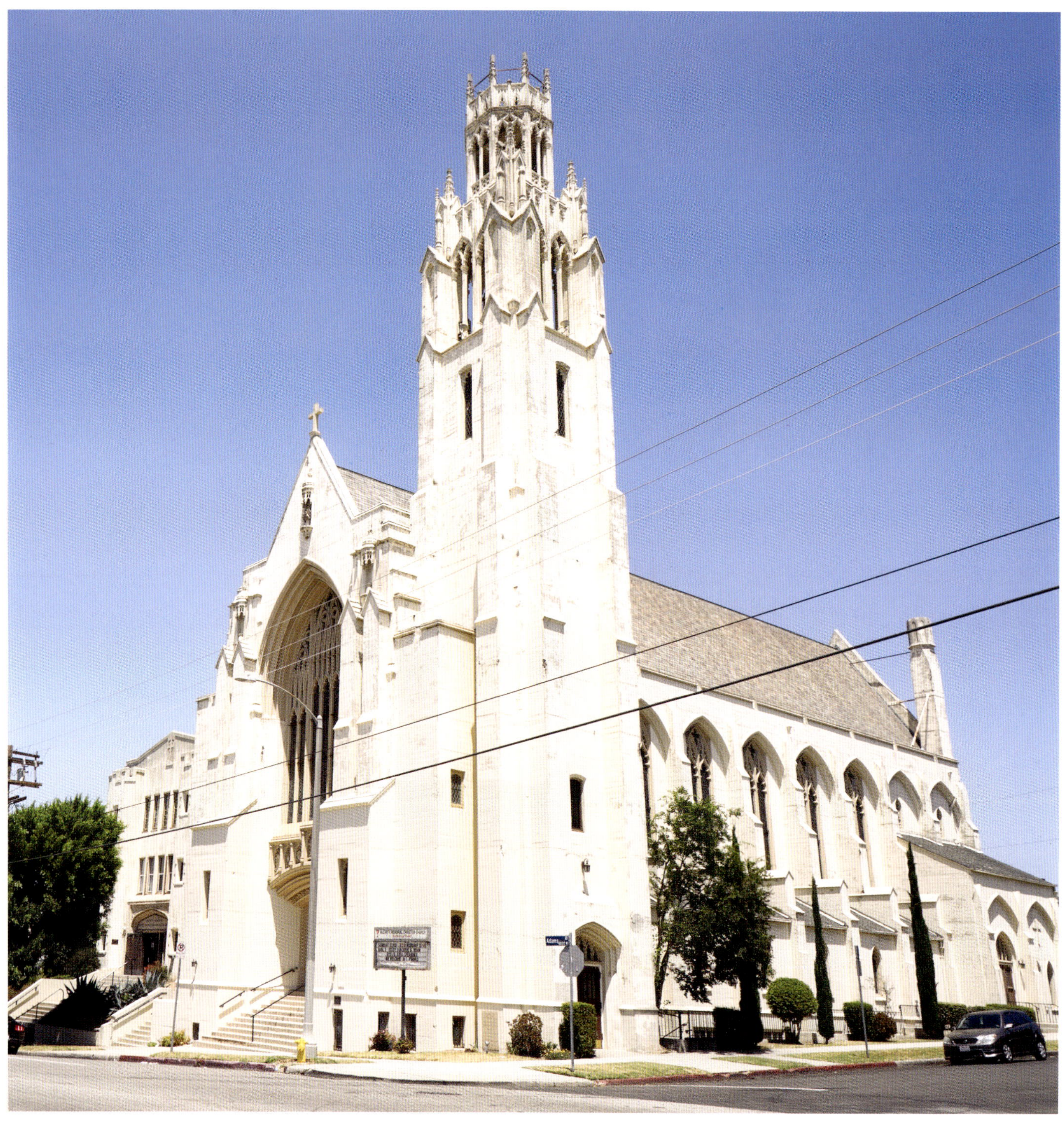

McCarty Memorial Christian Church

This grand Gothic Revival church is an important symbol of the Civil Rights Movement in Los Angles. Founded in 1932 as a white church, it became a multi-racial congregation in the 1950s under plans considered "radical" at the time. It is modeled after Exeter Cathedral in England.

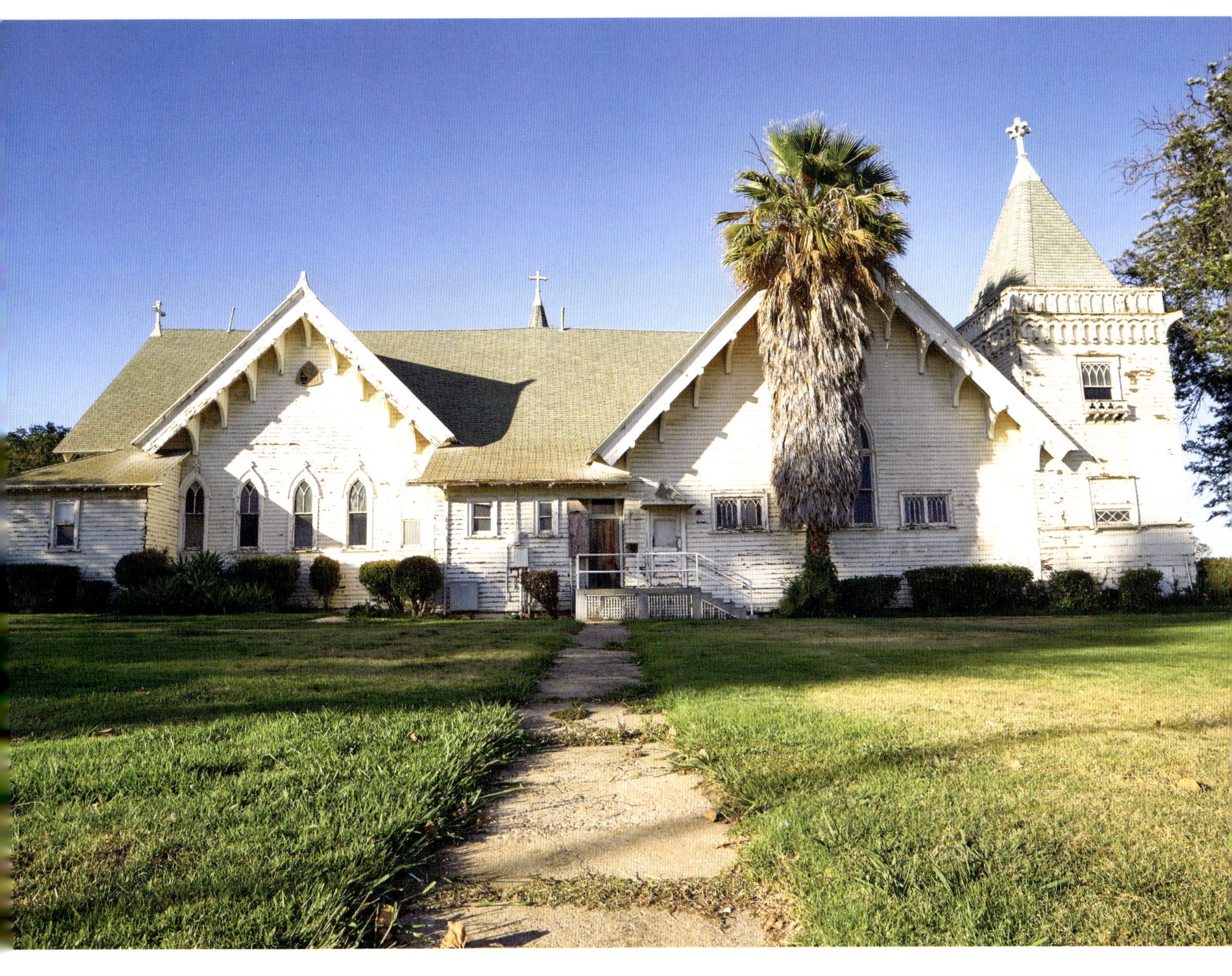

Wadsworth Chapel

Built in 1900 and the oldest remaining building on Wilshire Boulevard, this forlorn-looking chapel once provided a place of worship for injured soldiers. Containing two chapels, it was uniquely designed to serve Protestants on one side and Catholics on the other. Each chapel has its own separate entrance.

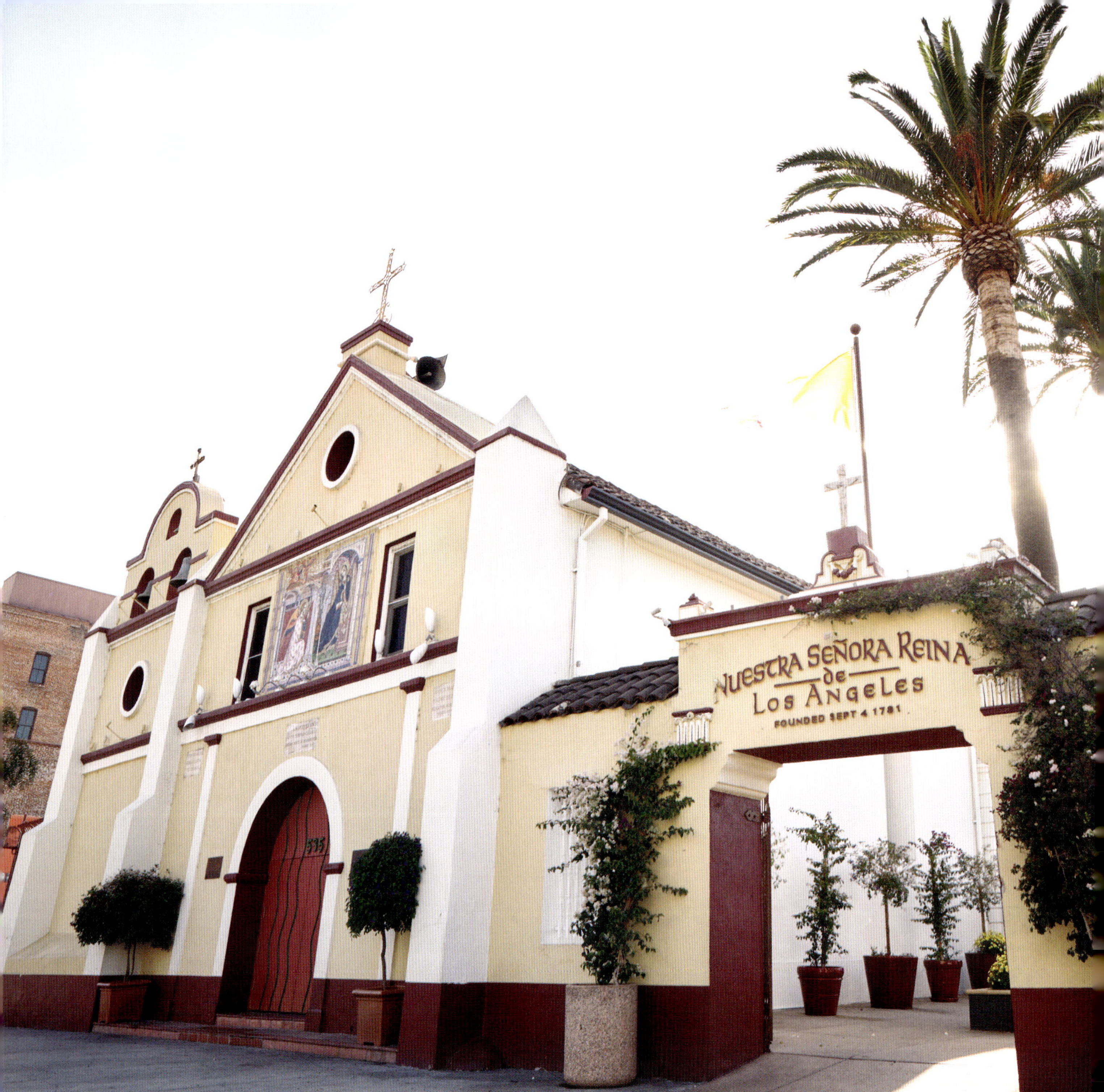

Our Lady Queen of Angels Church

The colorful chapel, "La Placita," was for years the sole Catholic church for Los Angeles' growing Hispanic community. Known in Spanish as La Iglesia de Nuestra Señora la Reina de los Ángeles, this historic Roman Catholic church dates back to 1784, although the current church building was erected in 1822.

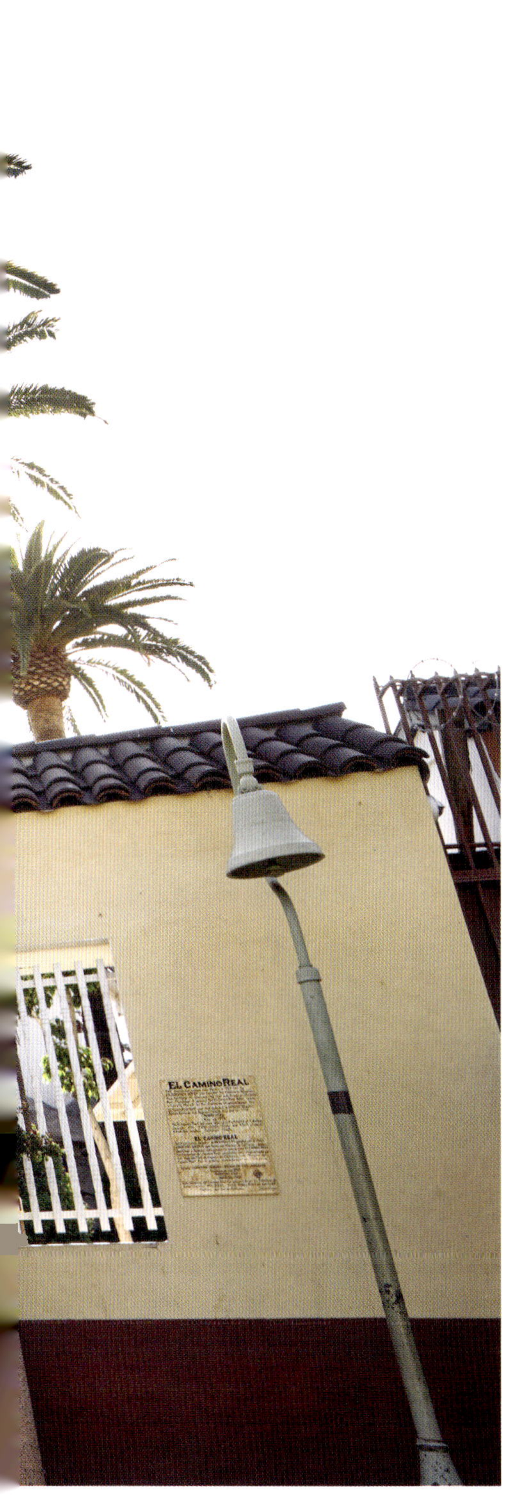

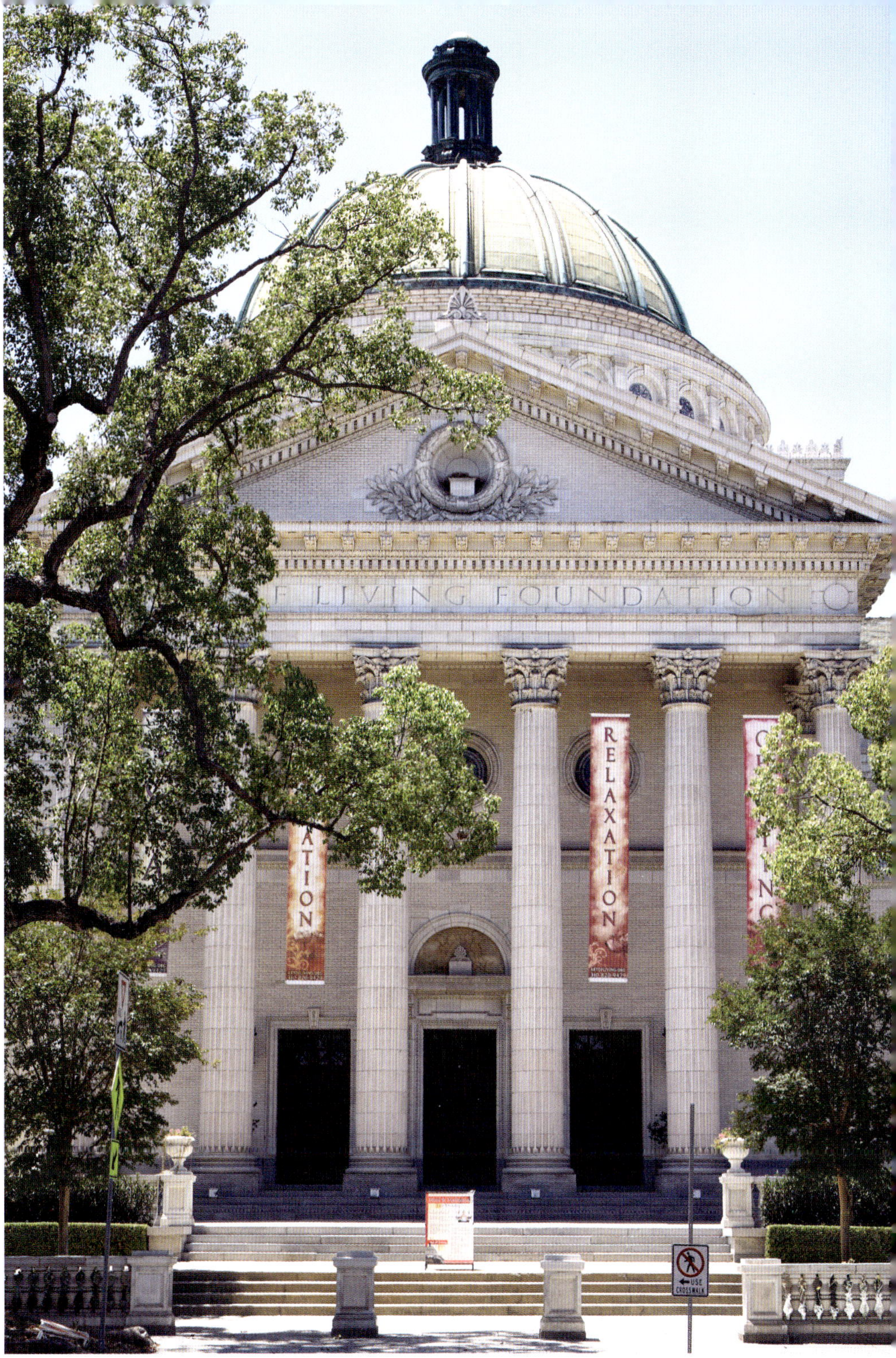

Second Church of Christ Scientist

This wonderful Classical Revival-style building was erected in 1910 as a Christian Science church in the West Adams district of Los Angeles. After the congregation's numbers dwindled the building was bought by the Art of Living Foundation, which teaches meditation, yoga, and stress management.

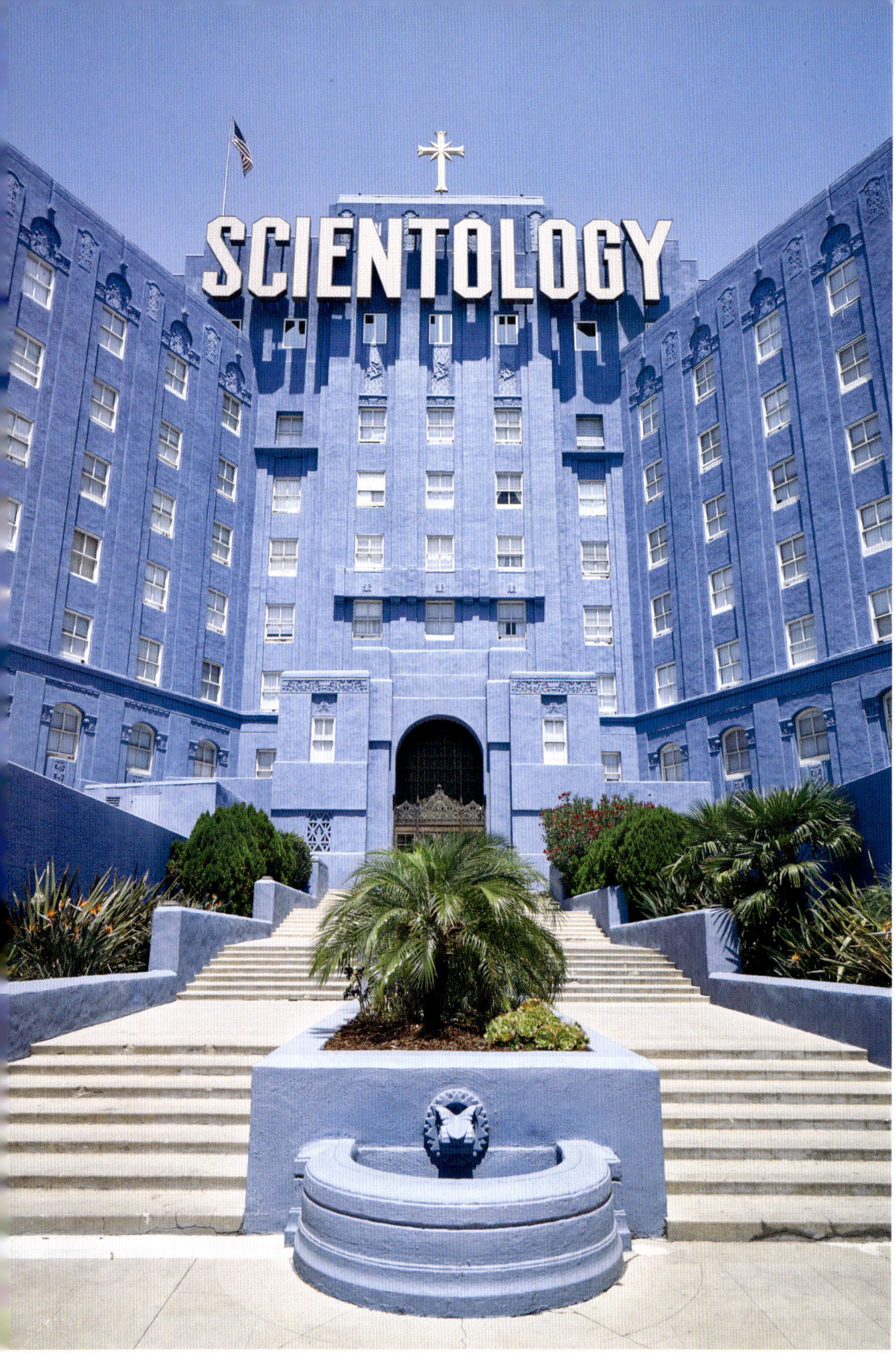

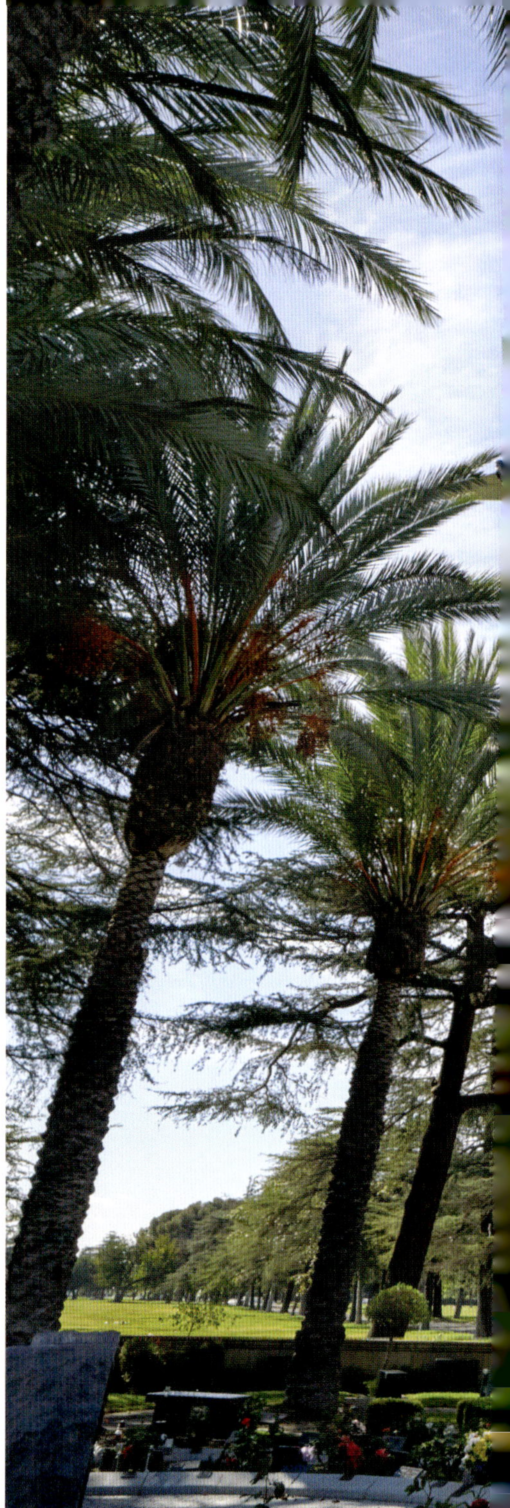

Church of Scientology

The pale blue facade of the West Coast headquarters of the Church of Scientology closely matches the azure skies above. Located in a former hospital on Fountain Avenue, it serves Los Angeles, which has the largest concentration of Scientologists and related organizations in the world.

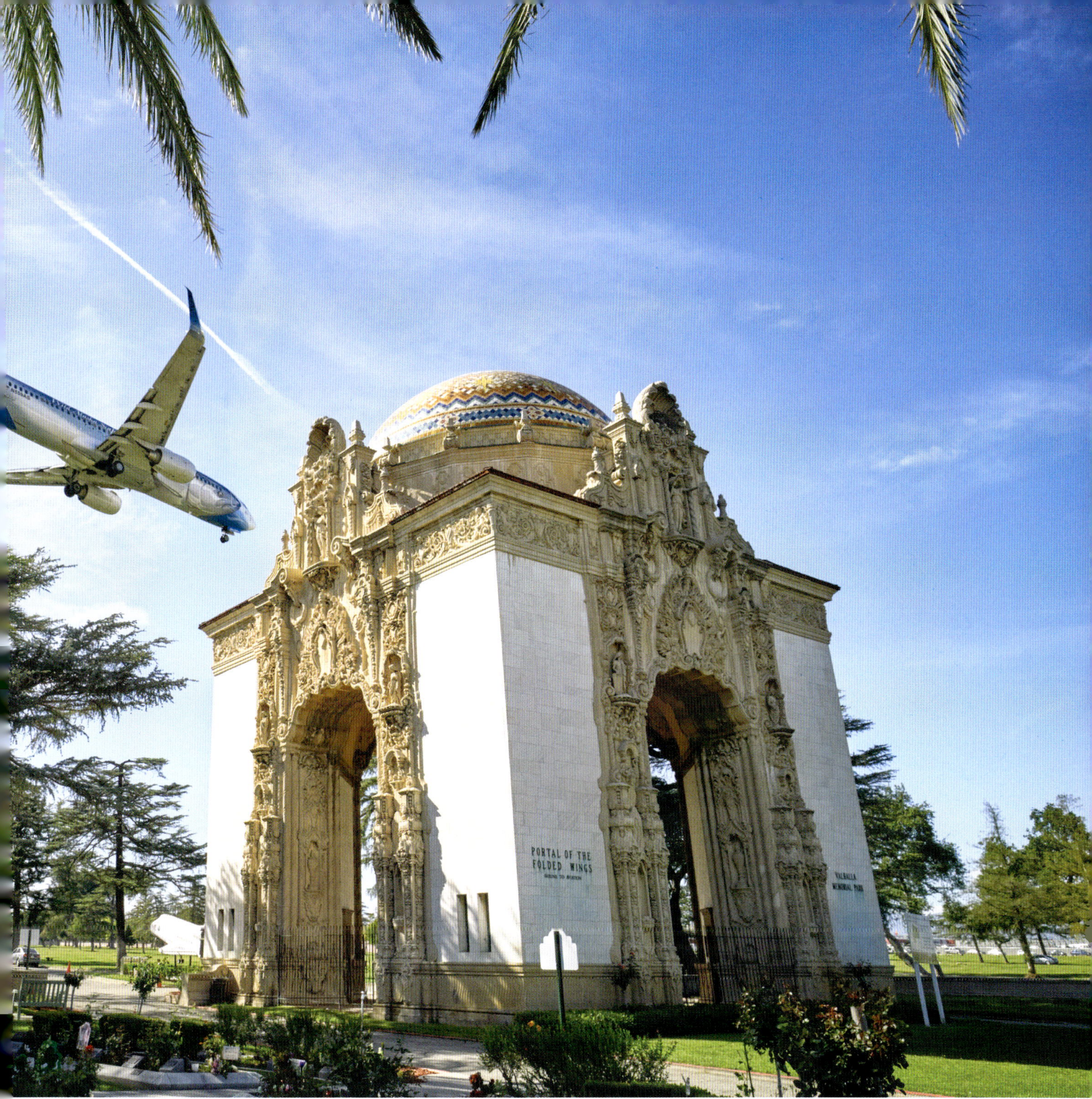

Portal of the Folded Wings

A passenger jet roars over Portal of the Folded Wings Shrine to Aviation, a poignant and beautiful tribute to pioneers of aviation. The 75-foot-tall structure of mosaic, marble, and sculptures is the burial site for 15 men and women who devoted their lives to the advancement of flight.

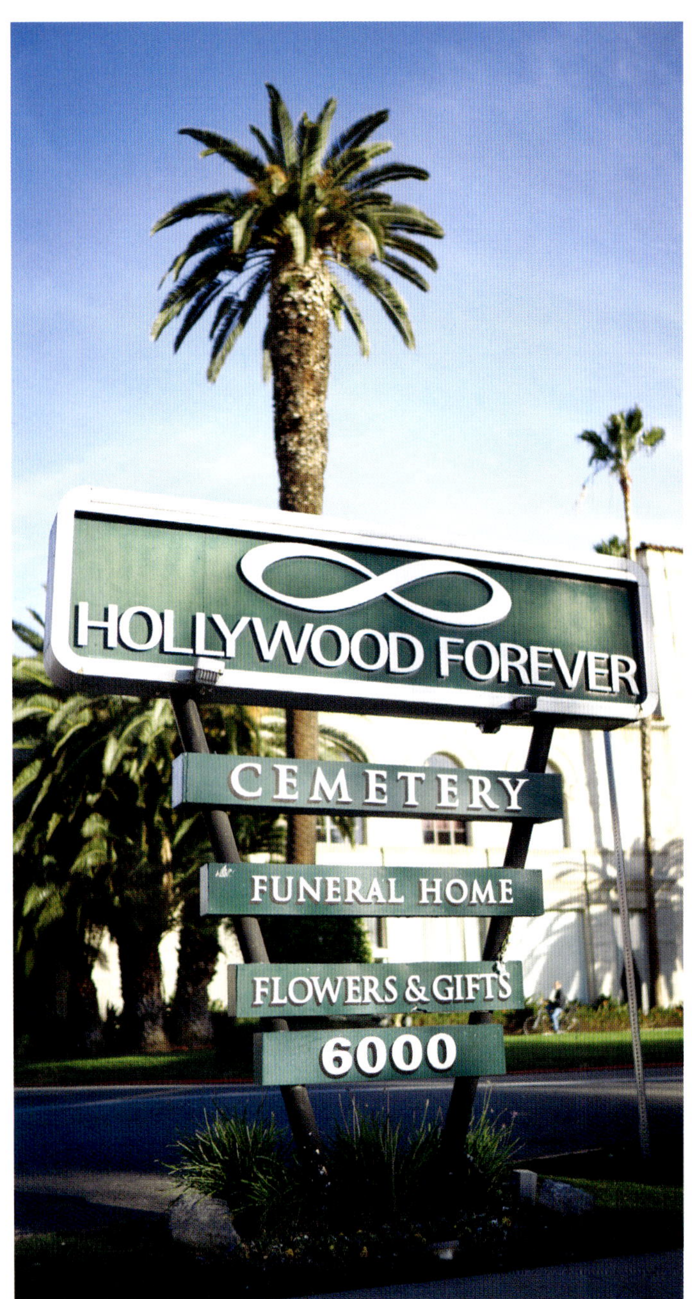

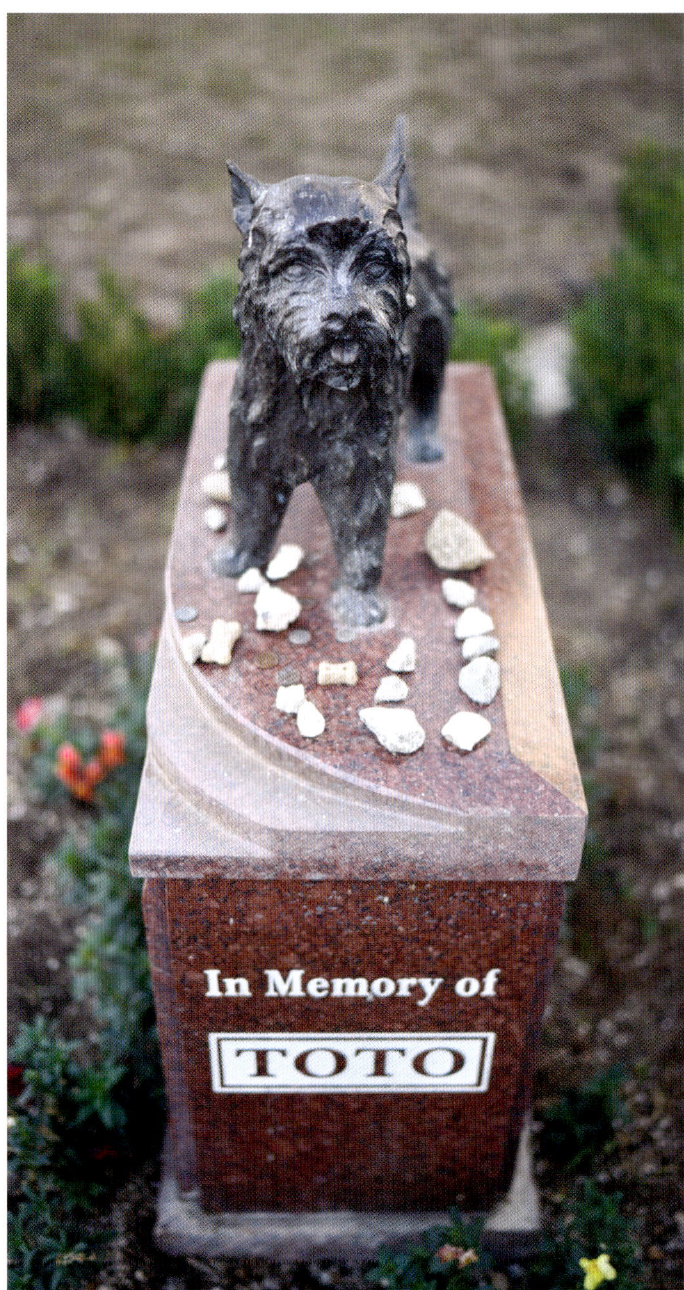

Hollywood Forever Cemetery

(left and right)

The final resting place of Hollywood's great stars. The cemetery has been featured in movies, TV shows, and songs – with rock band LA Guns even naming an album after it. Among the graves of movie stars lies a memorial to Terry, the dog who played Toto in the *The Wonderful Wizard of OZ*.

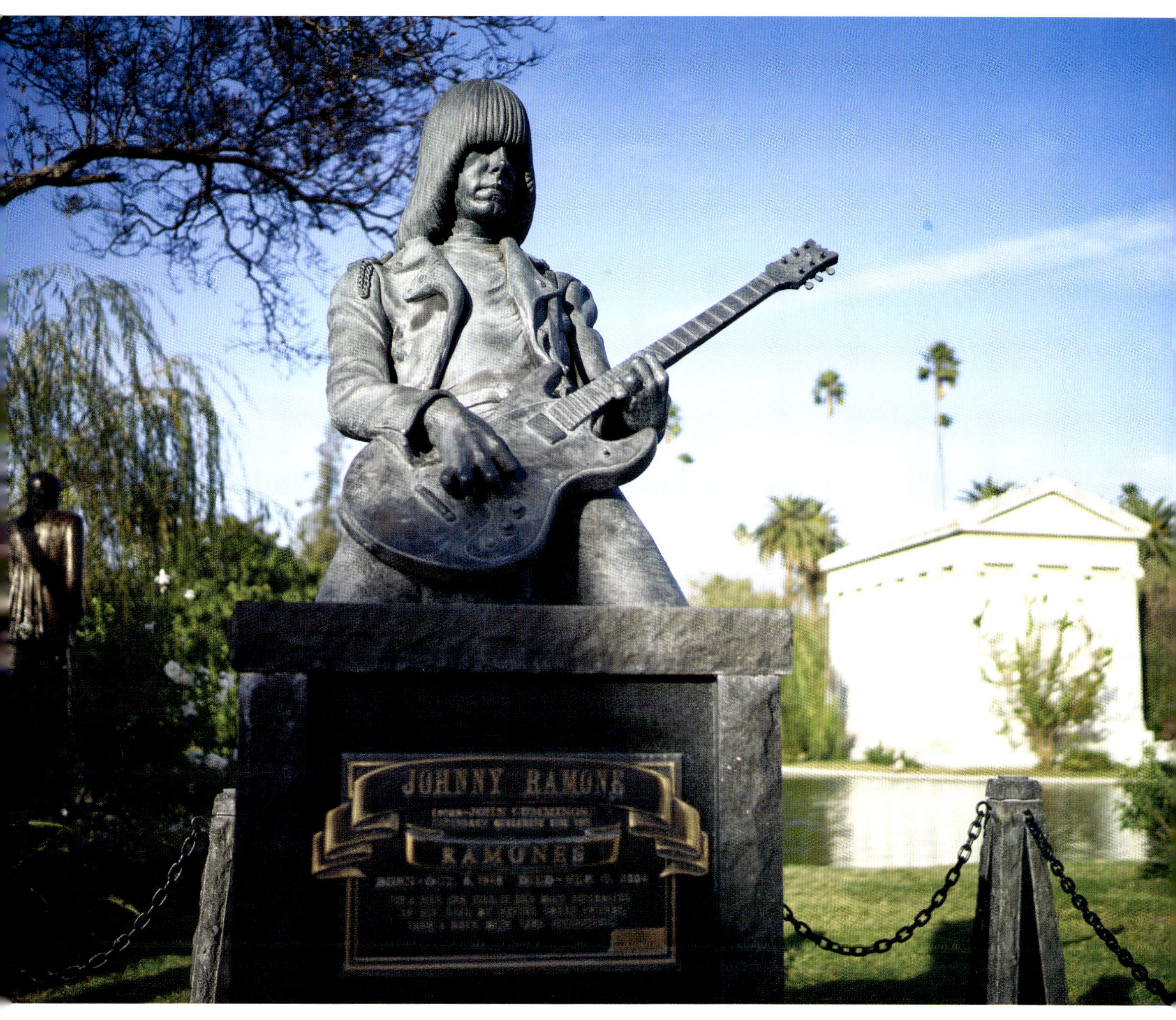

Hollywood Forever Cemetery *(above)*

Music fans travel from all over the world to pay homage to punk pioneer Johnny Ramone, who is immortalized in this 8-foot-tall bronze statue by Wayne Toth. Best known as the guitarist for the Ramones, *Time* magazine included him on the list of the 10 Best Electric Guitarists of All Time.

Self-Realization Fellowship Lake Shrine Temple *(pages 52–53)*

Just a few minutes from the Pacific Ocean lies the serene Lake Shrine. Founded by Paramahansa Yogananda, the site is open to all and designed as a place to mediate and find peace. By the lake sits this reproduction of a 16th-century Dutch windmill, now converted into a chapel.

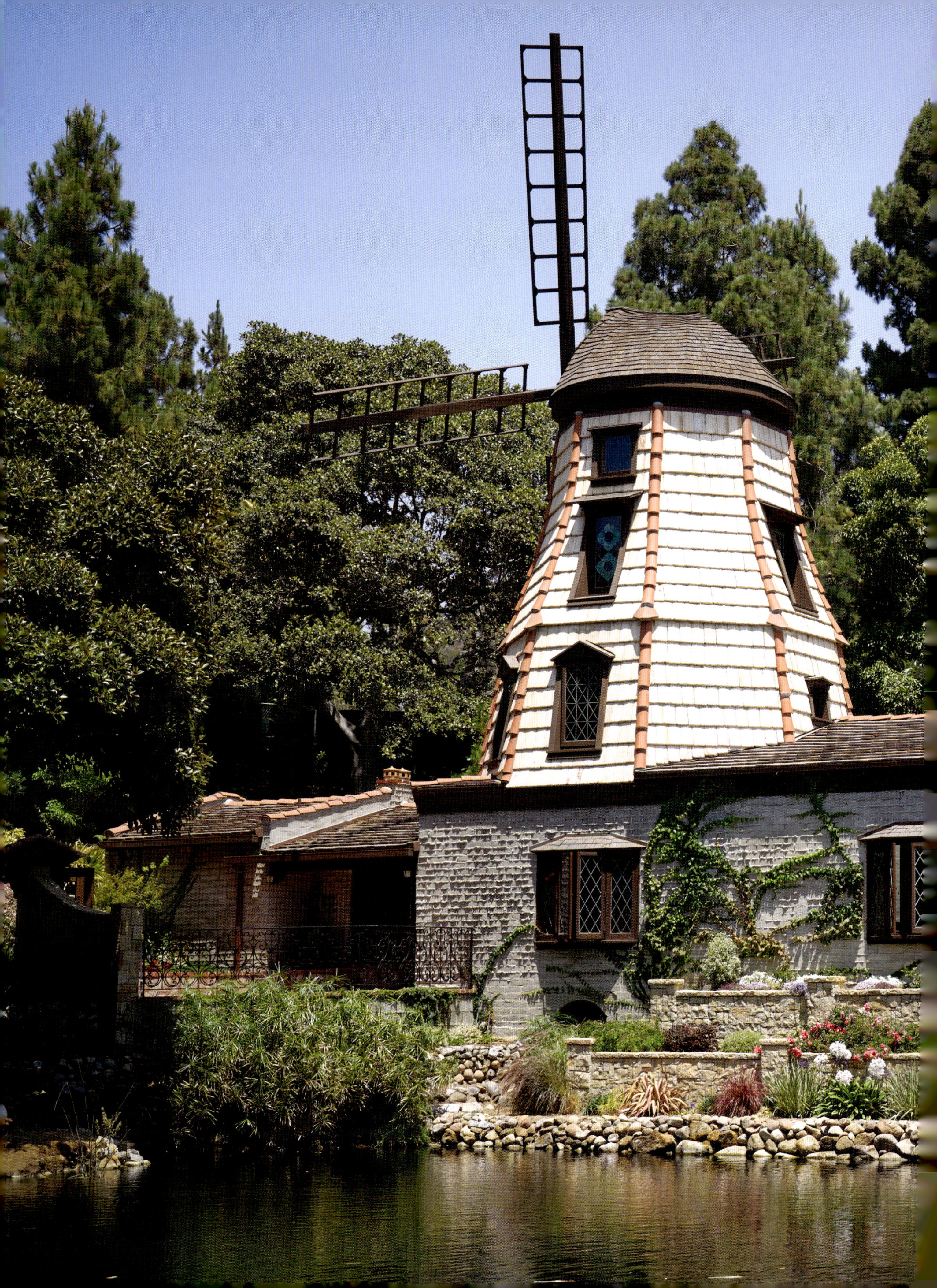

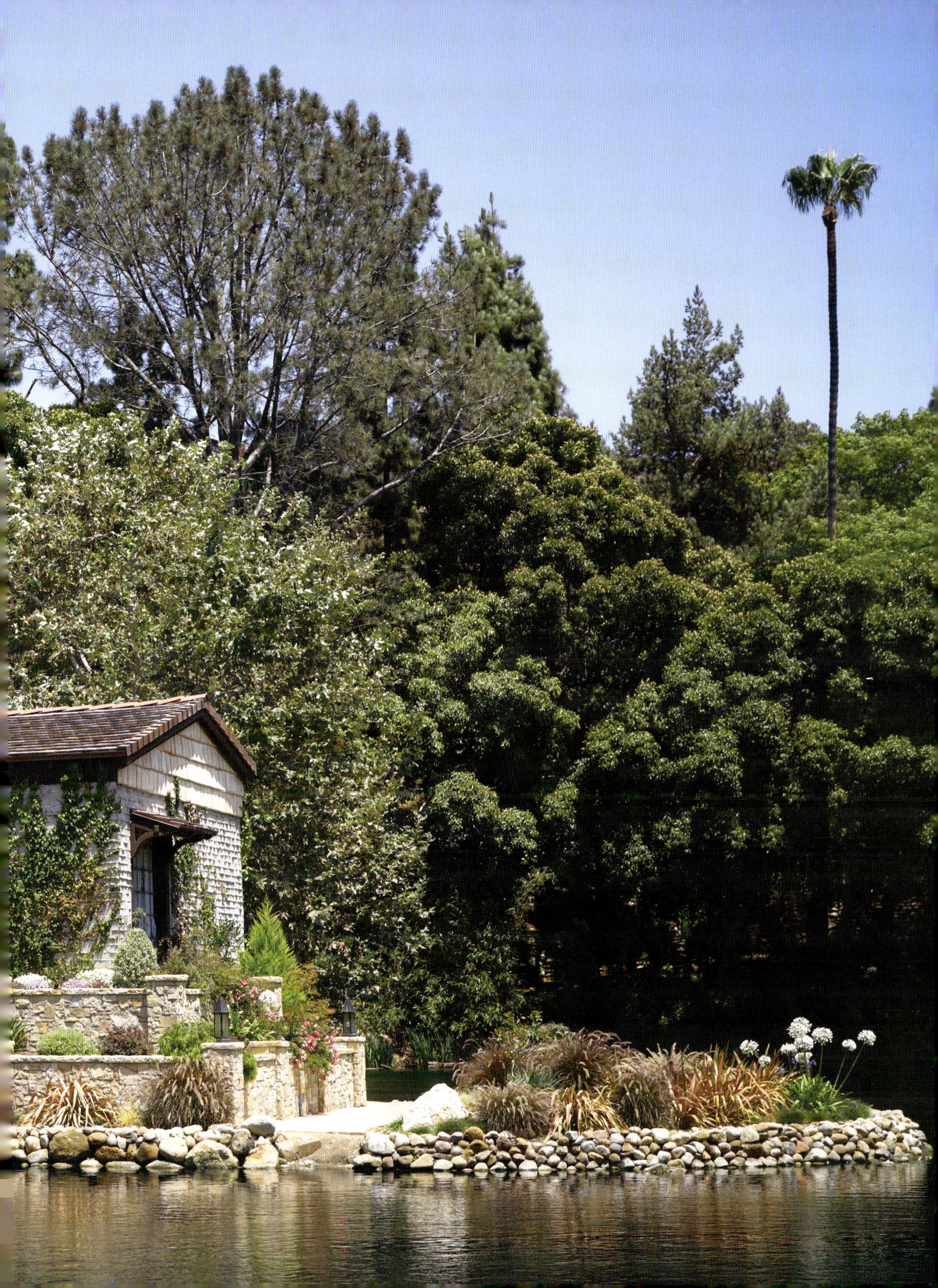

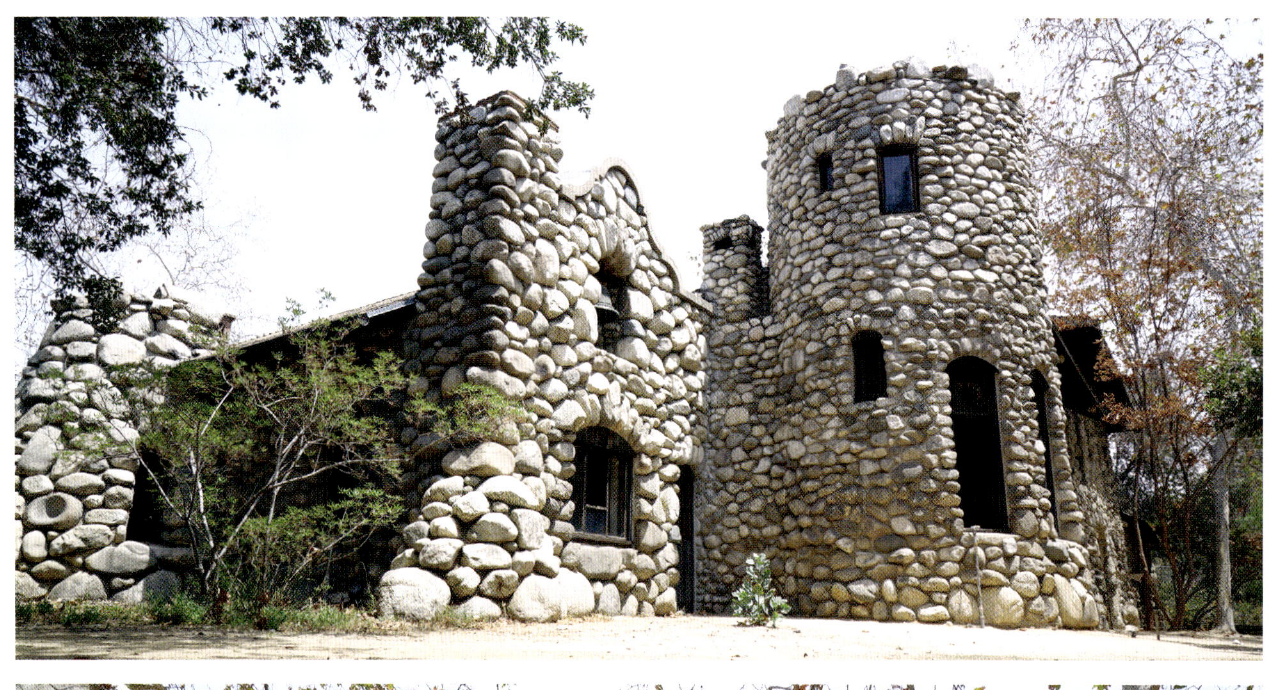

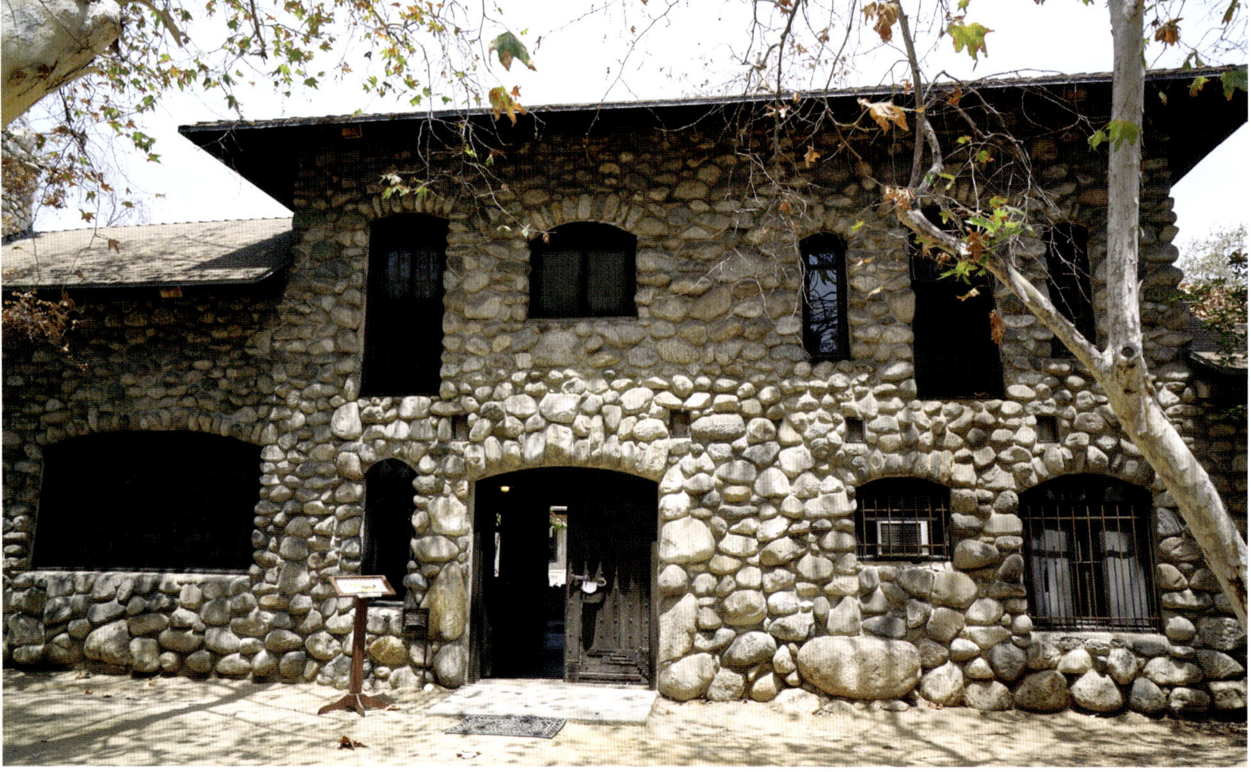

Lummis House *(top, bottom, and opposite)*

Step back in time to this 19th-century river-rock house, built in the Rustic American Craftsman-style by Charles Fletcher Lummis, a journalist and activist for Indian rights. Also known as "El Alisal," after the sycamore and alder trees surrounding the property, it is now a historic house museum.

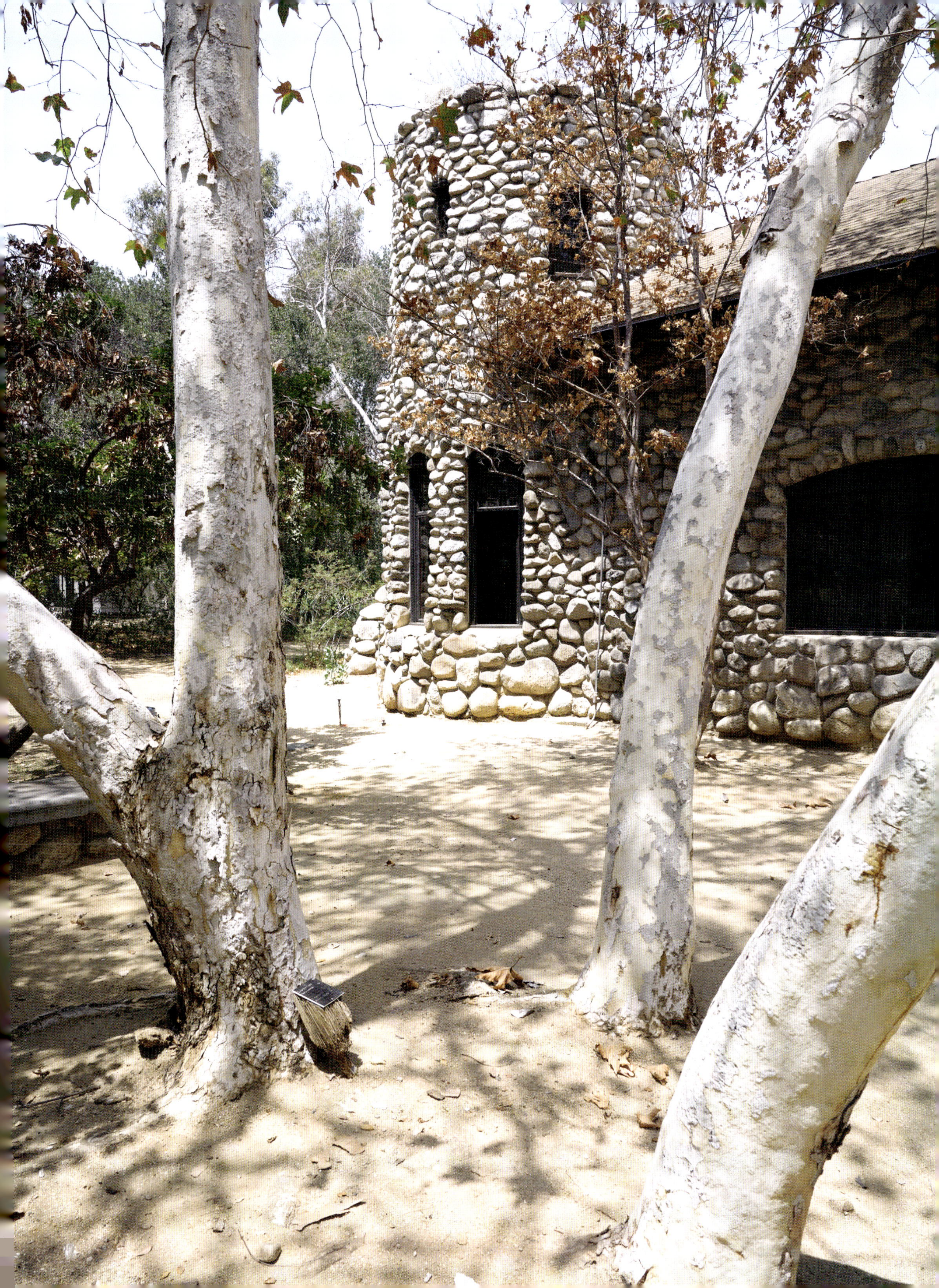

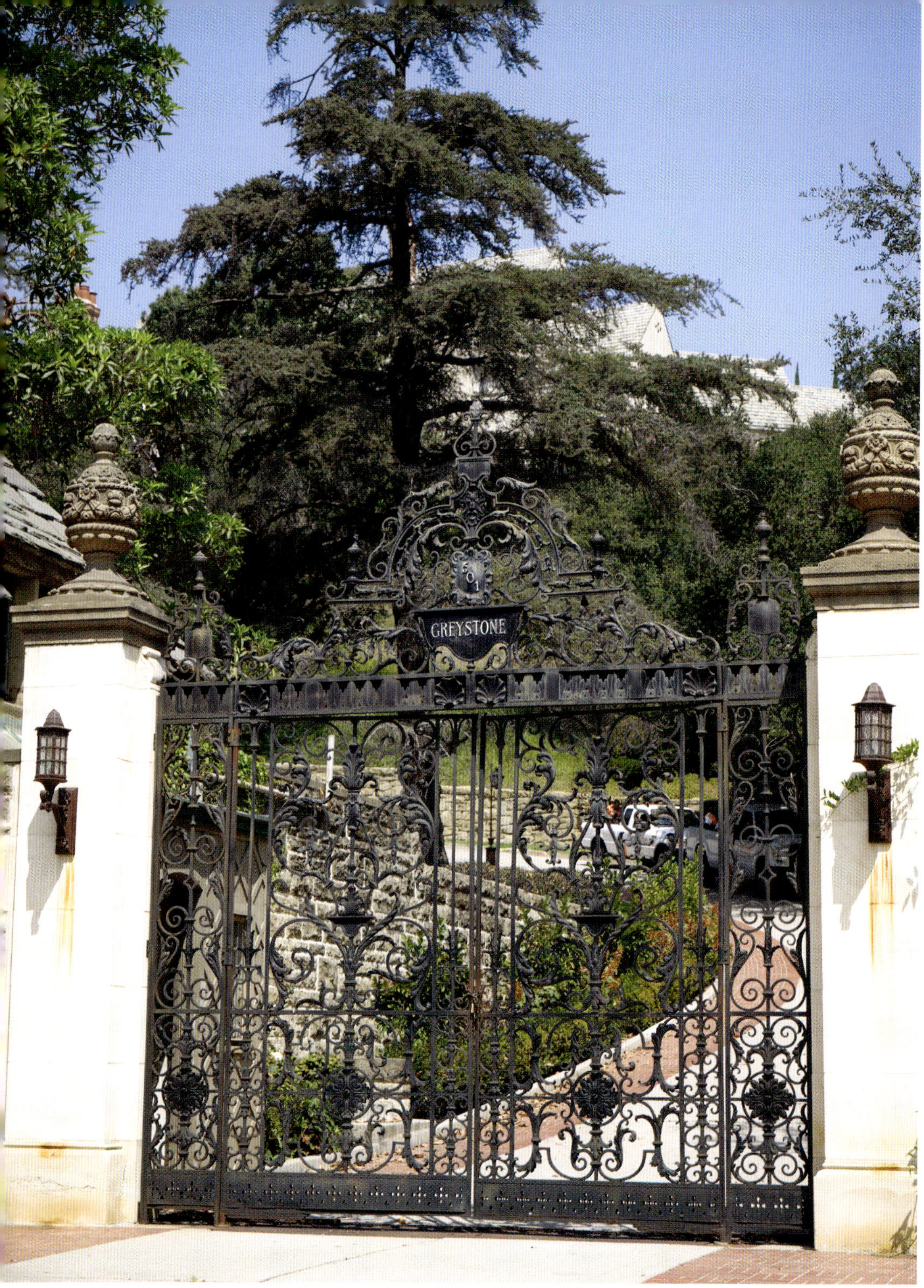

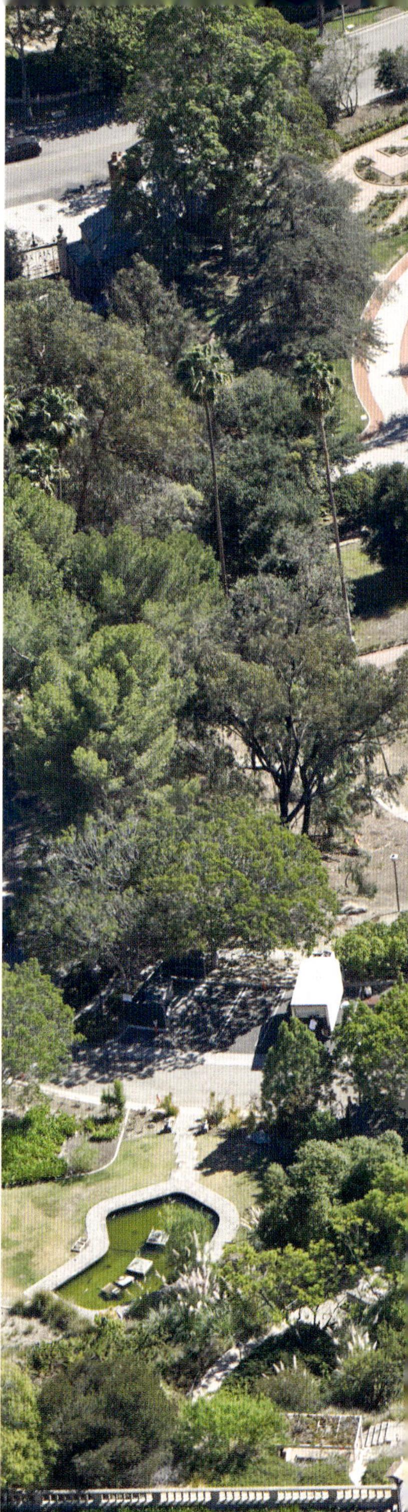

Greystone Mansion Gates

The wrought iron gates of the Greystone Mansion. Named Greystone for its abundant use of stone and its gray appearance, the mansion alone cost over 1.2 million dollars, an unimaginable sum at the time. Visitors are welcome to stroll through public areas, the formal gardens, and the inner courtyard.

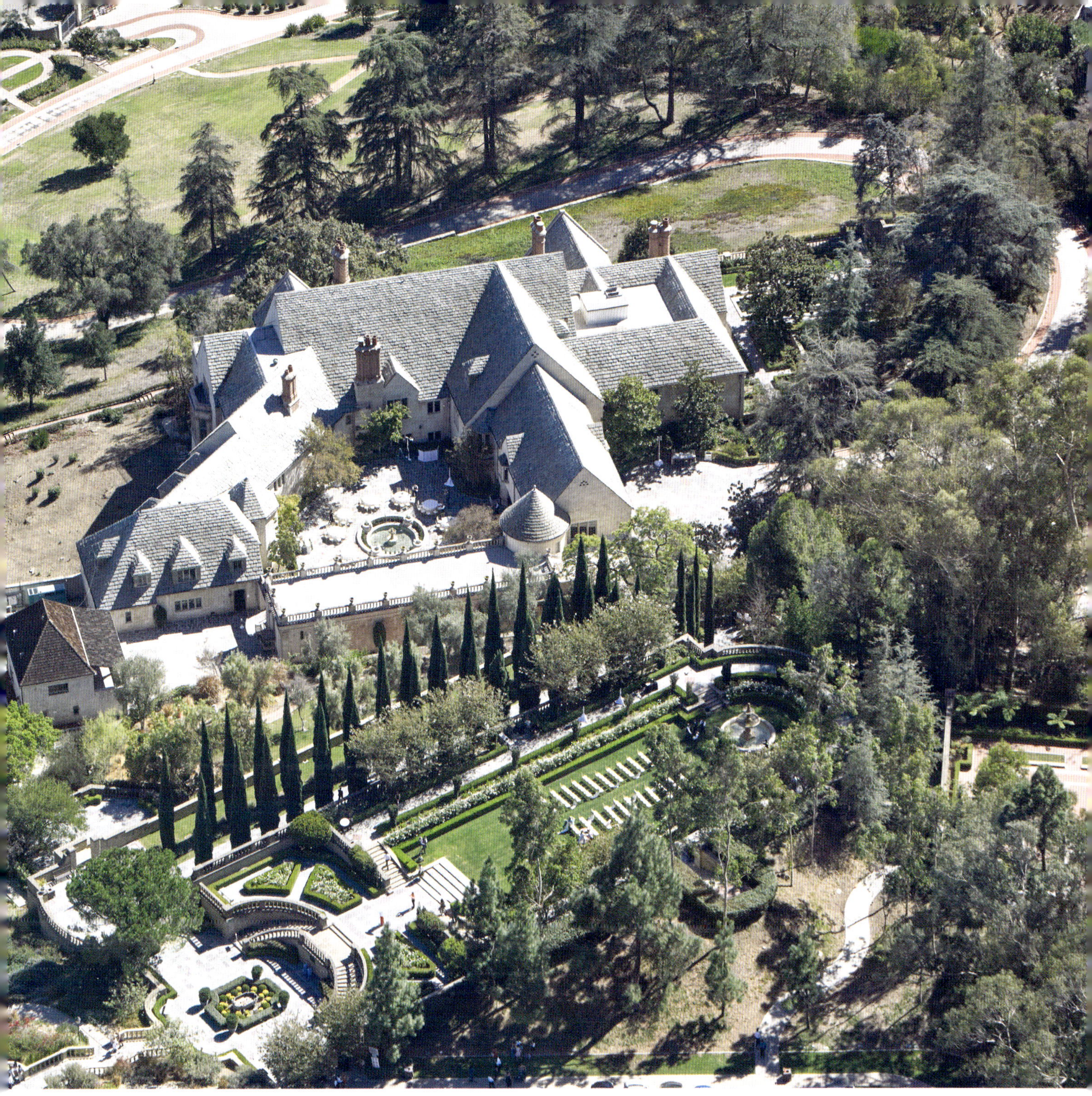

Greystone Mansion and Gardens

This hidden gem was constructed in 1928 by oil tycoon Edward L. Doheny. After his death, the city purchased the property and dedicated it a public park. Situated on 18.3 acres, it is a popular site for weddings and events. In 1976 it was registered into the Registry of Historic Places.

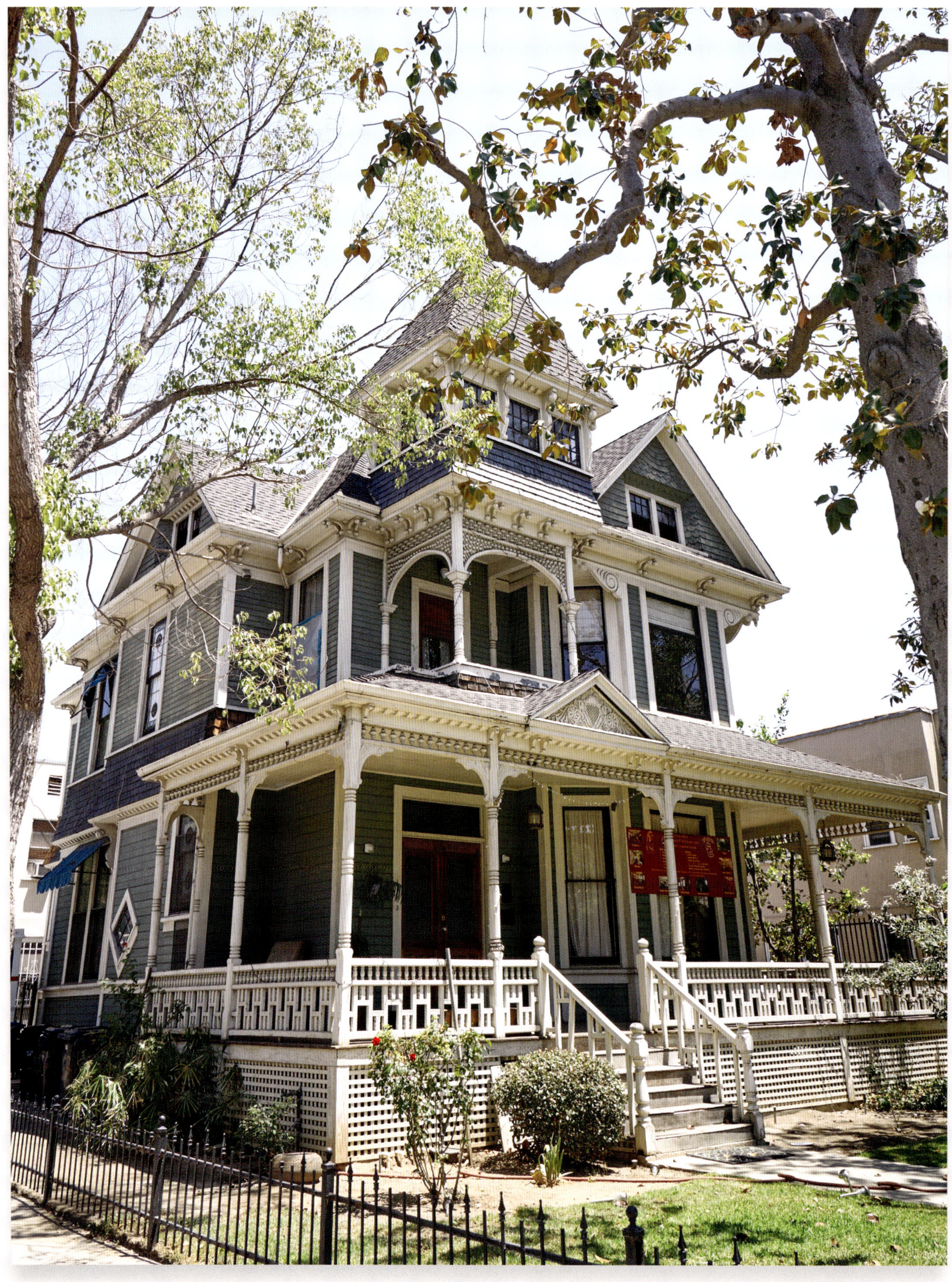

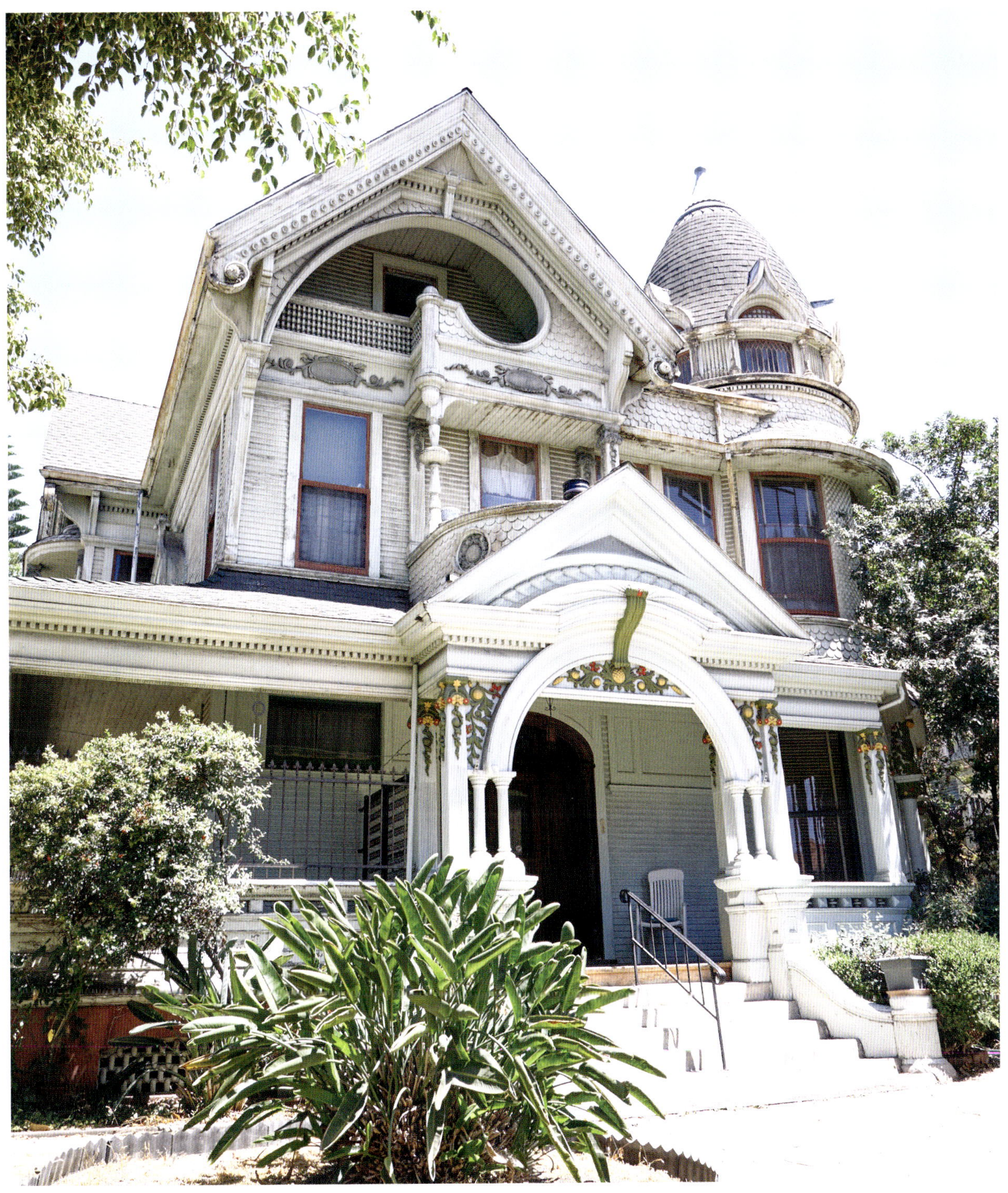

Frederick Mitchell Mooers House *(above)*

This quirky and ornately decorated Victoria-era house in Westlake was built in 1894 for Frank and May Wright. It was sold four years later to Frederick Mitchell Mooers. It features a three-story tower and onion dome. In 1967 it was designated a Los Angeles Historic-Cultural Monument.

Miller and Herriott House *(opposite)*

Used in the filming of the sitcom *Modern Family* during a Halloween episode, this is believed to be the oldest surviving tract house in Los Angeles. Situated in the North University Park area of the city, this 1890 Victorian house is now used for student housing.

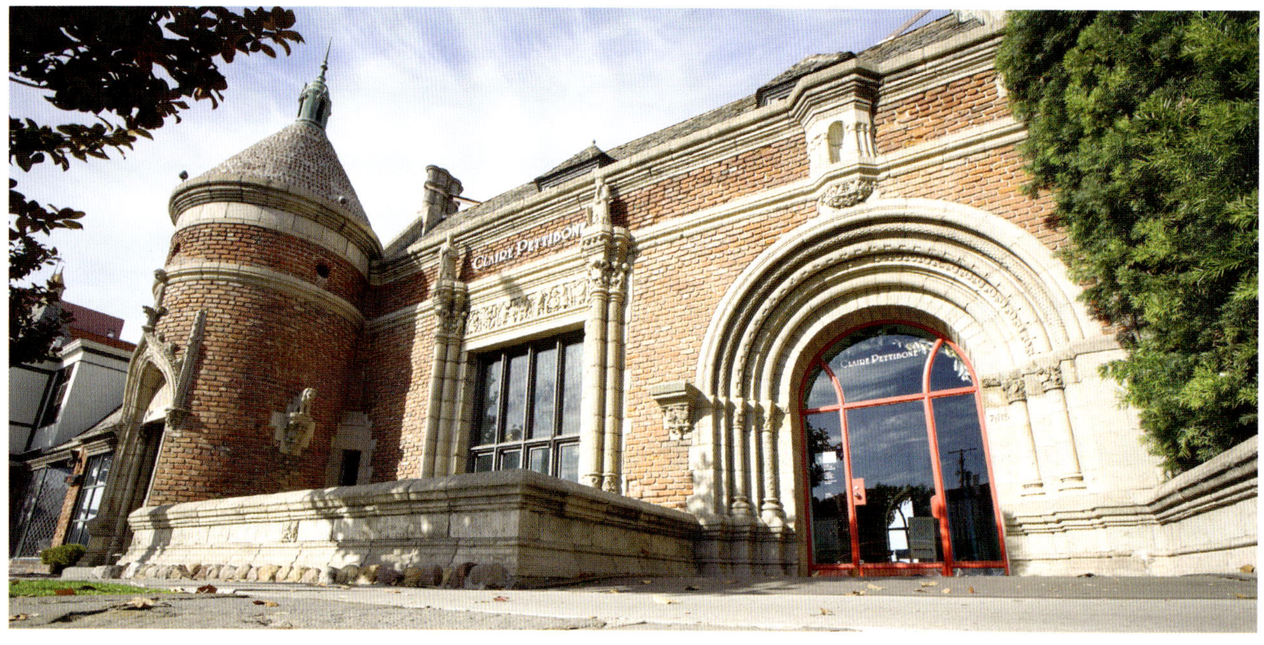

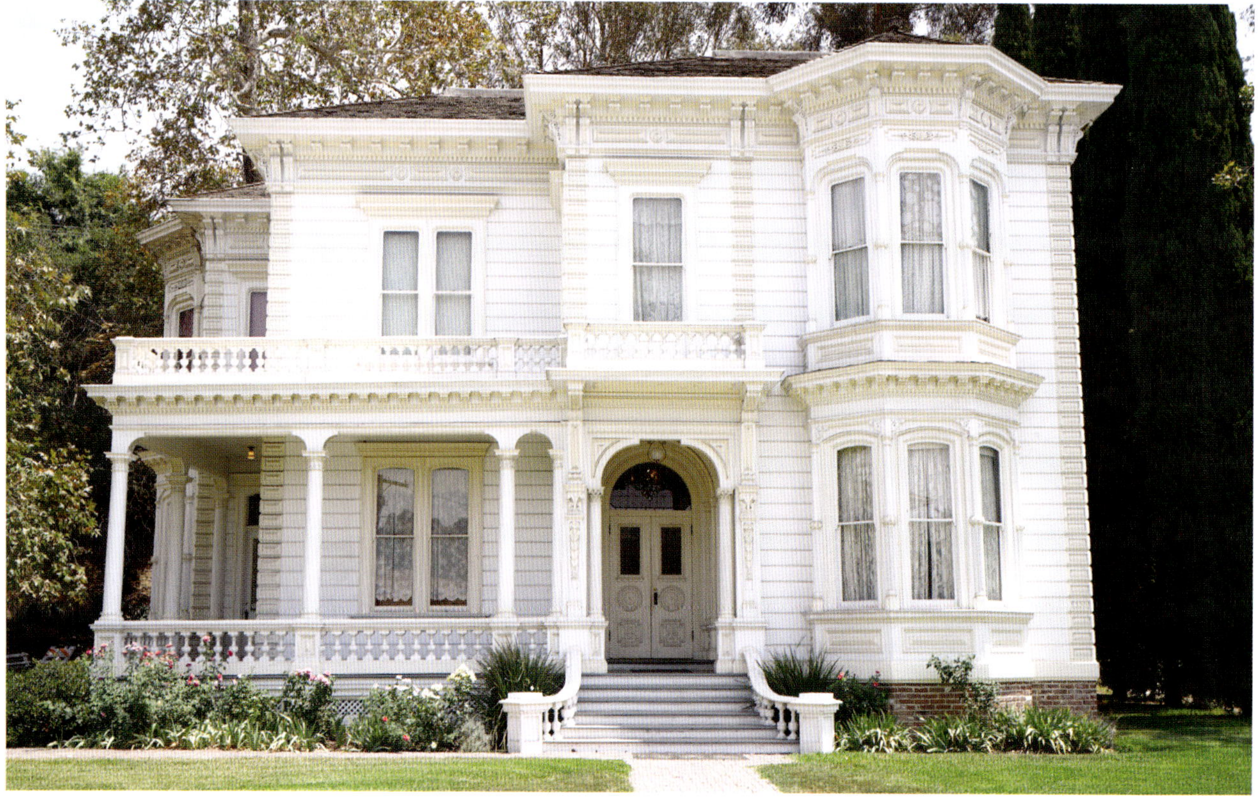

Heinsbergen Decorating Company *(top)*

Built using red bricks from the old City Hall, this castle-like Beverly Hills property was erected in 1928 for muralist Anthony Heinsbergen, a notable artist who created murals for theaters, civic halls, churches, and other important buildings. It is now the flagship store for bridal fashion designer Claire Pettibone.

Heritage Square Museum

(bottom and opposite)

The past comes back to life at this living history museum in Montecito Heights, which explores SoCal's past from the Civil War to the 20th century. The red and green Hale House and the white Greek Revival William Hayes Perry Residence are two of eight exquisite properties at the museum.

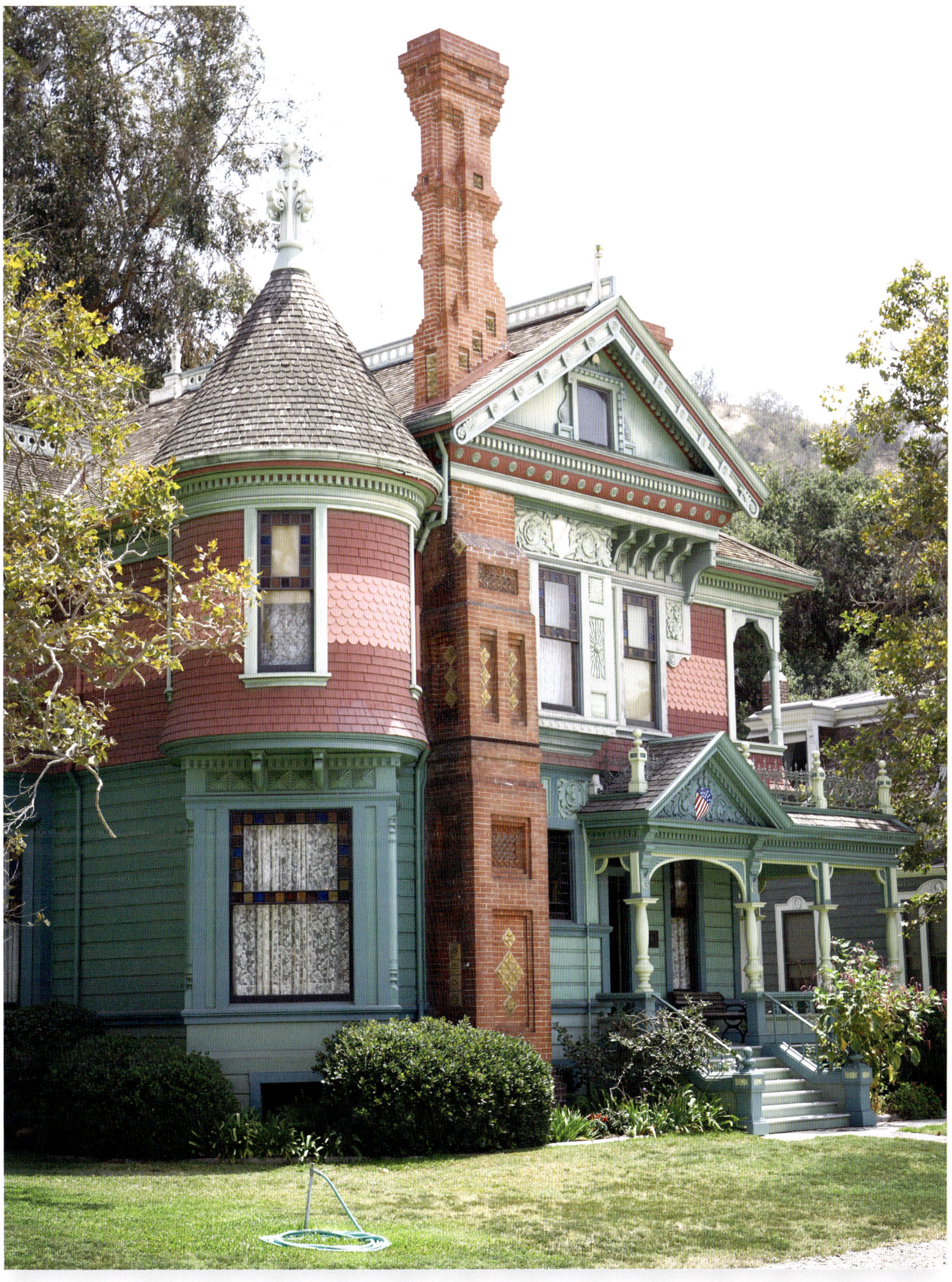

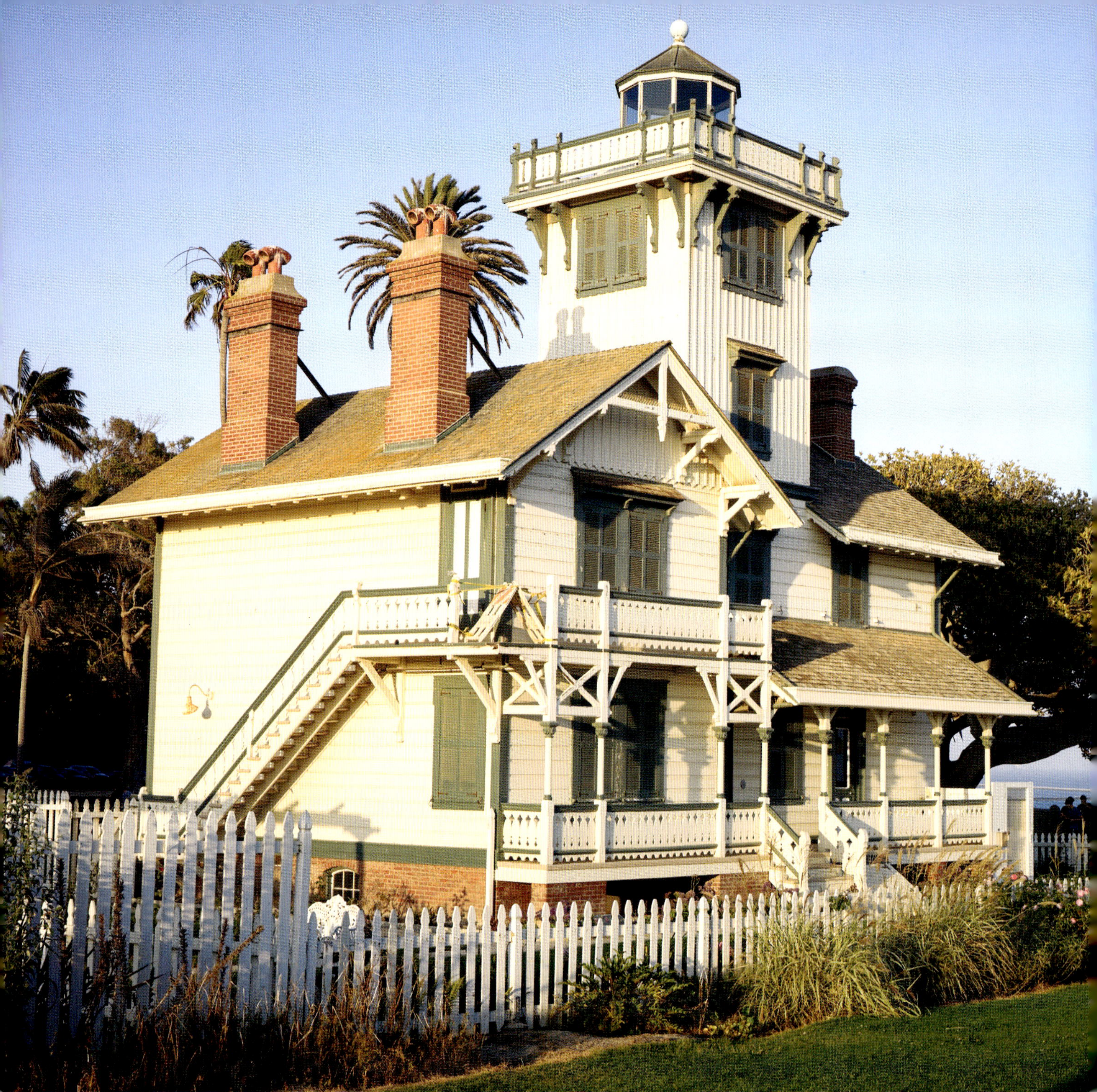

Point Fermin Lighthouse

Designed in the Victorian Stick style, with gabled roofs, overhanging eaves and crisscrossing brackets on the porch and balcony, Point Fermin Lighthouse has stood on a bluff overlooking San Pedro Bay since 1874, where it was the first navigational light into the bay.

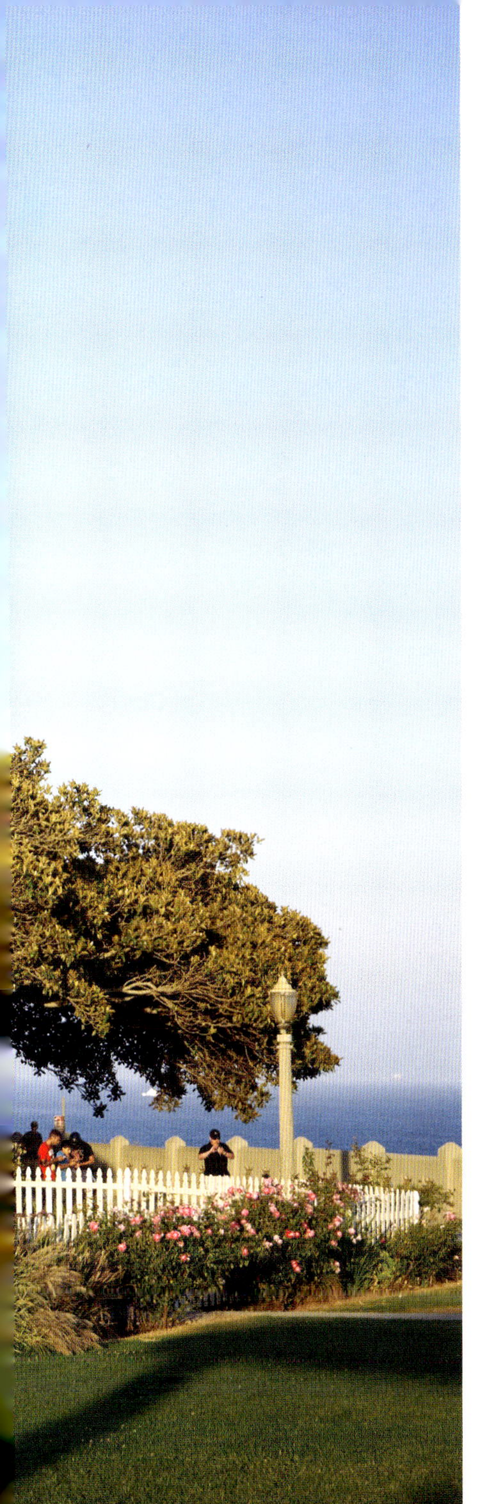

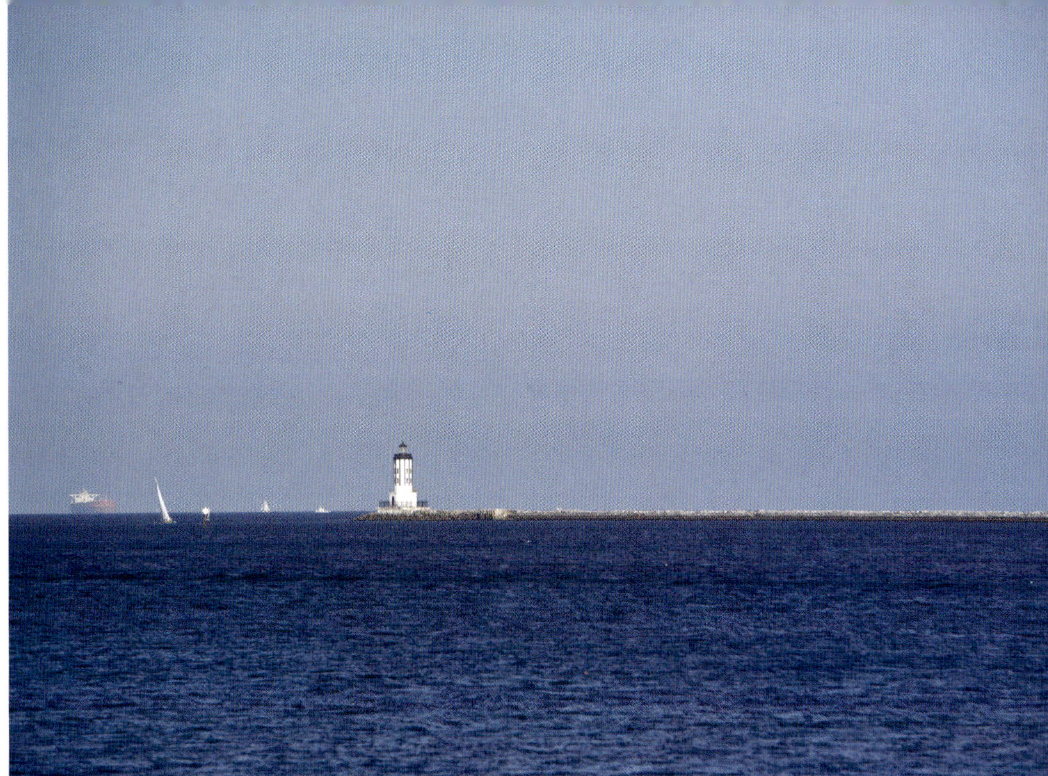

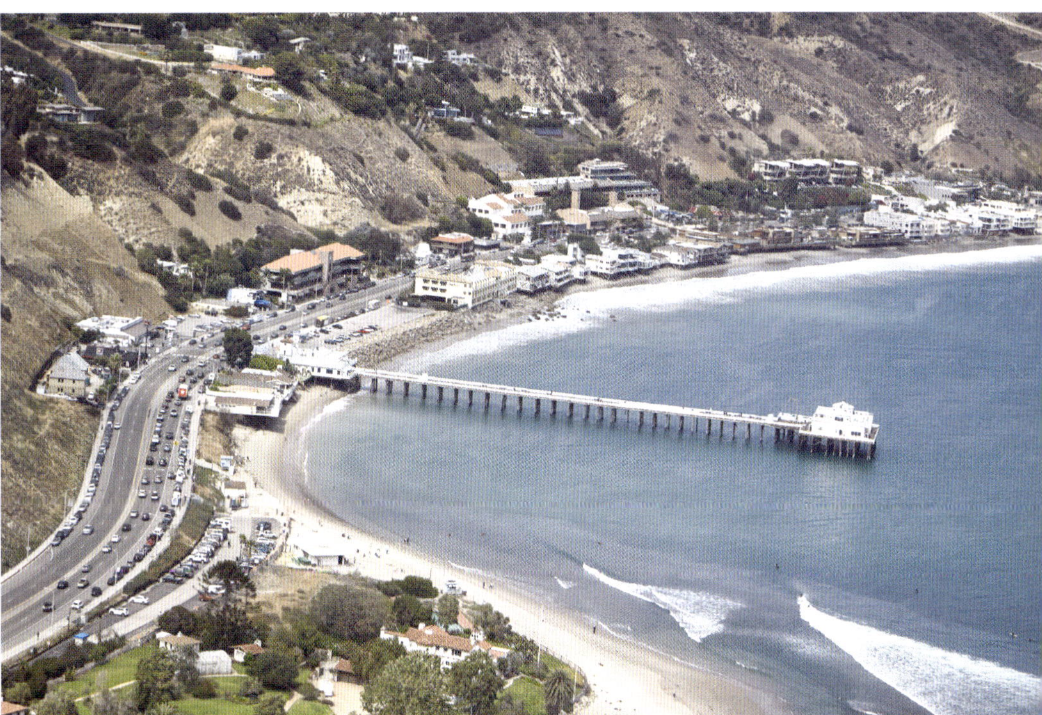

Los Angeles Harbor Light Station *(top)*

Also known as "Angels Gate Light," this solitary lighthouse can just be seen on the horizon over the wide expanse of blue ocean. Sitting at the end of the 9,250-foot San Pedro breakwater, the lighthouse has been welcoming ships into the harbor of Los Angeles since 1912.

Malibu Pier *(bottom)*

Watch surfers riding waves at the adjacent Surfrider Beach; enjoy a bite to eat by the ocean, or go fishing on the historic Malibu Pier. The 780-foot-long pier was extended to its current length in 1934. After WWII, the familiar twin buildings were added.

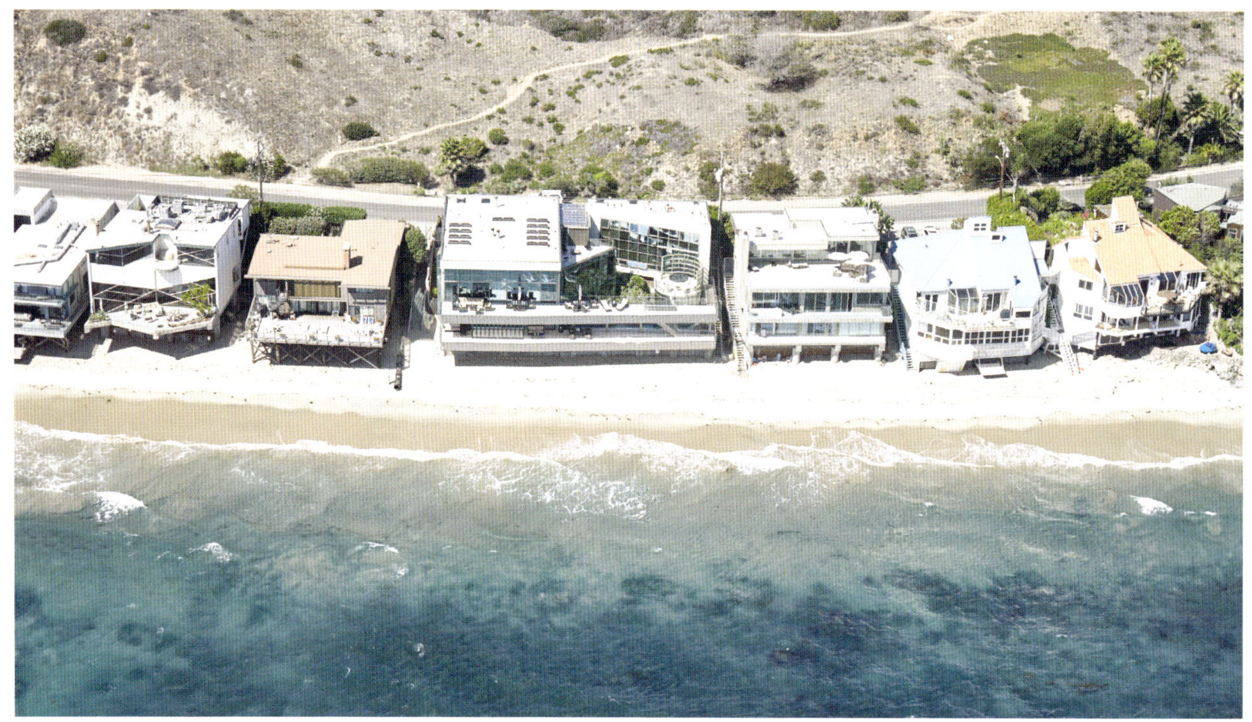

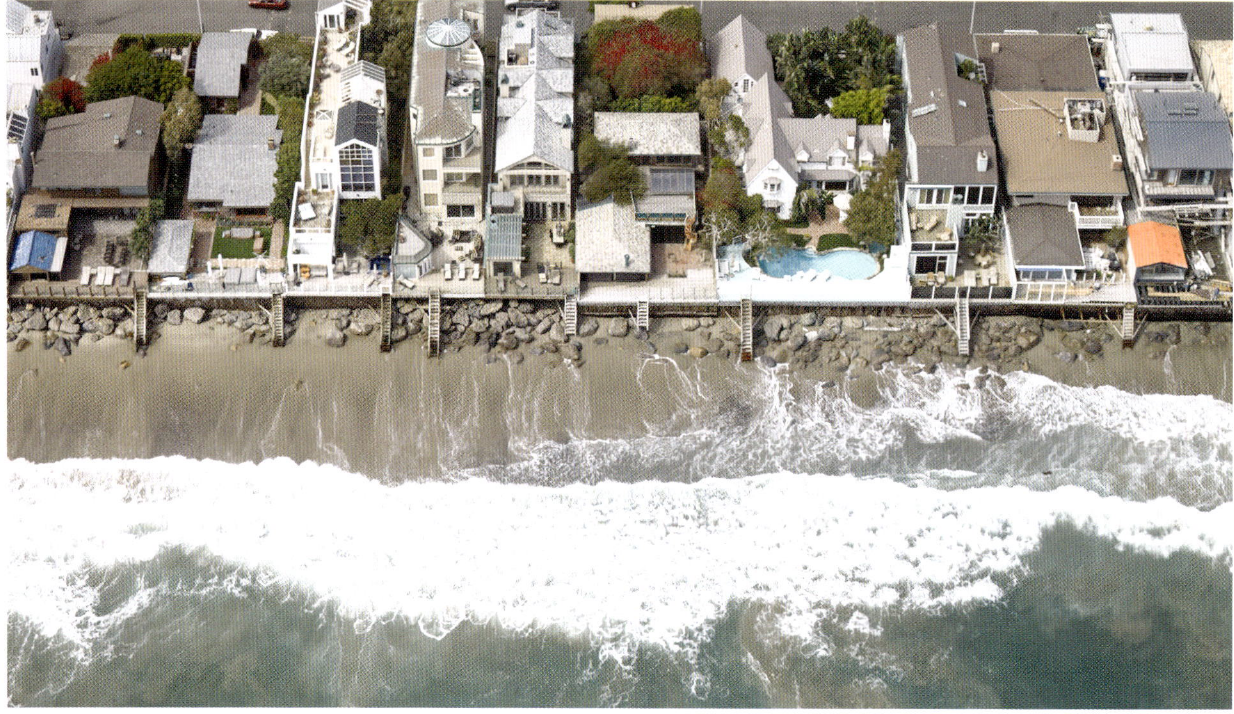

Beach Front Homes *(top and bottom)*

Exclusively reserved for the rich and famous, these Malibu beach front homes go for millions of dollars apiece. Situated between the Pacific Ocean and the Pacific Coast Highway, it is easy to see the allure of the white sandy beaches and clear blue water of this stunning stretch of coastline.

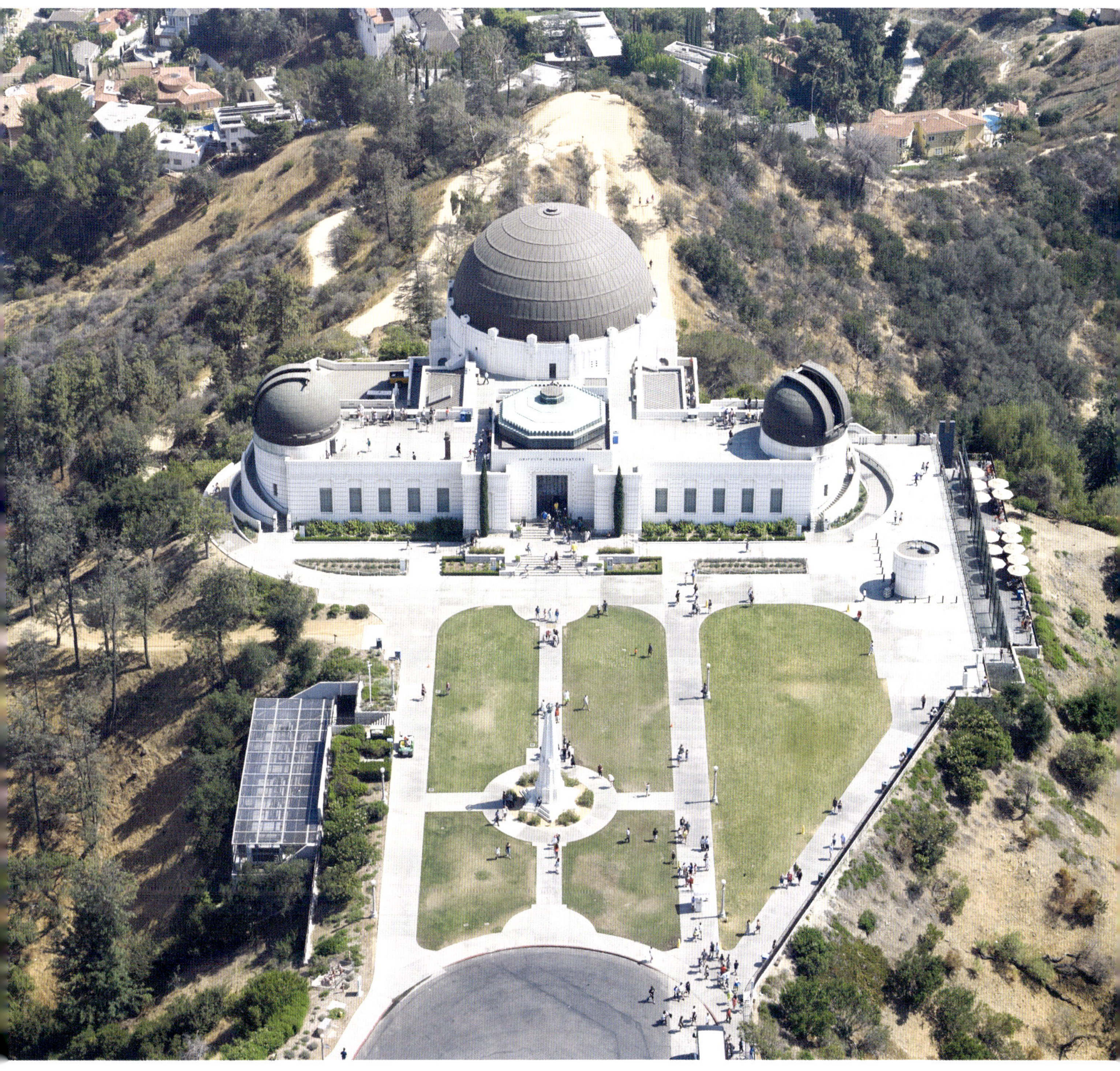

Griffith Park Observatory

Described as Southern California's "gateway to the cosmos," the Griffith Observatory sits on the slopes of Mount Hollywood, offering spectacular views of Los Angeles and the Hollywood Sign. Since its opening in 1935, the grounds, exhibits, and telescopes are free to the public.

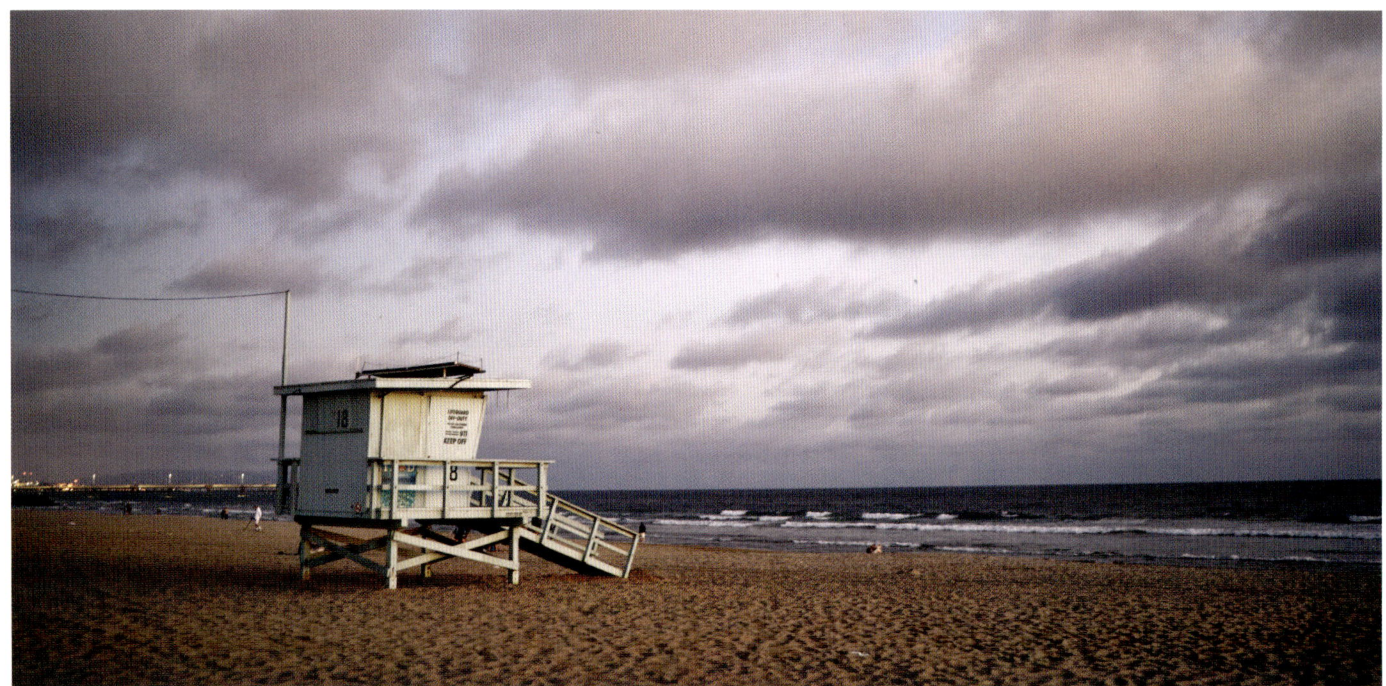

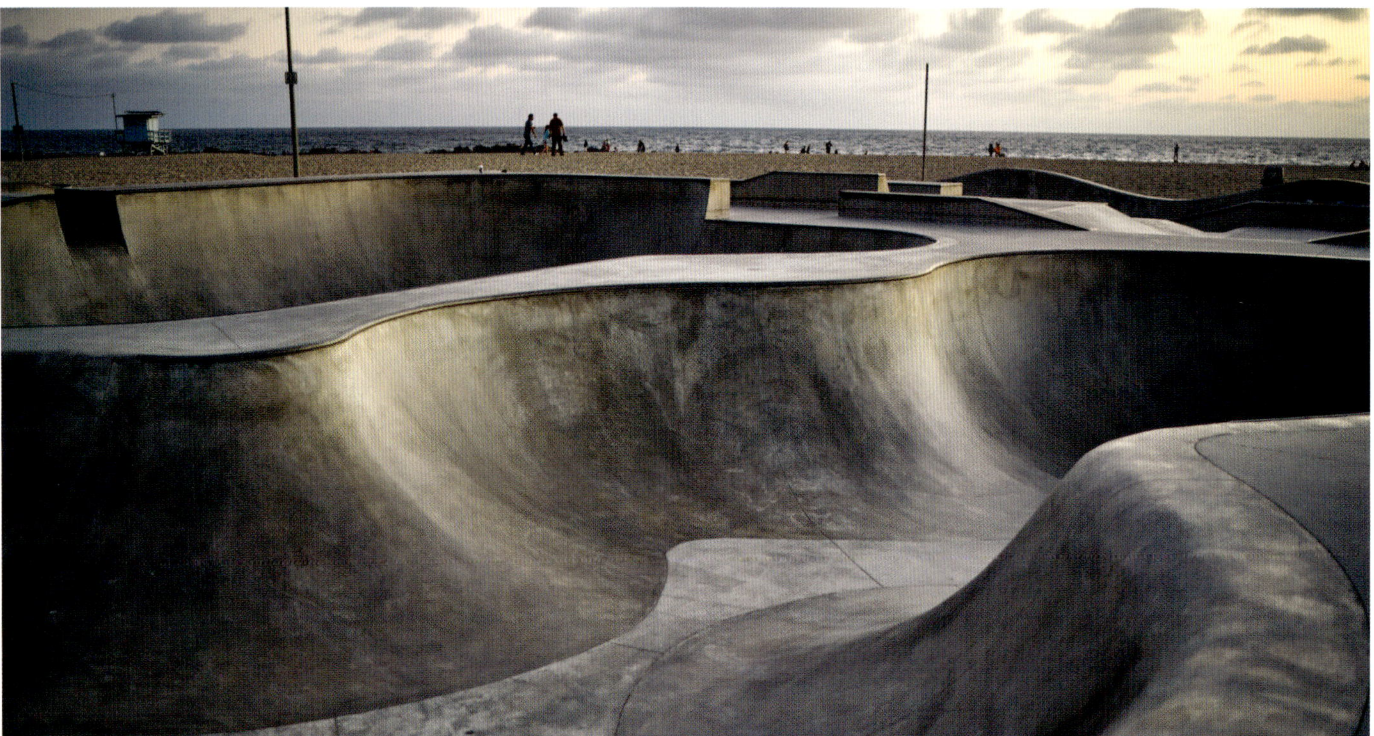

Venice Beach *(top)*

An unusually grey, sunless day on the famous Venice Beach, the rolling clouds loom over the ocean in a dramatic effect. This 3-mile-long beach is manicured daily and overseen by lifeguards. Surf, skim, and body boards are all readily available for rent or just stroll along the beach and people watch.

Venice Beach Skate Park *(bottom)*

The curved concrete of the skate park gleams in the dusk light. Known as the "Breeding Ground," the park honors Venice's rich skateboarding heritage, featuring bowls that resemble empty swimming pools in homage to the early "dogtown" days when skateboarders would crash neighbors' backyard pools to hone their art.

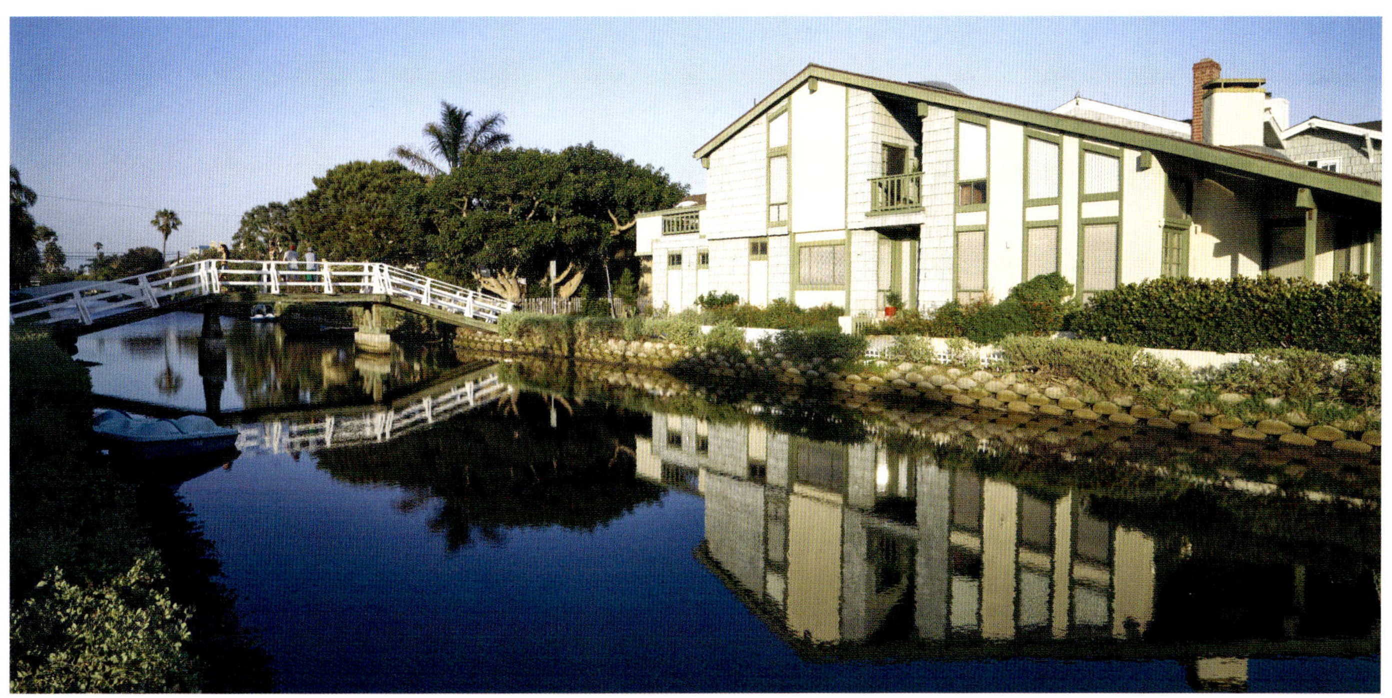

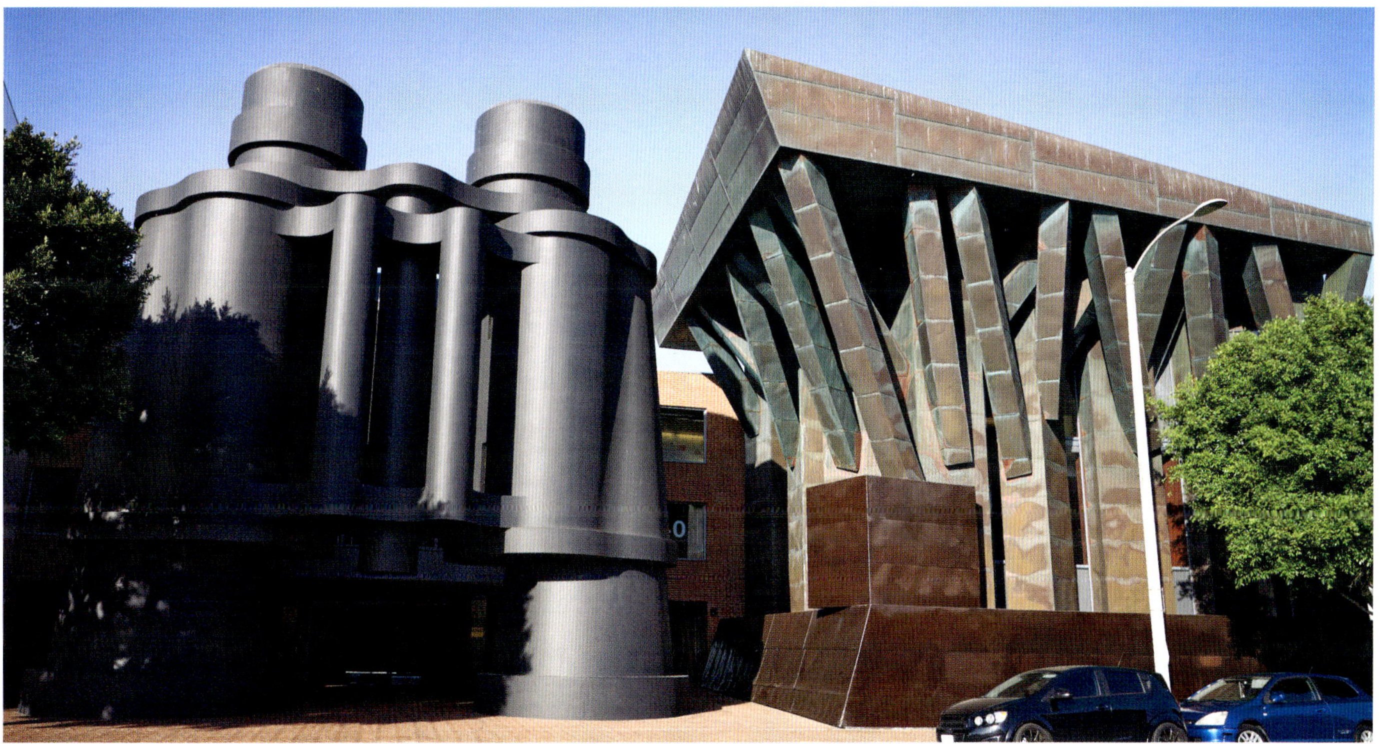

Venice Canals *(top)*

A perfect reflection is seen in the water of one of the Venice Canals. Designed as part of developer Abbot Kinney's plan to create the "Venice of America," the canals and arched bridges aimed to recreate the look and feel of Venice, Italy. Once upon a time visitors enjoyed gondola rides here.

Venice Giant Binoculars *(bottom)*

Part public art and part office block, you cannot miss the striking Binoculars Building, designed by acclaimed architect Frank Gehry. Once the headquarters for the Chiat/Day advertising agency and now leased by Google, the quirky design allows cars to drive through the binoculars to get to the parking garage.

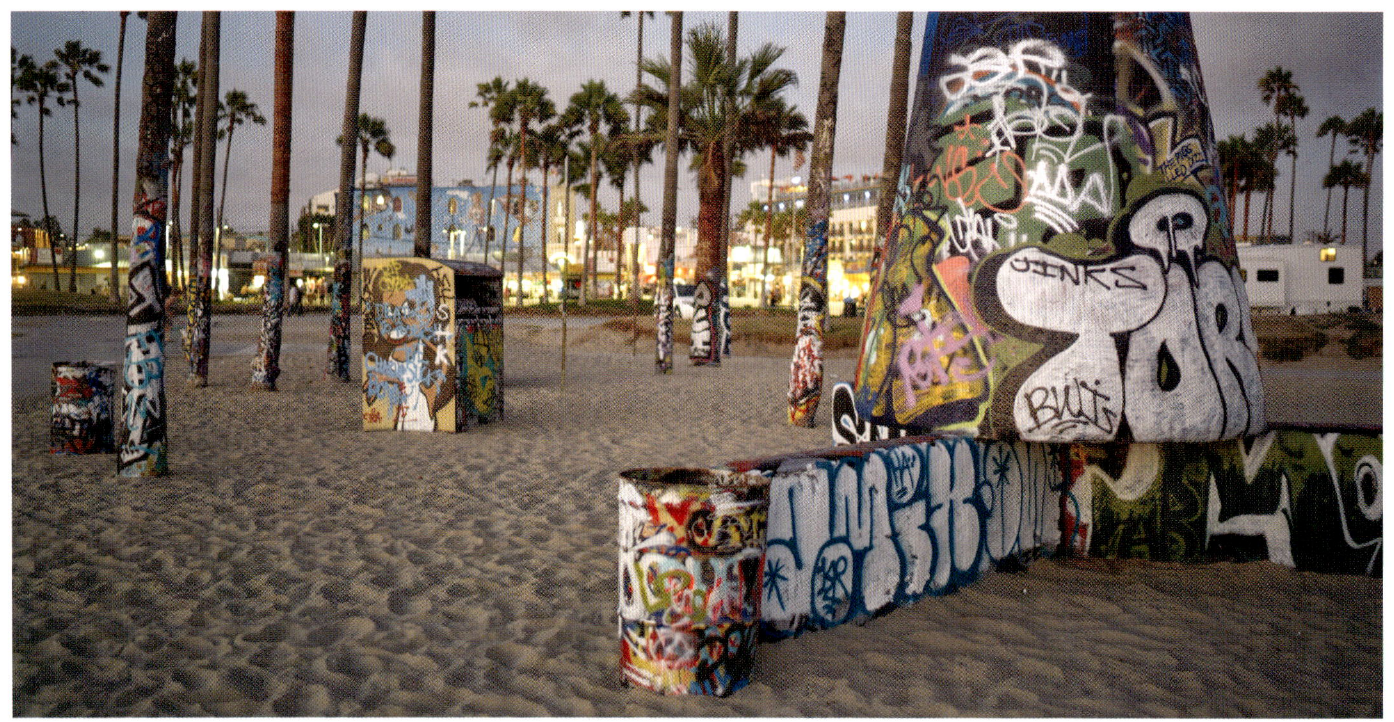

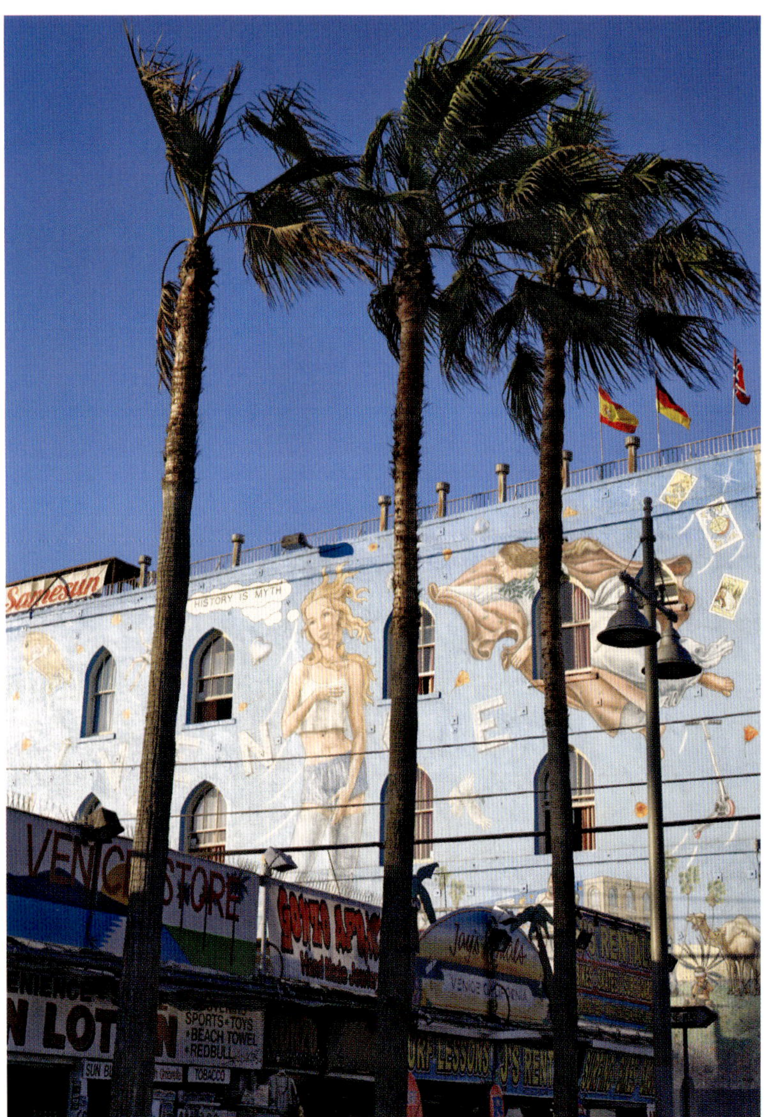

Venice Beach *(above and left)*

As well as its world-famous boardwalk, where bikini-clad tourists on roller skates rub shoulders with street performers weird and wonderful, Venice is renowned for its vibrant street art scene. Murals and graffiti occupy every blank space with even the palm trees doubling as a canvas for local artists.

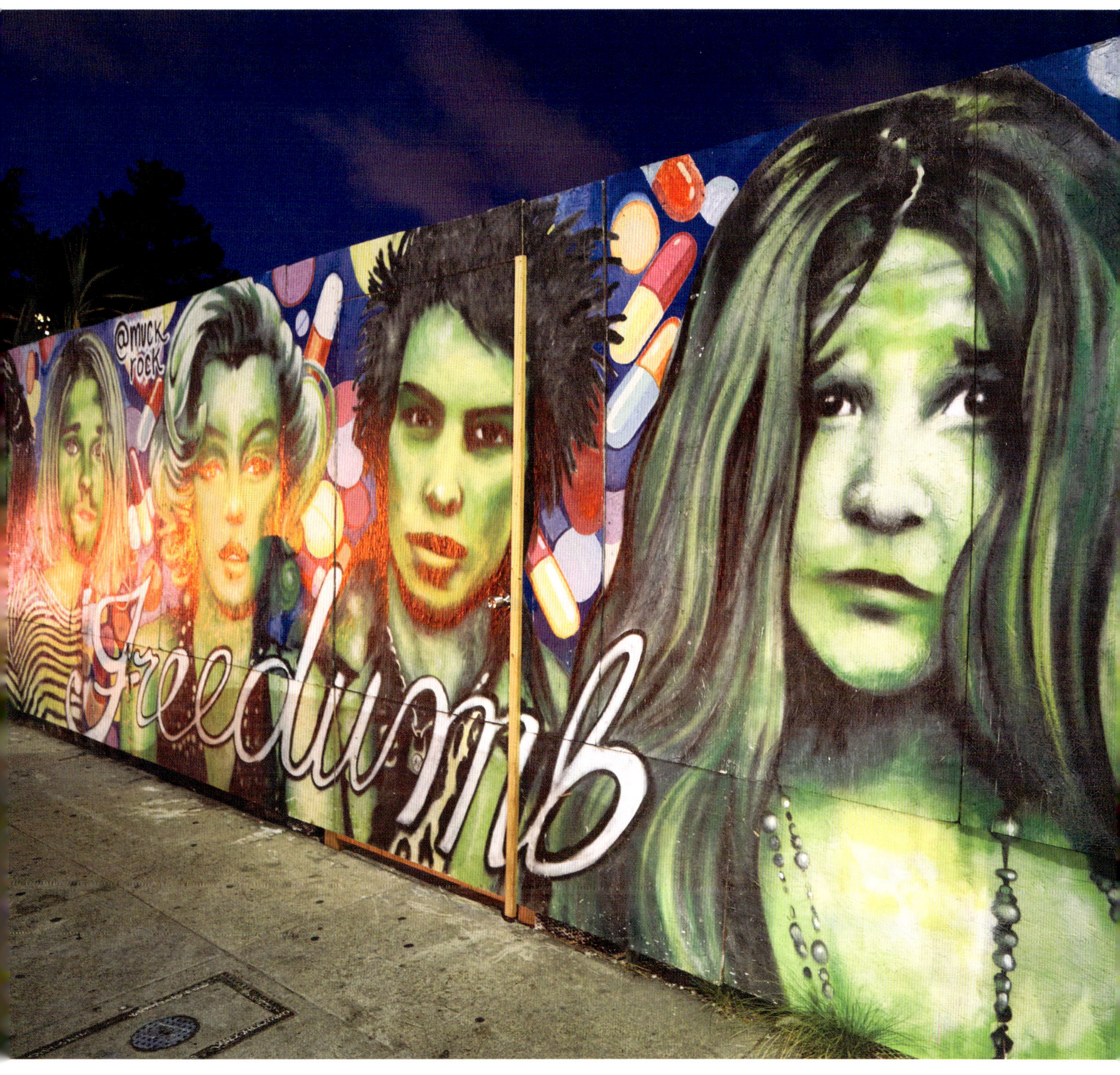

Freedumb

The *Freedumb* mural, by renowned street artist Jules Muck, depicts five icons who prematurely lost their lives to drugs. The lights from passing cars on Main Street, Venice, bounce off the compelling green portraits of Jim Morrison, Kurt Cobain, Marilyn Monroe, Sid Vicious, and Janis Joplin.

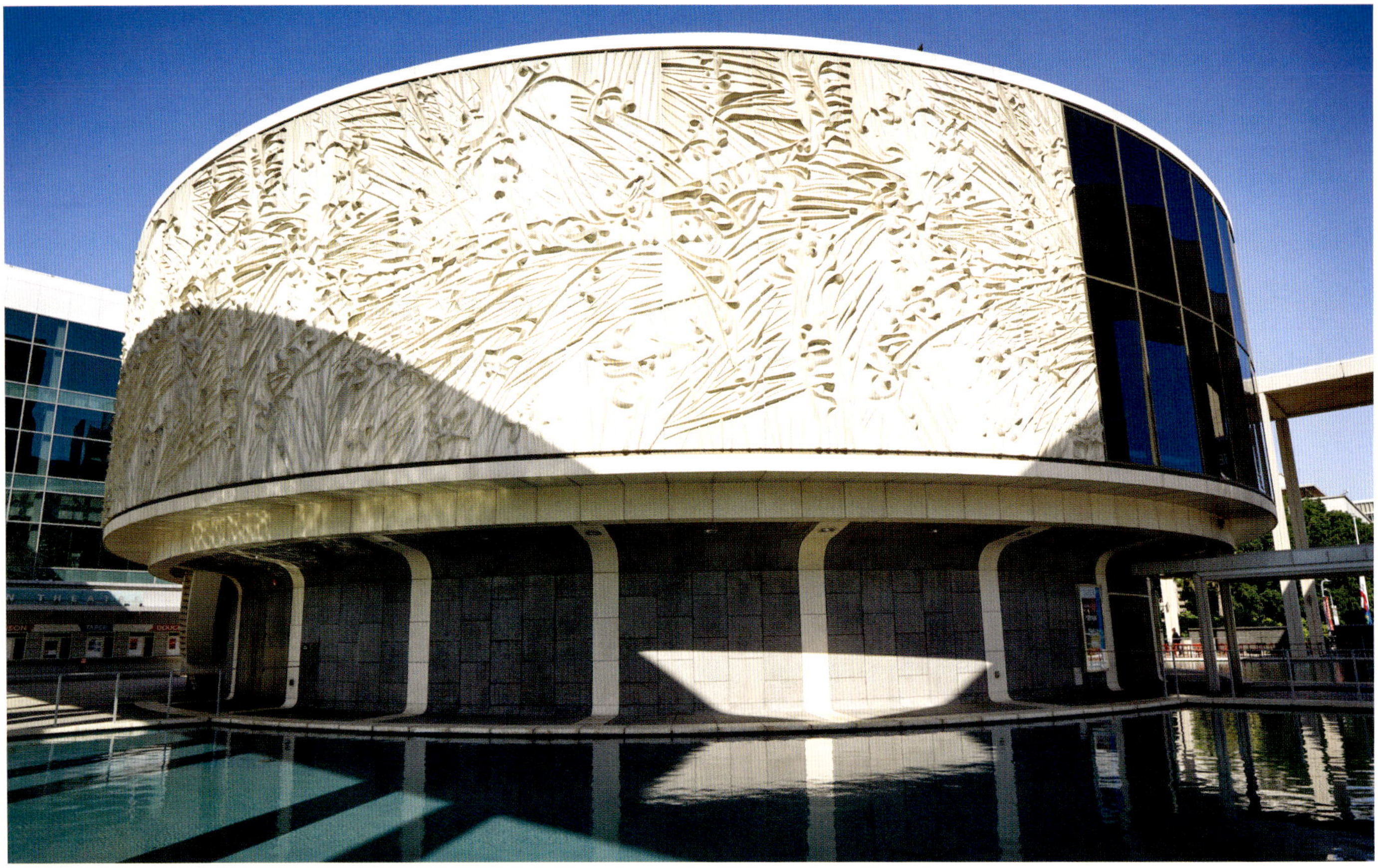

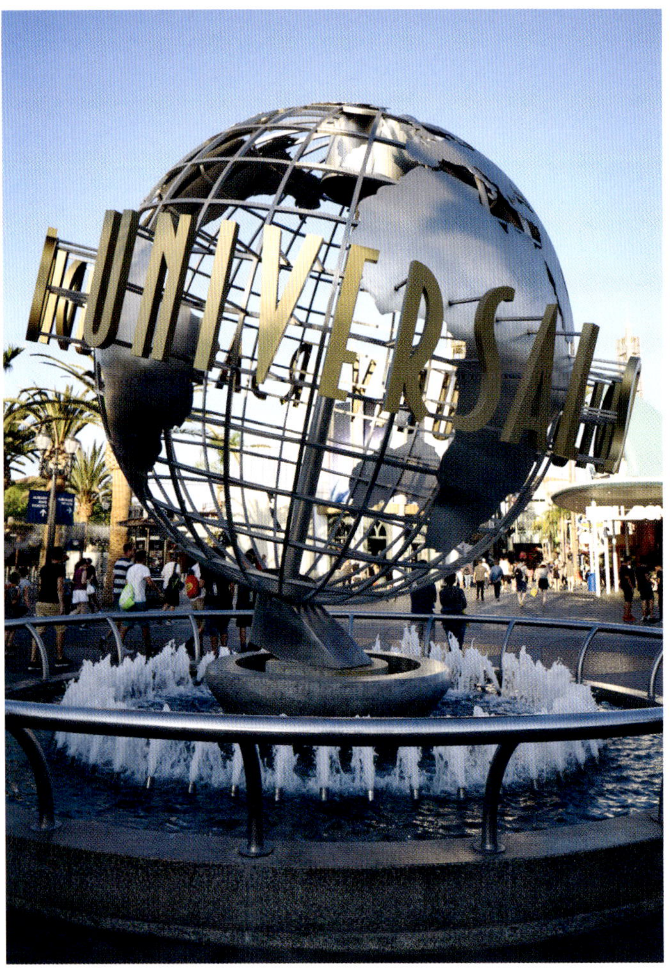

Mark Taper Forum *(above)*

This circular drum, decorated with a lacy precast relief giving the impression of icing on a cake, is a 739-seat stage at the Los Angeles Music Center. Designed by Welton Becket, the theater has presented many innovative plays since it opened in 1967 and has won five Tony Awards.

Universal Studios Hollywood *(left)*

The iconic Hollywood Globe and Fountain marks the main entrance to one of Hollywood's most famous theme parks. In 1964 Universal formally opened Universal Studios Hollywood, allowing a glimpse into movie making. Today, the theme park is a world-class destination with immersive lands, thrill rides, and shows.

Walt Disney Concert Hall *(opposite)*

The gravity-defying silver sails of the iconic Walt Disney Concert Hall shimmer in the midday sun. Designed to bring music to the city of Los Angeles, the Deconstructivist-style building is just as innovative inside. Frank Gehry claimed he designed the architectural marvel "from the inside out."

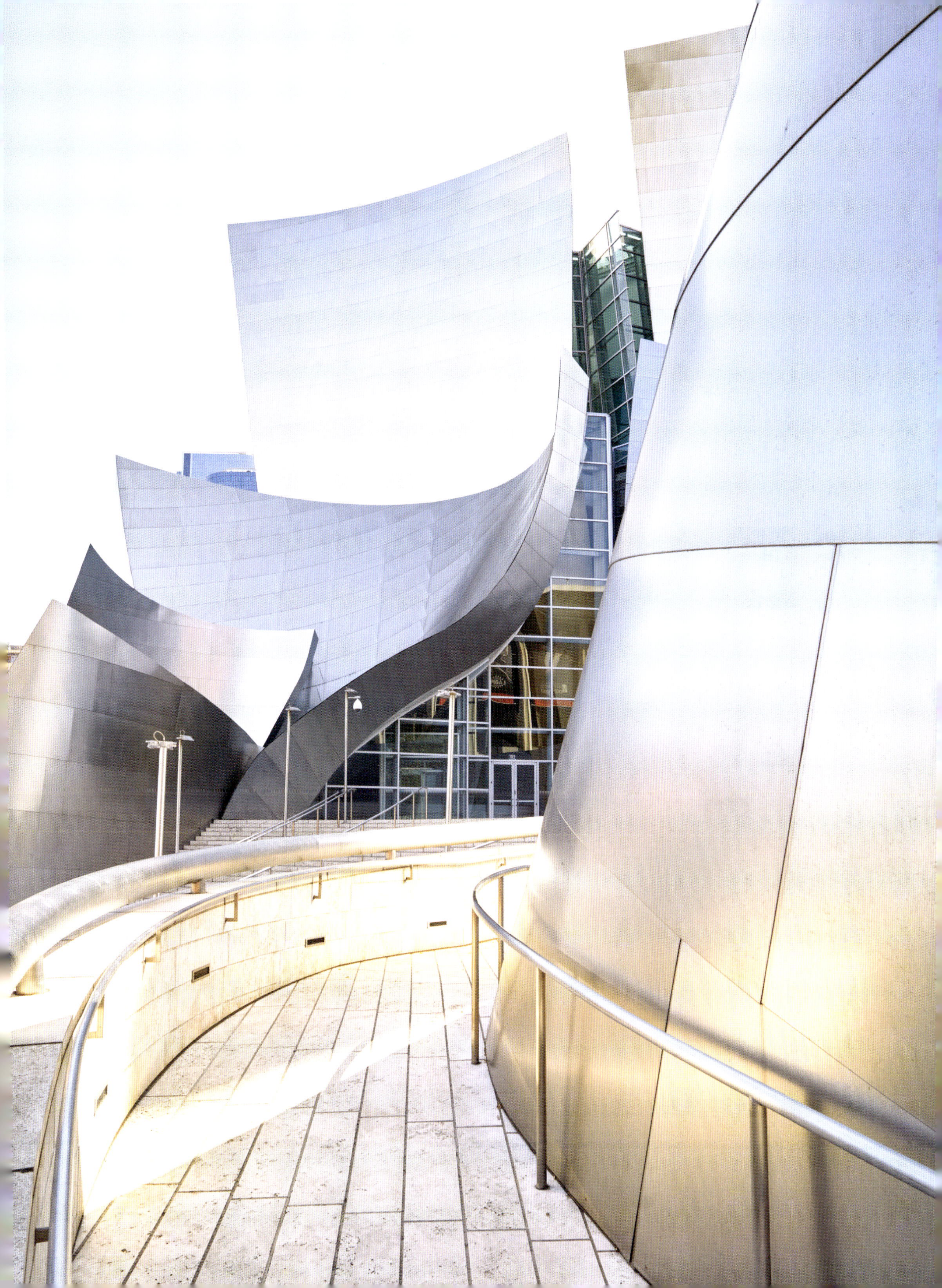

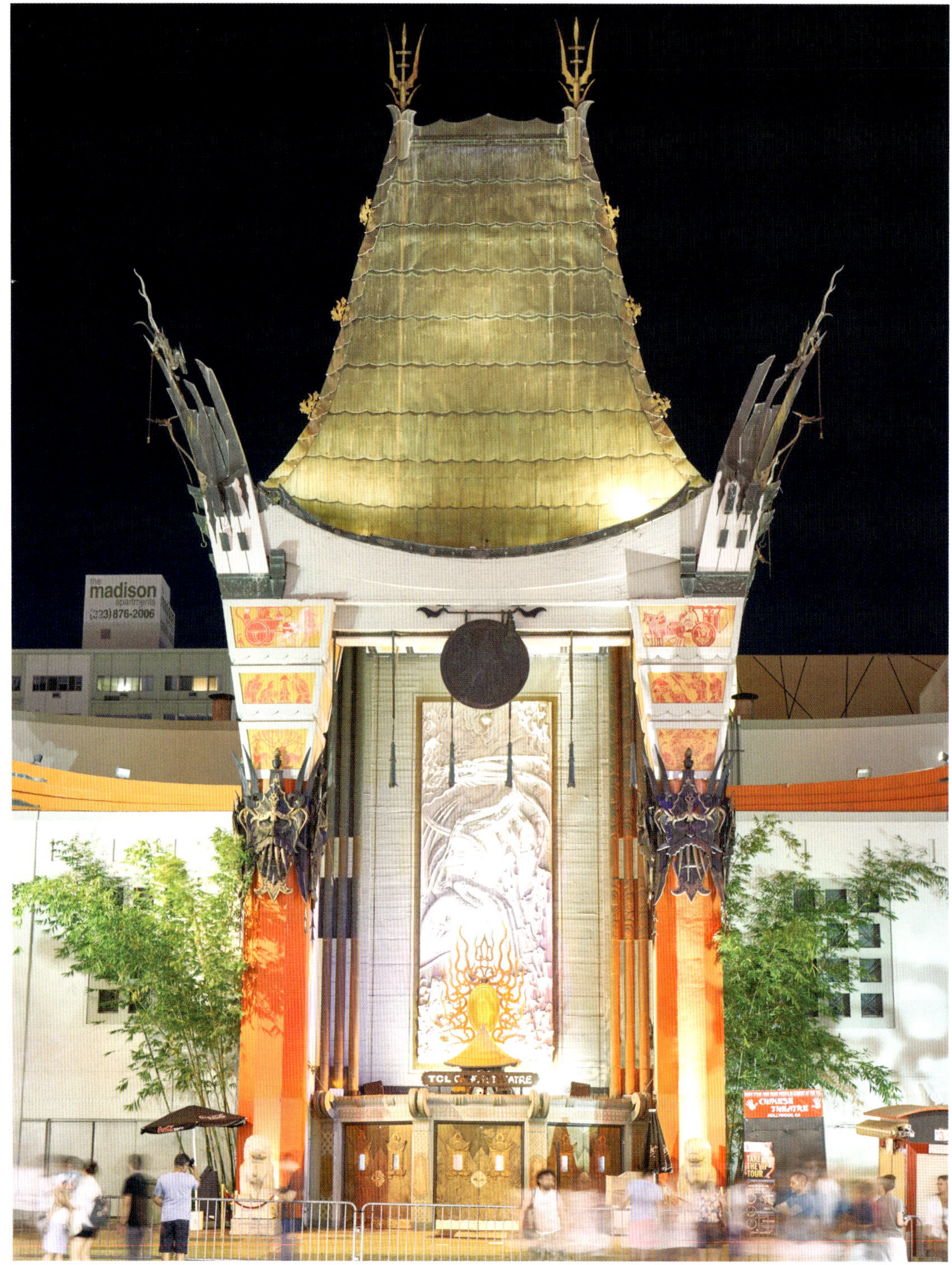

TCL Chinese Theatre *(above)*

Originally known as Grauman's Chinese Theatre, this 1927 Hollywood landmark buzzes with visitors on a warm Hollywood evening. It is famous for the celebrity hand and footprints set in concrete in front of the building. Declared a Historic-Cultural Monument in 1968, artifacts from China are integrated into its design.

Alex Theatre *(opposite)*

This neon Art Deco gem glows in the dusk light. Opened in Glendale in 1925, the theatre showed vaudeville performances, plays, and silent movies. Today, the theatre holds 250 events a year including the annual "Three Stooges Big Screen Event" held every Thanksgiving and attended by relatives of the Stooges.

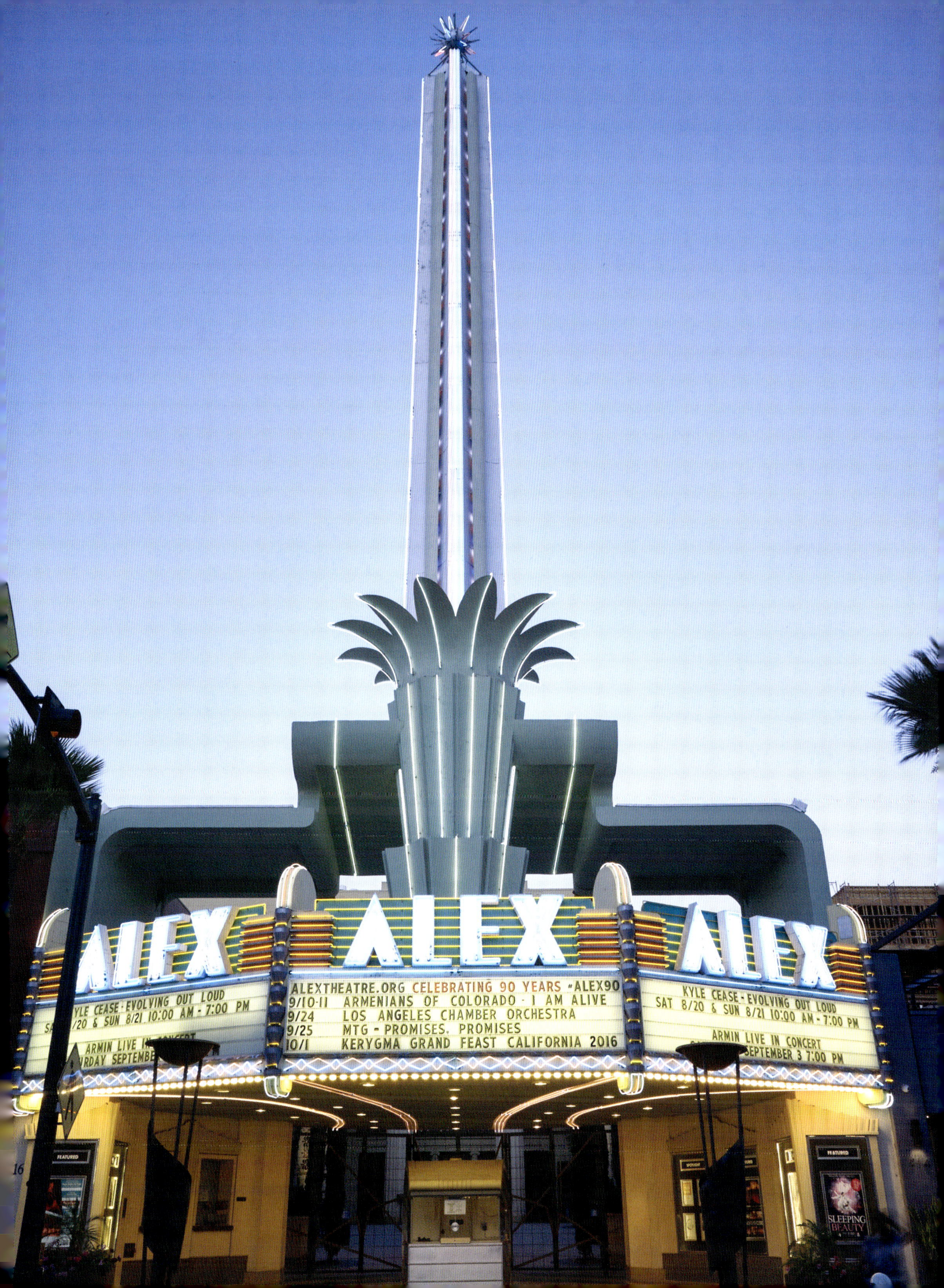
ALEX
ALEX
ALEX
ALEXTHEATRE.ORG CELEBRATING 90 YEARS #ALEX90
9/10-11 ARMENIANS OF COLORADO - I AM ALIVE
9/24 LOS ANGELES CHAMBER ORCHESTRA
9/25 MTG - PROMISES, PROMISES
10/1 KERYGMA GRAND FEAST CALIFORNIA 2016
KYLE CEASE - EVOLVING OUT LOUD
SAT 8/20 & SUN 8/21 10:00 AM - 7:00 PM
ARMIN LIVE IN CONCERT
FEATURED
FEATURED
SLEEPING BEAUTY

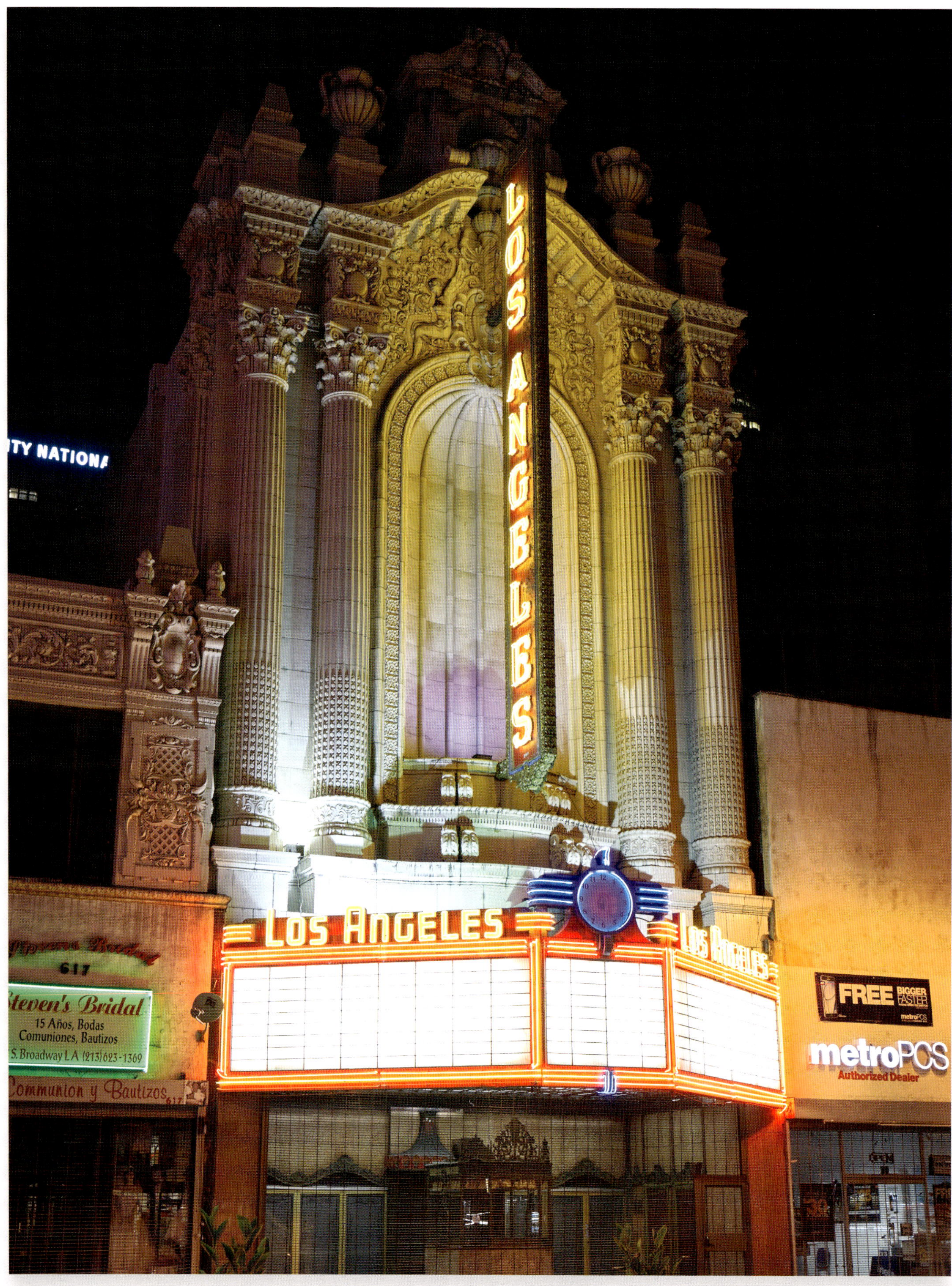
LOS ANGELES
LOS ANGELES
LOS ANGELES
617
Steven's Bridal
15 Años, Bodas
Comuniones, Bautizos
S. Broadway LA (213) 623-1369
Communion y Bautizos
FREE
BIGGER FASTER
metroPCS
Authorized Dealer

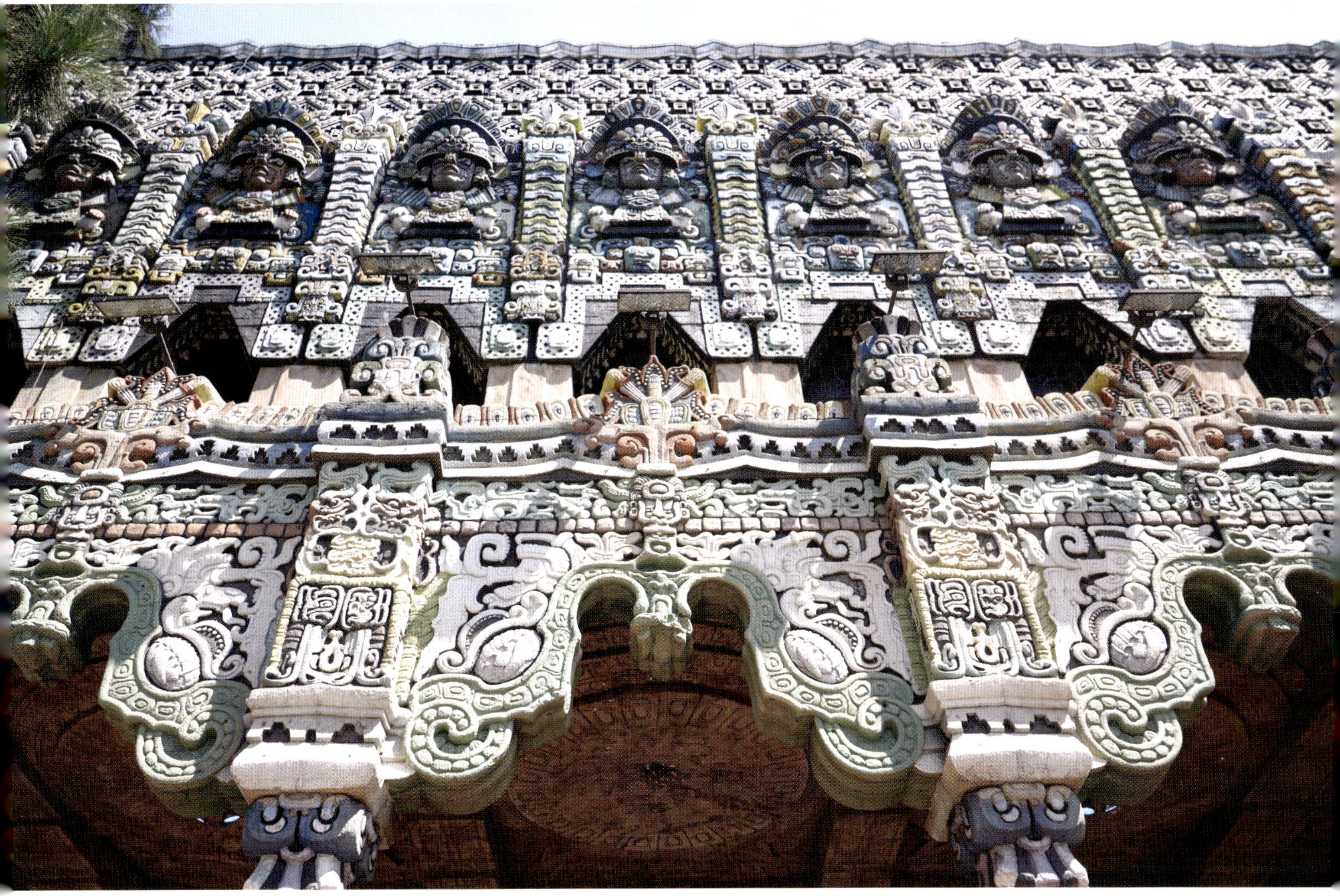

Mayan Theater *(above and right)*

The intricate Mayan-inspired facade of this former theater is a stunning example of the Exotic Revival style that was popular in the 1920s. Sculptor Francisco Cornejo designed the exterior and it is considered his most famous work. Today, it is a popular Downtown nightclub.

Los Angeles Theater *(opposite)*

This ornate French Baroque-style theater is located in the Broadway Theater District. The theater is equally lavish inside, modeled after the Hall of Mirrors in the Palace of Versailles, France. Built in 1930, it has changed ownership just two times. Today, it is used as a filming location.

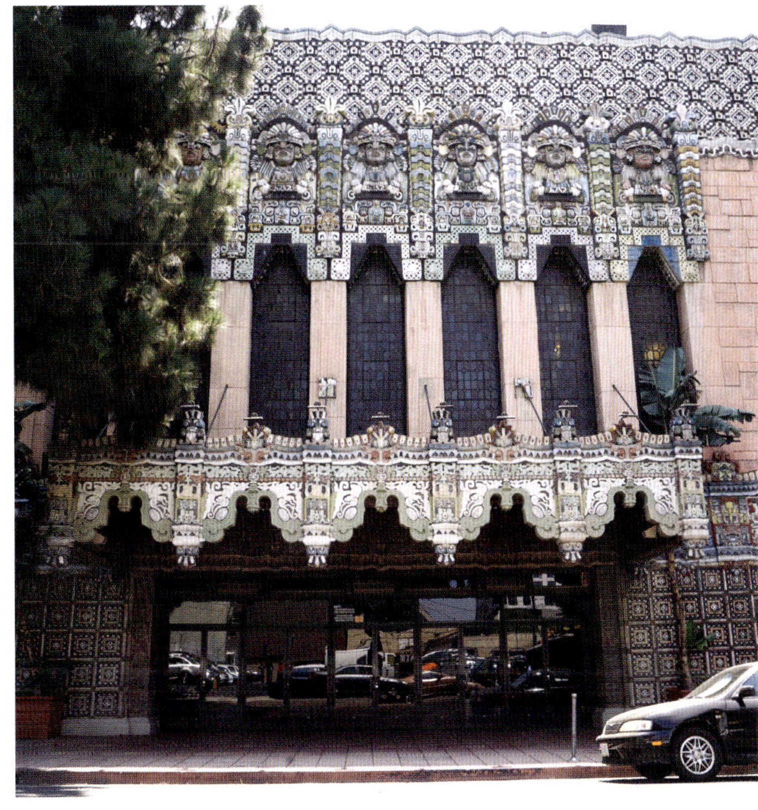

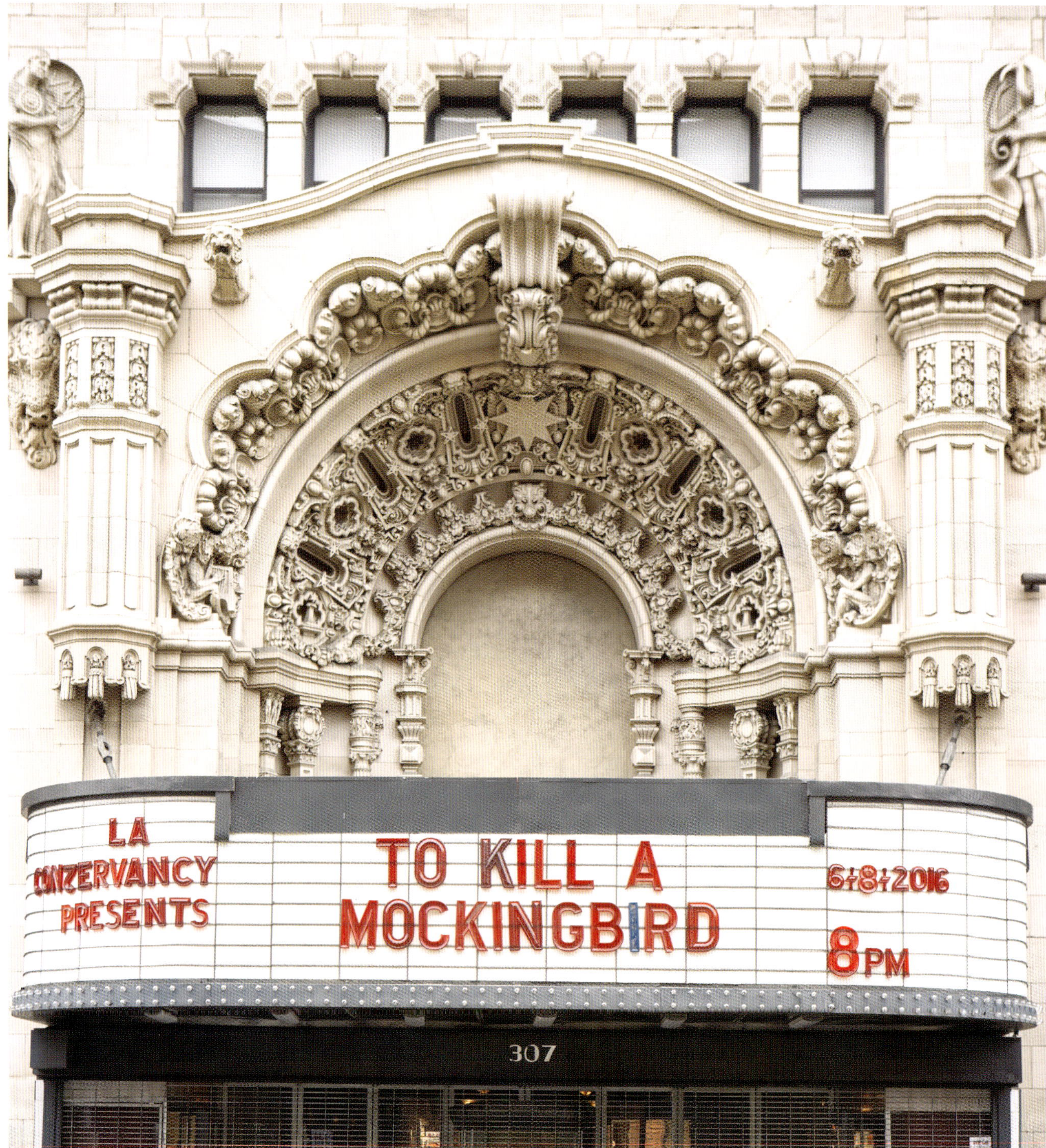

Million Dollar Theater *(above)*

Classic movie *To Kill a Mockingbird* showing at the historic Million Dollar Theater, one of the first movie theaters in the United States. Built in 1918 by Sid Grauman, who later opened Grauman's Chinese Theatre in Hollywood, the Spanish Baroque Revival-style building sits opposite the Bradbury Building in Downtown.

Pellissier Building and Wiltern Theatre *(opposite)*

The distinctive blue-green terra cotta exterior of the Wiltern Theatre is one of Los Angeles' most loved Art Deco buildings. Ear-marked for demolition in 1979, the theater and adjoining 12-story Pellissier Building were saved from the wrecking ball by the Los Angeles Conservancy.

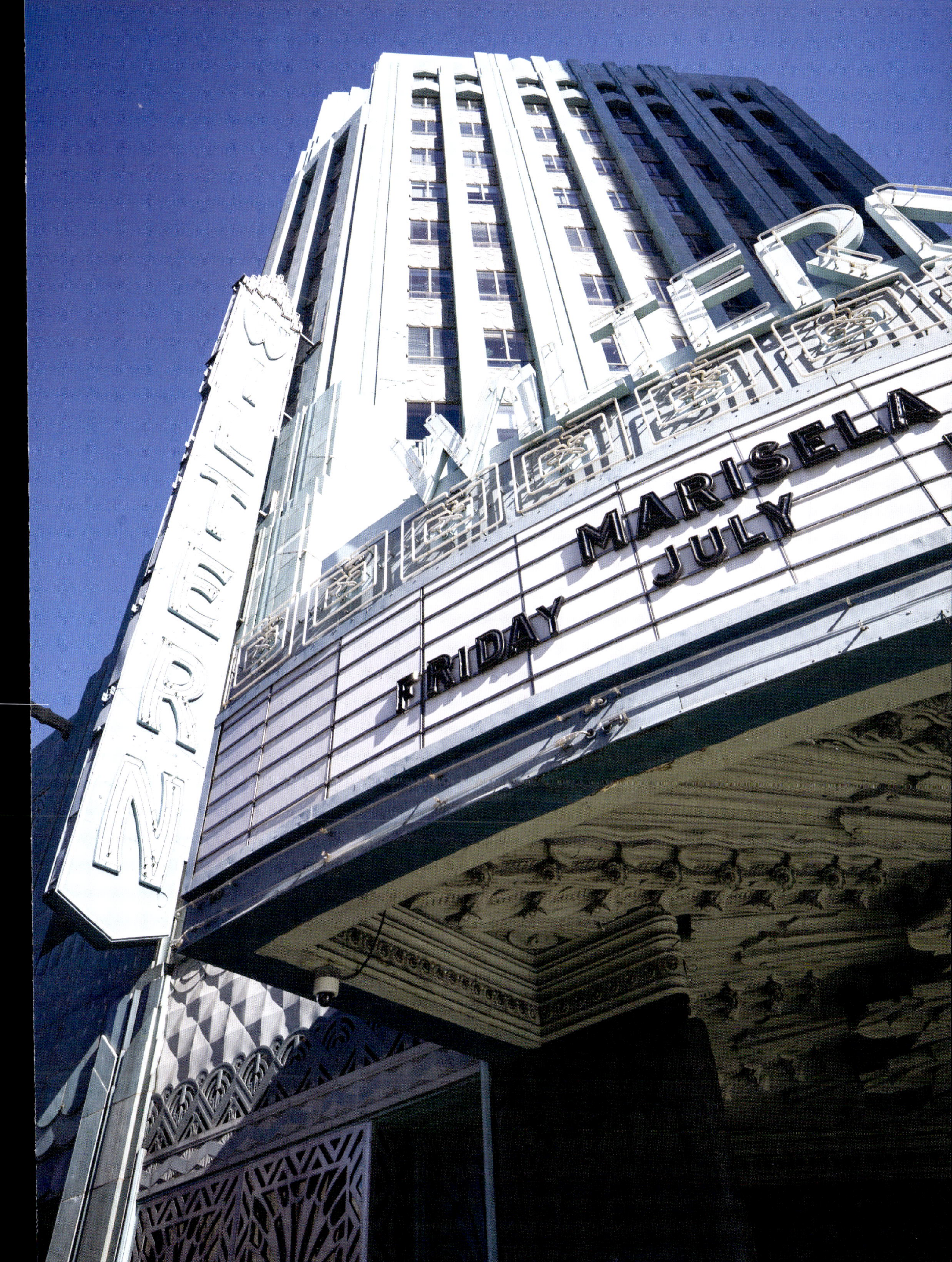
WILTERN
MARISELA
JULY
FRIDAY

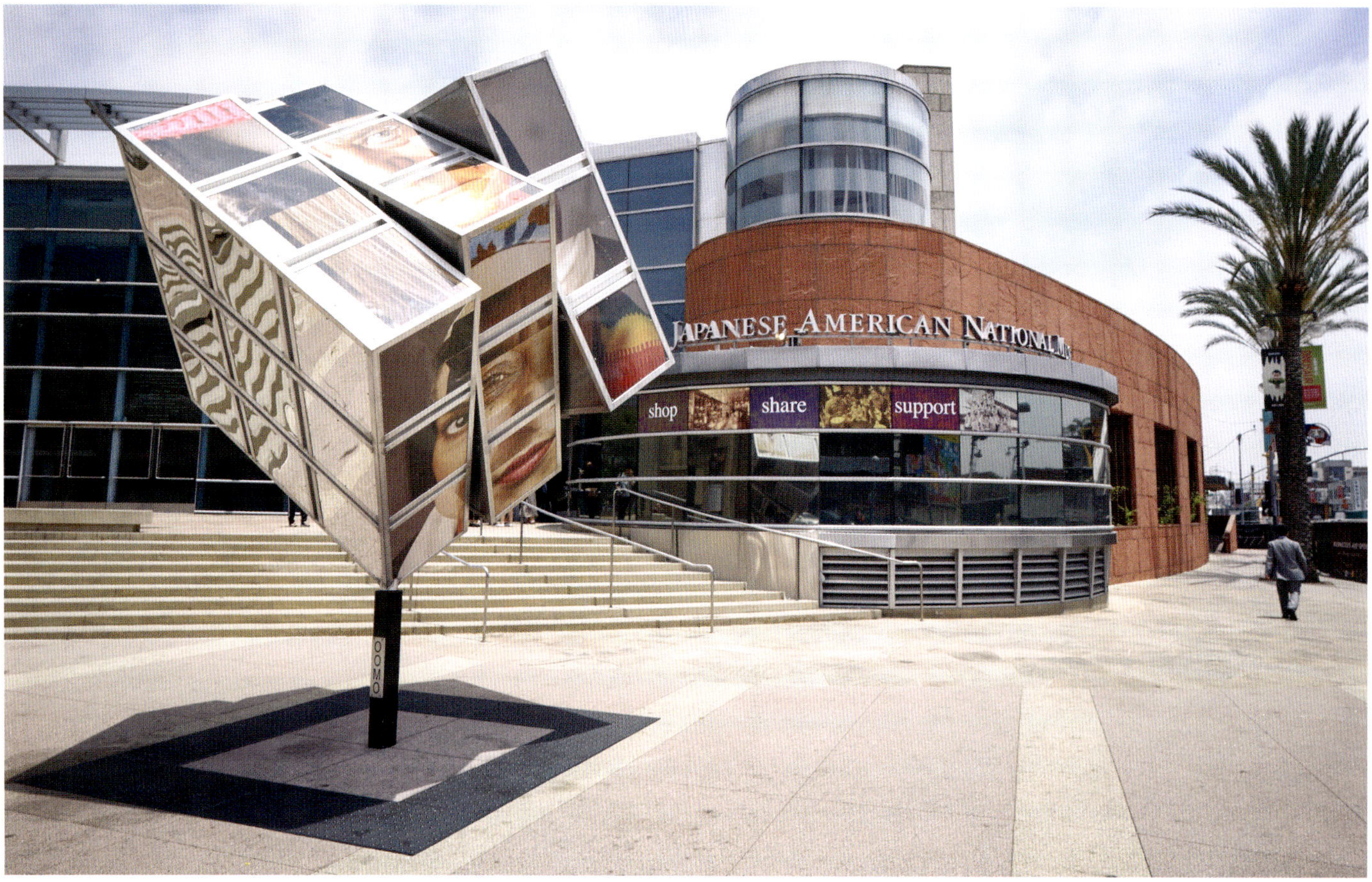

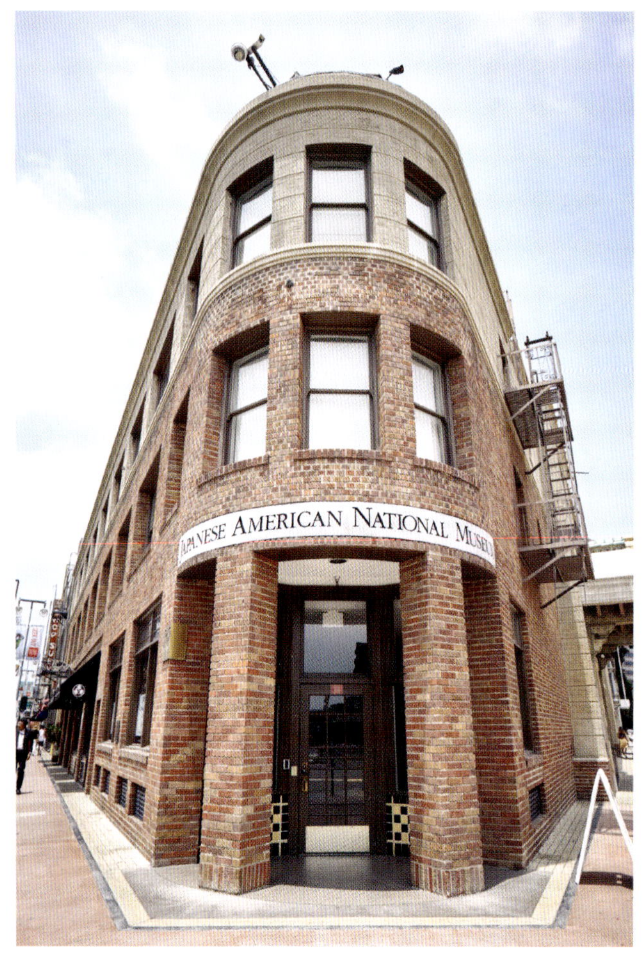

Japanese American National Museum

(above and left)

The OOMO cube outside the Japanese American National Museum is a public art installation, containing the faces of 30 Angelenos that visitors can twist and turn like a Rubik's cube. Located in the Little Tokyo area near Downtown, the museum contains over 130 years of Japanese American history.

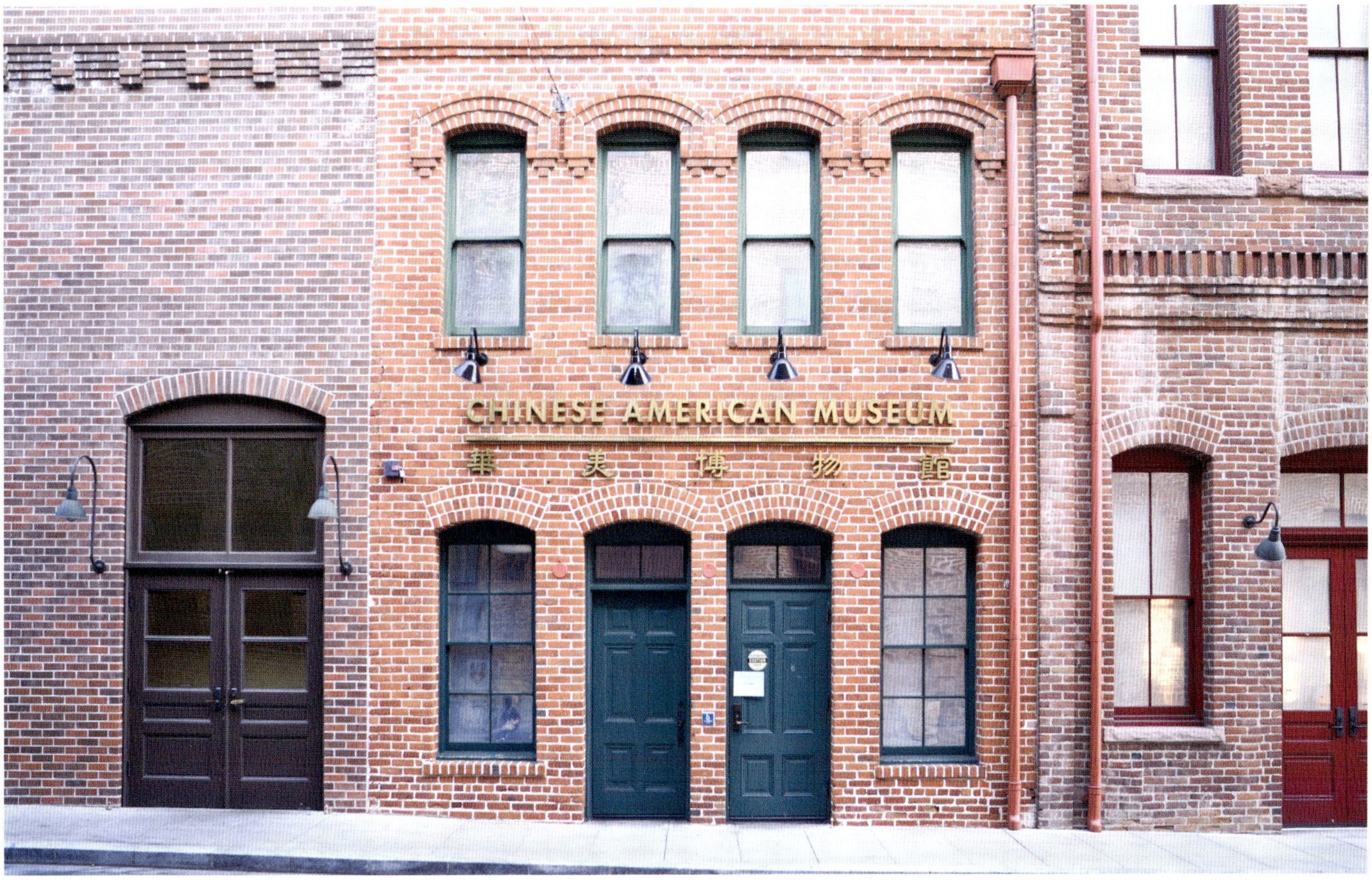

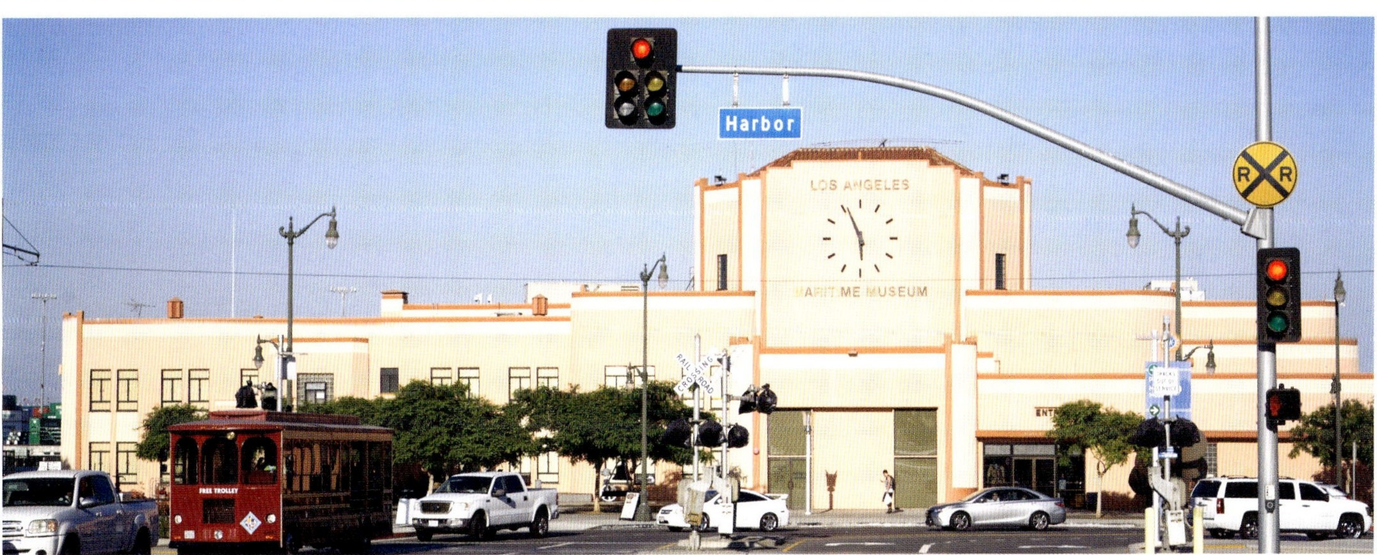

Chinese American Museum *(top)*

Aiming to celebrate the vibrant history of Chinese Americans, this museum is symbolically housed in the oldest remaining structure of Los Angeles' original Chinatown. The museum is dedicated to preserving and sharing the rich contribution of Chinese Americans who have lived in Los Angeles for over 150 years.

Los Angeles Maritime Museum *(bottom)*

Learn how Los Angeles Harbor grew from a lonely mudflat to a huge trade hub at this museum, located in the former Municipal Ferry Terminal Building on the main channel of Los Angeles Harbor in San Pedro. The museum also offers tours on its very own harbor tug, *Angels Gate*.

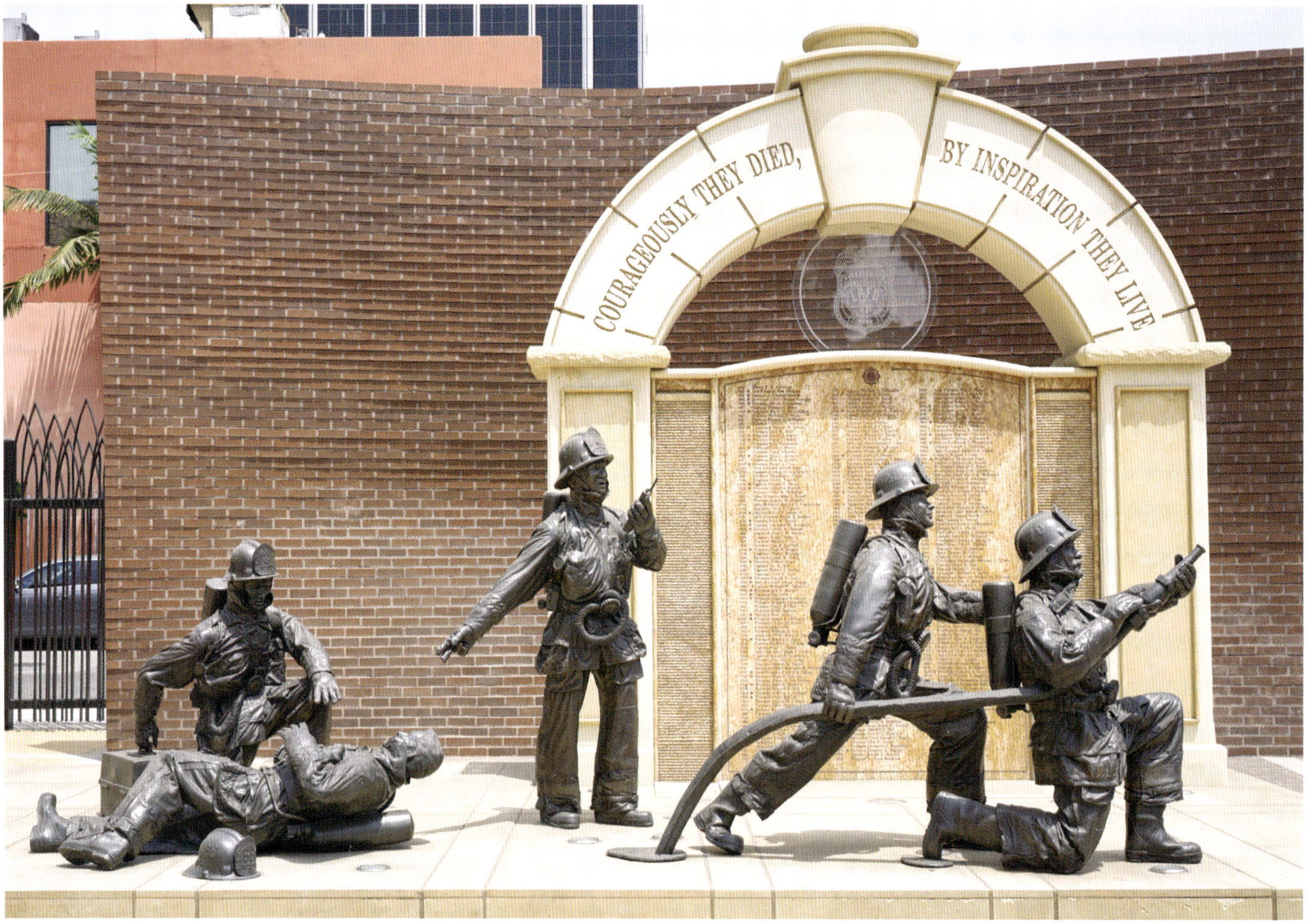
COURAGEOUSLY THEY DIED,
BY INSPIRATION THEY LIVE

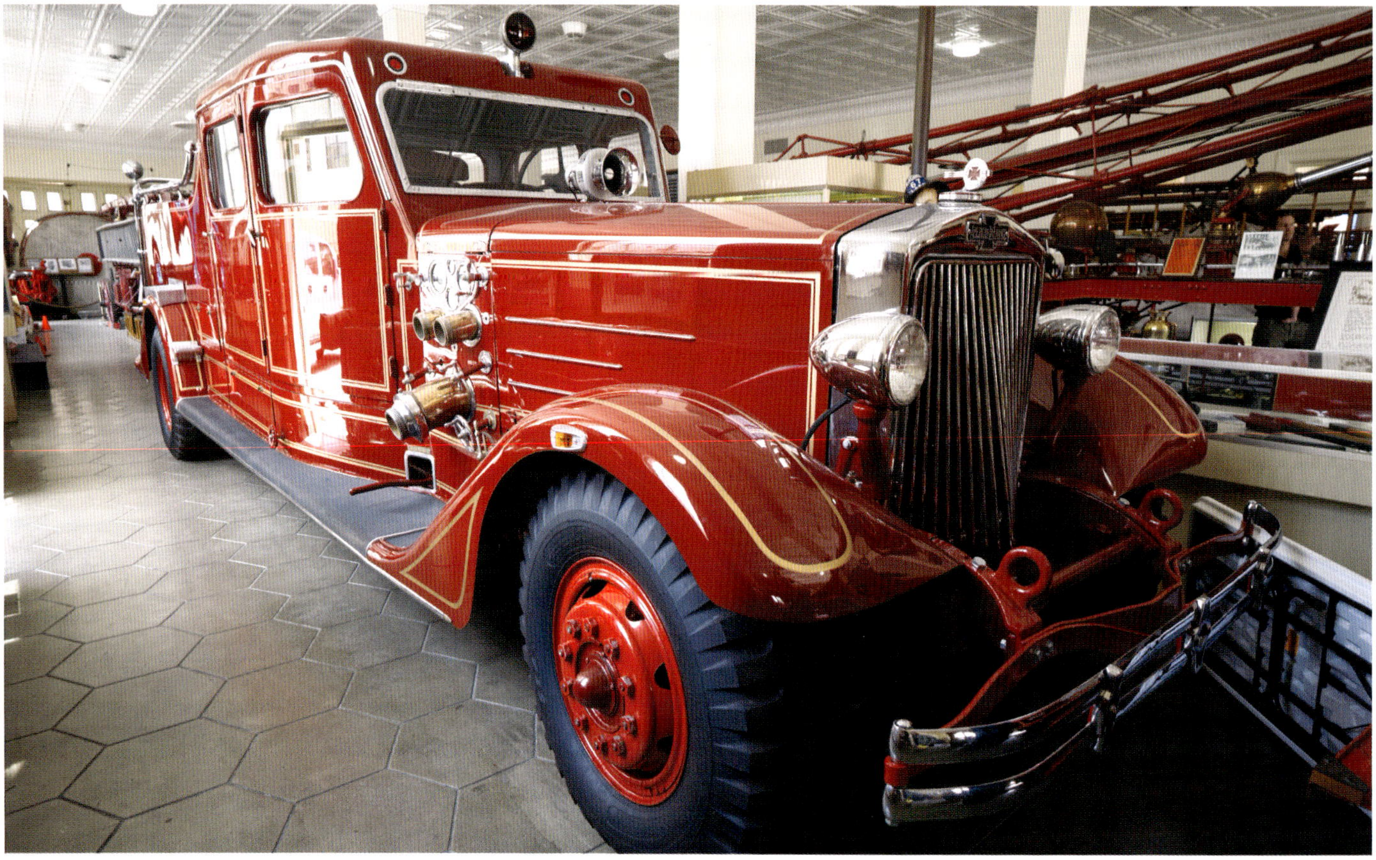

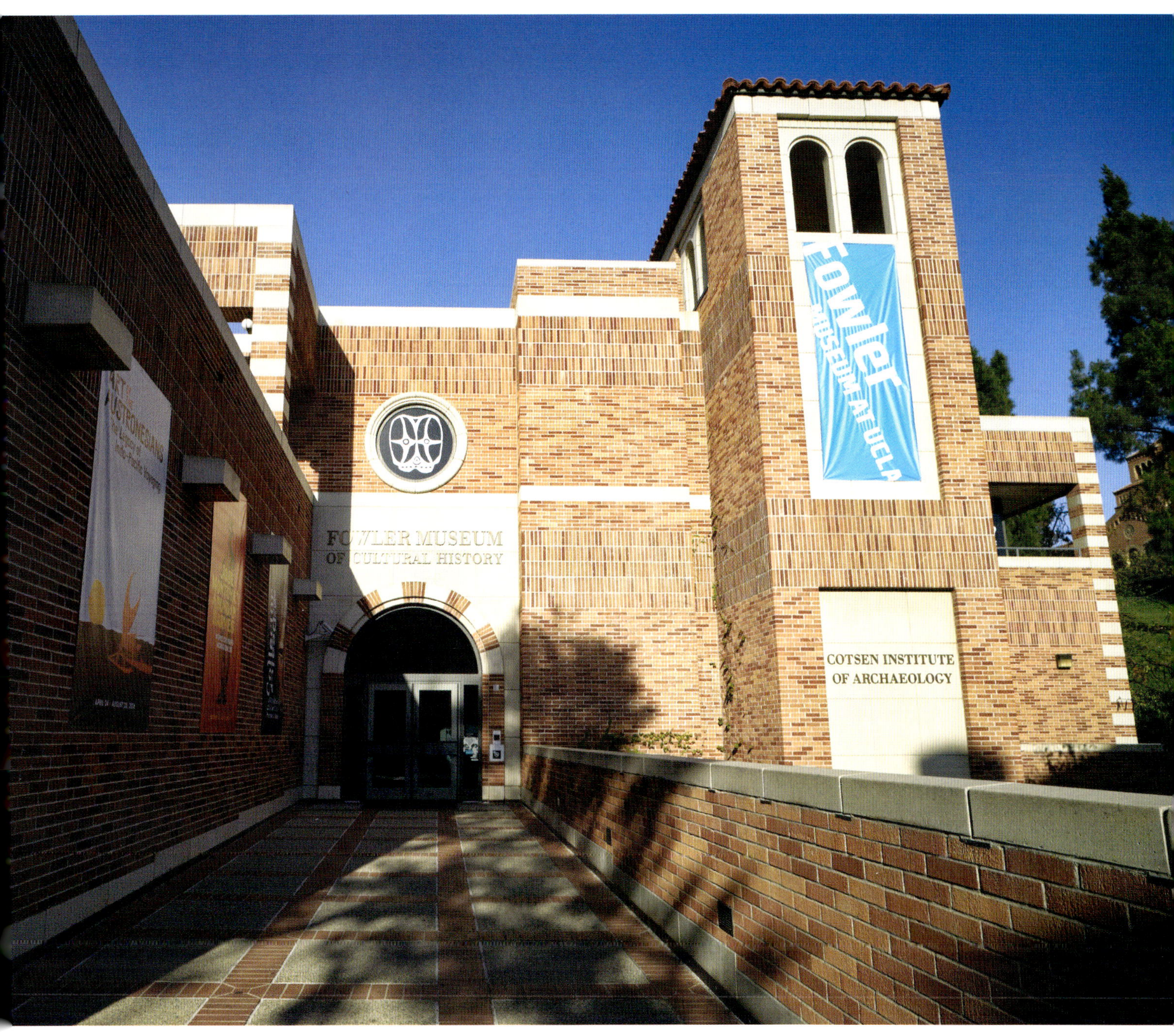

Los Angeles Fire Department Museum *(opposite, top and bottom)*

A poignant tribute to the city's fallen firefighters, this memorial outside Old Fire Station 27 in Hollywood is a series of beautifully rendered bronze statues. Below is *Lulubelle*, a wonderfully restored 1937 American LaFrance fire engine that is housed at the museum.

Fowler Museum at UCLA *(above)*

Exploring local arts and cultures, particularly work from Africa, Asia, the Pacific and the Americas, the Fowler Museum is located at UCLA's campus in Westwood. It boasts a collection of 120,000 art and 600,000 archaeological objects.

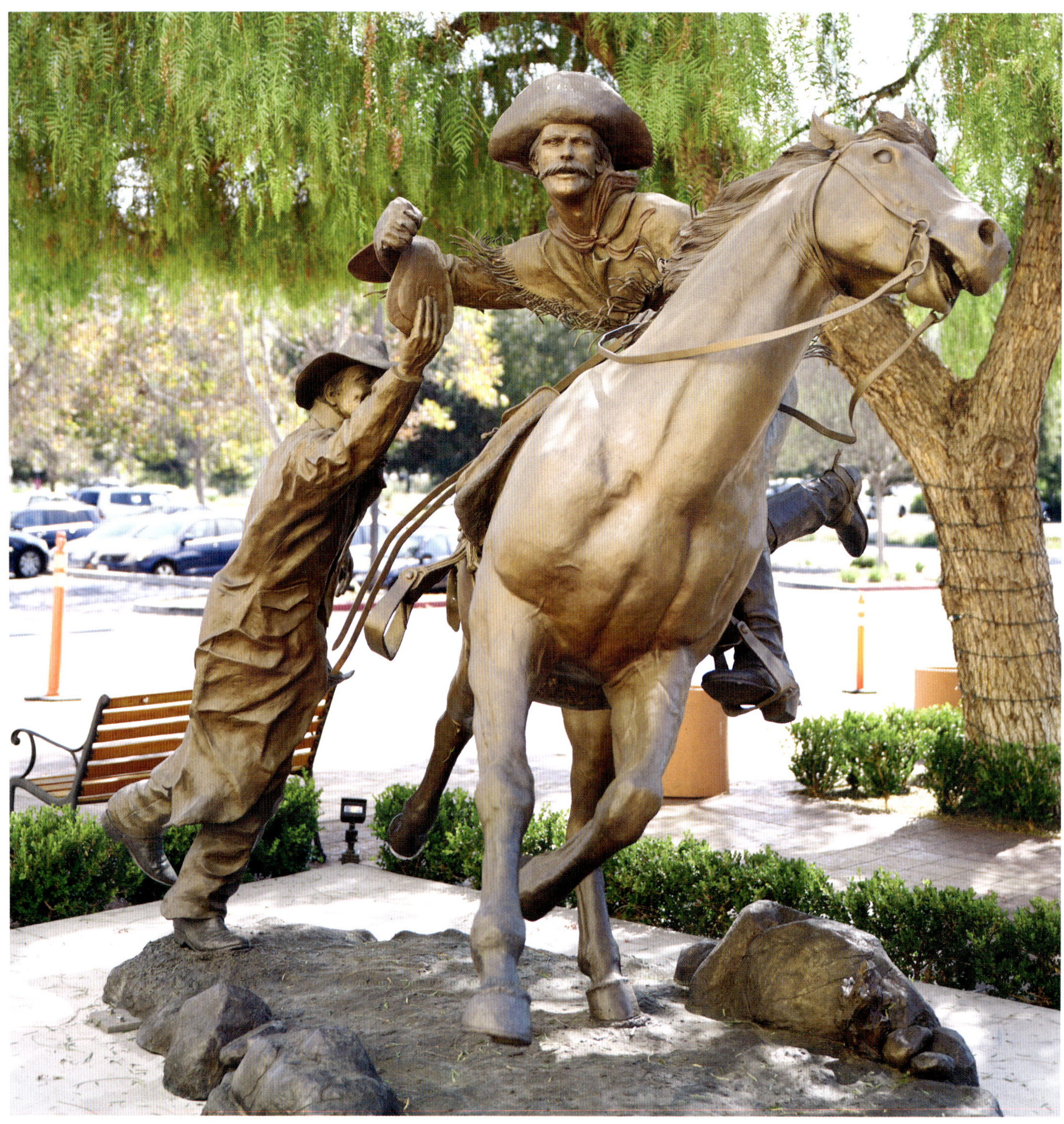

Pony Express *(above)*

The excitement of the fastest ride in the history of the Pony Express is captured in this statue outside the Autry Museum in Glendale. Starting in St. Joseph, Missouri and ending in Sacramento, California the ride carried the news that Abraham Lincoln had been elected president.

Autry Museum of the American West *(opposite)*

Located across from the Los Angeles Zoo, this inclusive museum is dedicated to bringing together the stories of all peoples in the American West. Founded in 1988, it is home to over 21,000 paintings, sculptures, costumes, instruments, tools, toys, and other objects..

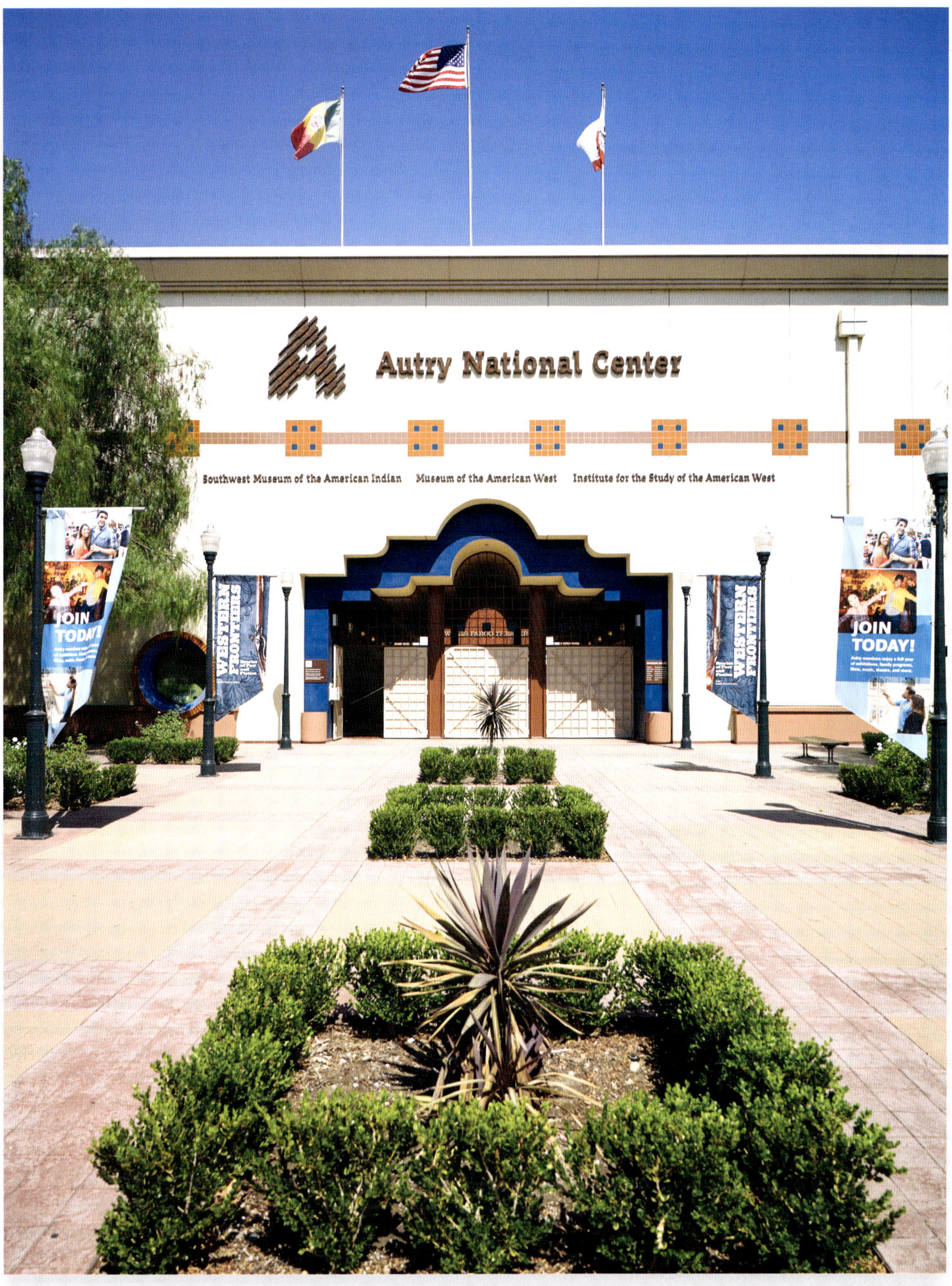
Autry National Center
Southwest Museum of the American Indian
Museum of the American West
Institute for the Study of the American West
JOIN TODAY!
WESTERN FRONTIERS
WESTERN FRONTIERS
JOIN TODAY!

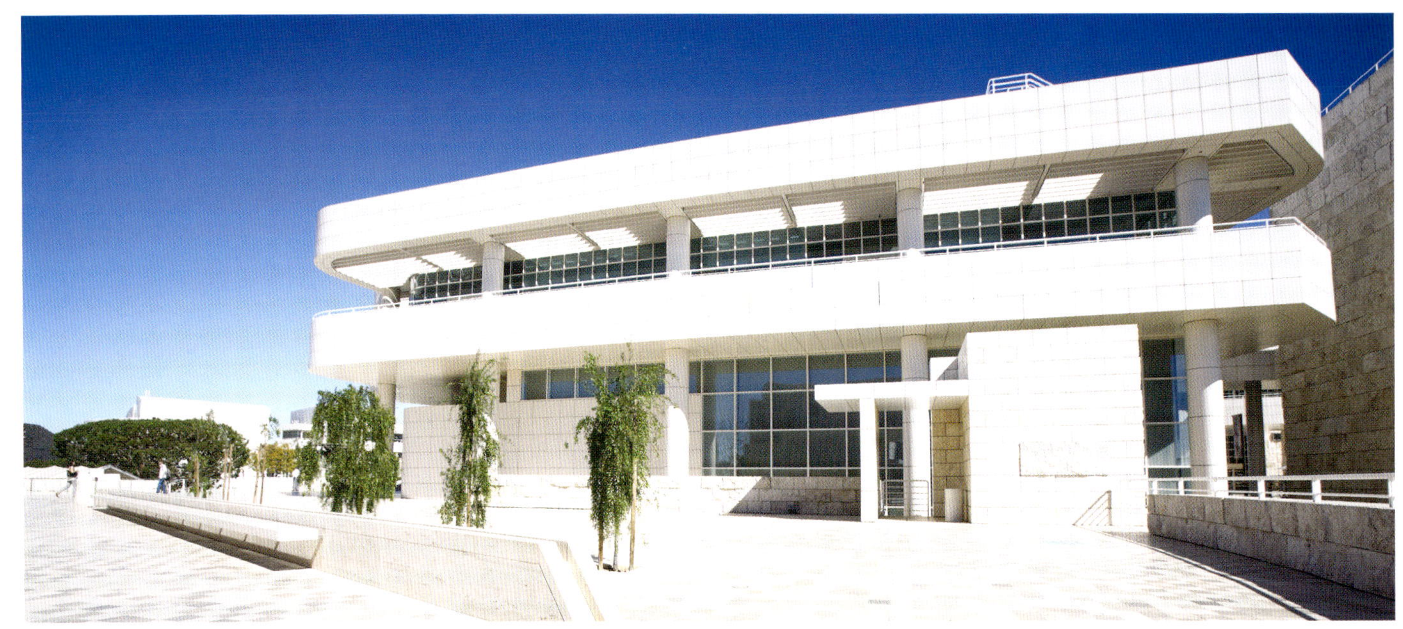

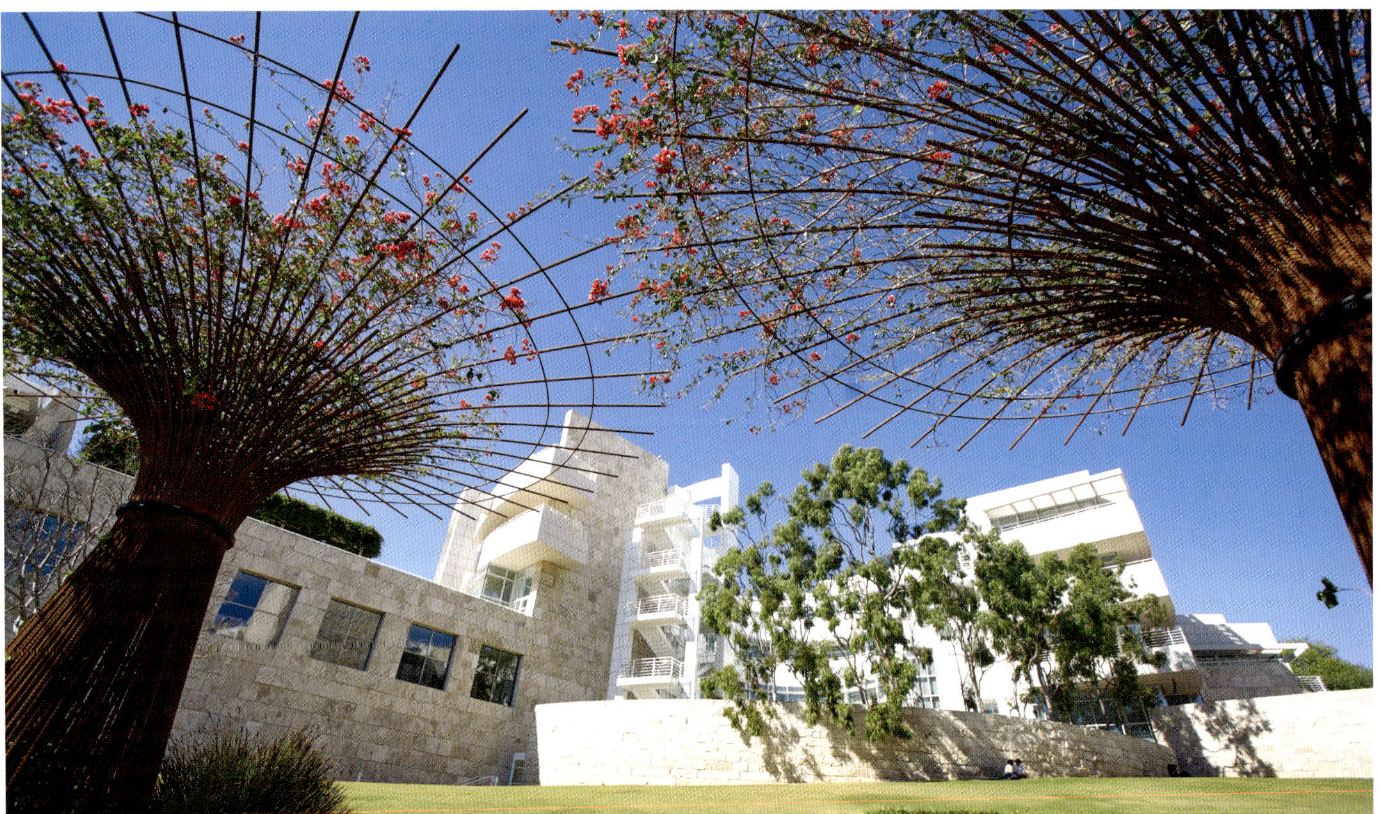

Getty Center *(top and bottom)*

Opened in 1997, the Getty Center showcases a collection of European paintings, sculpture, and decorative arts that span from the Middle-ages to present. The museum also houses a collection of manuscripts, prints, drawings, photographs, rare books, and more. Today, it is one of the most visited museums in the world.

Museum Entrance Hall *(opposite)*

The curved features of the museum's main entrance hall cast shadows along the terrace. Designed by Richard Meier, the museum's most remarked-upon element is its use of stone. The hilltop center in the Santa Monica Mountains offers spectacular views of the Pacific Ocean and Los Angeles.

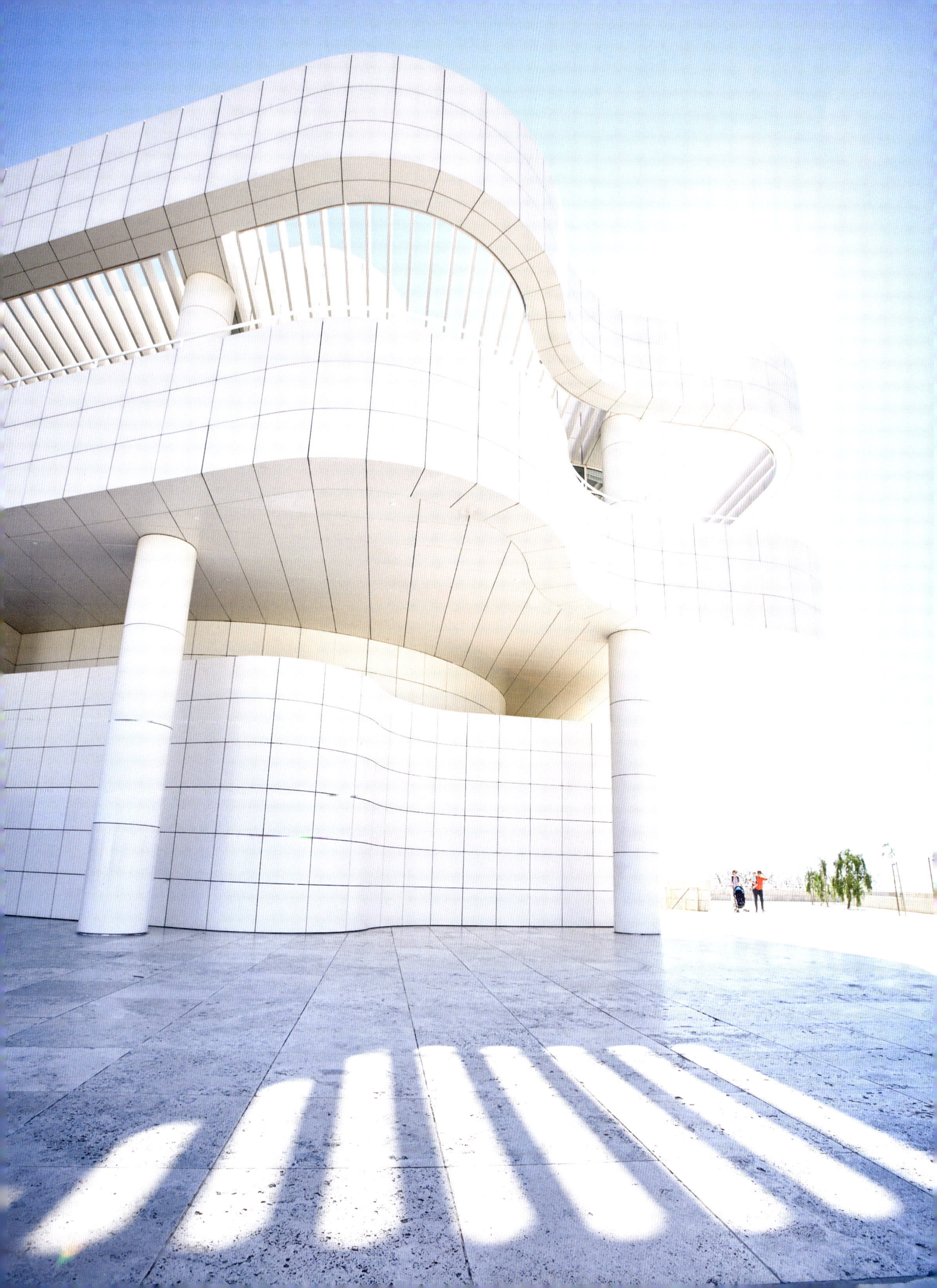

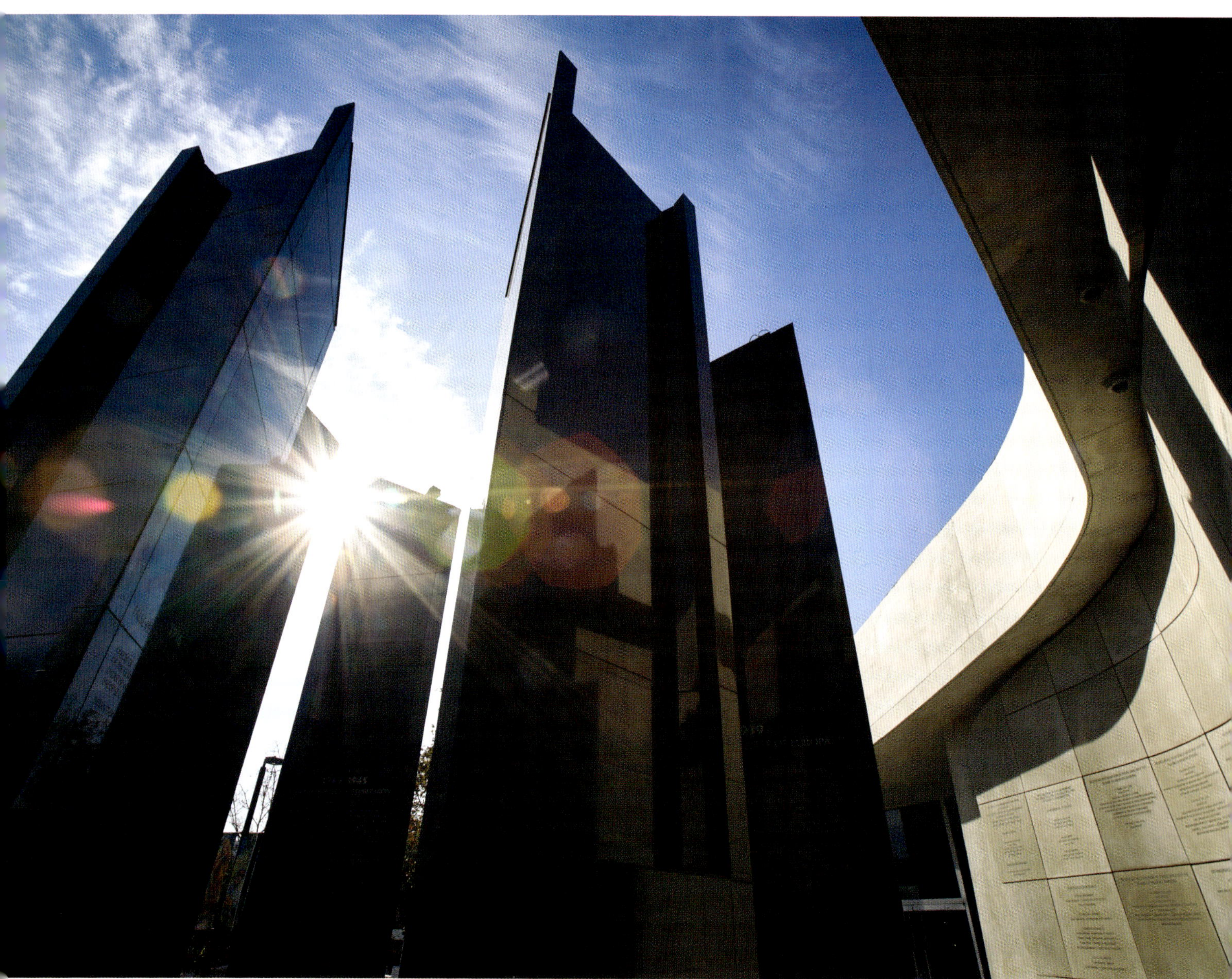

Martyrs Memorial

Sunlight streaks through the six black, triangular granite columns of the Martyrs Monument on the grounds of the Los Angeles Museum of the Holocaust. The columns, designed to resemble crematoria smoke stacks, honor the six million victims of the Holocaust. In the center is an "invisible" seventh column, which represents the living.

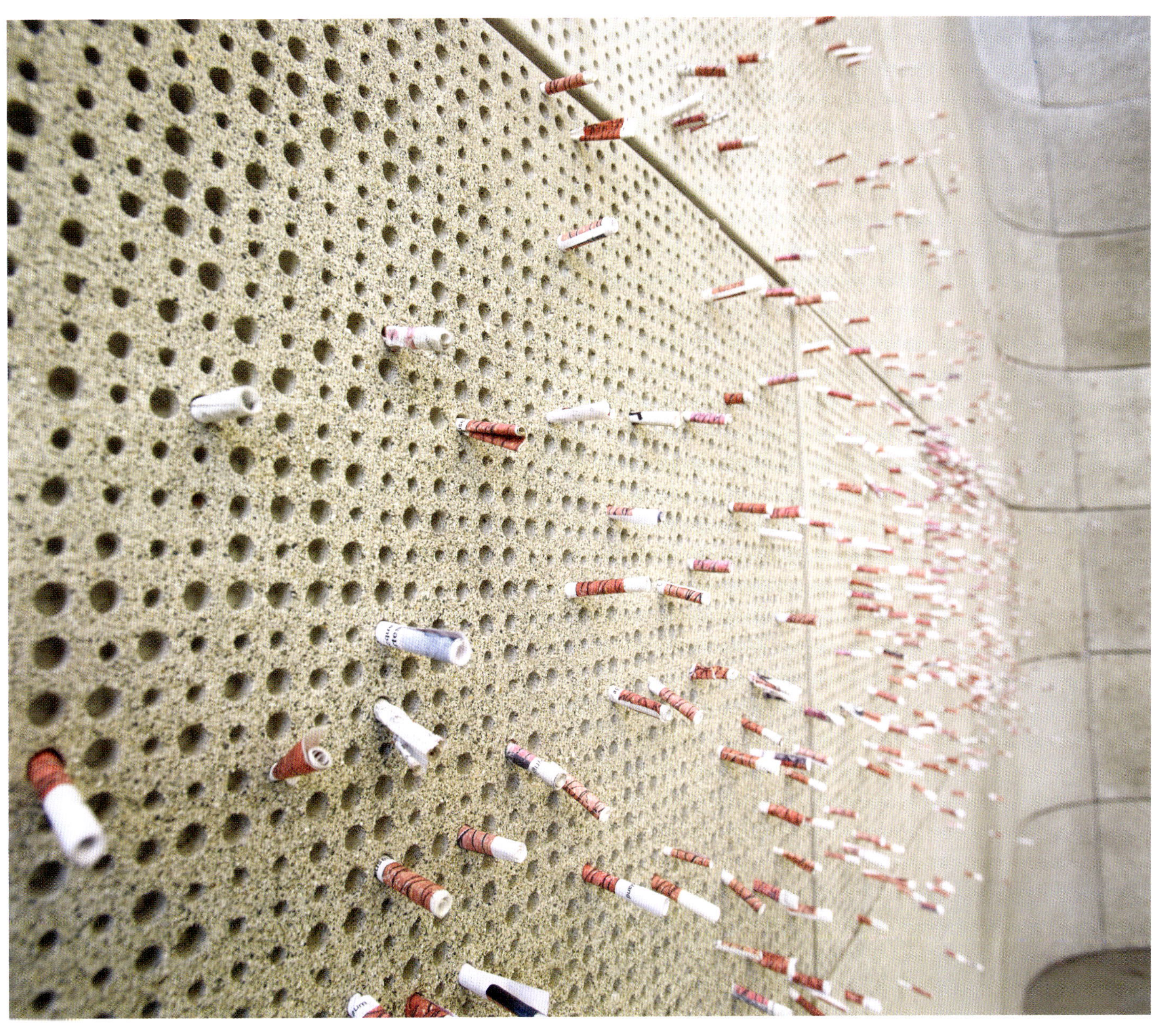

Los Angeles Museum of the Holocaust

In 2010, the museum opened its doors with exhibits marking momentous phases in Jewish life between 1932-1948. The 1.2 million holes drilled into this wall represent each child who perished in the Holocaust. Inspired by the *Wailing Wall* in Jerusalem, visitors are invited to place a note into one of the holes.

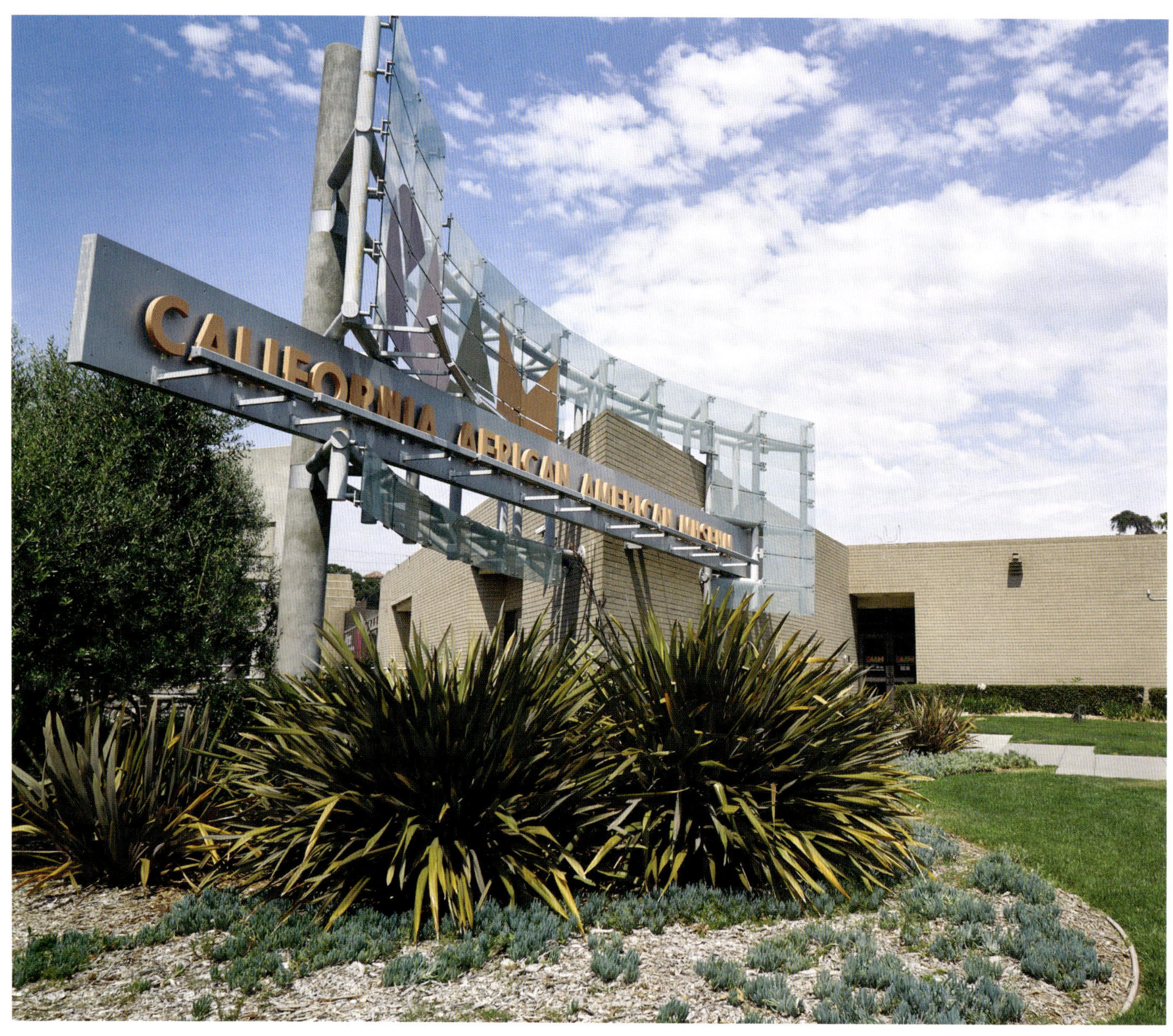

California African American Museum

Designed by African American architects Jack Haywood and Vince Proby, this museum opened during the 1984 Olympics. Free to the public, the museum sets out to collect and preserve the art, history and culture of African Americans, particularly those in California.

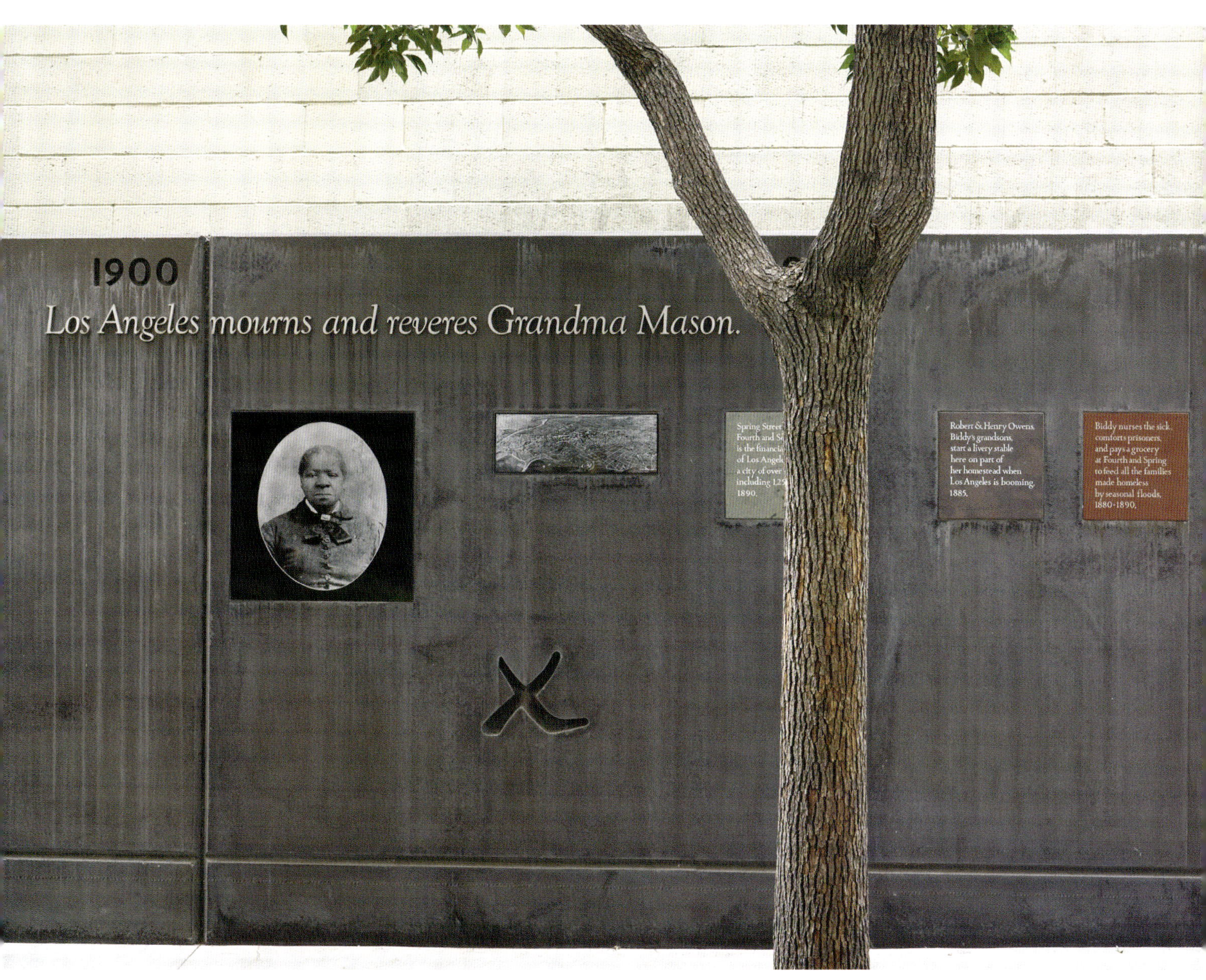

Biddy Mason Memorial Park

This Downtown park memorializes the "Grandmother of Los Angeles," Bridget "Biddy" Mason. Born a slave, Biddy spent most of her childhood working on plantations in Georgia, Mississippi, and South Carolina. She was brought to California where she was eventually freed and became an inspirational midwife, landowner, and philanthropist.

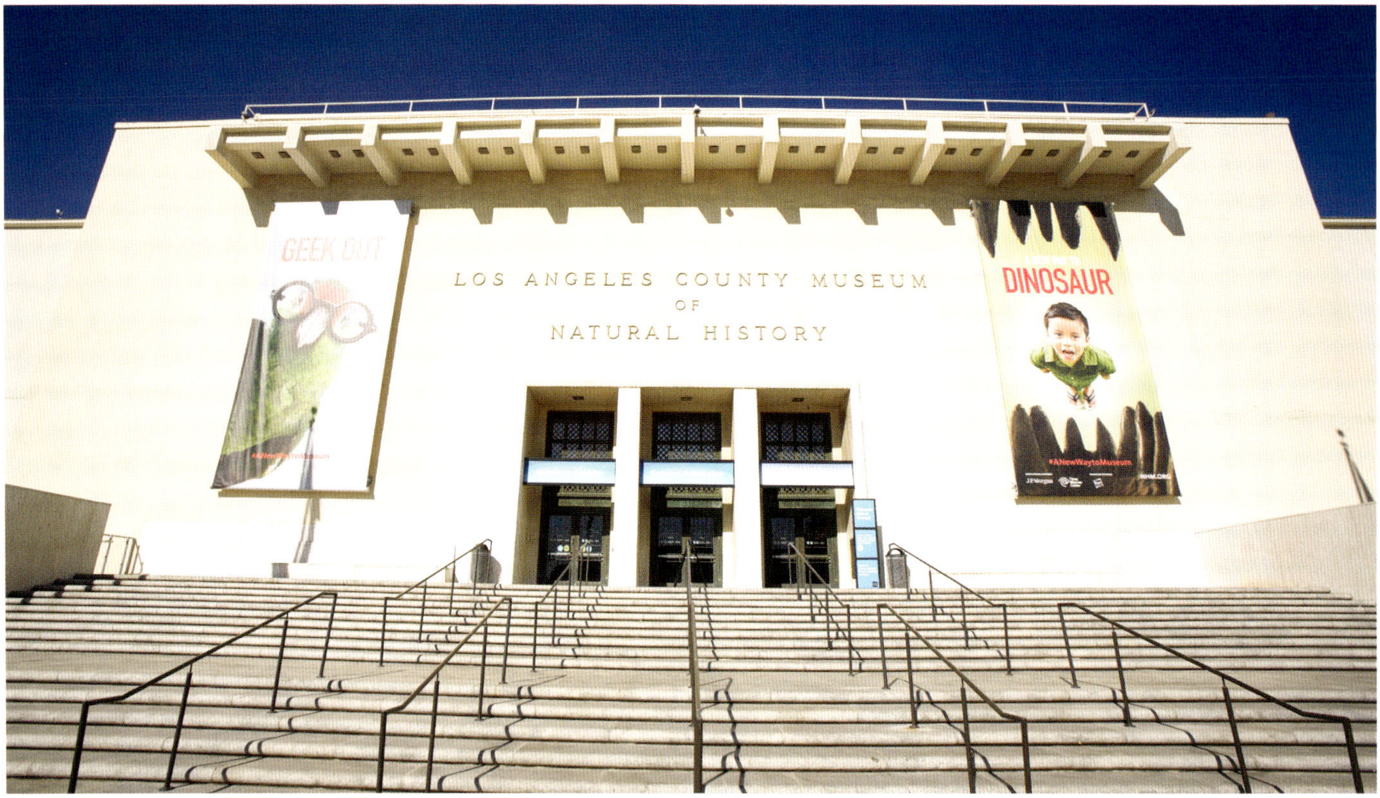

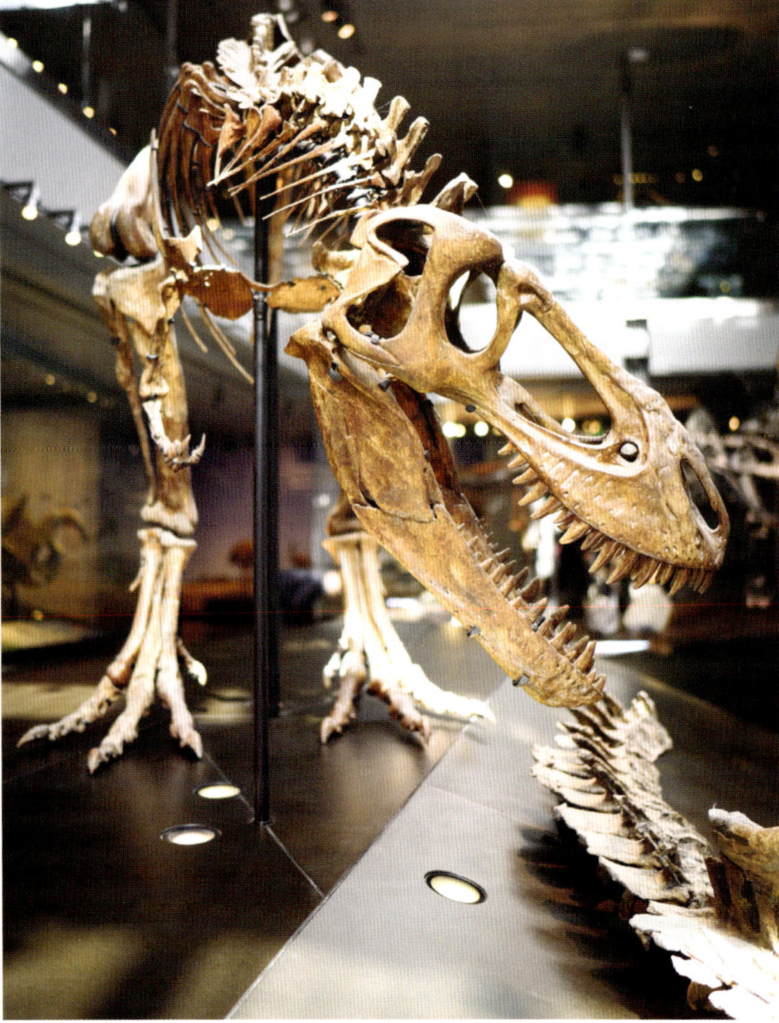

Museum of Natural History

(above and left)

Inspiring wonder, discovery and responsibility for the natural world, the Museum of Natural History in Exposition Park protects over 35 million specimens. The highlight for many is Dinosaur Hall, where visitors can come face to face with 20 complete dinosaurs and ancient sea creatures.

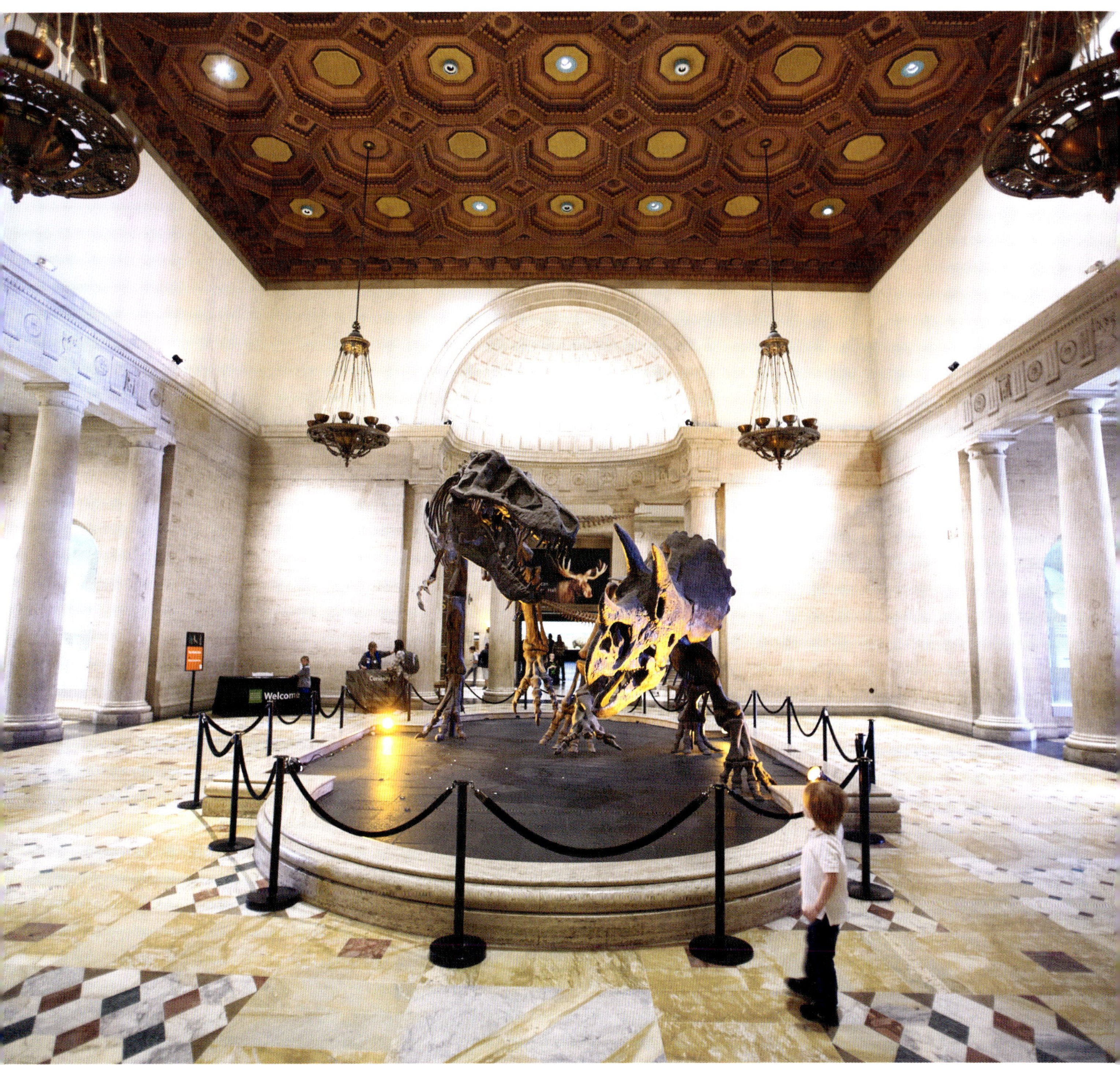

Dinosaur Hall

It is Tyrannosaurus v Triceratops in a spine-chilling battle bound to terrify and delight visitors to Los Angeles' Natural History Museum, a fascinating collection of artifacts covering 4.5 billion years of history. It has been 66 million years since these dueling dinosaurs roamed earth - yet their allure never grows old.

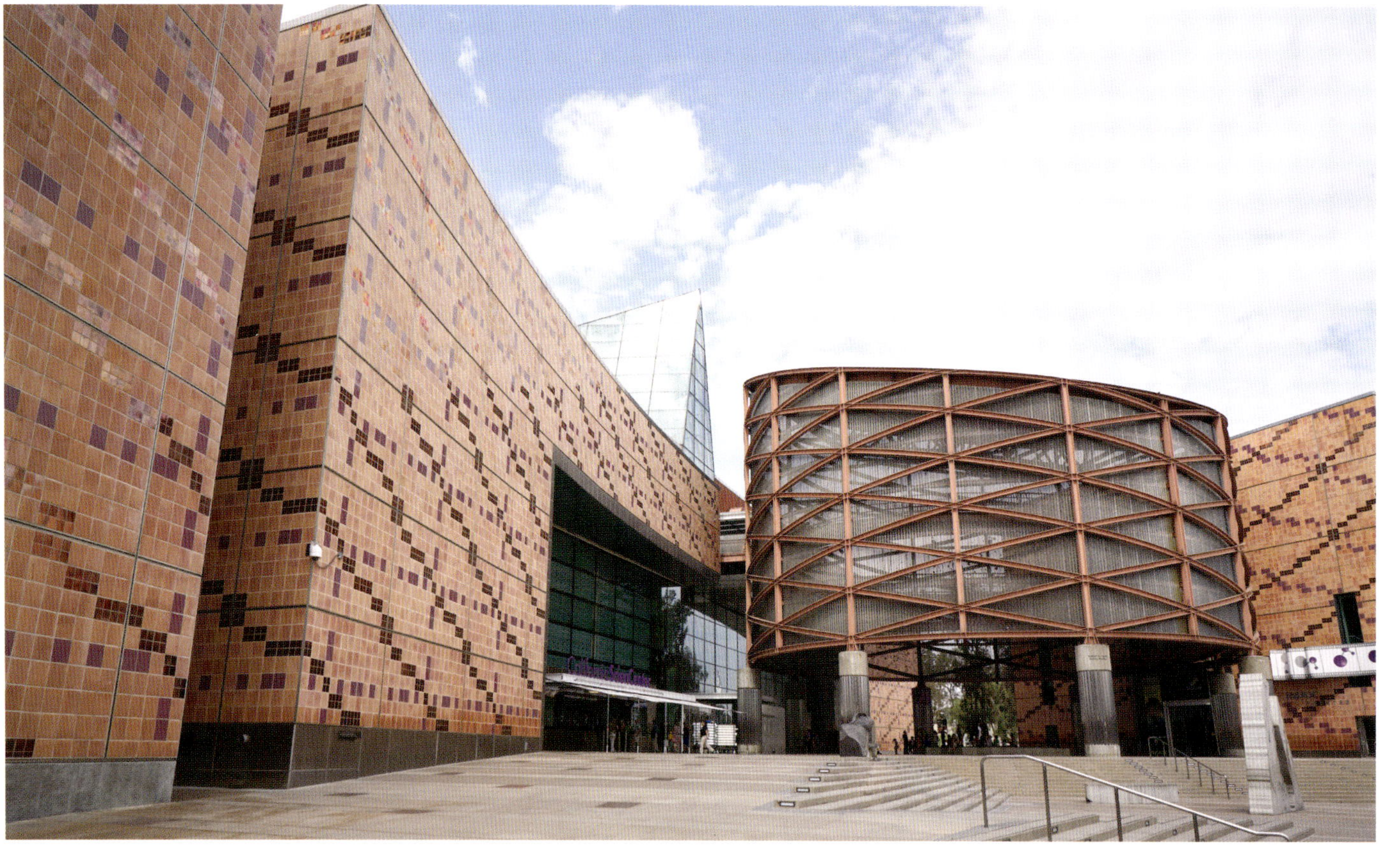

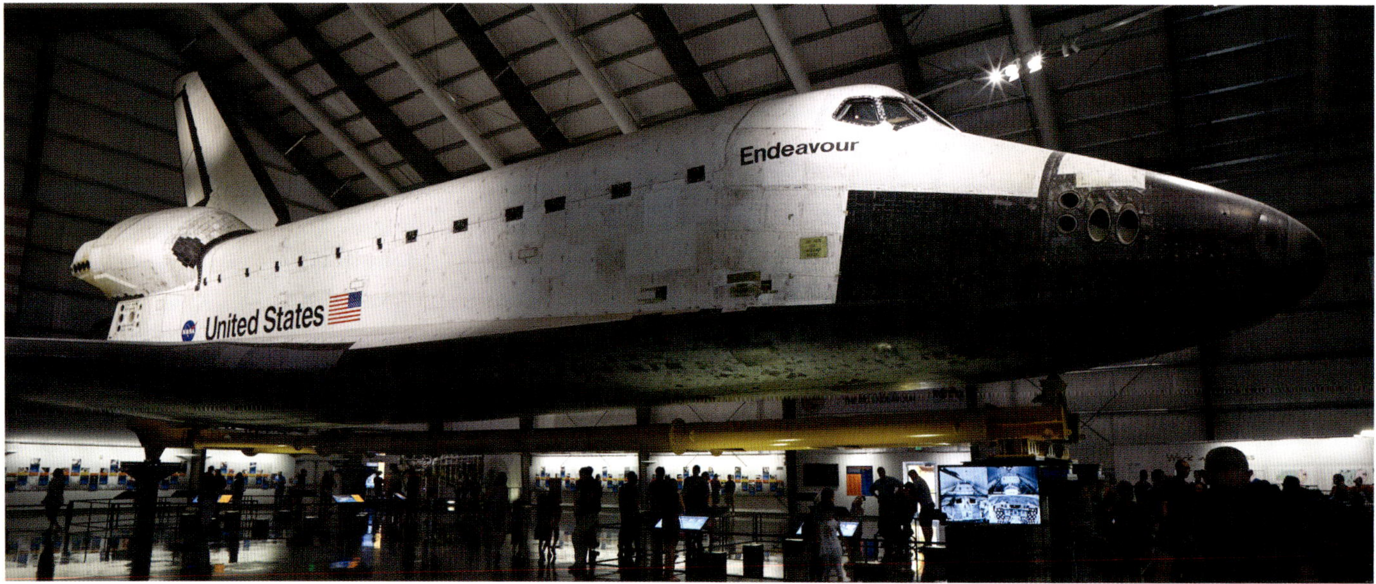

California Science Center *(top)*

Billed as the largest hands-on science center on the West Coast, the California Science Center boasts an IMAX theater, a high wire bicycle, climbing wall, and motion simulator. It also has a two-story Ecosystems exhibit featuring live animals and aquariums.

Space Shuttle Endeavour *(bottom)*

After successfully completing 299 days in space, 25 missions, and a total of 122,883,151 miles, the spectacular *Endeavour* space shuttle is now enjoying a well-earned retirement in its permanent new home at the California Science Center in Exposition Park, where visitors can learn about the shuttle's awesome space legacy.

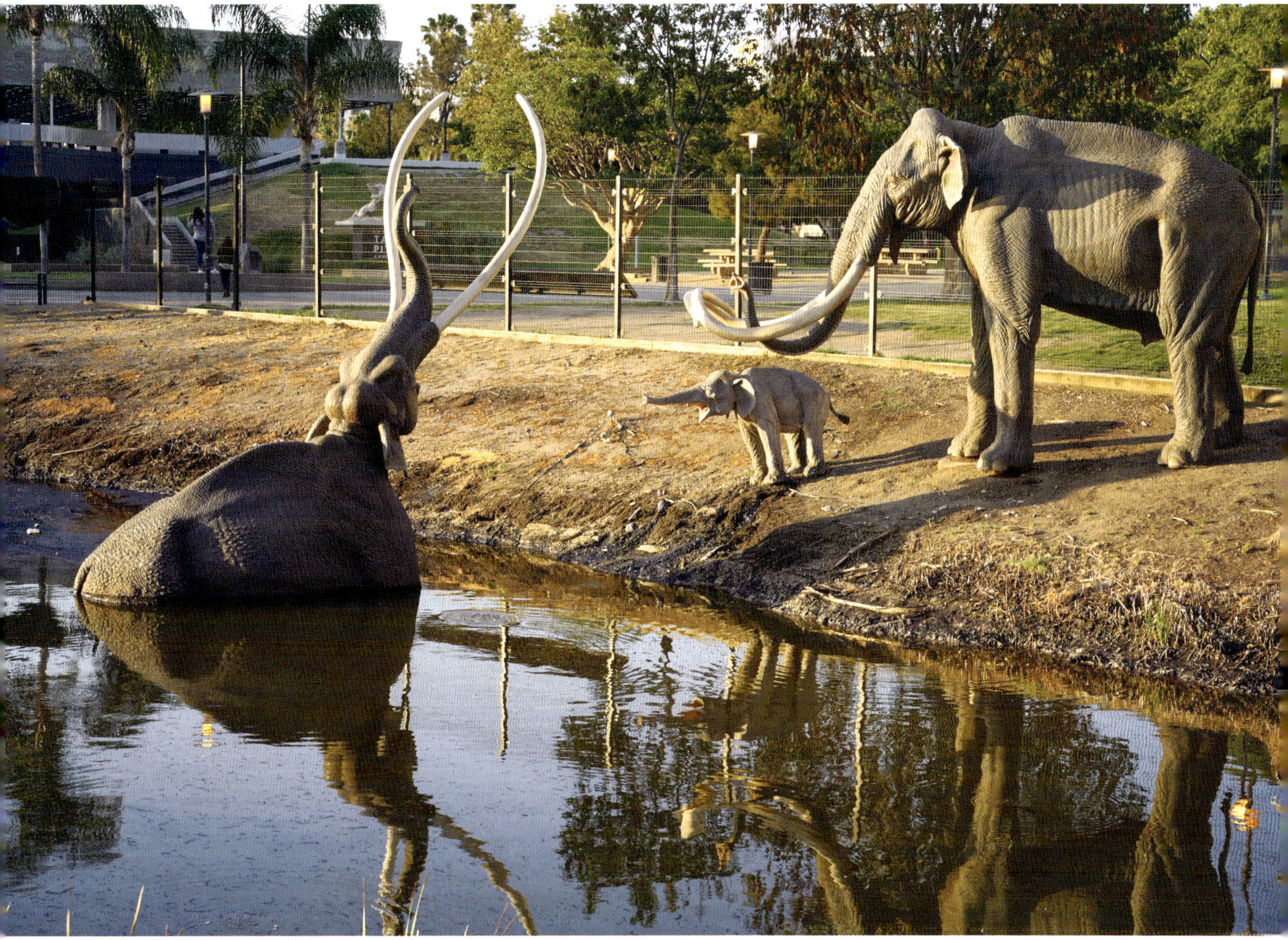

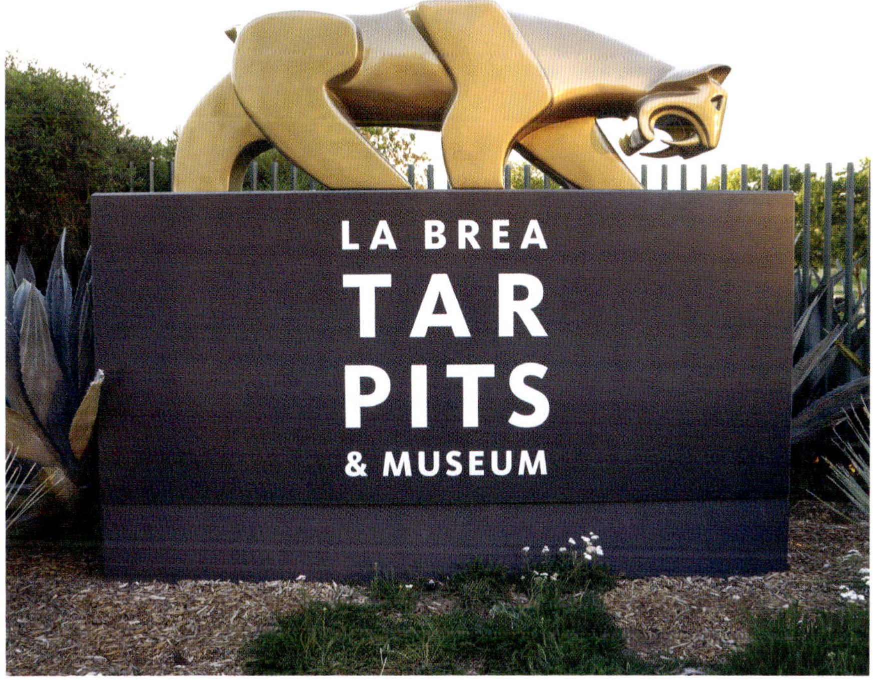

La Brea Tar Pits and Museum

(above and right)

Giant mammoths and mastodons once roamed the now bustling hub of central Los Angeles. Although these Ice Age beasts became extinct around 10,000 years ago, the tar pits where they once lived still bubble. These fiberglass models are based on real skeletons that were found in the oily pits.

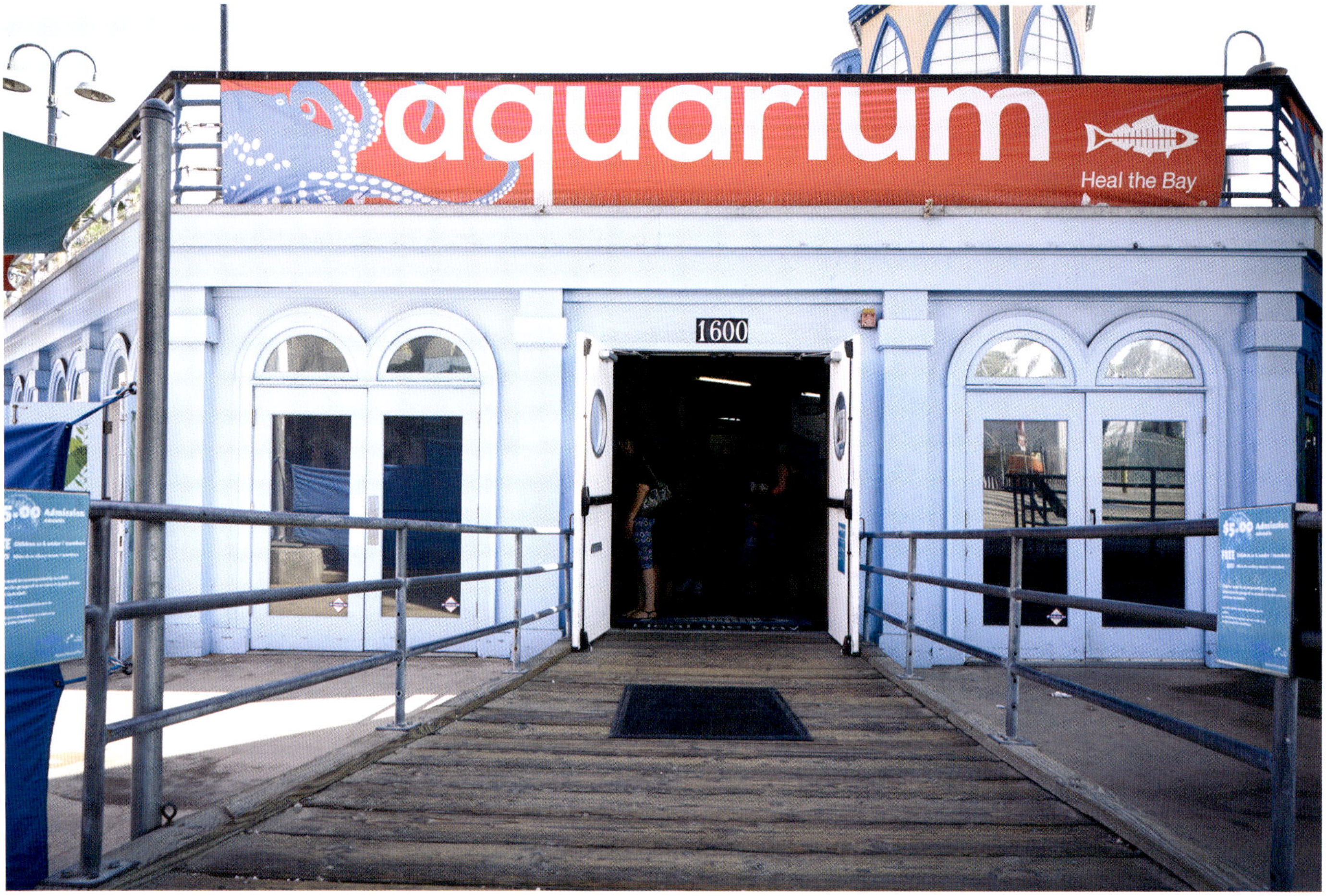

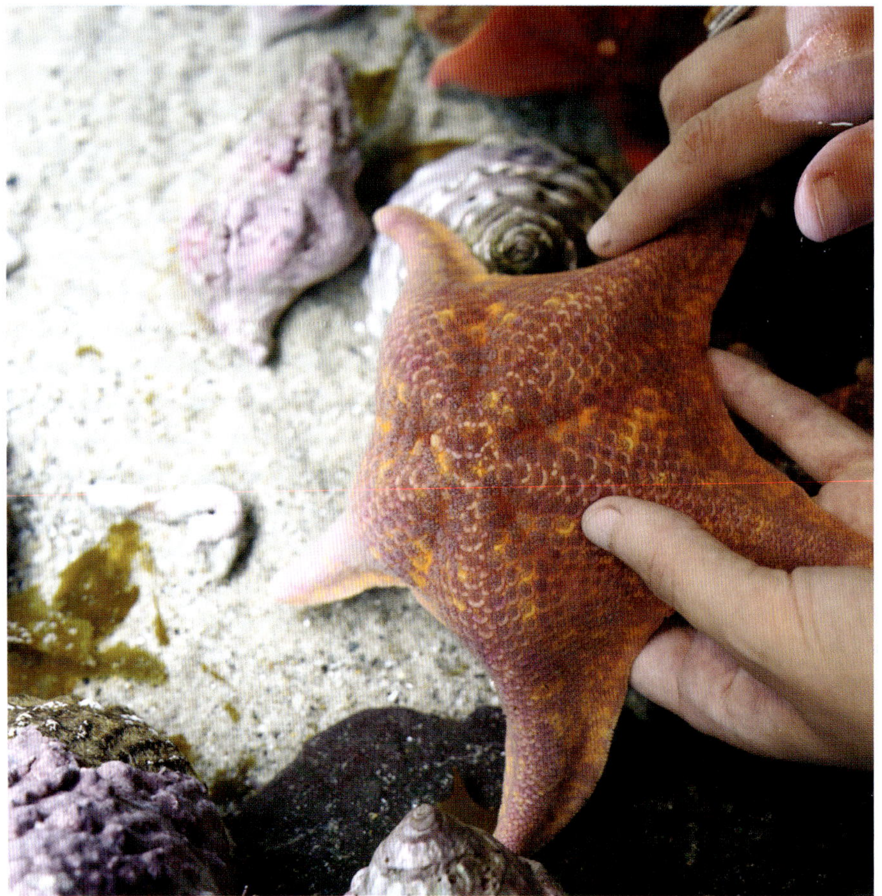

Santa Monica Pier Aquarium

(above and left)

Come face to face with creatures of the deep at this much-loved aquarium and marine conservation center, which sits below Santa Monica Pier. This bright red and orange bat star lives in the petting tank, where visitors can touch and hold star fish, sand crabs, and other ocean creatures.

Santa Monica Pier *(opposite)*

The world-famous Santa Monica Pier from above. Popular with tourists and locals for over 100 years, the pier boasts fairground rides, including a one-of-a-kind solar powered Ferris wheel, an original 1920s carousel, pubs, and restaurants. During the summer months, it is a venue for outdoor events.

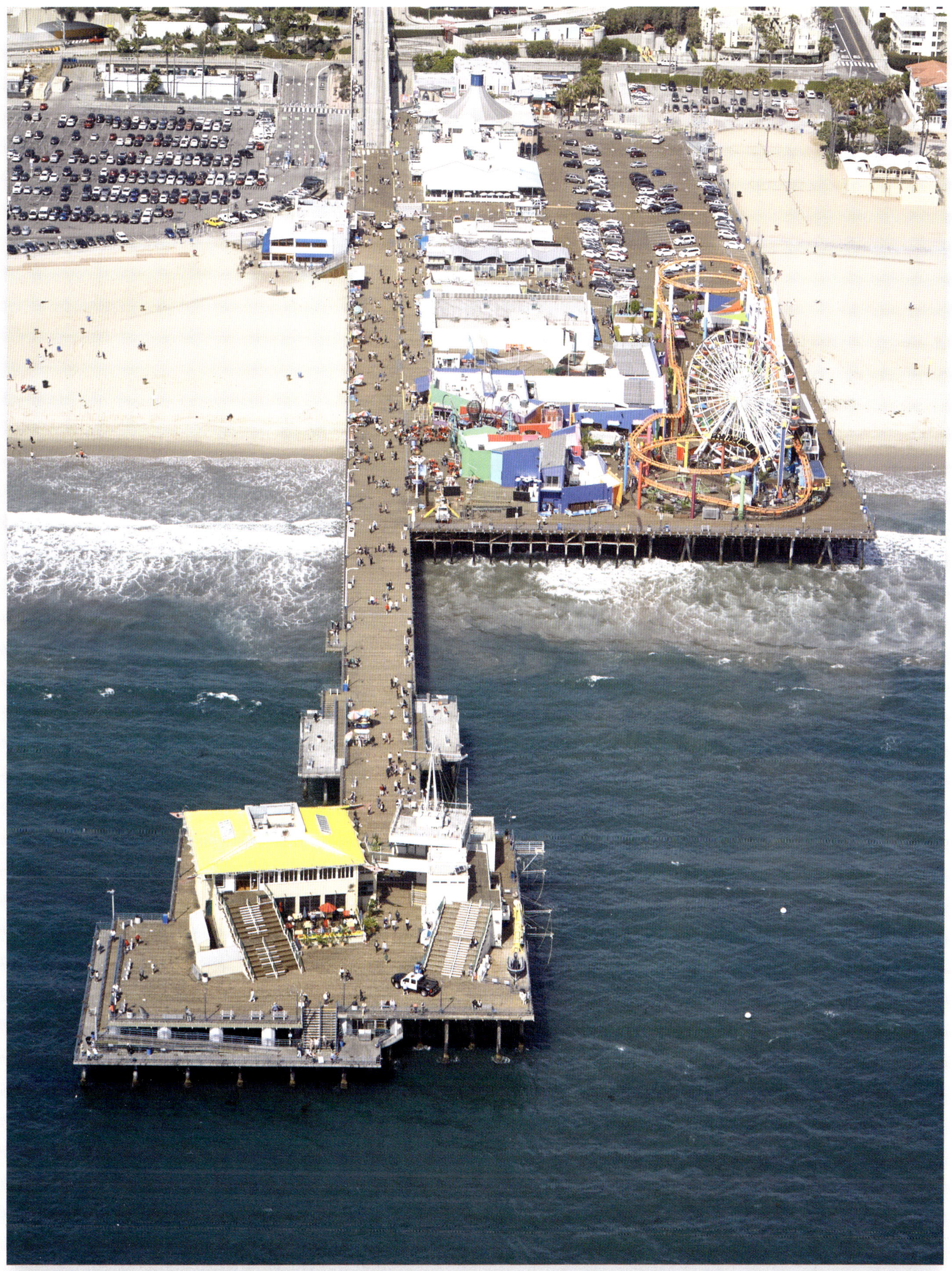

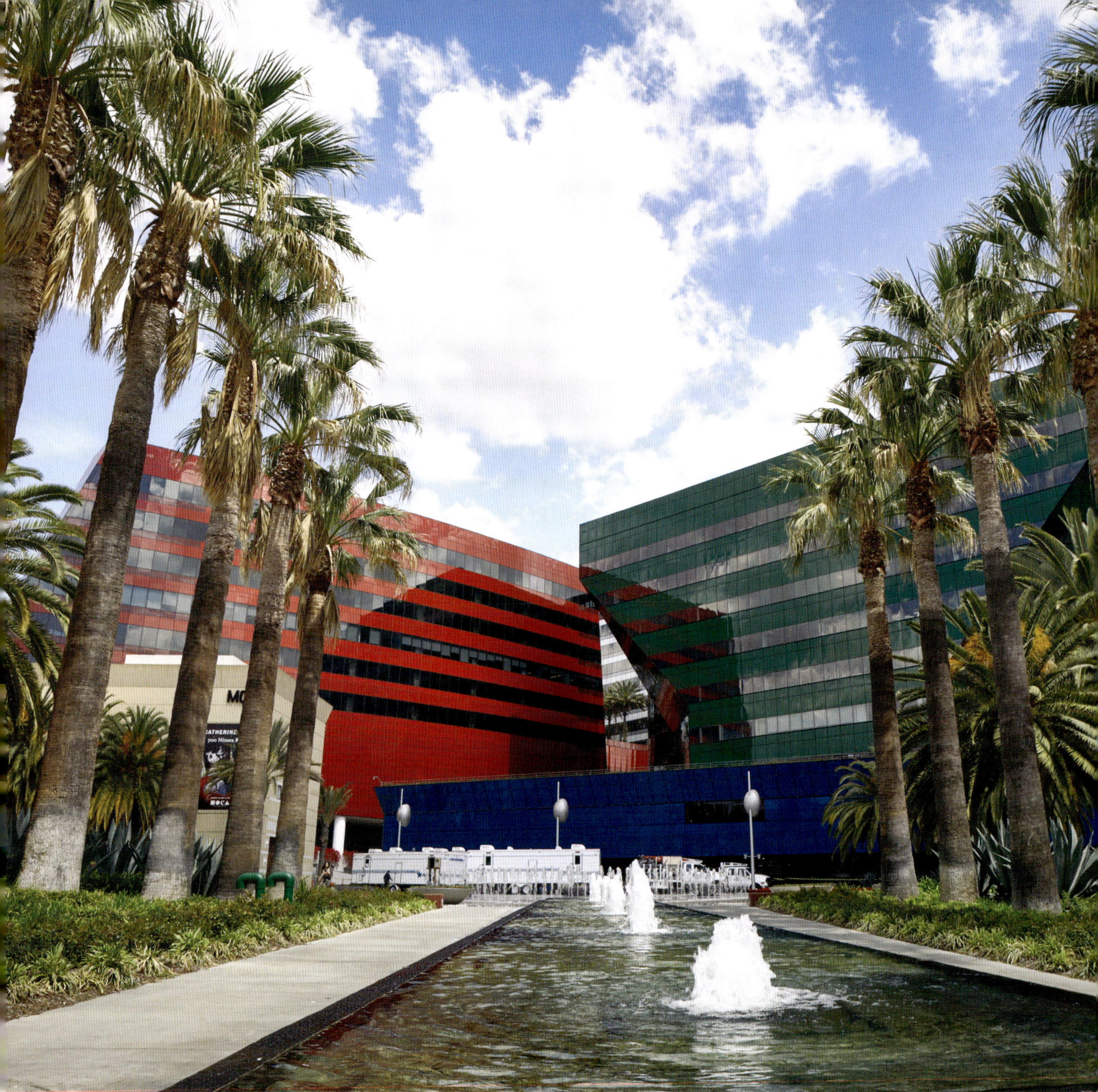

Pacific Design Center

The red and green buildings of the Pacific Design Center in West Hollywood starkly contract against the pale blue sky. This mega 1.6 million-square-foot campus is a multi-use center, which houses 130 showrooms of furniture and interior design products, an art museum, and two restaurants.

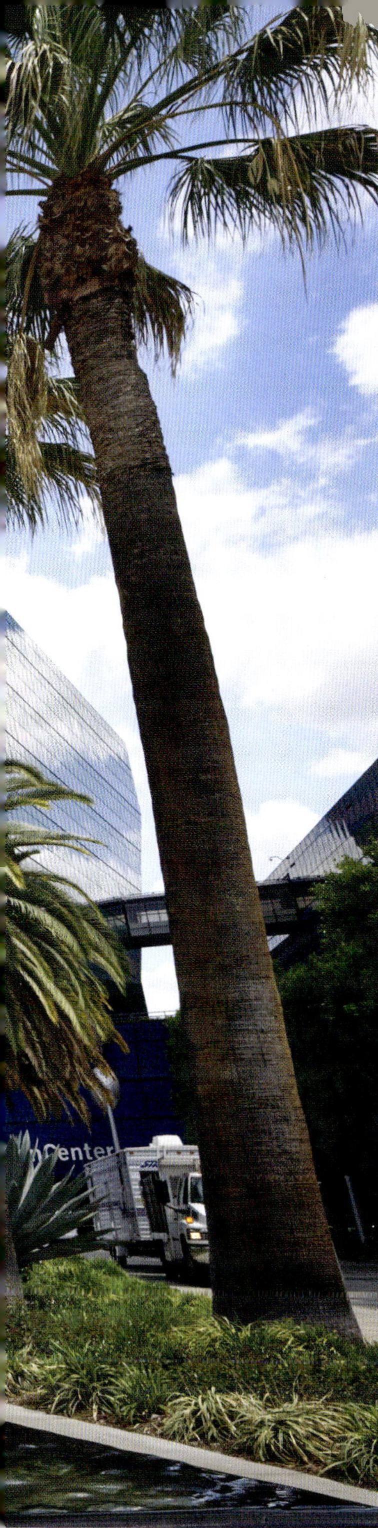

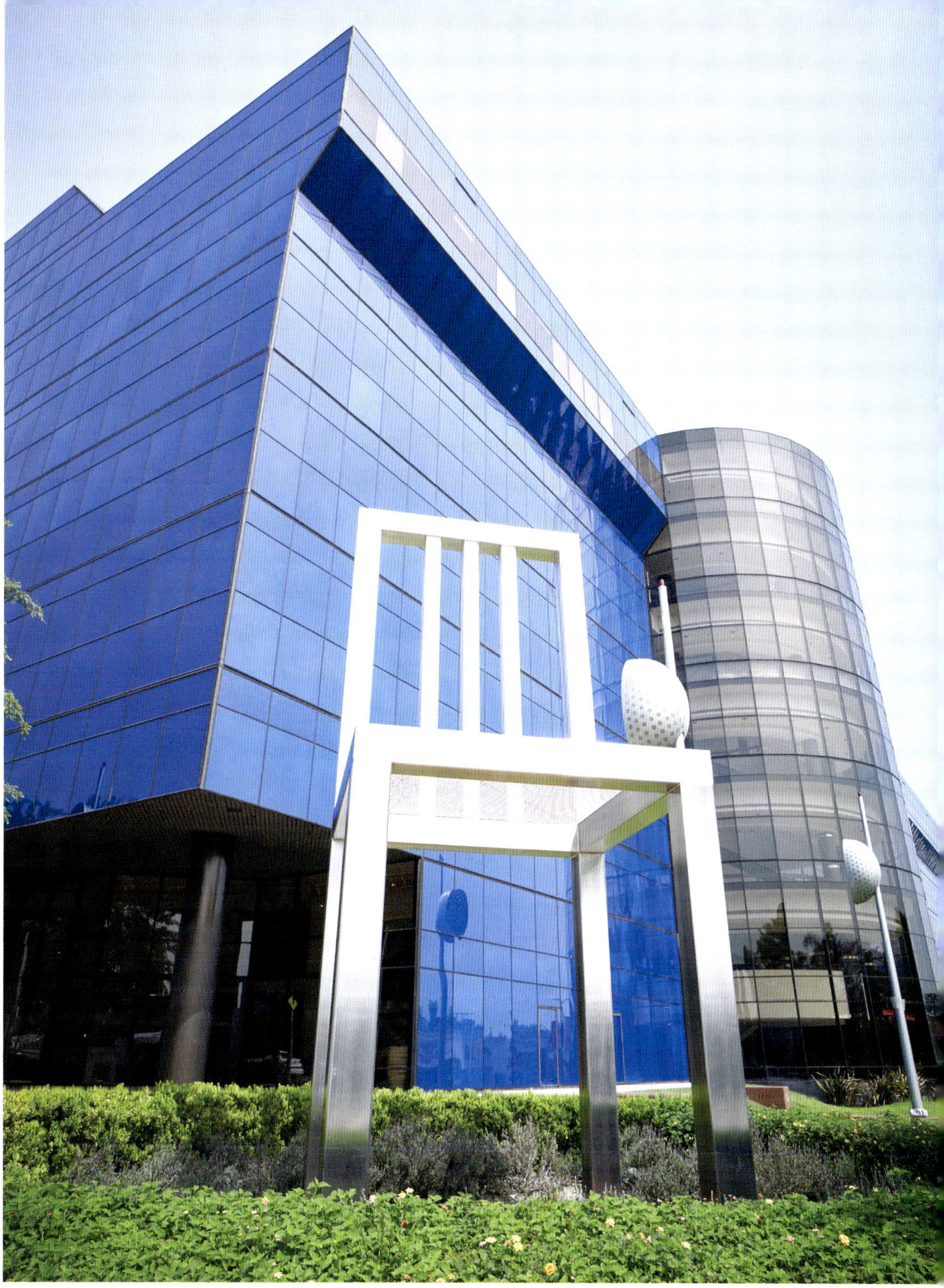

Pacific Design Center

Nicknamed "The Blue Whale" because of its large size and bright blue glass cladding, this vivid blue structure was the first of the center's three buildings to open in 1975. Designed by Cesar Pelli, the building has received several awards, including the 25 Year Award from AIA Los Angeles.

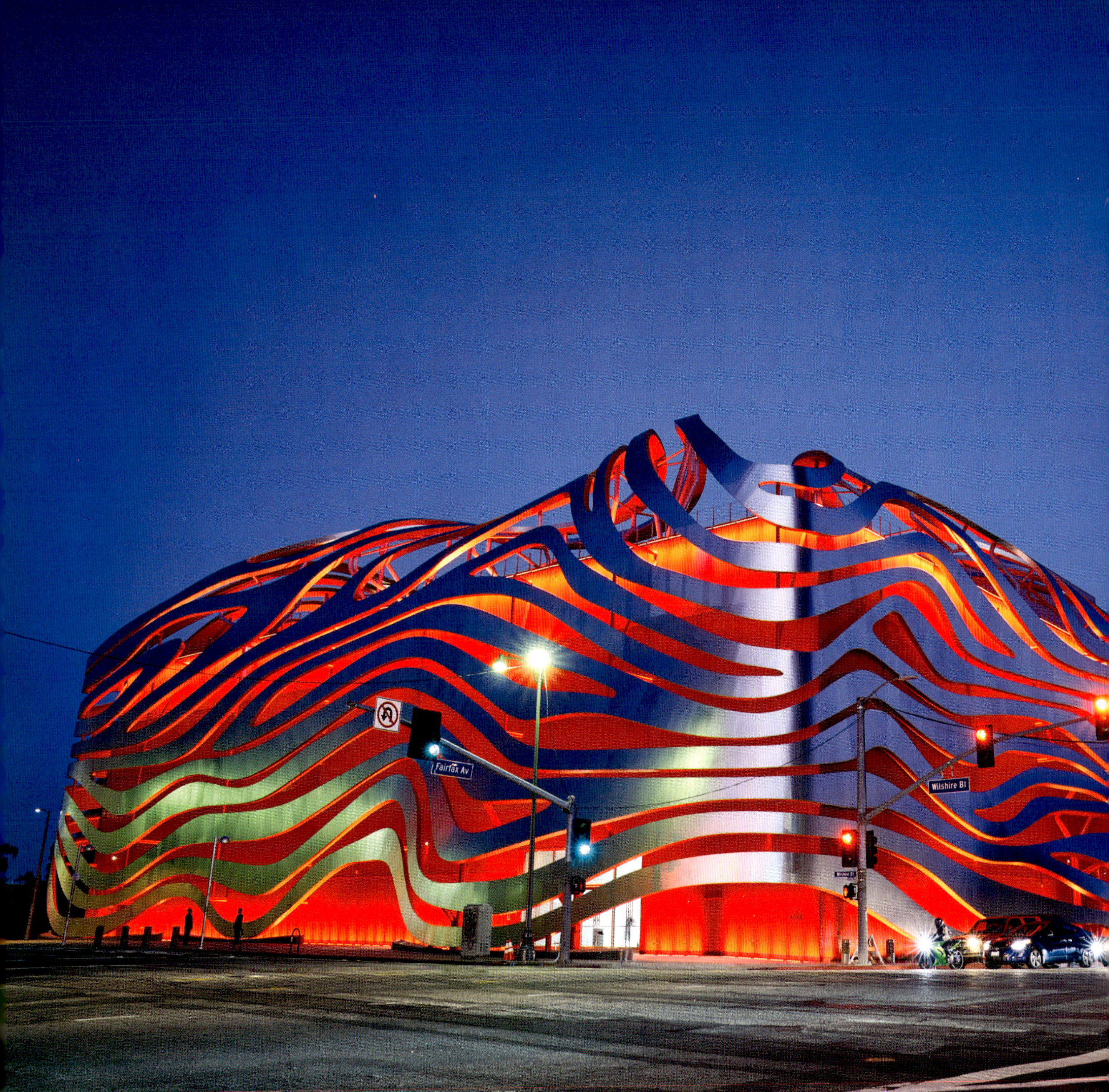

Petersen Automotive Museum

Redesigned in 2015 by the architectural firm Kohn Pedersen Fox, the eye-catching exterior of the Petersen Automotive Museum glows red against the bright blue evening sky. The stainless-steel ribbons completely transformed the building and are designed to evoke the imagery of speed.

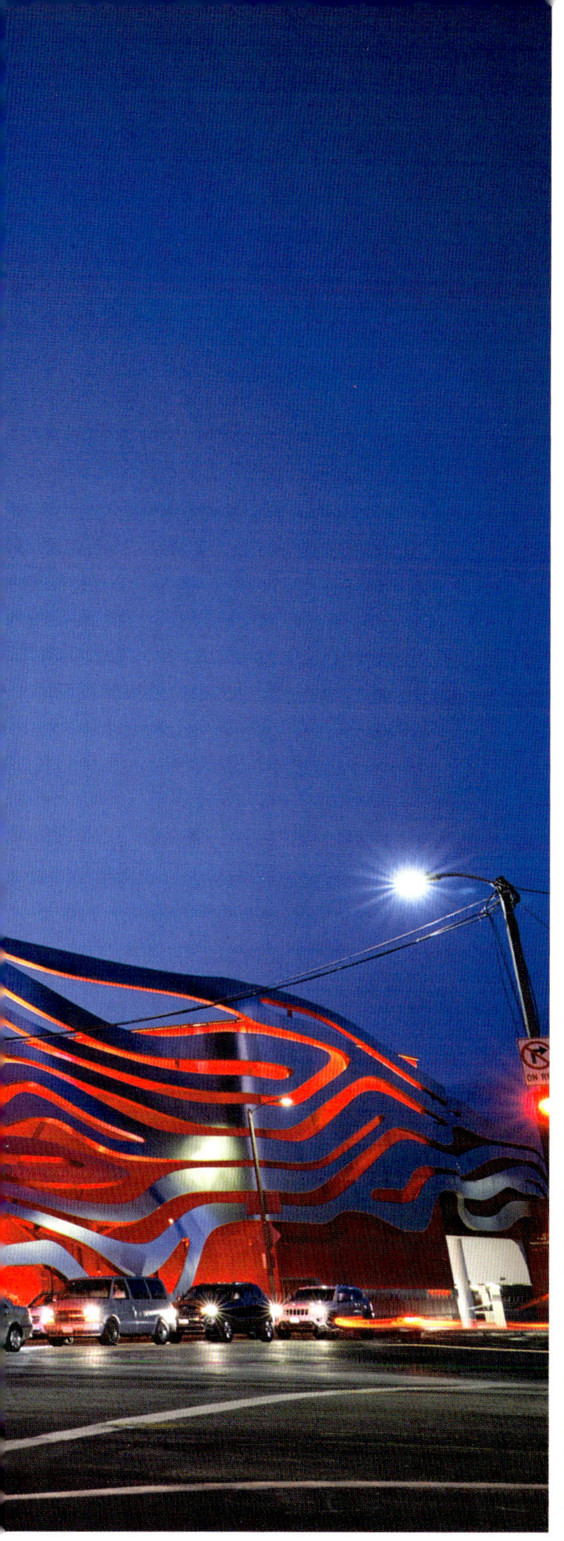

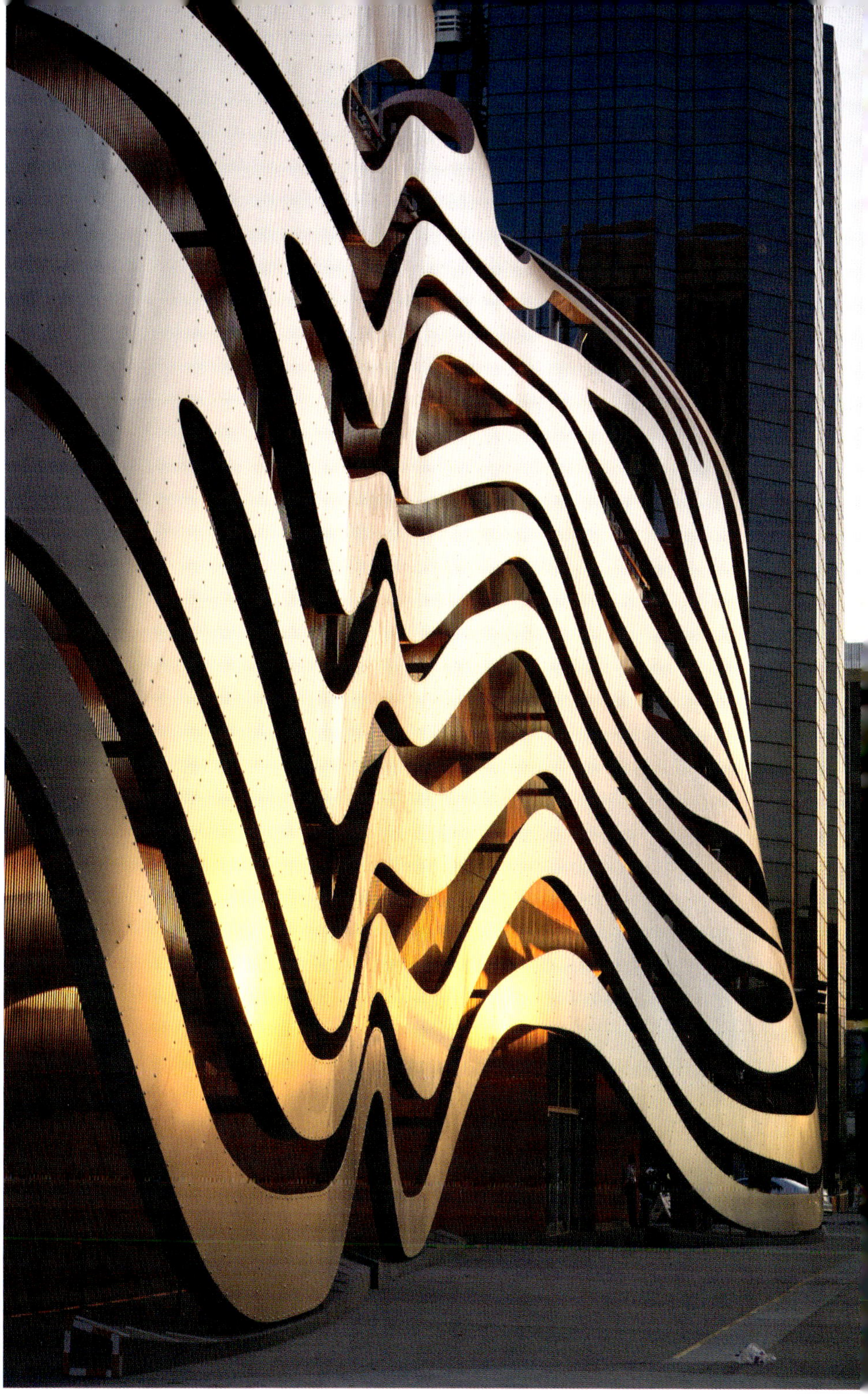

Petersen Automotive Museum

Founded in 1994 and located in the Miracle Mile, the museum has been described as the "world's greatest automotive museum" by *Top Gear*. Three hundred pristine vehicles, old and new, are displayed on two floors, presenting the history of the automobile and its impact on American life.

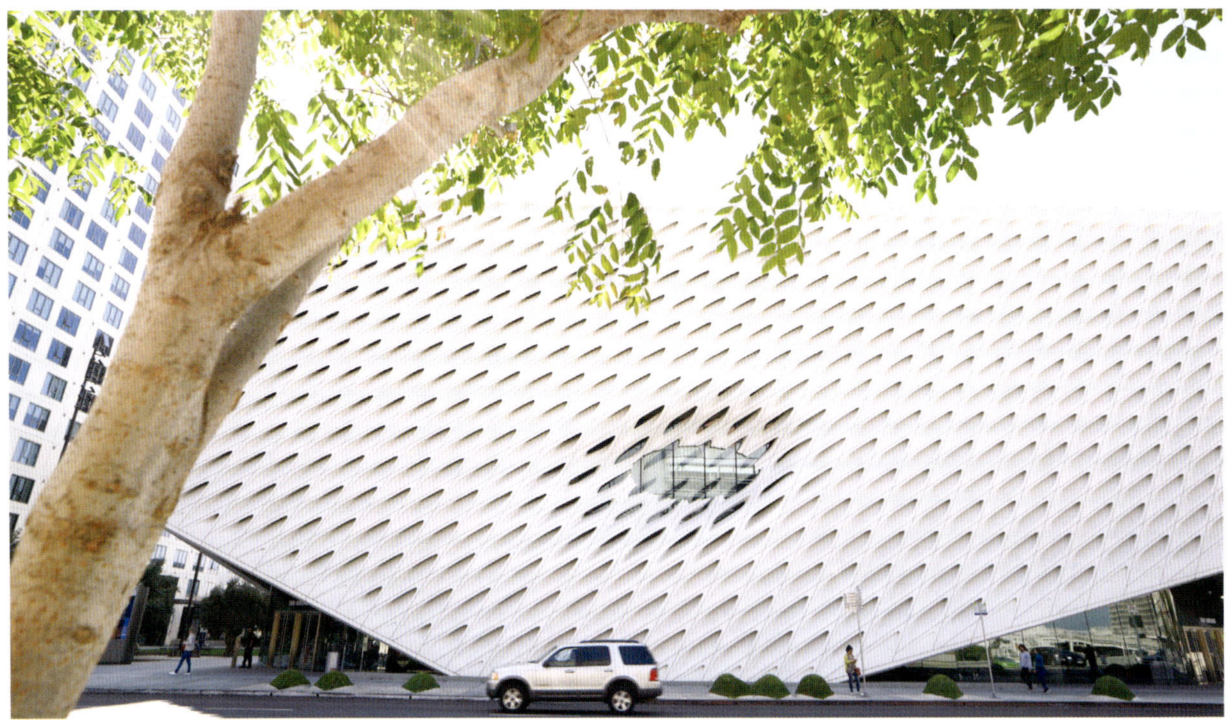

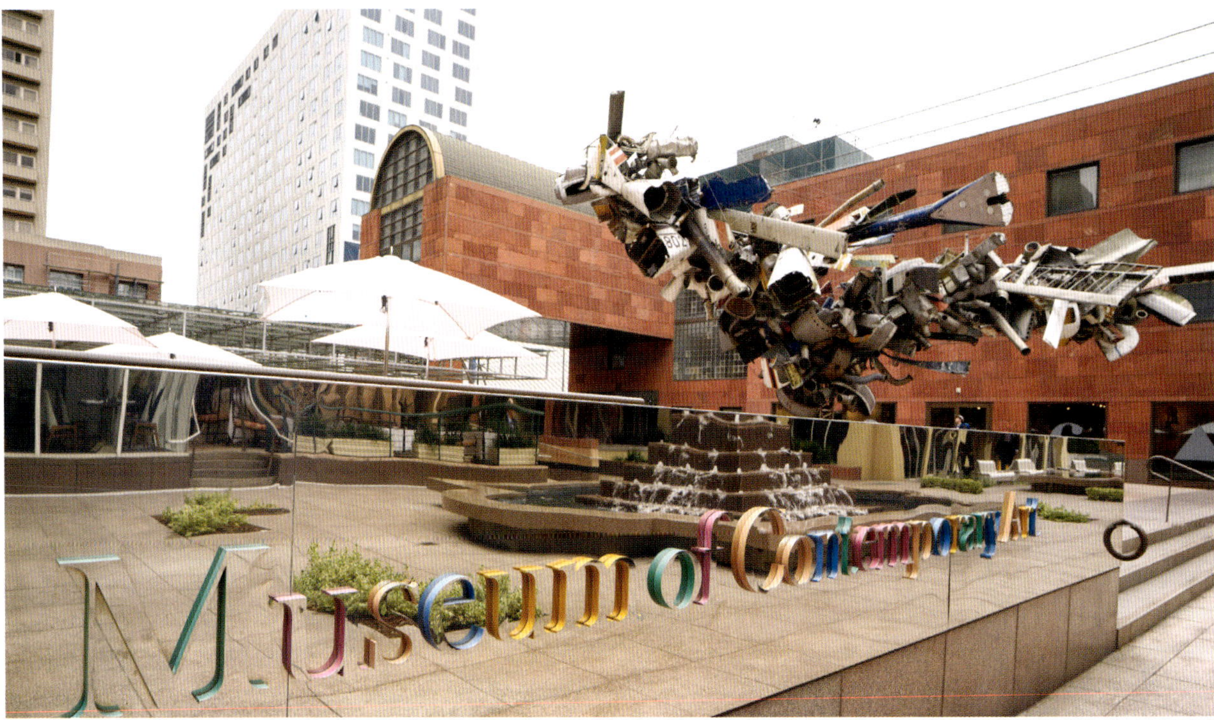

The Broad *(top)*

The striking, perforated metallic exterior of this art museum is designed to allow natural light to pass freely inside. Its design concept was named "the veil and the vault," with the "veil" being the honeycomb-like envelope that wraps the building, and the "vault" being the concrete core that houses the art.

Museum of Contemporary Art *(bottom)*

The sprawling sculpture by artist Nancy Rubins rises over 25 feet in front of the popular museum. This chaotic "junk tree" sculpture, made from scraps of old airplanes, greets visitors to the Museum of Contemporary Art, also known as MOCA, the only artist-founded museum in Los Angeles.

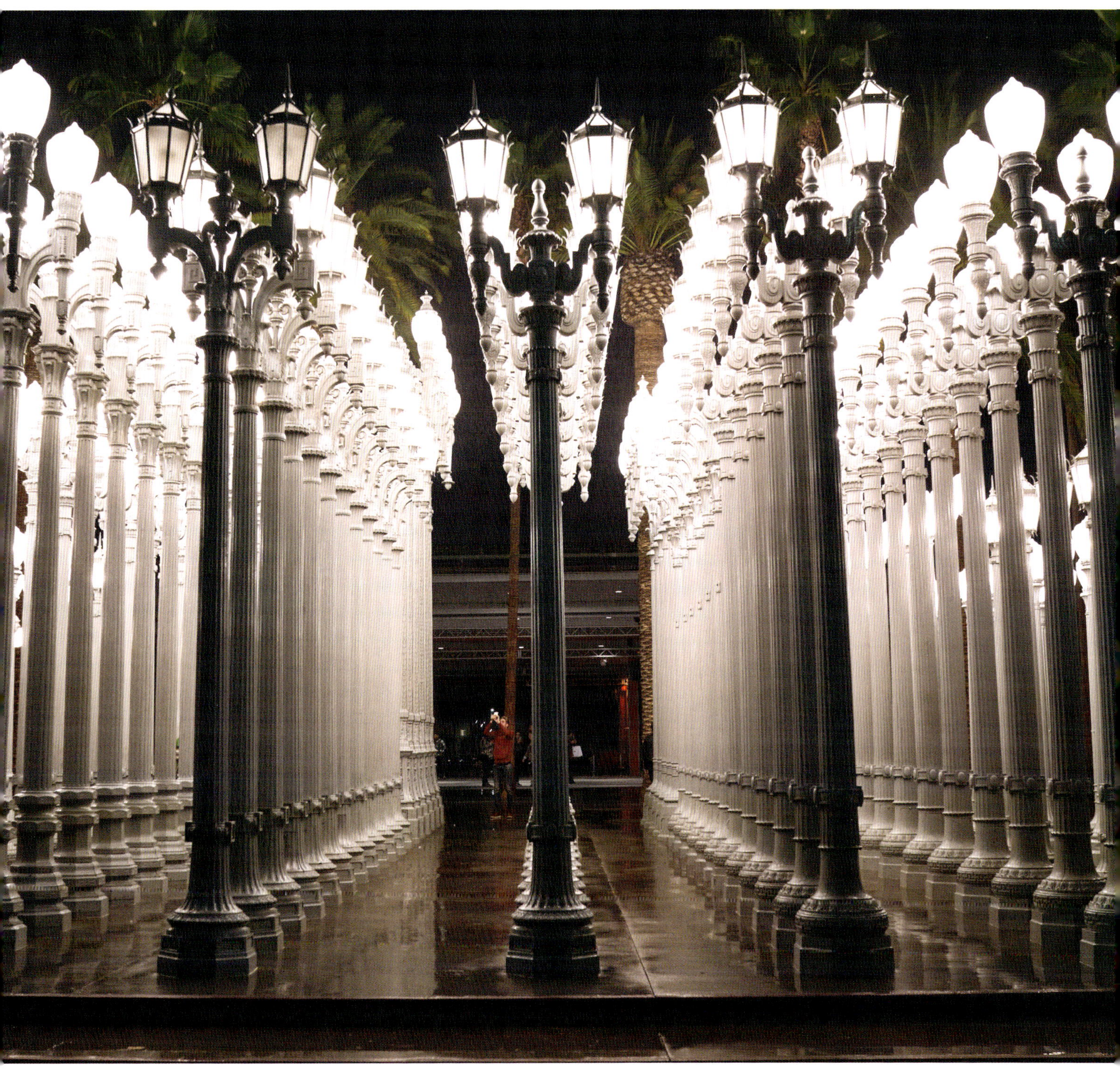

Los Angeles County Museum of Art

These pristine rows of restored street lamps are part of "Urban Lights," a breathtaking installation outside the LACMA by artist Chris Burden. A favorite with visitors to the museum, children can often be seen chasing each other through the 202 light poles, screeching with delight.

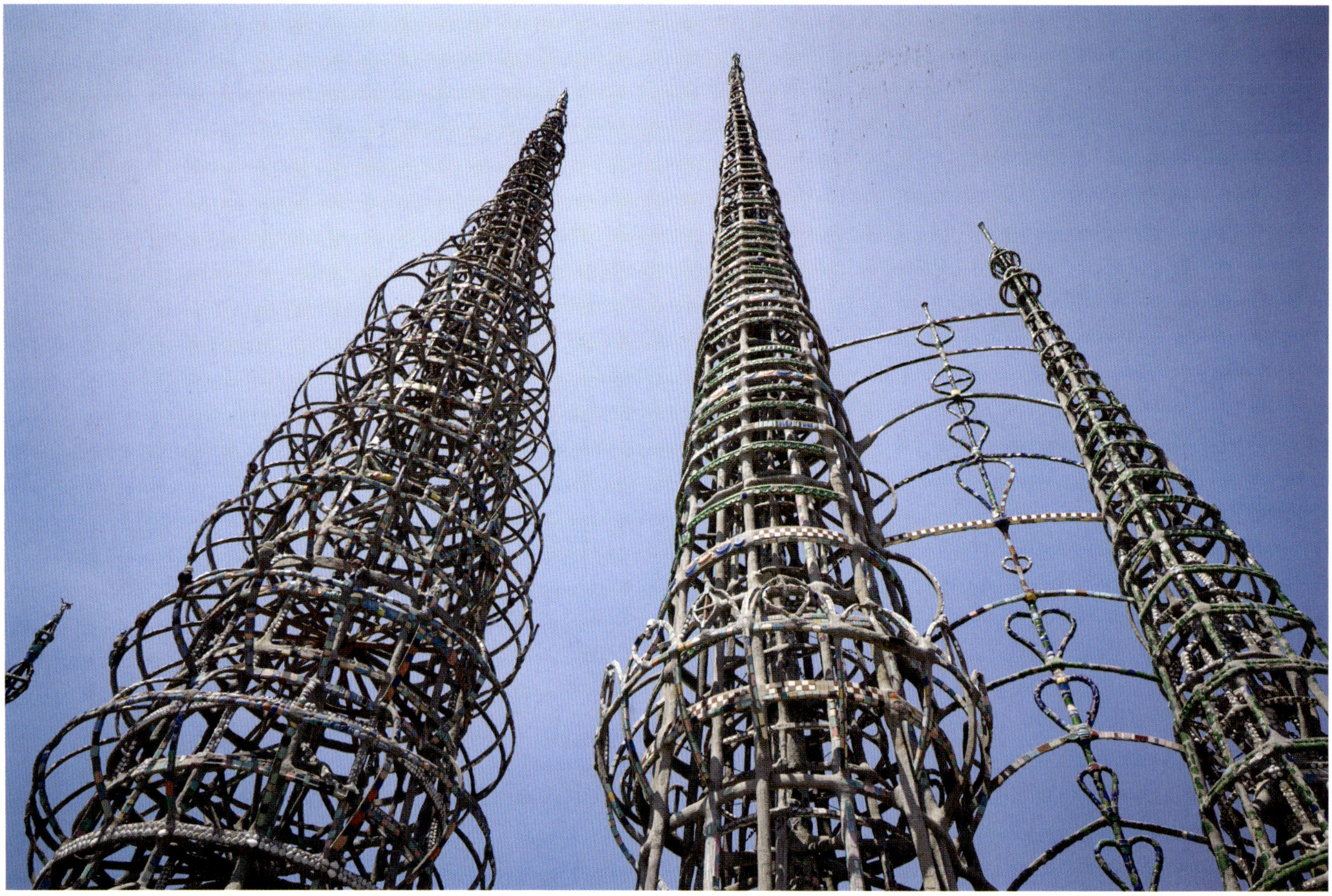

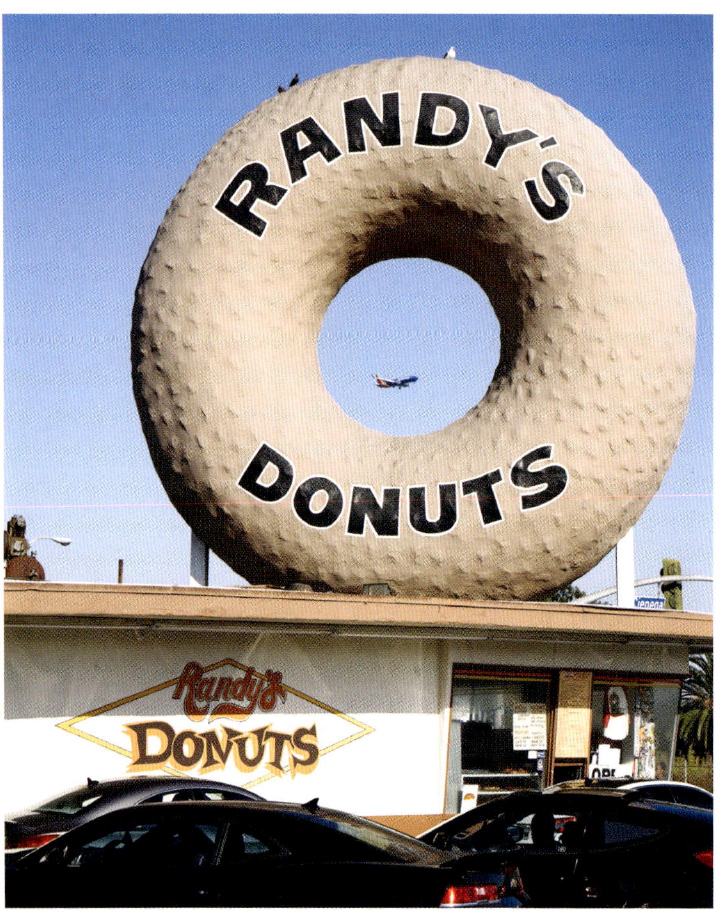

Watts Towers *(above and opposite)*

Using "found objects" such as bottles, seashells, mirrors and tiles, artist Simon Rodia, an Italian immigrant construction worker, created 17 sculptures, which are proudly displayed in the Simon Rodia State Historic Park in the Watts area of Los Angeles. The tallest of his towering creations reaches almost 100 feet.

Randy's Donuts *(left)*

Randy's iconic 32-foot-tall donut has made many movie appearances over the years, which makes it instantly recognizable. Built in 1953, this drive-through shop offers a variety of 35 homemade donuts. Randy's Donuts has been named one of the top donut shops in the country for over 60 years.

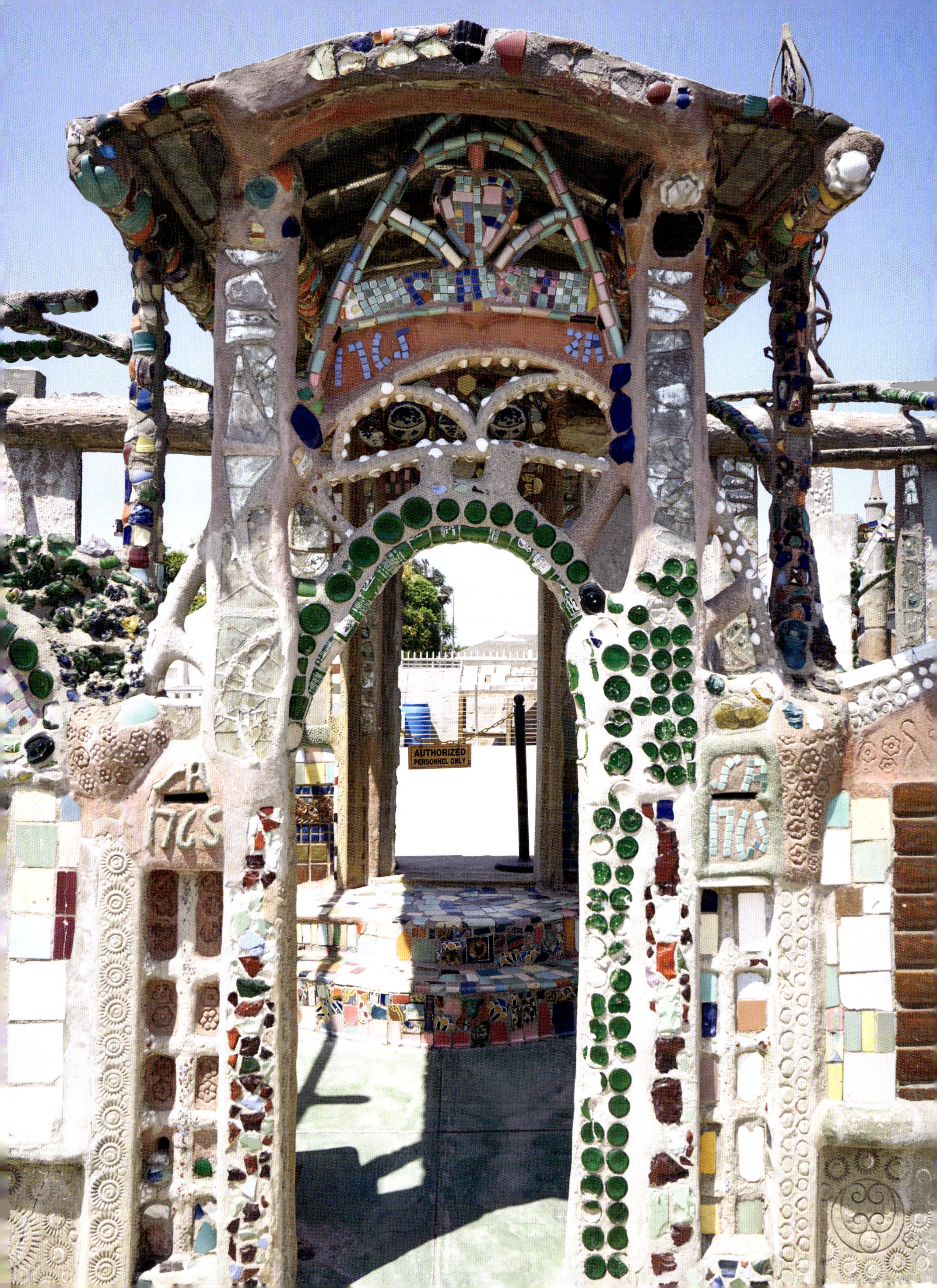
AUTHORIZED
PERSONNEL ONLY

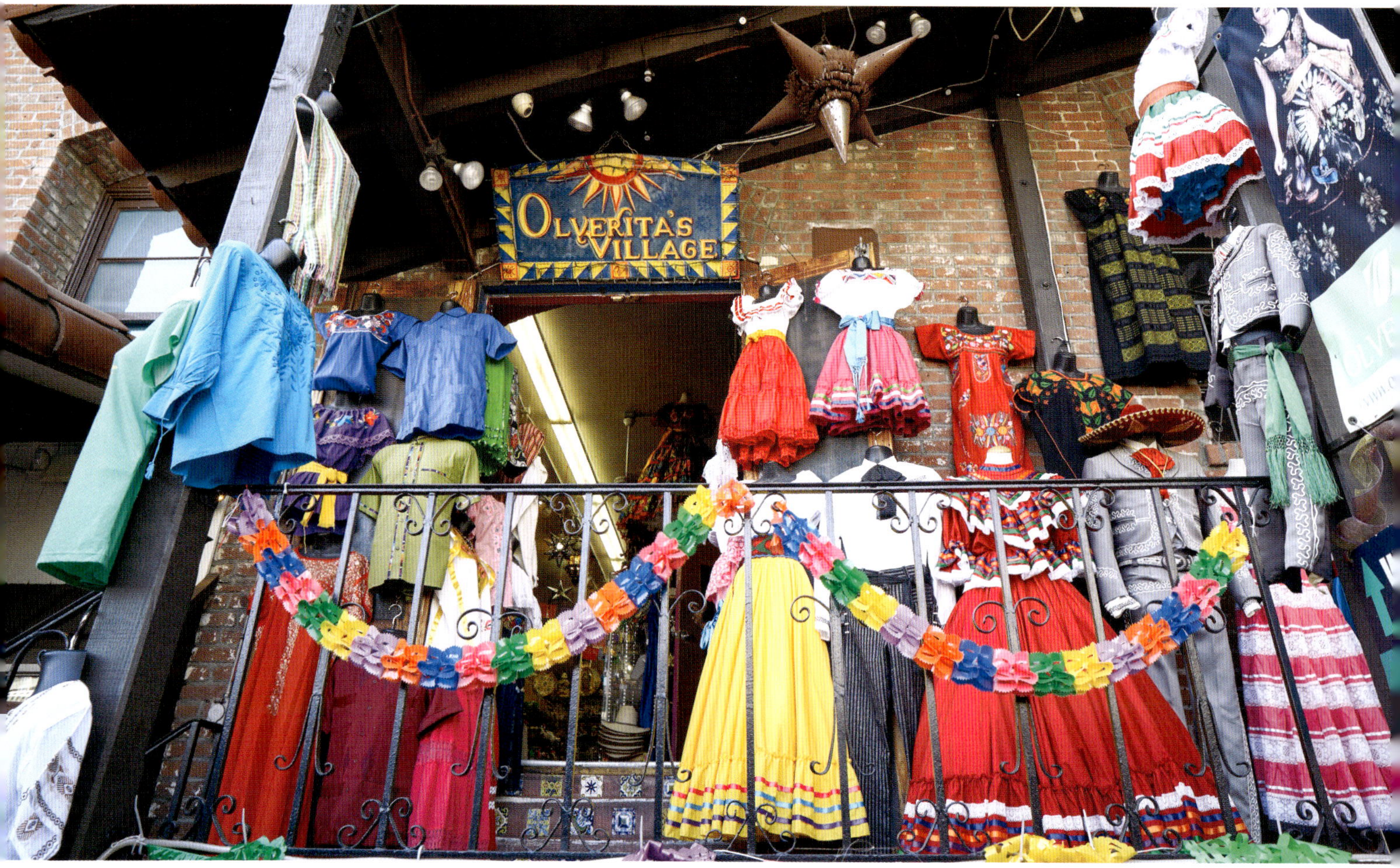

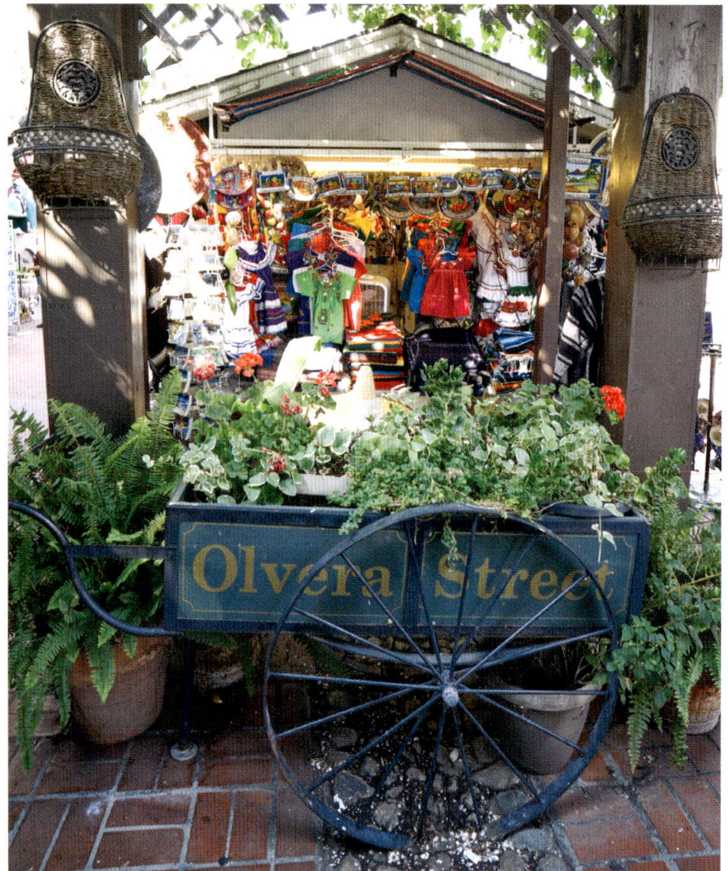

Olvera Street *(above and left)*

Welcome to Olvera Street, Los Angeles' "first street." Known as "the birthplace of Los Angeles," this vibrant and colorful area is a Mexican marketplace where visitors can enjoy authentic taquitos and tacos and buy handcrafted items. Many of the stall-holders are descendants of the original vendors.

La Plaza United Methodist Church

(opposite)

A hot pink customized lowrider - part of a quirky and unique Mexican-American subculture - sits at the entrance of Olvera Street. La Plaza United Methodist Church, seen in the background, was built on the site of the adobe home of Agustín Olvera, after whom the historic street is named.

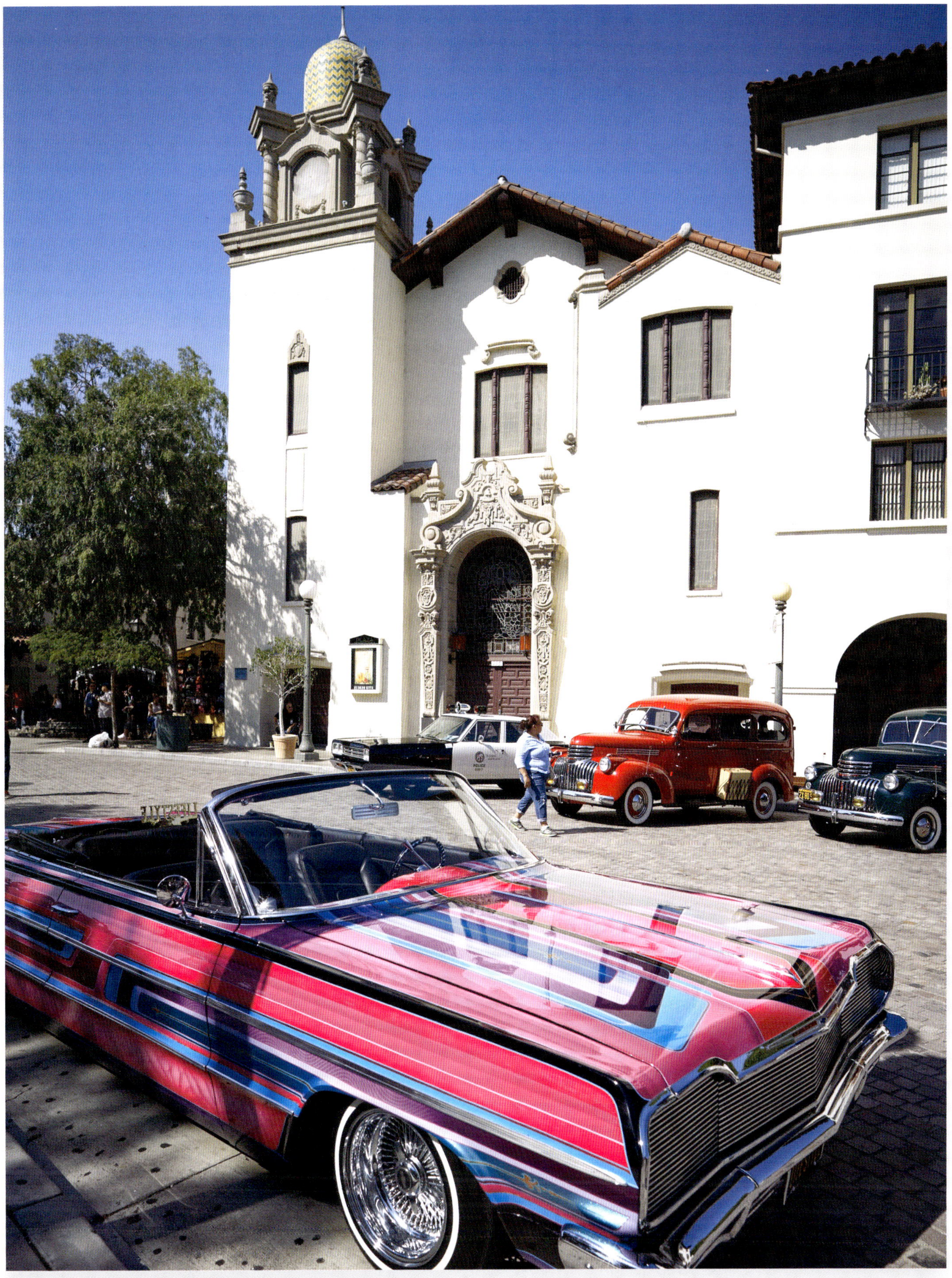

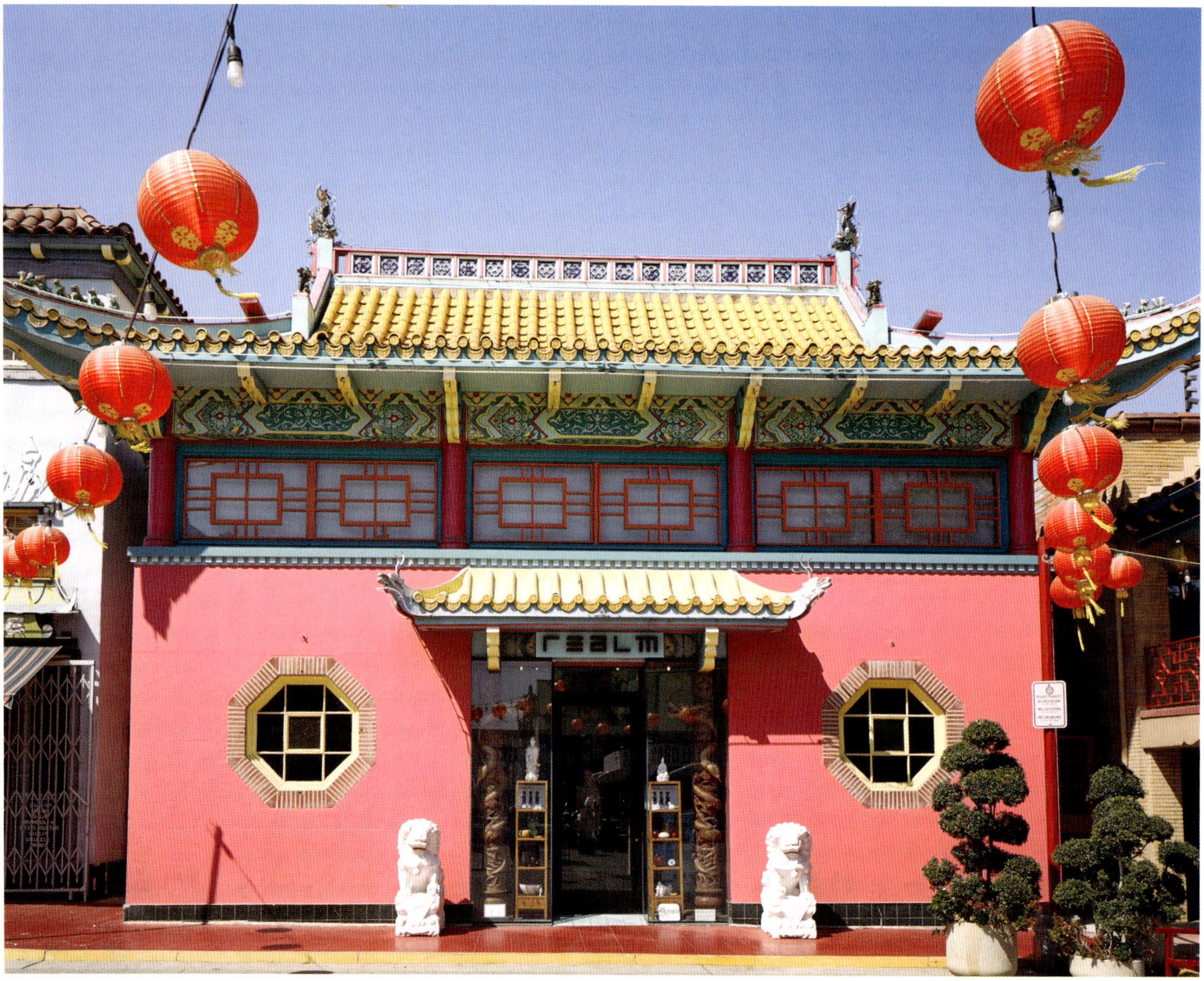

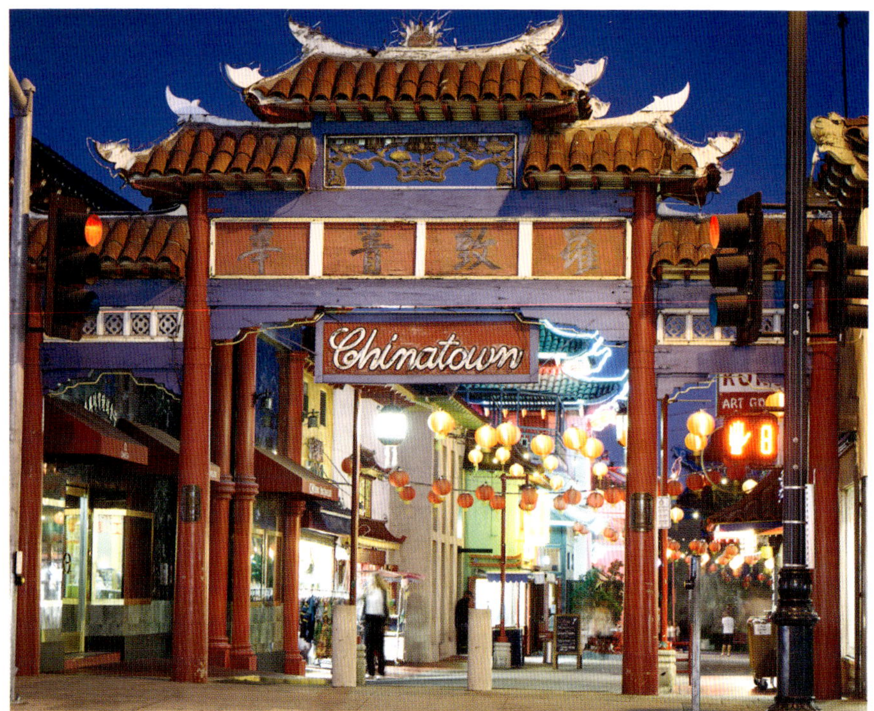

Chinatown *(above and left)*

Established in 1938 as New Chinatown after the original one was demolished to make room for Union Station, Downtown's Chinatown is a bustling hub for Chinese and Asian businesses. The first of four gates, the West Gate's inscription reads, "Cooperate to Achieve." Today, Chinatown has a population of around 10,000 residents.

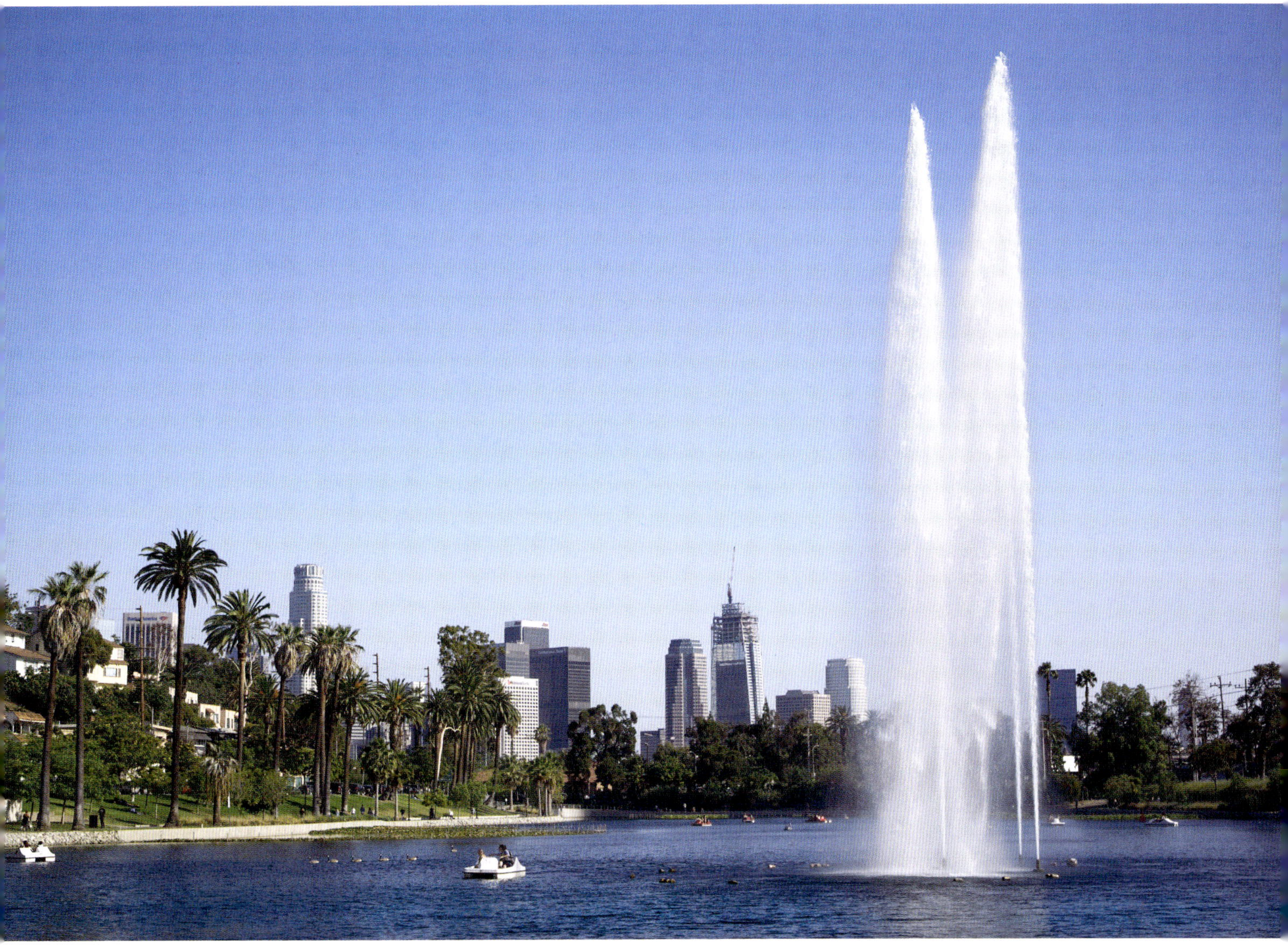

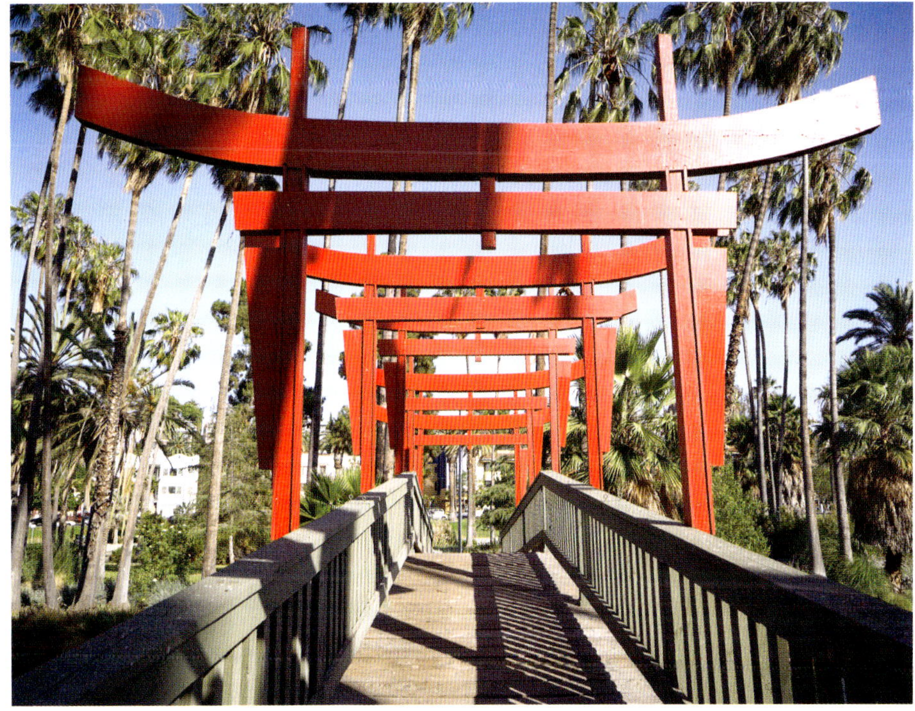

Echo Park Lake *(above and right)*

Named after the reverberations of the voices of workers who built the space, Echo Park Lake is a welcome retreat from the bustling city. The park includes a boat house, pedal boats, pathways, a fountain, lotus beds, and a bridge.

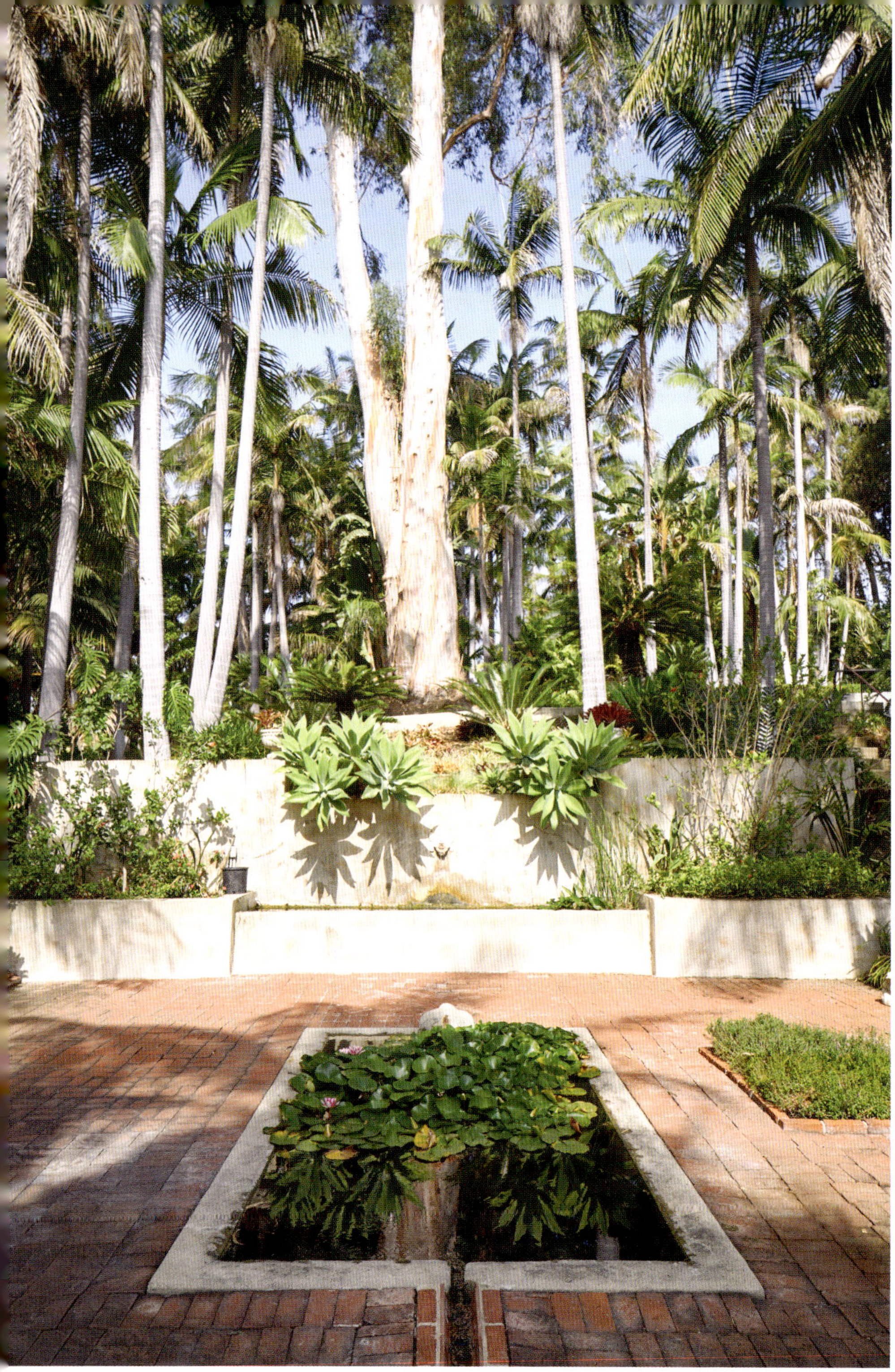

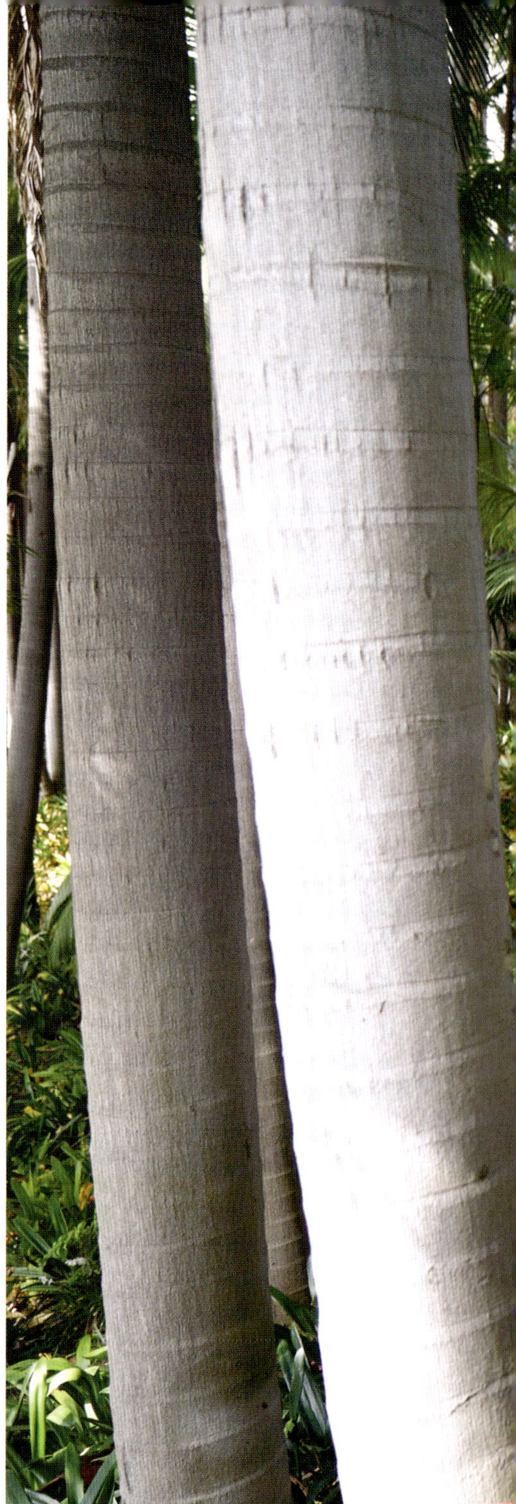

Virginia Robinson Gardens

An exotic paradise on the site of the first mansion in Beverly Hills, these stunning gardens include this awe-inspiring Australian King Palm Forest, a relaxing Italian Terrace Garden, and a lush pool pavilion. The fully restored estate offers a glimpse into the early history of Beverly Hills.

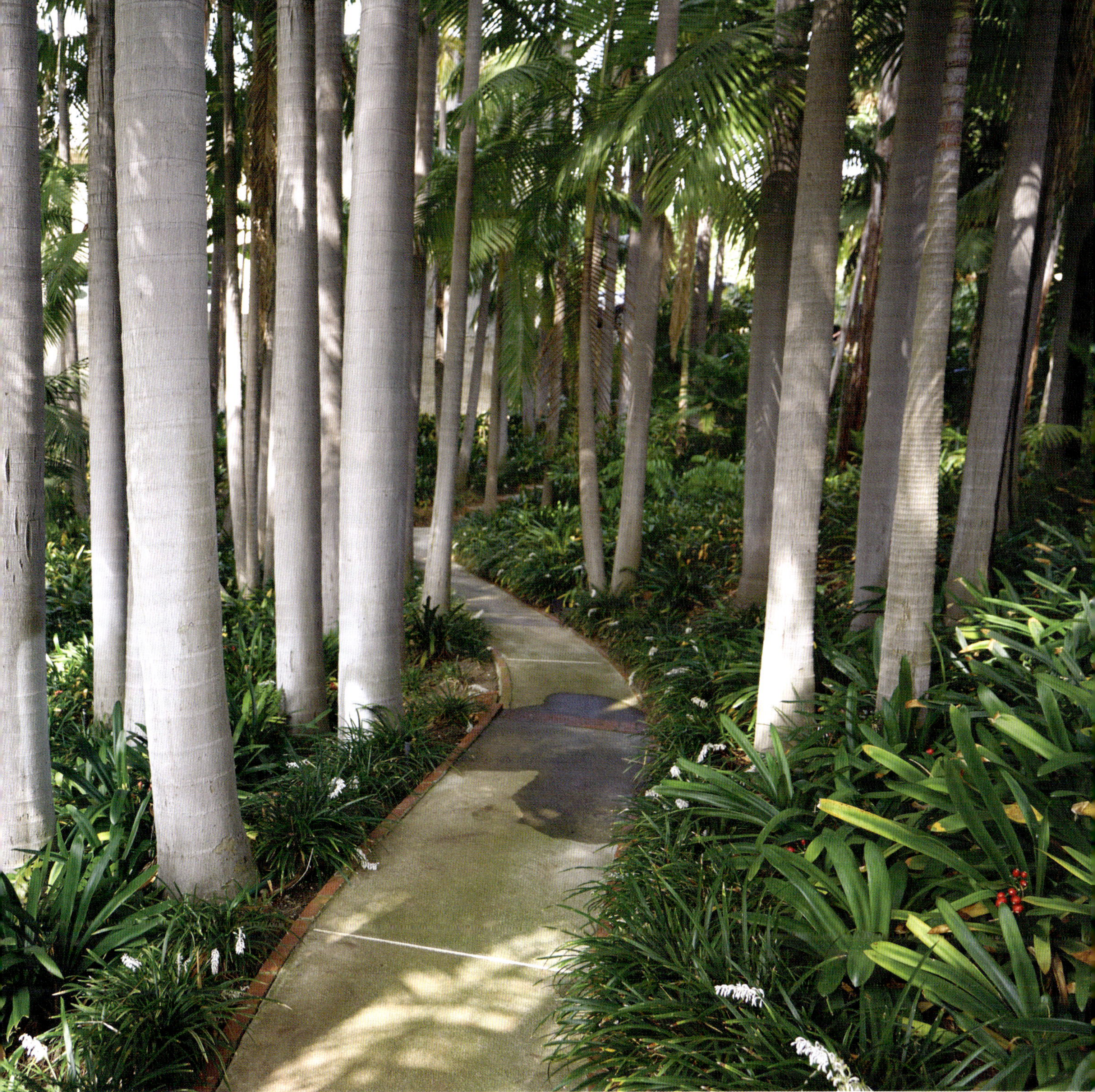

Virginia Robinson Gardens

(above and pages 110–111)

These gardens were once the site of lavish Hollywood parties, attended by glamorous guests such as the Duke and Duchess of Windsor, Marlene Dietrich, and Fred Astaire. They are named after former resident Virginia Robinson, a retail tycoon also known as the "First Lady of Beverly Hills."

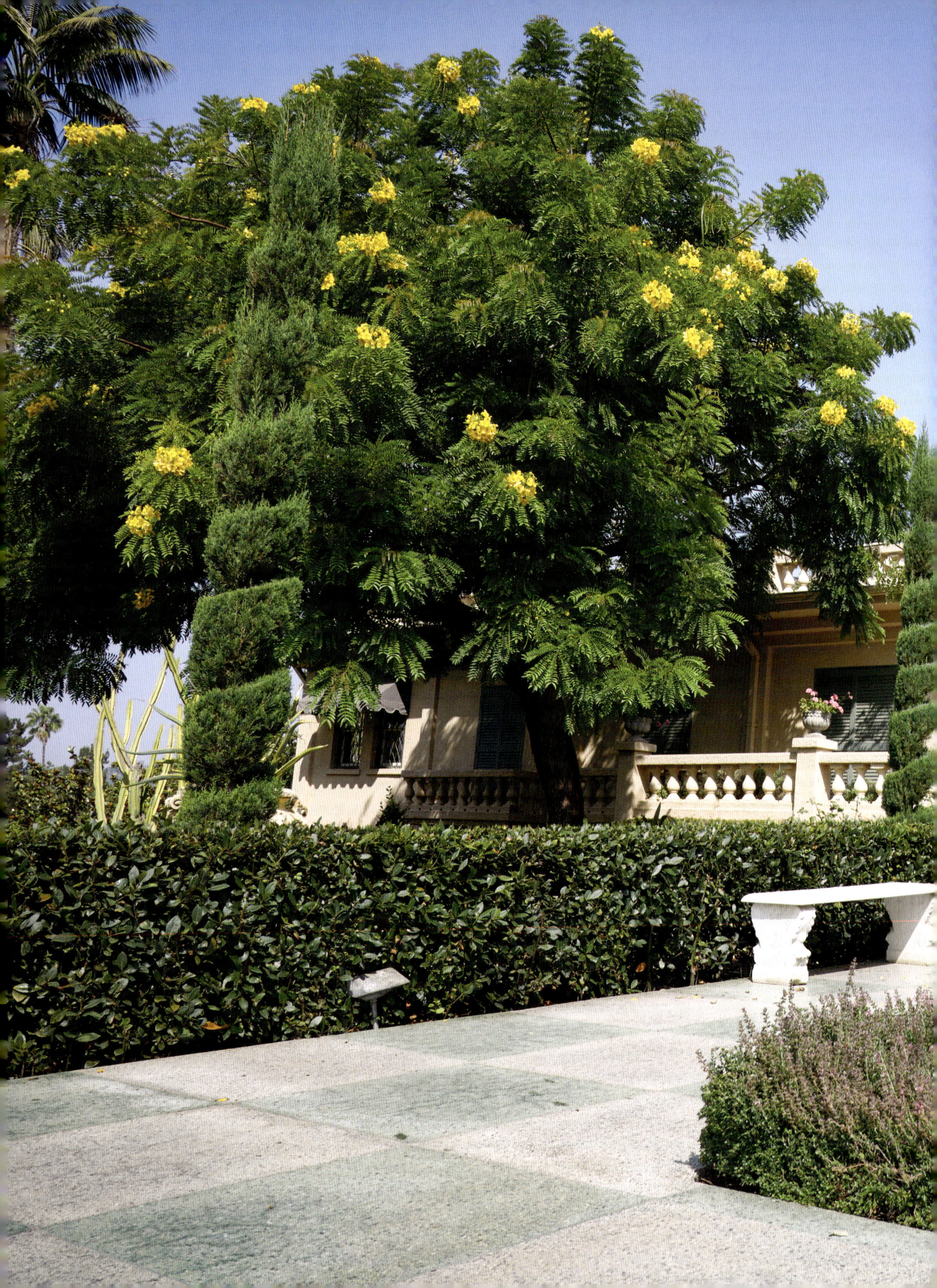

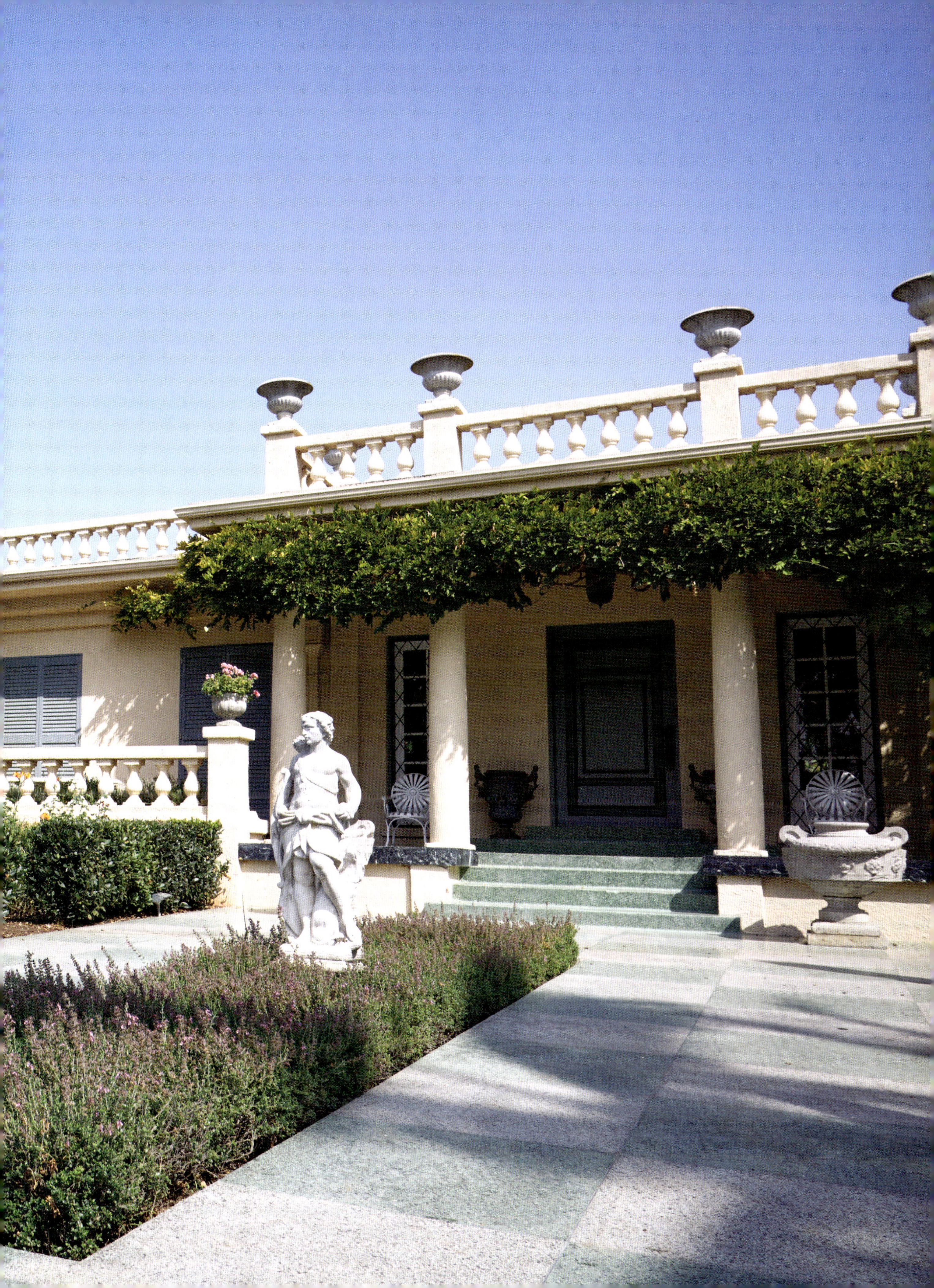

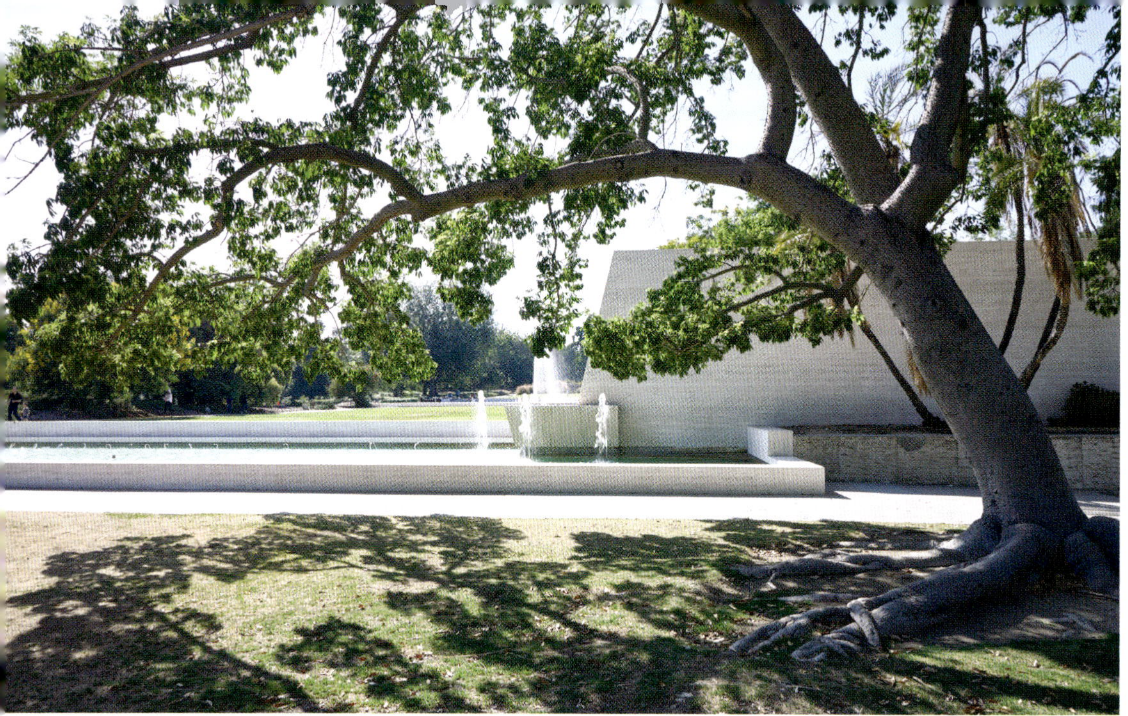

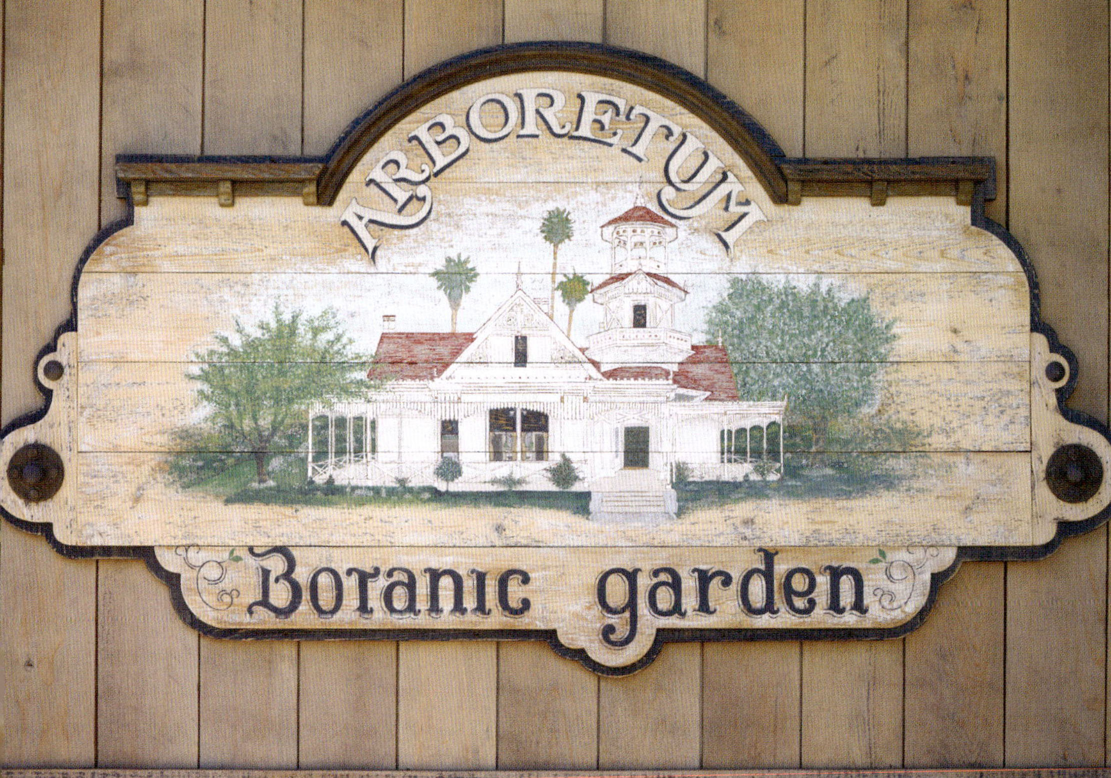

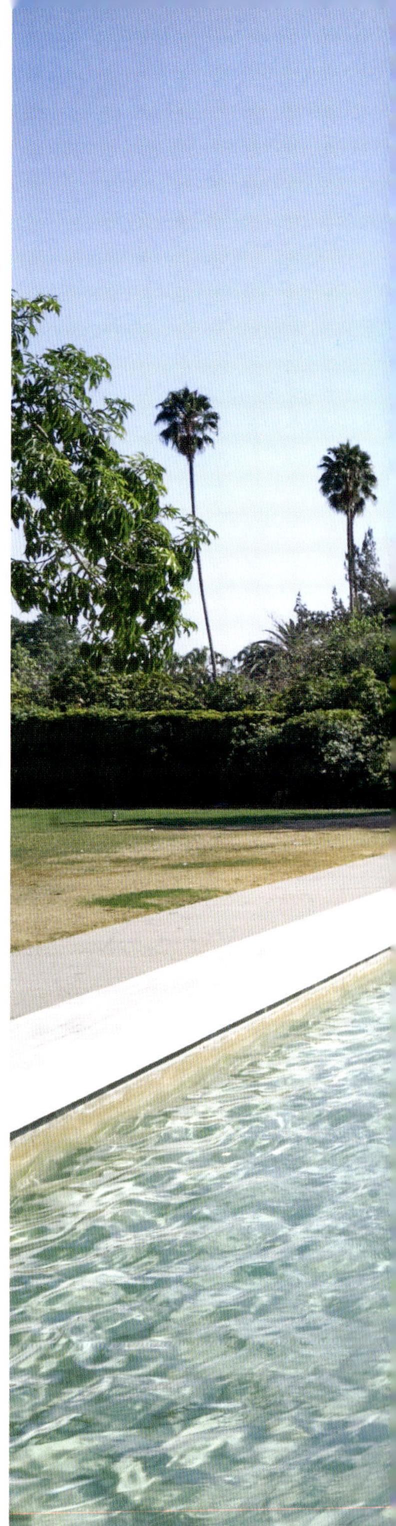

Los Angeles County Arboretum and Botanical Garden *(top and bottom)*

Once called Aleupkigna, "the place of many waters," by the original inhabitants of this site, these lush gardens are built around Baldwin Lake in Arcadia. The arboretum is said to be haunted with visitors reporting strange sights and sounds.

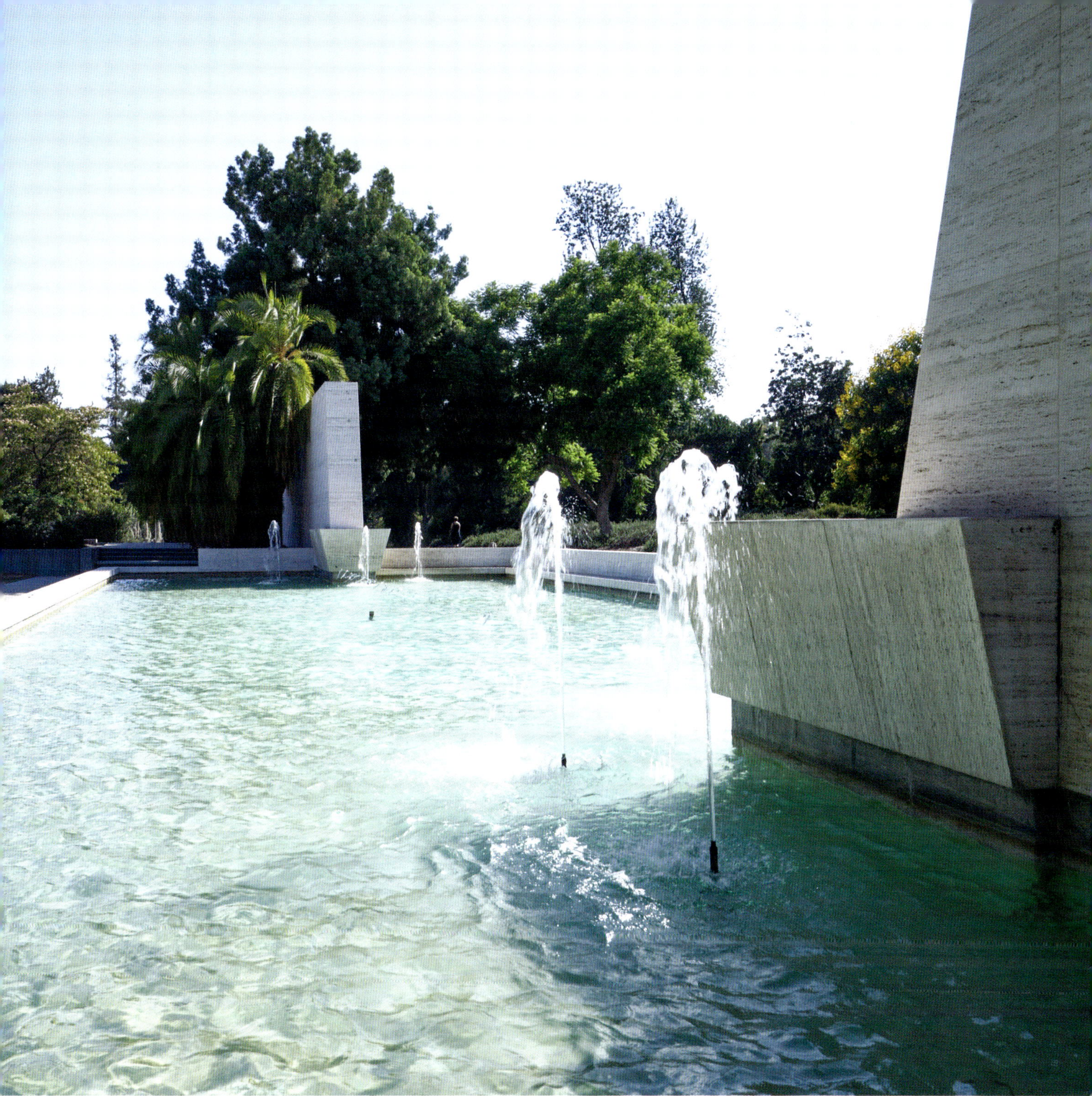

Los Angeles County Arboretum and Botanical Garden

Shimmering waters of the Bauer Lawn and Fountains greet visitors to the gardens, which are also a popular spot for weddings. The 127-acre site is grouped into sections including bio-geographical collections showcasing botanicals from Africa, Madagascar, the Canary Islands, and Australia.

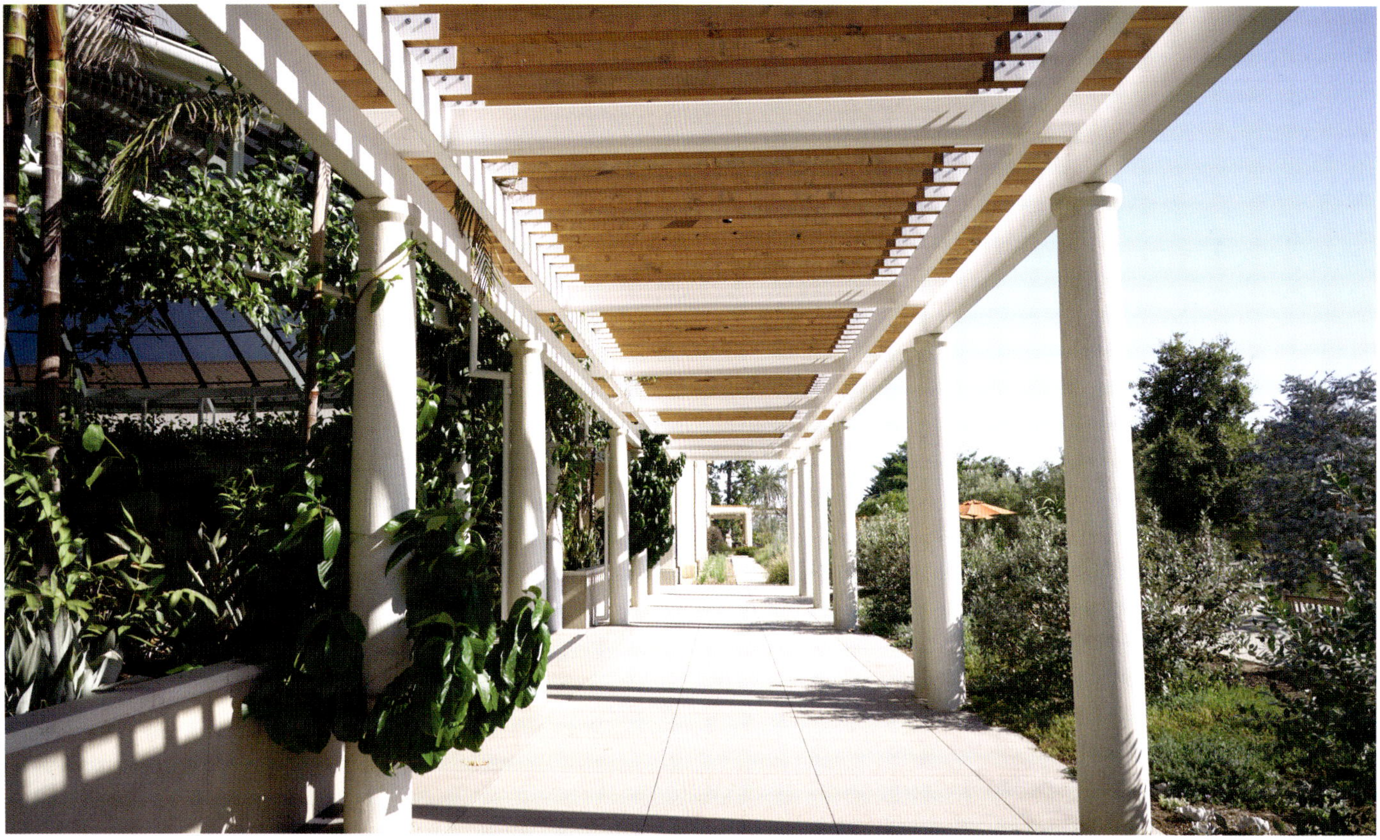

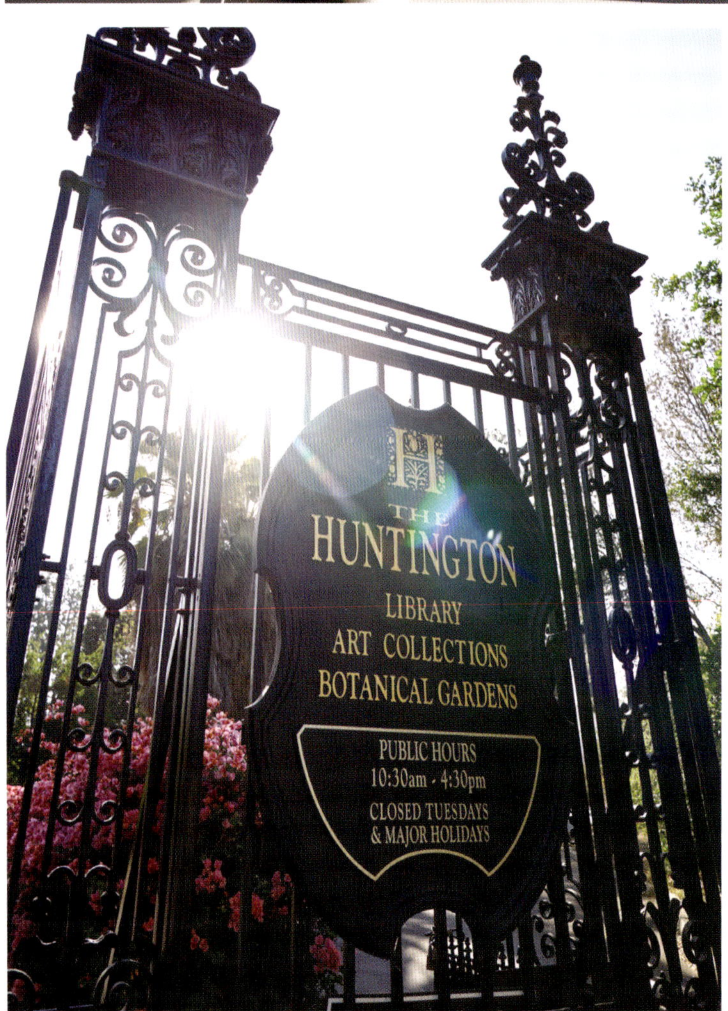

Huntington Library, Art Collections, and Botanical Gardens *(above and left)*

Sunlight streaks through the pillars of the library building, built in the Mediterranean Revival-style in 1920. Located in San Marino, this collection of books, art, and botanical plants was founded by railroad tycoon Henry Huntington.

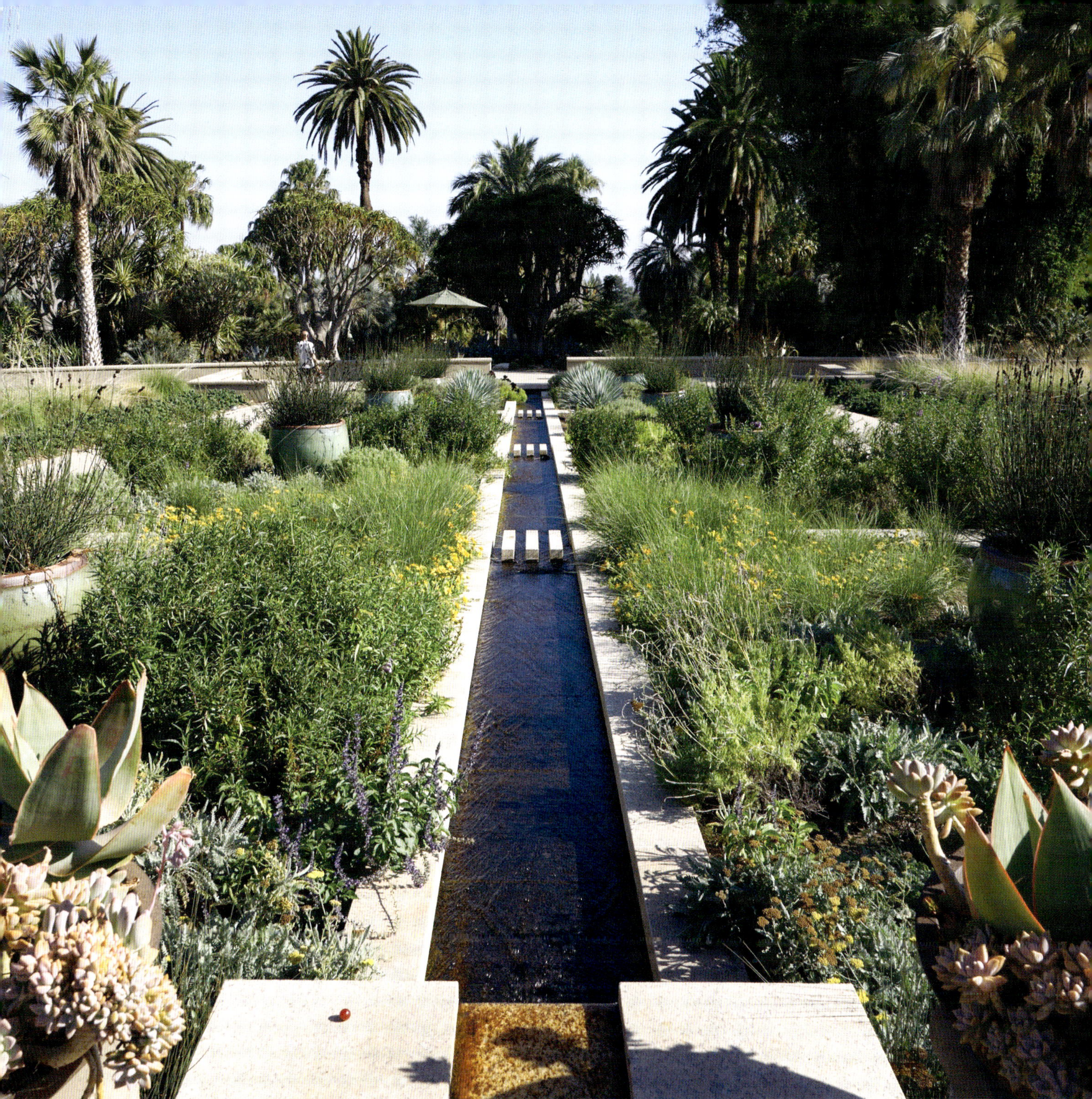

Celebration Garden

Located near the Steven S. Koblik Education and Visitor Center, the Celebration Garden is defined by its stone-lined water feature and terraced beds of seasonal blooms. Situated on 6.5 acres of gardens, the "Huntington" features 12 distinct gardens, outdoor sculptures, and art collections of European and American art.

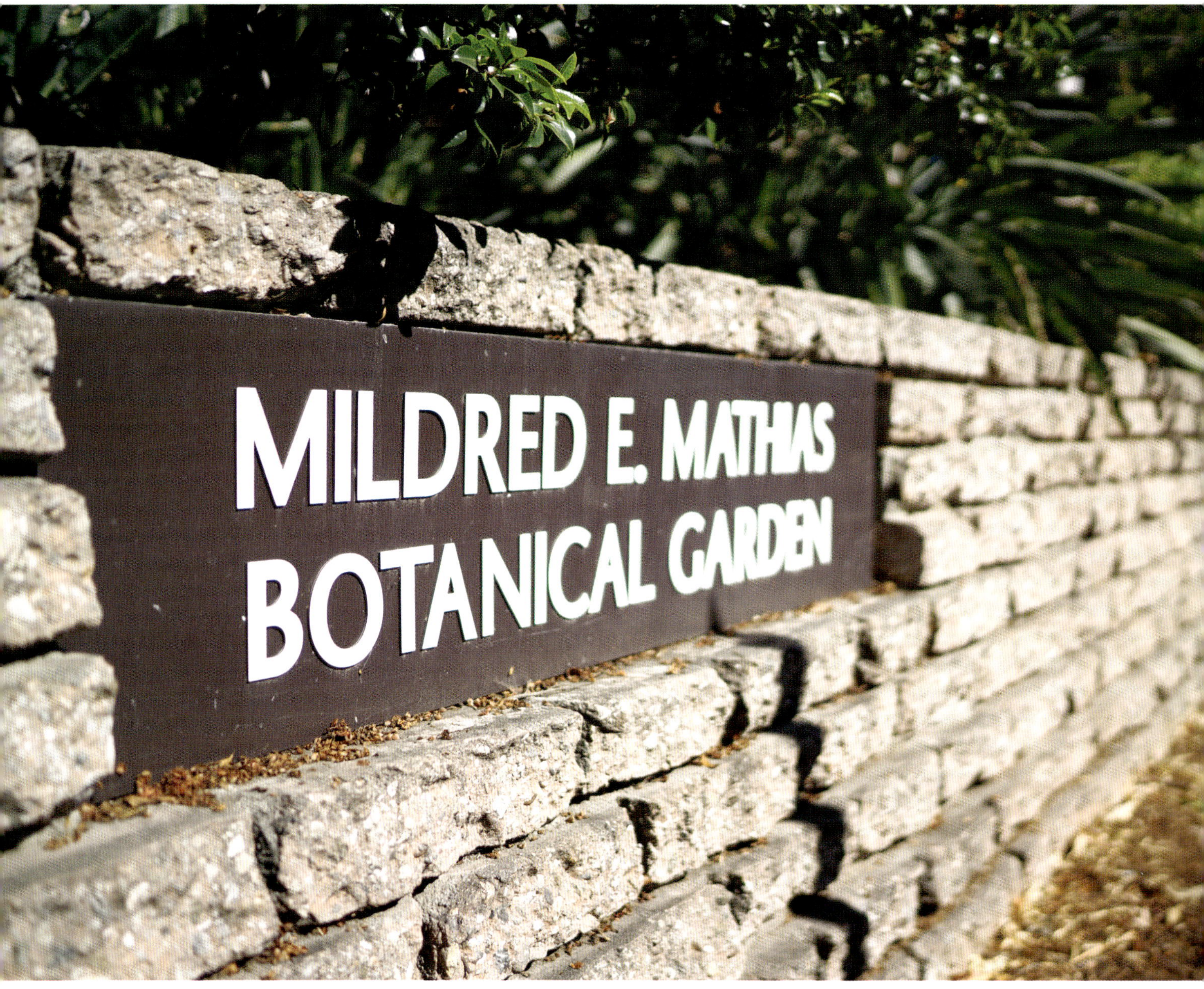

Mildred E. Mathias Botanical Garden *(above and opposite)*

Close ups of two plant species that make up the extensive collection at the Mildred E. Mathias Botanical Garden, part of the UCLA campus in Westwood. The garden, named after its former director, has special collections of ferns, palms, eucalyptus, and figs.

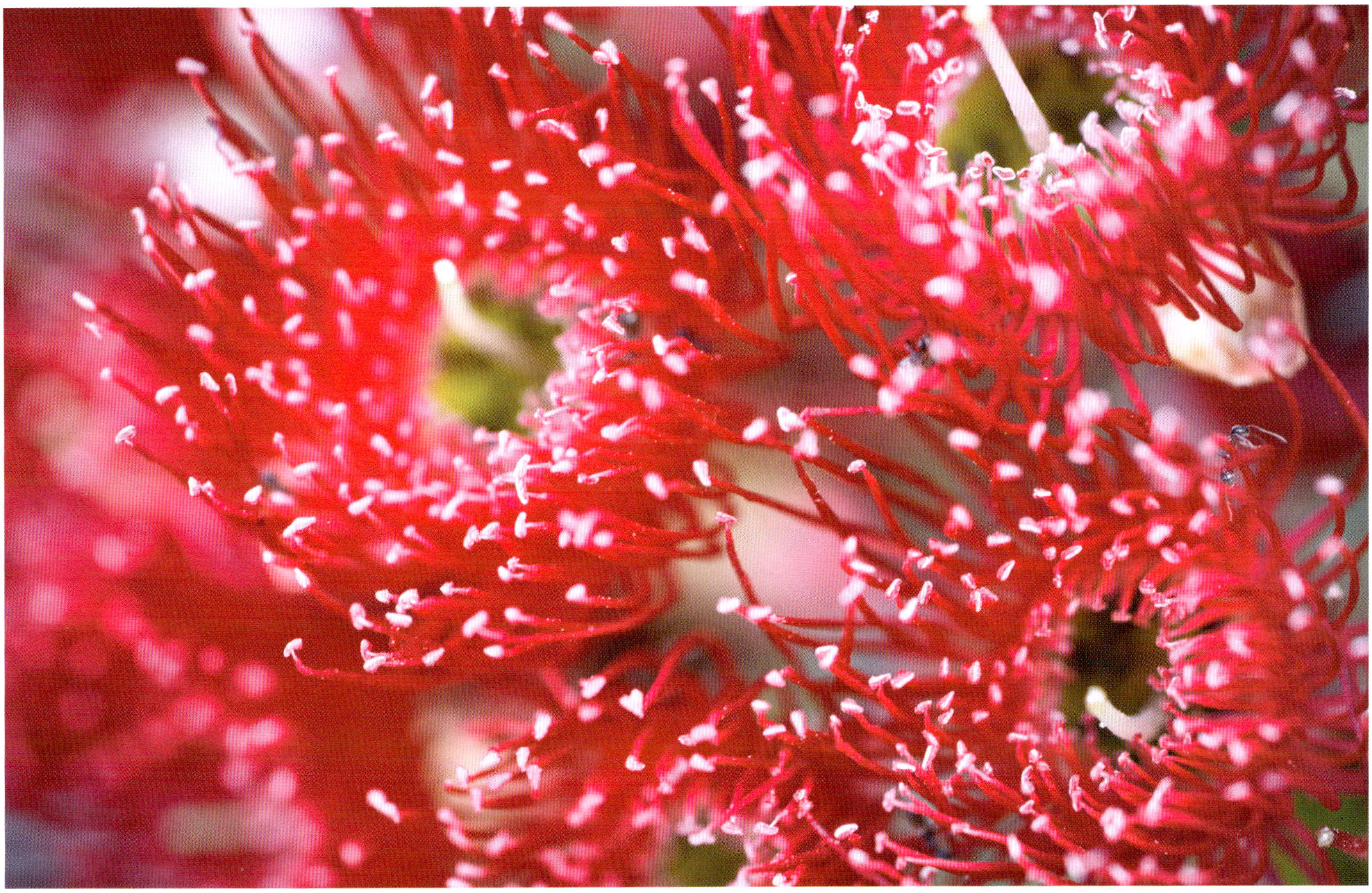

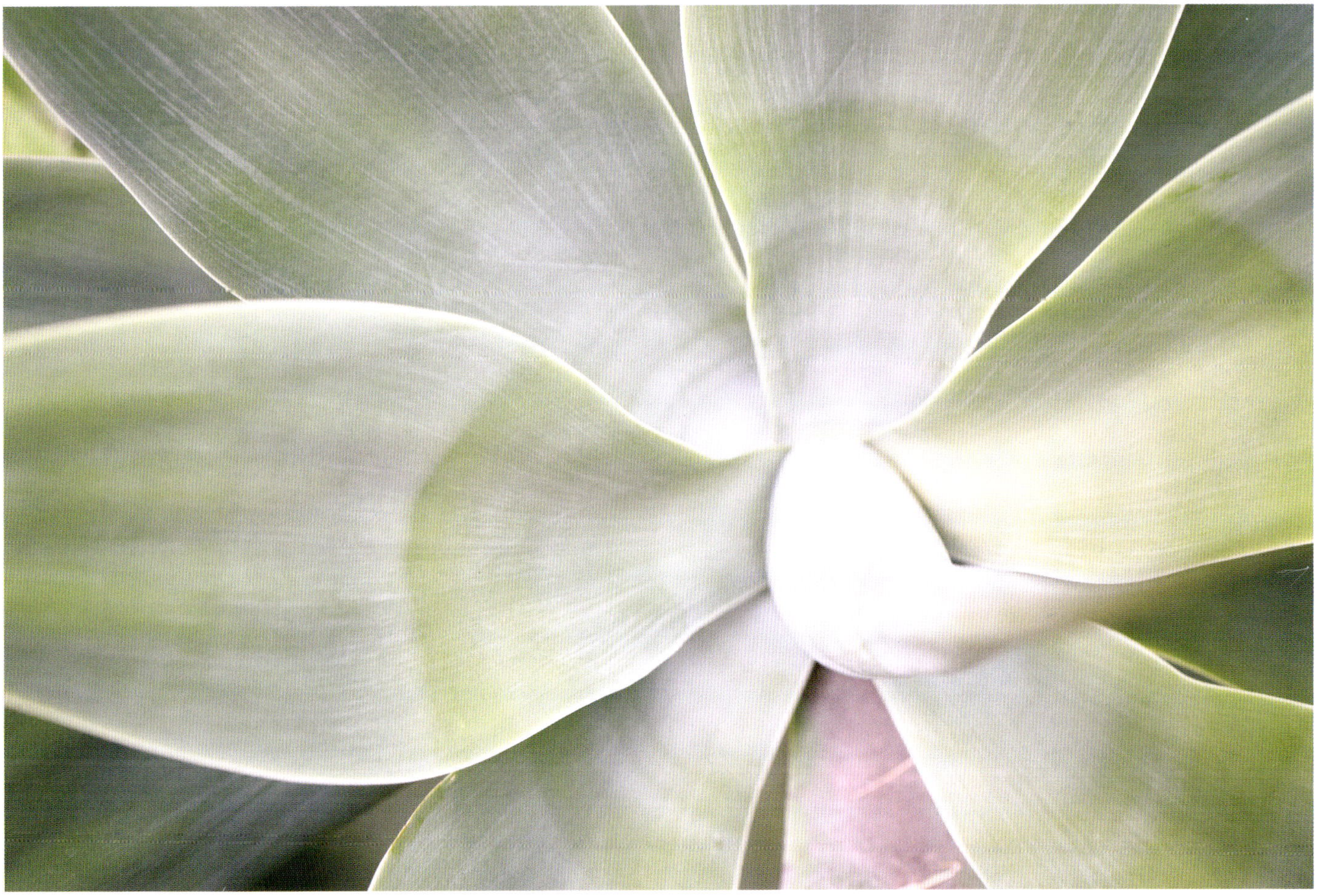

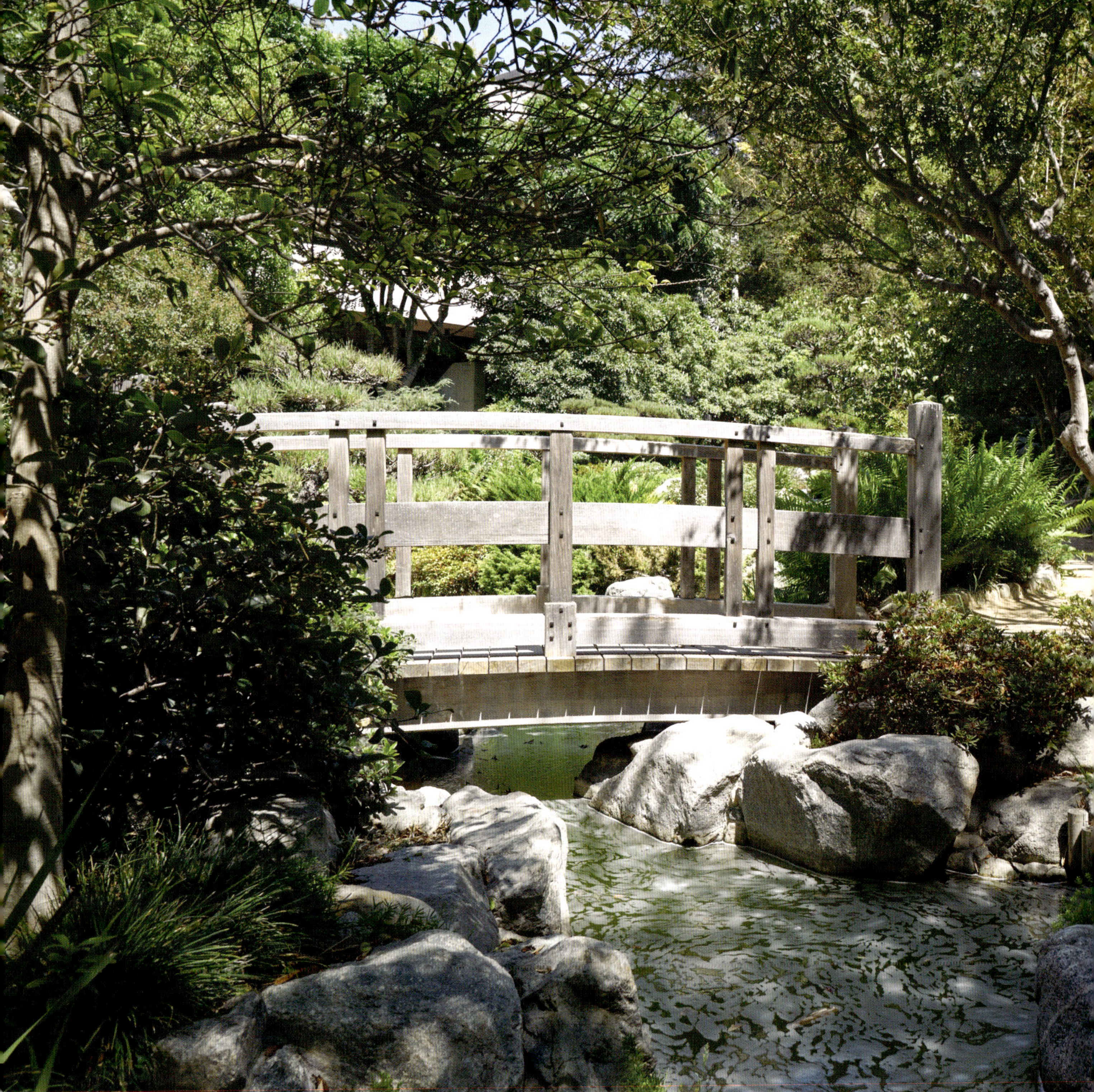

JACCC James Irvine Japanese Garden, Little Tokyo

Known as Seiryu-en or "Garden of the Clear Stream," this peaceful garden was designed in the Zen tradition of the famous gardens of Kyoto. A cascading stream, handcrafted cedar bridges, stone lanterns, and a handwashing fountain make it a hidden gem in Downtown Los Angeles.

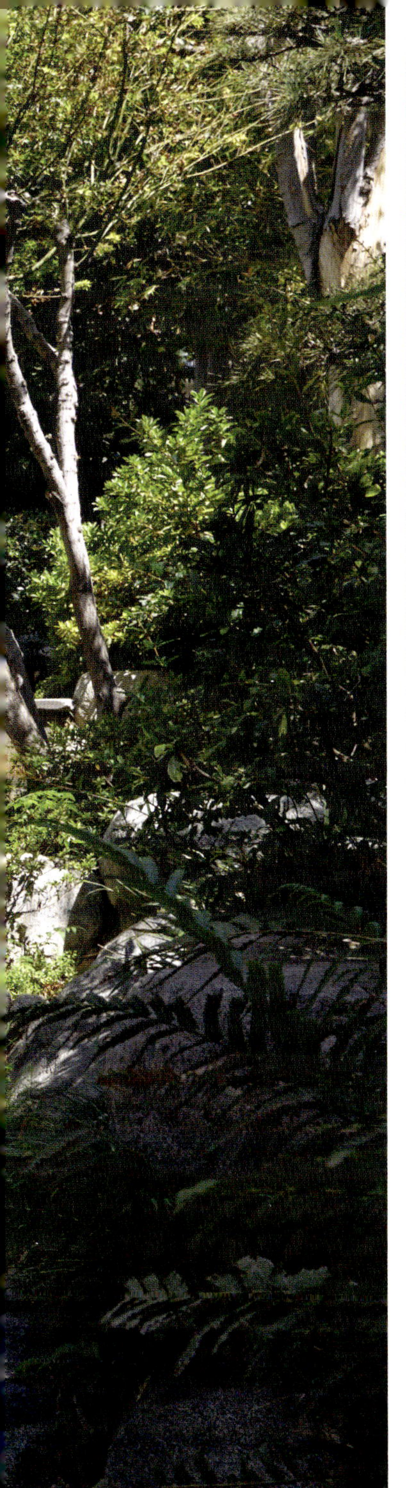

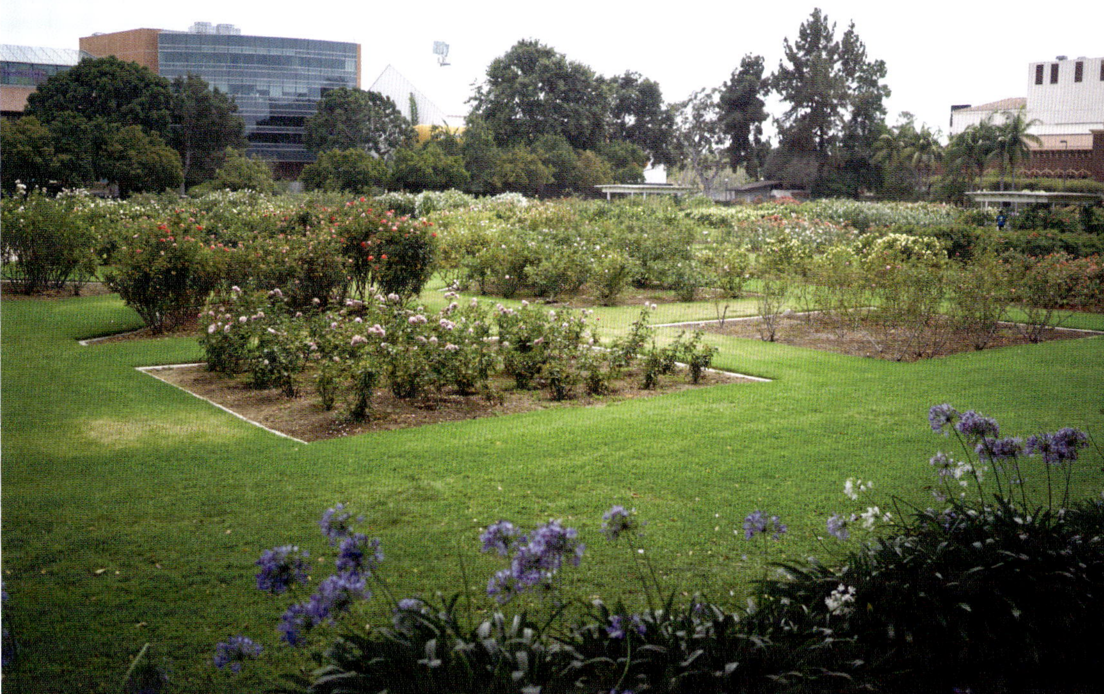

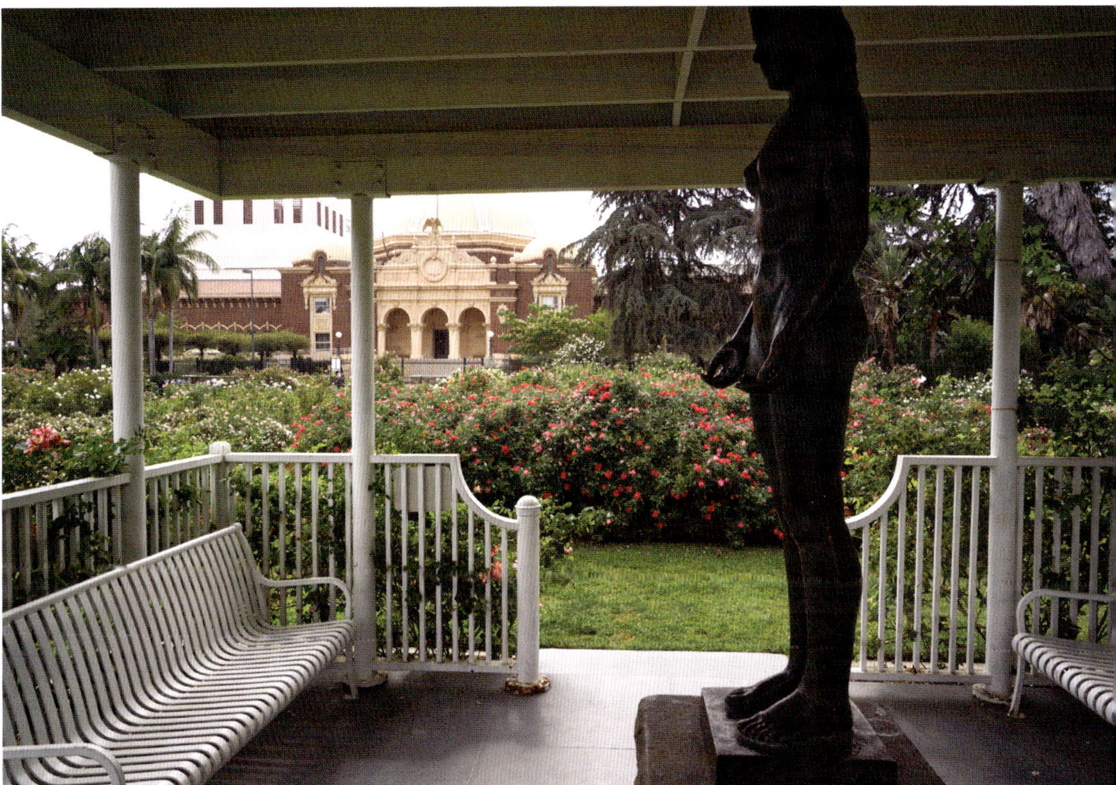

Exposition Park Rose Garden

(top and bottom)

This marble statue is one of four installed on pedestals at the corners of the Exposition Park Rose Garden. Created by Danish sculptor, Thyra Boldsen, the statues *Nymph Finding Pipes of Pan*, *Terpsichore*, *The Blessing*, and *The Start* are dedicated to all the women and mothers of the world.

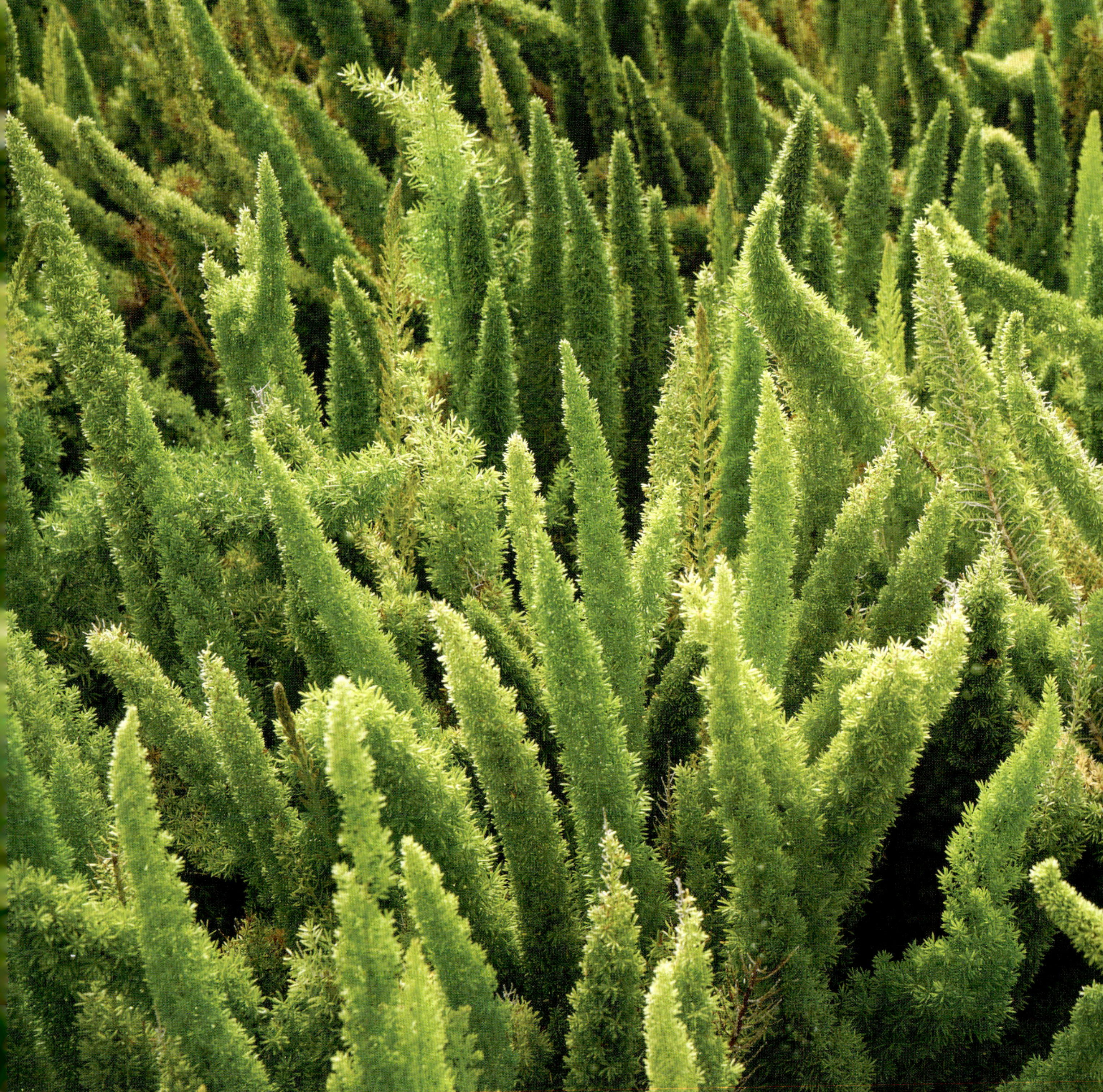

Exposition Park Rose Garden

Located between the Natural History Museum and the California Science Center on the USC campus, this iconic garden sits on 7 acres and features over 200 varieties of roses surrounded by other plantings. In 1991 it was added to the National Register of Historic Places.

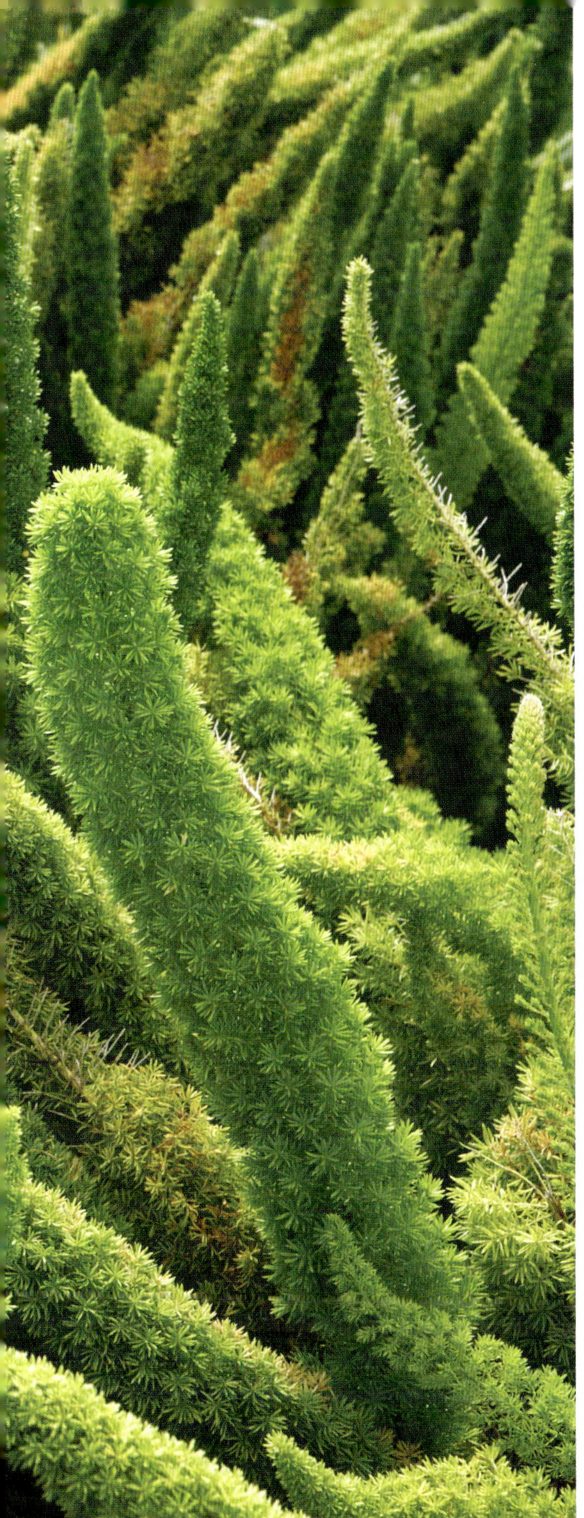

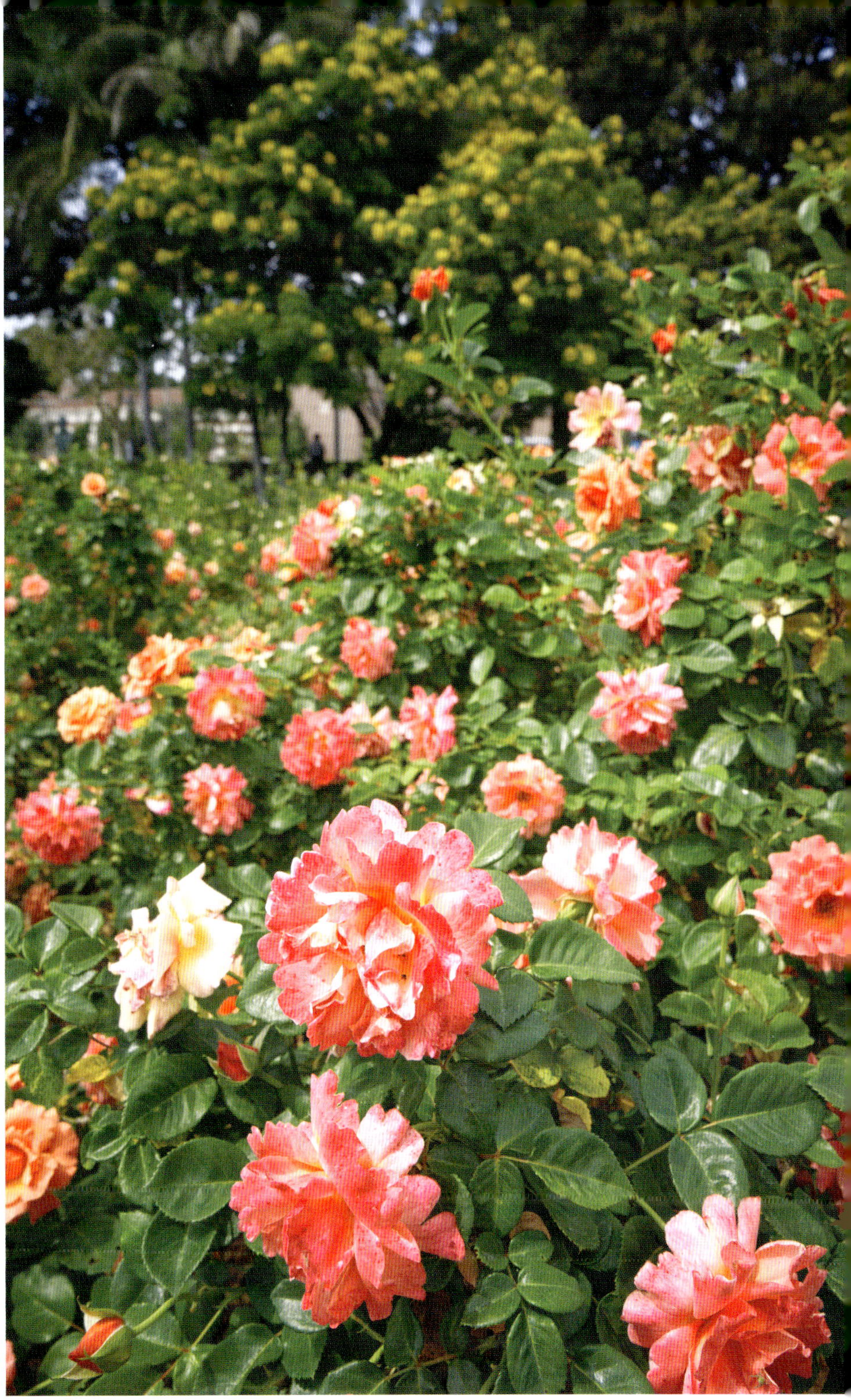

Exposition Park Rose Garden

(above and pages 122–123)

Between 1872 and 1910, a racetrack known as Agricultural Park was located at this site. Demolished in 1913, the renovated space was renamed Exposition Park. Today, Sunken Garden, with rose bushes laid in a grid that extend from both sides of a fountain, is considered one of the city's best kept secrets.

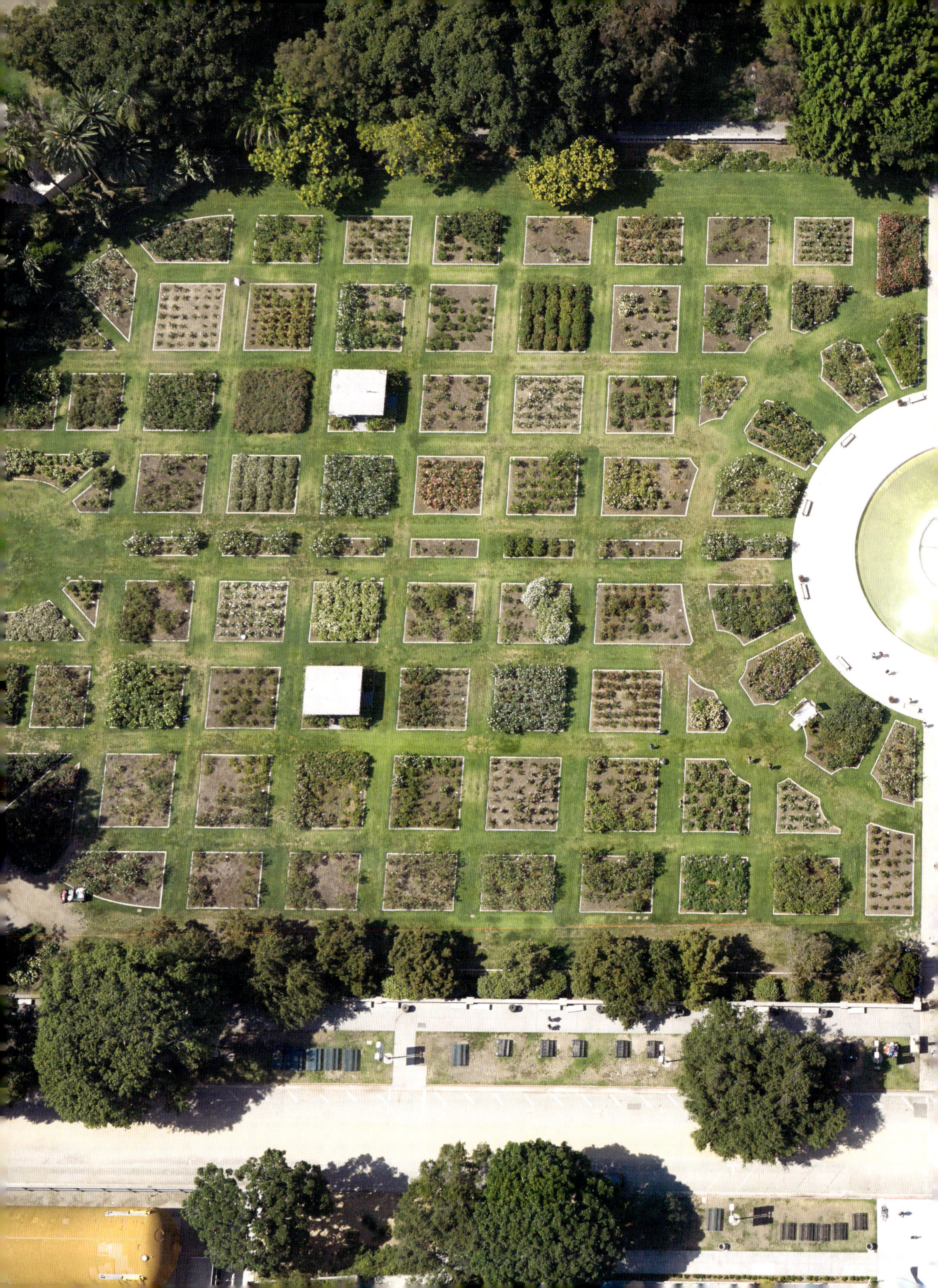

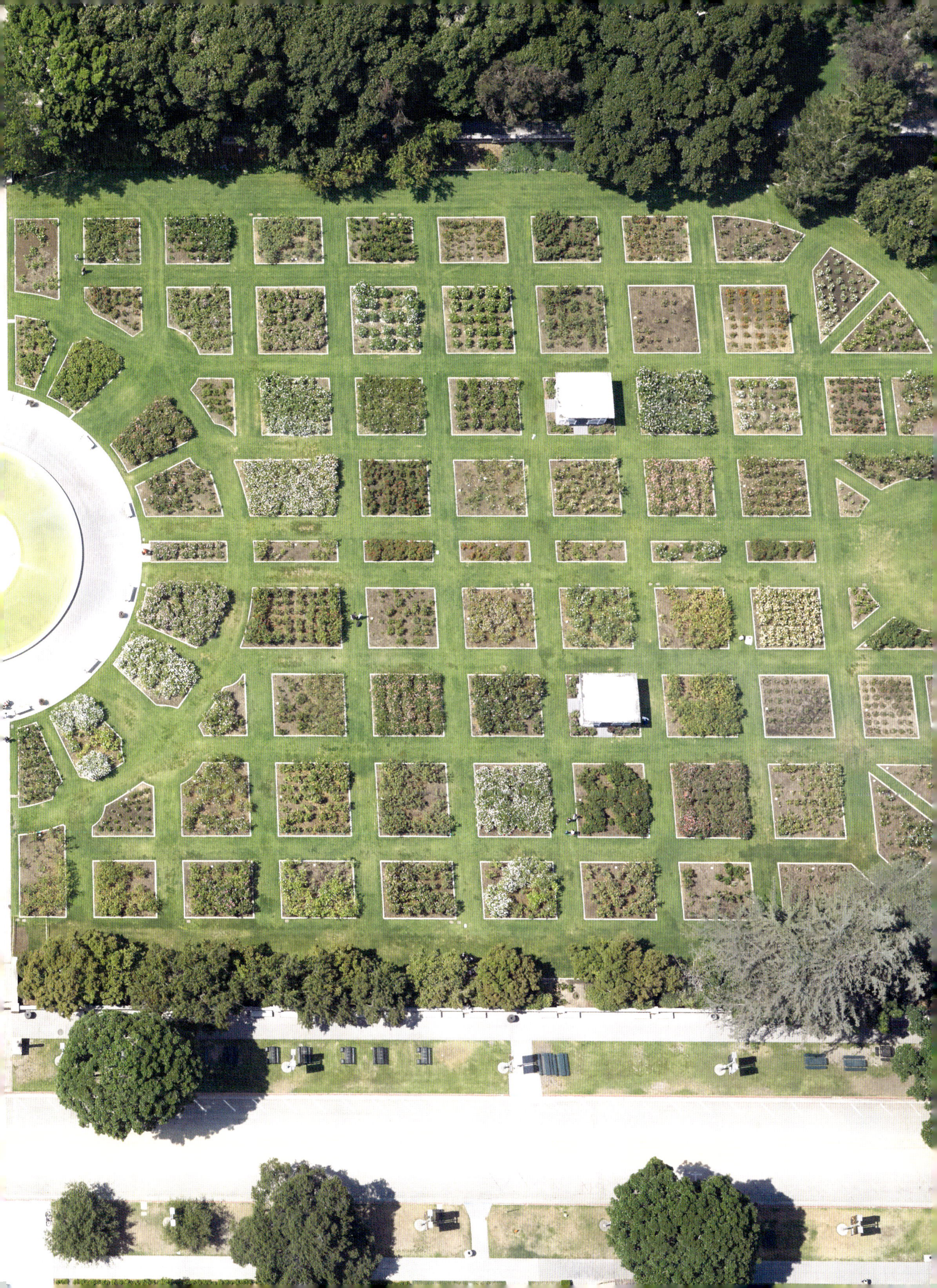

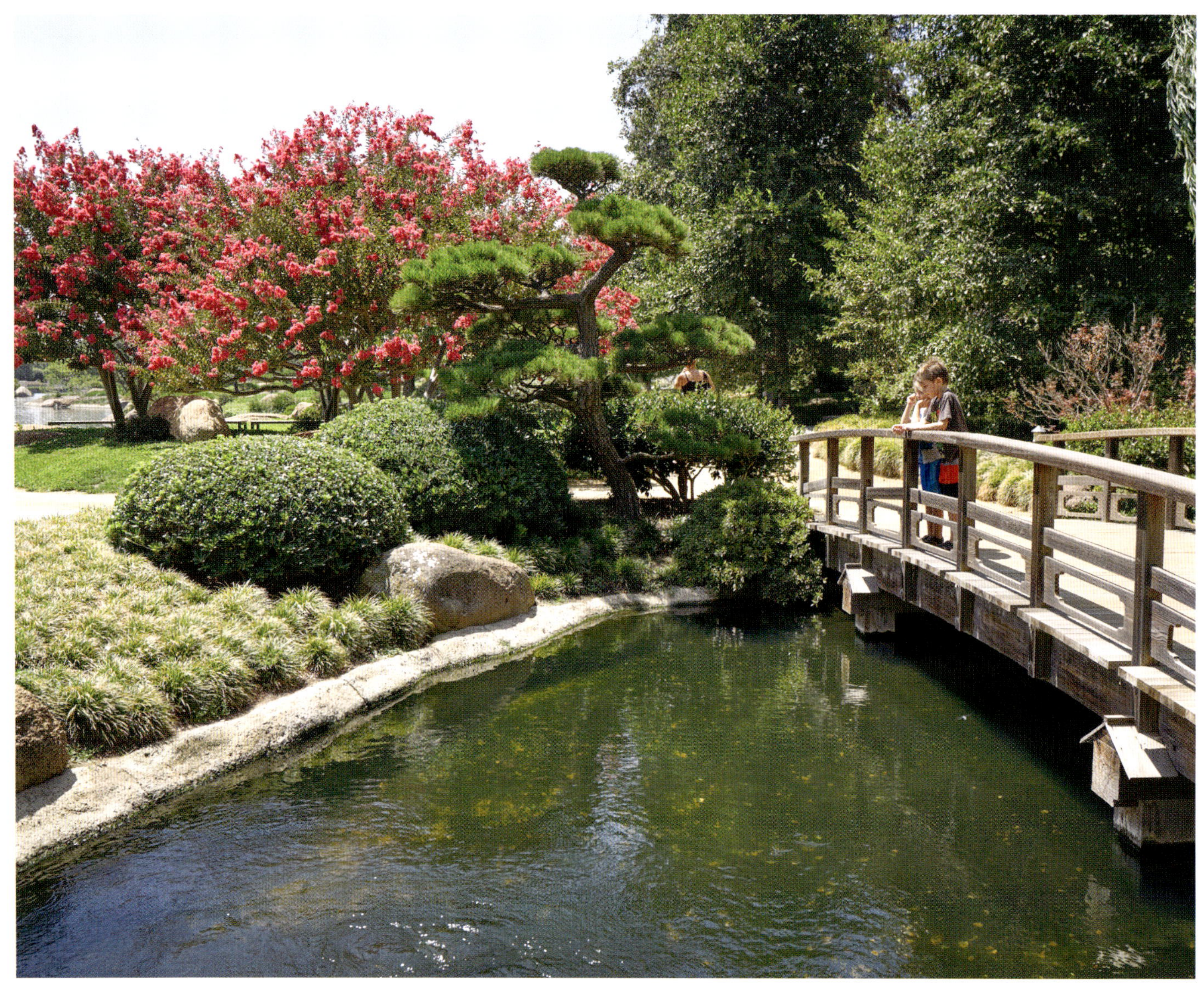

The Japanese Garden *(above and opposite)*

A wooden bridge and a cascading waterfall at the Japanese Garden, a peaceful oasis in the busy San Fernando Valley. Also called SuihoEn, "the garden of water and fragrance," this Zen-inspired garden was designed by Dr. Koichi Kawana and uses reclaimed water from the adjacent Tillman Water Reclamation Plant.

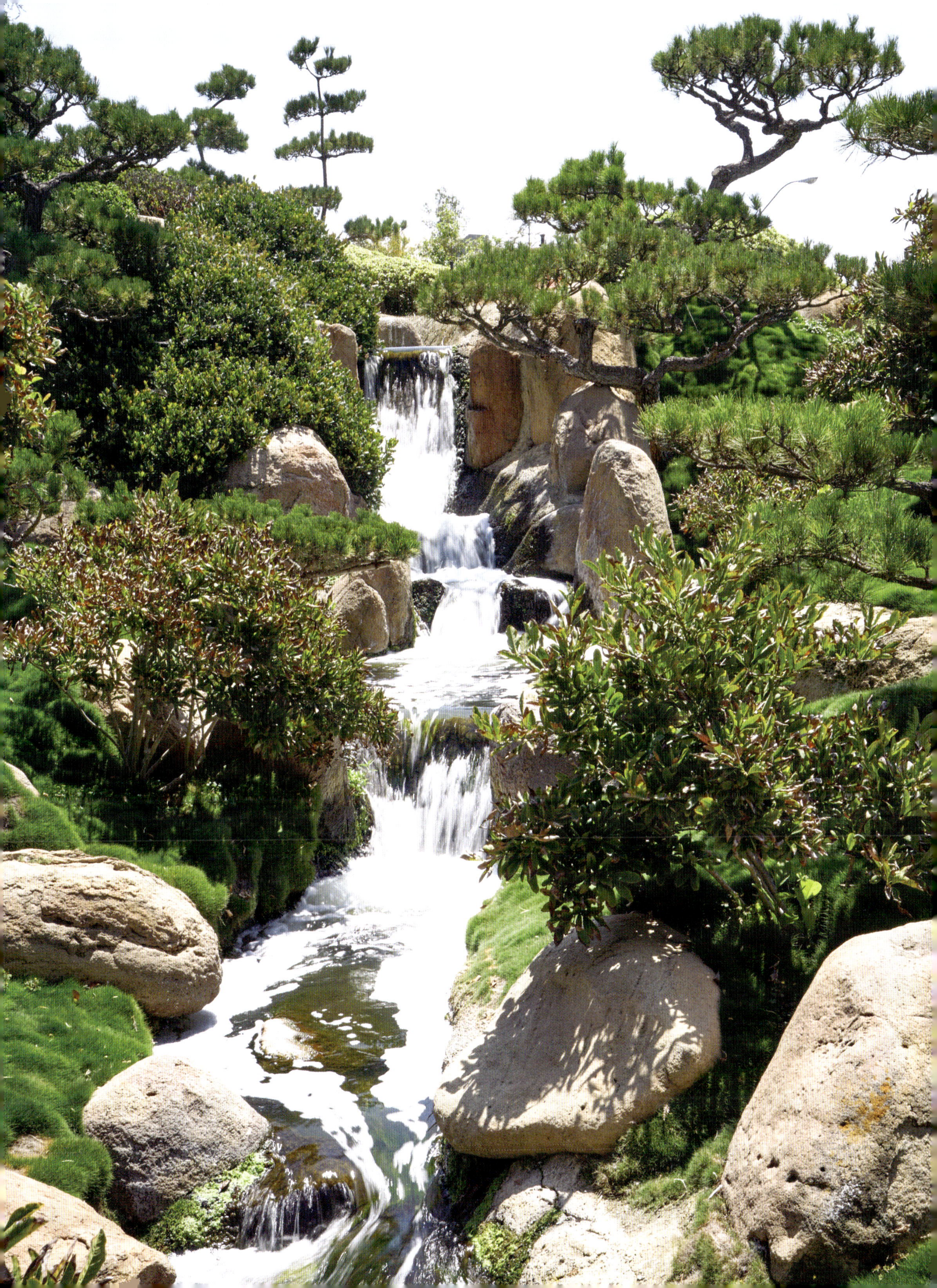

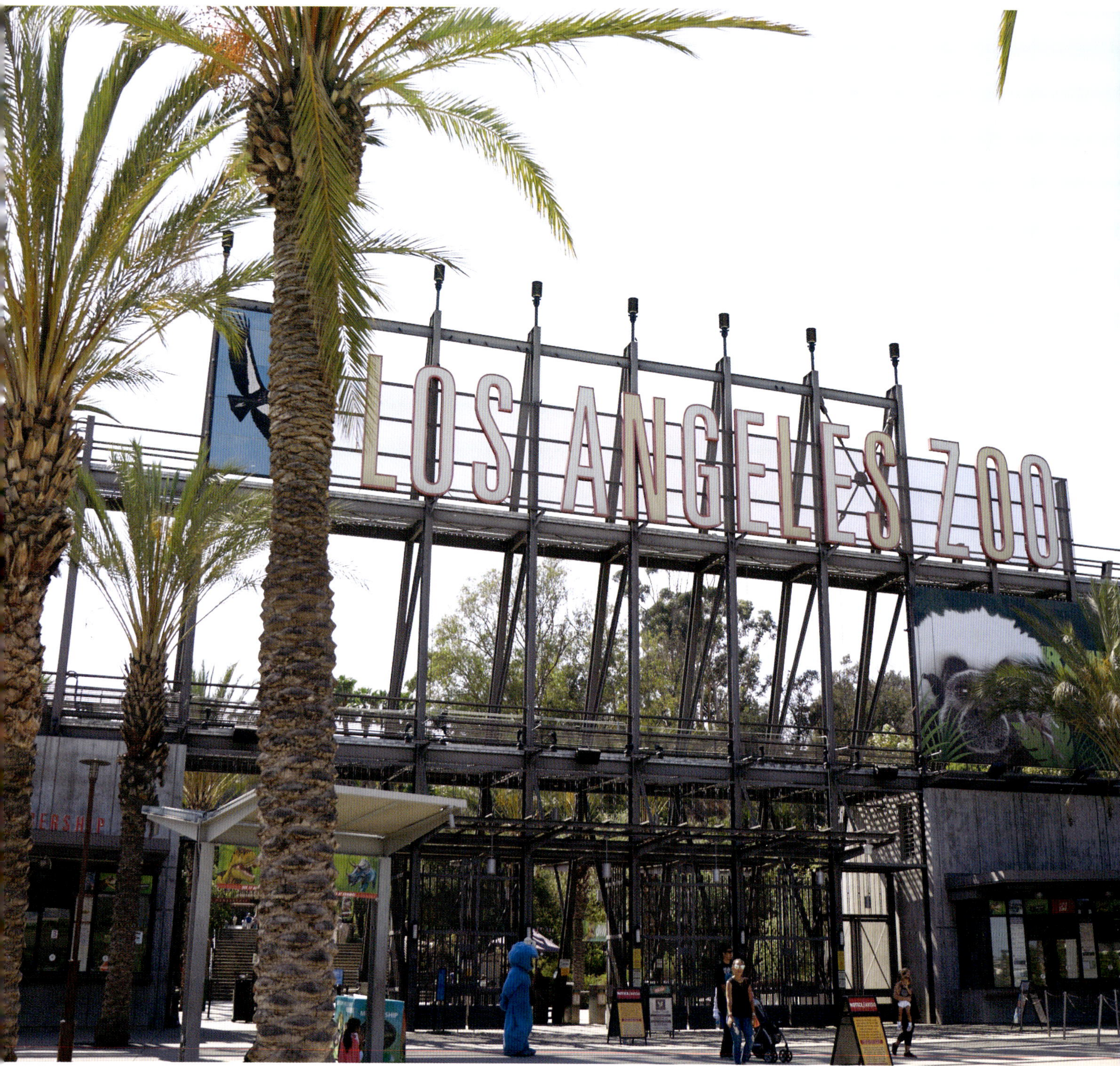

Los Angeles Zoo *(above)*

A variety of animals have been delighting visitors to the city's zoo since its founding in 1966. Today, the zoo sits on 133 acres and is home to 800 different plant species and 250 different animal species, of which 29 are endangered. Over 1.8 million people visit the zoo each year.

Los Angeles Memorial Coliseum

(opposite top and bottom)

This hallowed sports ground has played host to Olympic Games, Super Bowls, World Series, a Papal Mass, and was even the site of Nelson Mandela's 1990 triumphant return to the United States. Built in 1923, the coliseum is credited with helping to form professional sports teams on the West Coast.

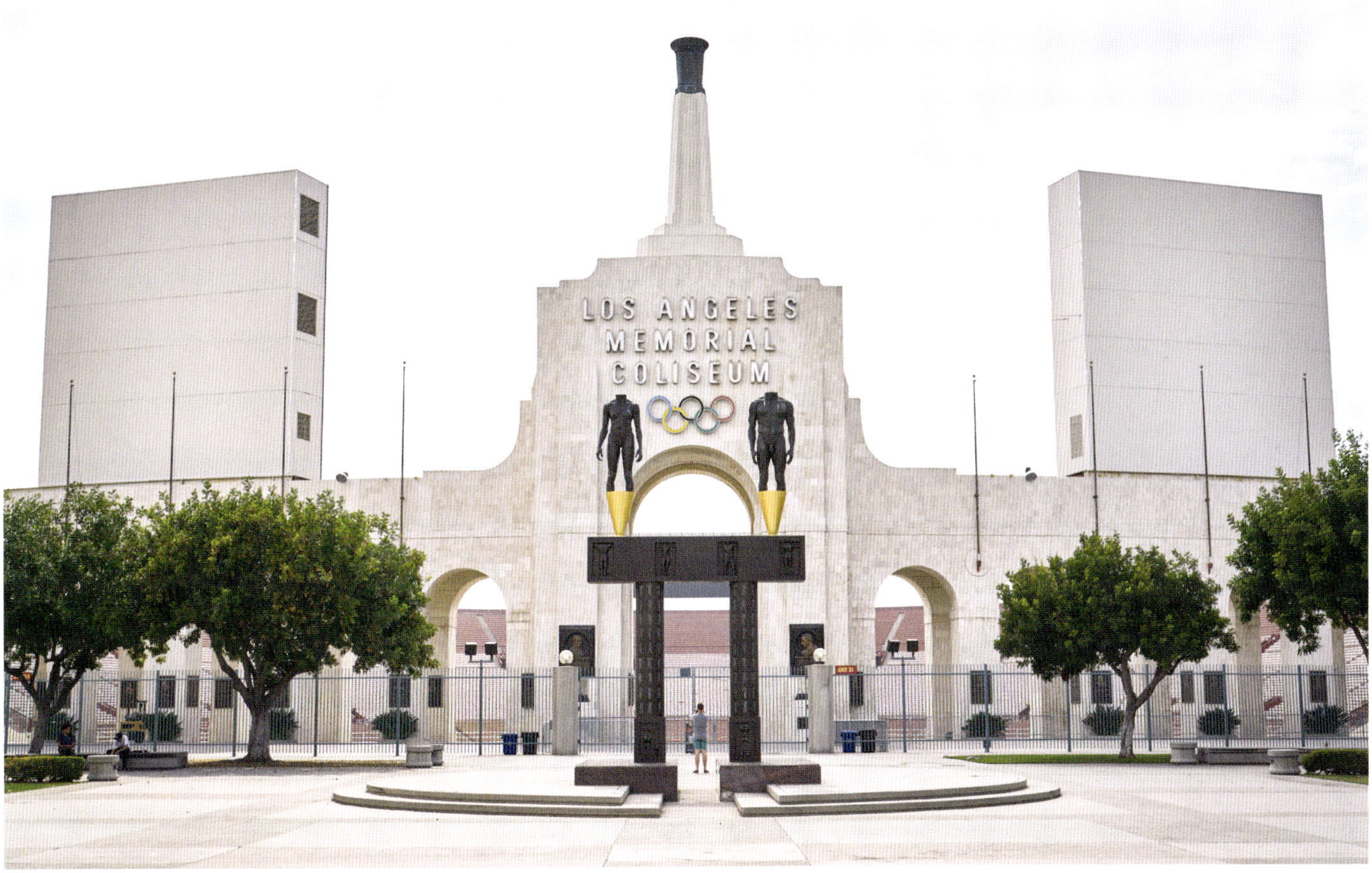

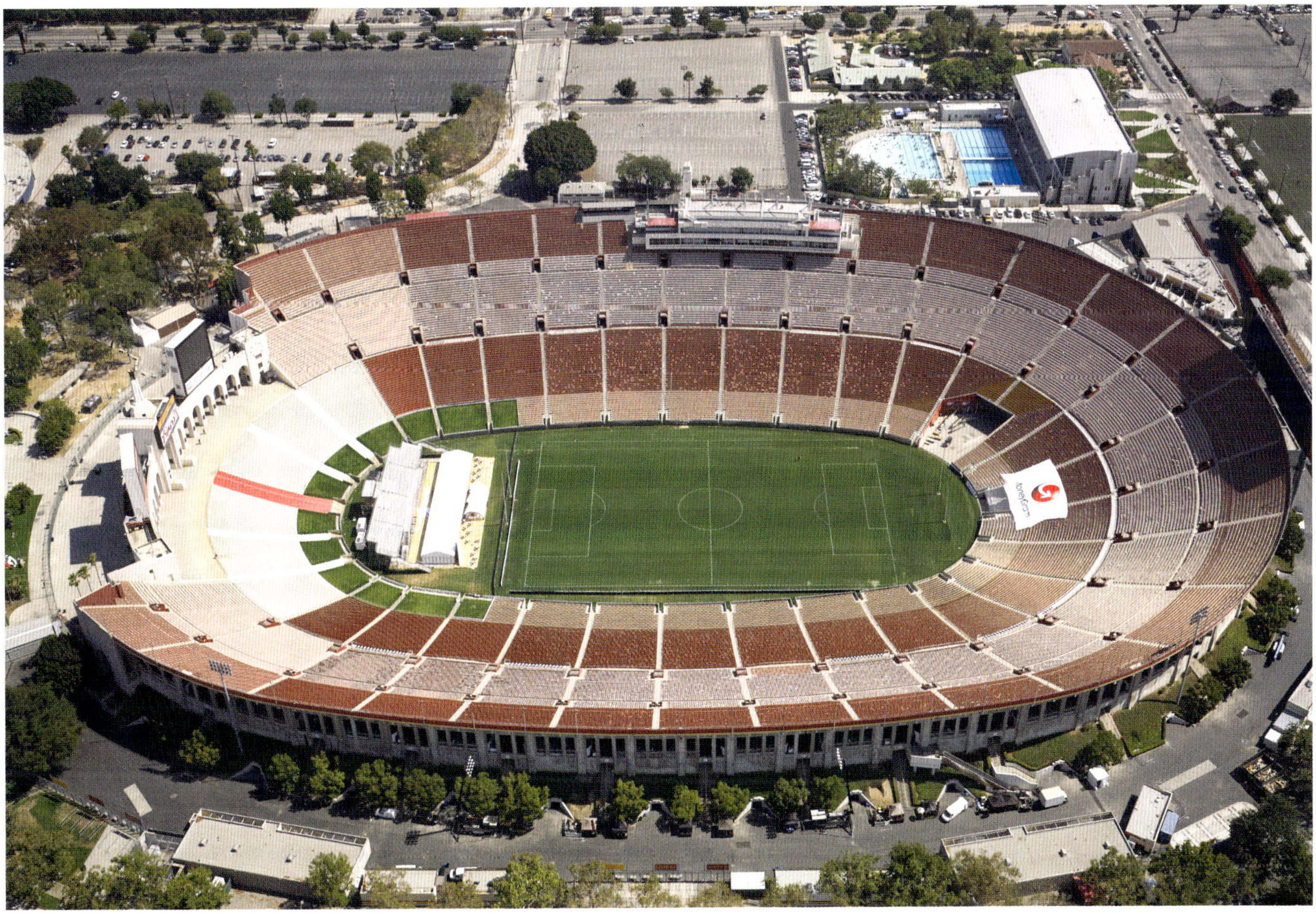

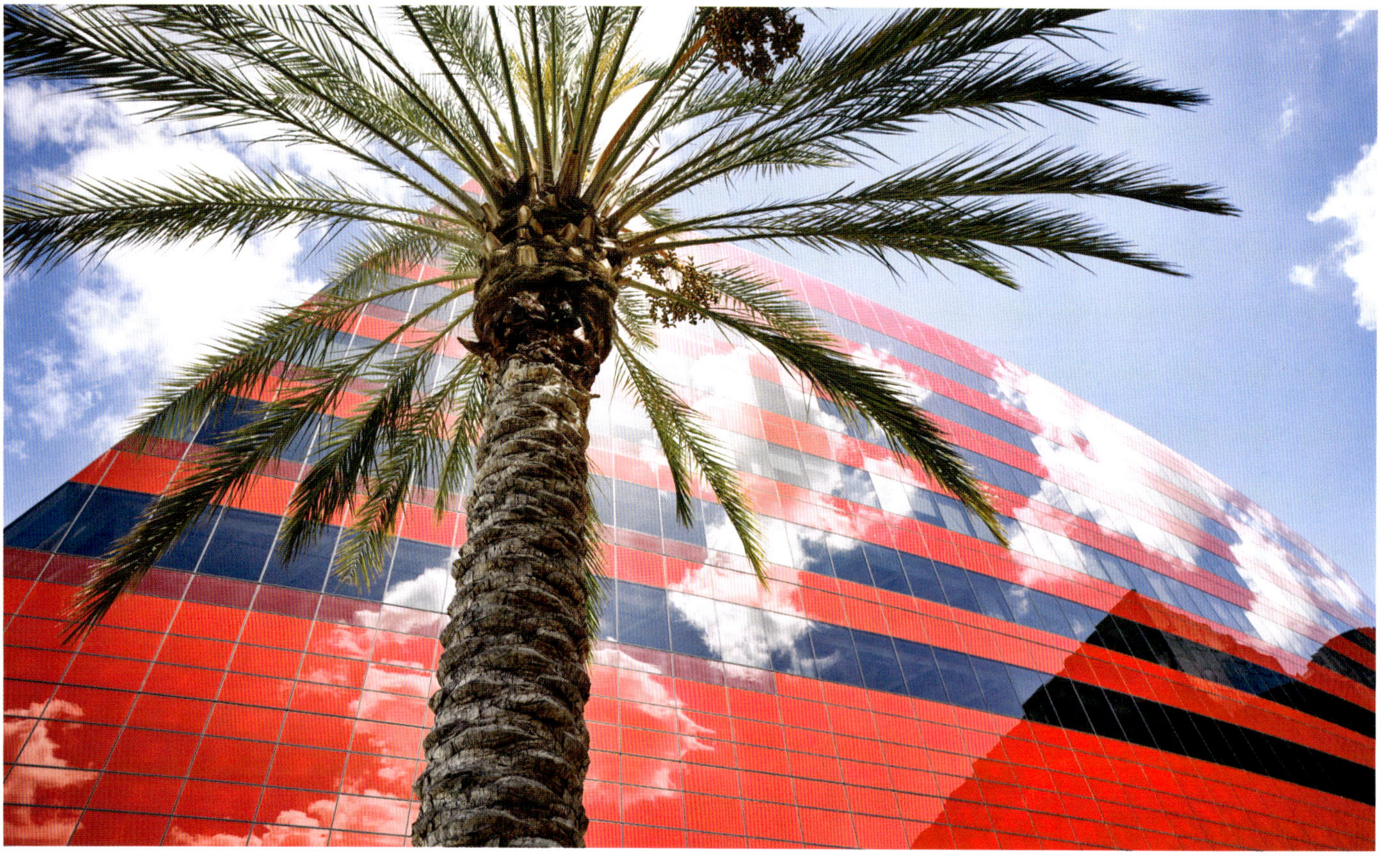

Pacific Design Center

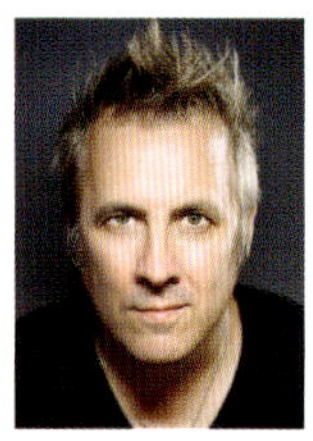

John Chapple was born and raised on the North Devon coast of England, where the spectacular scenery inspired him to pick up a camera at the age of 14. Self-taught, John has enjoyed an incredibly varied and successful career as a news, celebrity portraiture, and landscape photographer - contributing to the *New York Post*, DailyMail.com, the *Discovery Channel*, and many others. He has photographed iconic celebrities including Charlie Sheen, Jon Bon Jovi and Samuel L Jackson, and won multiple awards for his stunning landscape work. During his 30-year career, John has traveled all over the world to cover major news stories such as the 9/11 atrocities in New York and Hurricane Katrina in New Orleans. The married dad-of-two currently lives in Tarzana, Los Angeles. Learn more about John's work at www.johnchapple.com or www.chapple.biz.

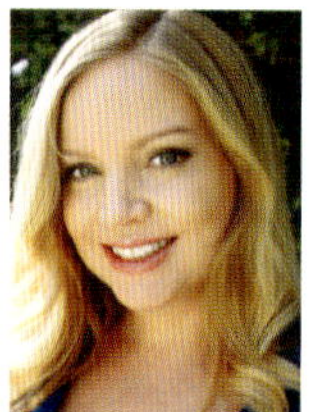

A journalist by trade, **Emma Foster** has traveled extensively to cover the biggest news and showbiz stories of the day for a range of publications. Originally starting out as a reporter in the north of England, where she grew up, Emma worked for national news agency *Press Association* and the popular newspaper *The Sun*, among others. She moved to the United States in 2014 and is now a successful freelance journalist and writer, contributing to newspapers, magazines, and websites in the US, UK, and Australia. Los Angeles is Emma's adopted home, and she currently lives in the West Hills area of the city with her husband and two children.